BIBLE STUDY NOTES

Volume 6

BIBLE STUDY NOTES

MEMORIAL EDITION

By Anita S. Dole

Edited By Wm. R. Woofenden

AMERICAN NEW CHURCH
SUNDAY SCHOOL ASSOCIATION
1979

Sales Agent:

Swedenborg Library
79 Newbury Street
Boston, Massachusetts 02116

"Well done, good and faithful servant."
—*Matthew 25:23*

Printed in U.S.A.

TABLE OF CONTENTS

INTRODUCTORY NOTES FOR TEACHERS

As we may see by the accompanying chart, this program was planned as a four-year Bible course, but it was originally arranged so that the whole Word was covered by periods each year, in order that the child might early realize that the Bible is one book—not only a continuous story but a completed one—and also that children might not so often enter the Sunday School for the first time in the middle of the Bible story with no idea of what has gone before. While this plan might in any one year seem to leave many important stories untouched, the retelling of the background of the successive periods from year to year in the context of different stories built up gradually in the child's mind both a surer knowledge and a better understanding of the whole letter of the Word. The plan insured that the beginning of the Bible story was not forgotten before the end was reached, and that the Old and New Testaments were seen in their proper relation and proportion. Although the lessons are now arranged in Bible sequence, it is still possible, by using the chart, to use the original four-year plan.

The notes for the various age groups are written with two purposes in view. It is *not* intended that the teacher should read them to the class. Neither is it intended that copies should be given out to the pupils in advance. Only the Bible reading should be done in advance. For the teacher, the notes are meant to suggest the points to be covered in the lesson, a possible order of presentation, and the general level of meaning which pupils in the particular age group may be expected to comprehend. For the pupil, if he has his own set of the books, they are meant to be taken home, read as a review during the week, and preserved for future reference.

It is very important that the teacher plan his use of the class time carefully. Five minutes or less at the beginning of the period are enough for review questions. Then give five minutes to a carefully thought-out covering of the background of the lesson for the day before going into the lesson proper. In the Old Testament build the background as far as possible about persons and places in order to fix these in their proper sequence in the pupils' minds. In the New Testament the background should be the factual story of the Lord's life on earth.

The writings of the church tell us that "generals" must be grasped before "particulars" can be understood in their proper context; so we may feel sure that our first object in the Sunday School should be to impress the general outline of the whole Bible story on the minds of our pupils. The covering of the whole story each year has this objective in view.

The two survey lessons (nos. 22 and 24 on the accompanying chart) are general lessons but are based on a different passage each year in order to give the pupils a wider variety in the study of the Prophets than has been possible in previous courses. They are also optional lessons, written in such a way that Sunday Schools with a school year of less than forty sessions may omit them without losing continuity. Each series also contains fifteen lessons from the New Testament. A different Gospel is studied each year. Two of the fifteen lessons are written as optional lessons; three are the special lessons for Christmas, Palm Sunday, and Easter; and three are from the book of Revelation.

FOUR-YEAR LESSON COURSE FOR NEW CHURCH SUNDAY SCHOOLS

Assignments in the Old Testament

Lesson	Subject	Series I	Series II	Series III	Series IV
1.	The Creation	General View	First Four Days	Days Five and Six	The Seventh Day
2.	The Most Ancient Church	The Garden of Eden	Helpmeet for Adam	The Serpent	Cain and Abel
3.	The Ancient Church	Noah Builds an Ark	End of the Flood	The Rainbow	Tower of Babel
4.	Abraham	The Call of Abram	Abram and Lot	Birth of Ishmael	Abraham & the Angels
5.	Isaac	Birth of Isaac	Sacrifice of Isaac	Isaac and Rebekah	Isaac & Abimelech
6.	Jacob	Jacob & Esau	Jacob's Dream	Wives & Sons	Jacob's Return
7.	Joseph	Joseph & Brothers	Joseph in Prison	Ruler of Egypt	Sons and Death
8.	Moses	Birth of Moses	The Burning Bush	The Ten Plagues	The Passover
9.	Escape from Egypt	Crossing Red Sea	Marah & Elim	Quails and Manna	Rephidim & Amalek
10.	Mount Sinai	Ten Commandments	Ark of Covenant	The Tabernacle	The Golden Calf
11.	Wilderness Wanderings	Nadab & Abihu	The Twelve Spies	Korah, Dathan, Abiram	Aaron's Rod
12.	Entering the Holy Land	Balaam	Call of Joshua	Crossing the Jordan	Gilgal
13.	Conquest of Holy Land	Jericho	Ai	The Gibeonites	Conquest & Division
14.	The Judges	Deborah & Barak	Gideon	Jephthah	Samson
15.	Samuel	Birth of Samuel	Lord Calls Samuel	Capture of the Ark	Asking for a King
16.	Saul	Choosing of Saul	Saul's Impatience	Saul & Jonathan	Sparing Agag
17.	David	Anointing of David	David & Goliath	Ark to Jerusalem	David & Bathsheba
18.	Solomon	Wisdom of Solomon	Glory of Solomon	Building the Temple	Decline & Death
19.	Kingdom of Israel	Elijah & Ahab	Elijah at Horeb	Elijah's Mantle	Elisha & Naaman
20.	Kingdom of Judah	Reign of Asa	Hezekiah & Isaiah	Josiah	Zedekiah & Jeremiah
21.	Book of Psalms	Psalm 1	Psalm 19	Psalm 91	Psalm 119

Lesson	Series I	Series II	Series III	Series IV
*22. Major Prophets—Survey	Isaiah 6	Jeremiah 1	Ezekiel 47:1-12	Daniel 5
23. Major Prophets	Fiery Furnace	Ezekiel's Vision	Daniel & the Image	Daniel & the Lions
*24. Minor Prophets—Survey	Micah 6	Joel 3:9-21	Amos 8	Zechariah 4
25. Minor Prophets	Haggai 1; 2	Jonah & the Fish	Malachi 3: 4	Jonah & the Gourd

Assignments in the New Testament

Lesson	Series I	Series II	Series III	Series IV
26.	Matthew 1:18-25; 2:13-23	Mark 1	Luke 1	John 1
27.	Matthew 3	Mark 2	Luke 7:1-30	John 2:1-11
28.	Matthew 4:1-11	*Mark 3	Luke 9:1-36	*John 3:1-21
29.	*Matthew 4:12-25	*Mark 4	Luke 10:25-42	John 4:1-42
30.	Matthew 5; 6: 7	Mark 5	*Luke 11	John 5:1-16
31.	Matthew 8	Mark 6	Luke 14	John 9
32.	*Matthew 13	Mark 10	Luke 15	*John 10
33.	Matthew 17:1-13	Mark 14	*Luke 16	John 11:1-46
34.	Matthew 26: 27	Mark 15	Luke 24:13-53	John 15
35.	Revelation 1	Revelation 4	Revelation 6	Revelation 12
36.	Revelation 2: 3	Revelation 5	Revelation 8: 9	Revelation 13; 19:11-21
37.	Revelation 21; 22	Revelation 20:11-15; 21:1-7	Revelation 21:9-16	Revelation 22:8-21

Special Lessons

	Series I	Series II	Series III	Series IV
Christmas	Matthew 2:1-15	Luke 2:1-20	Matthew 2:1-15	Luke 2:1-20
Palm Sunday	Matthew 21:1-27	Mark 11	Luke 19	John 12:12-50
Easter	Matthew 28	Mark 16	Luke 24:1-12	John 20; 21

*Optional Lessons

BIBLE STUDY NOTES

JOHN - REVELATION

THE WORD MADE FLESH
John 1

Remind the children of Jonah's attitude toward the Ninevites, since it was that attitude among the people which finally necessitated the Lord's coming. The Christmas stories should be mentioned and the fact noted that no actual account of the external circumstances of the Lord's birth is given in the Gospel of John. The first verse of the chapter may be used in all classes as the basis on which to build the lesson.

―――――――

Doctrinal Points

The Lord came into the world as divine truth. Jesus Christ was God Himself incarnate.

The Lord's life on earth was the fulfillment of the Old Testament Scriptures.

We become "sons of God" as we make His truth the director of our thought and conduct. We receive the truth only when we want to obey it.

The Lord's love can come into our hearts only as we obey His truth.

―――――――

Notes for Parents

We should realize how closely the Old Testament and the New Testament are connected and how impossible it is to understand the New without knowing the Old. The attitude of Jonah toward the people of Nineveh continued to be the attitude of the religious leaders. They were proud of themselves and despised others and wanted to keep as a bit of personal property the inspired Scriptures which had been entrusted to them to teach to all the world. During the hundreds of years which followed the time of Jonah, the priests and scribes added to the Scriptures a great body of rules and regulations designed to minister to their own importance, so that finally not only the Gentiles but even the simple good people among the

Jews could no longer find out what the Scriptures really taught. The world had come into spiritual darkness. This was why the Lord Himself finally had to come into the world to live out the divine truth which was in the Word and bring light to the souls of men. Those who did not want to change their lives rejected Him, but those who really wanted to know how to live received Him gladly.

The Gospel of John is different from the other three Gospels because it tells us less of the outer story of the Lord's life and more of its deeper meaning. For instance, in this chapter instead of the familiar Christmas story we are told that it was God Himself who came into the world in Jesus Christ, the same God who made the world, and the same God who dwells within the inspired Scriptures, which He dictated. John the Baptist in our chapter calls Jesus "the Son of God" and while He was living in the human body He took on through Mary, He was often called the Son of God and He referred to God as His Father. But as little by little He put off the assumed humanity through overcoming its evils, He began to speak of Himself as one with the Father. He said, "I and my Father are one," and, "Believest thou not that I am in the Father, and the Father in me?" And when Philip said, "Lord, show us the Father, and it sufficeth us," Jesus answered, "Have I been so long time with you, and yet hast thou not known me, Philip? he that hath seen me hath seen the Father." This is what John is telling us in our chapter. Jesus Christ is the one God of heaven and earth.

Primary

After the introduction and the reading of the lesson an attempt should be made to show why we call the Bible "the Word," and what the first verse means. Impress upon them that Jesus Christ was God Himself come into the world. You will also be able to show them why we think of the Word on the altar in the church as the presence of the Lord with us, and why the minister opens it at the beginning of the service and closes it at the end.

Do you remember the story of Jonah? How did Jonah feel about people like the Assyrians who were not of his own nation? The religious leaders after Jonah's time went right on feeling the same way. They were the only people in the world who had the Scriptures, and the Lord had told them over and over again to teach the people around them, but they would not.

In time most of the people did not know what the Scriptures really said, because most of them could not read, and the learned men—the scribes and Pharisees—taught them instead a great many rules which they had made up themselves. So the Lord could no longer reach people here in this world through the Scriptures. He had to come into the world Himself to correct the false teachings of the scribes and Pharisees and show the people by His example just how they ought to live.

You know the stories about the Lord's birth in Bethlehem and about the Wise Men and the shepherds.

The Gospel of John tells us something still greater.

Let us read the first verse of our chapter.

This tells us two things: It tells us that the Bible is the Lord Himself speaking to us; and it tells us that the Lord Jesus was God Himself come into the world to live out the truth that is in the Bible, so that men can see it and always be sure what it is and what it means.

How did the Lord show John the Baptist that Jesus was the promised Messiah?

When you say something, you yourself are in the words you say. Speaking is the way you let other people know what you think and how you feel. So the Bible is the Lord speaking to us, telling us His thoughts and feelings, and we call it the Lord's Word. When the Lord came into the world, He came to show people the same things He had taught in the Word.

Junior

The Juniors are old enough to be given some explanation of this chapter, and an effort has been made in their notes to bring it within their mental reach, even though the ideas are in themselves abstract. Be sure the class looks up all the Bible references in their notes. It is a good exercise for them and will also help their understanding of the lesson.

With today's lesson we begin studying the Gospel of John. John was the brother of James and one of the first four disciples called by the Lord to follow Him. He was called "the beloved disciple," because he was always close to the Lord. He was also the one who in his old age was given the wonderful visions recorded in the book of Revelation.

The first chapter of John treats of the Lord's birth into the world, but in a very different way from the Gospels of Matthew and Luke, from which our Christmas lessons are always taken. You know that in the New Church we usually speak of the inspired books of the Bible as "the Word," and many other people use the expression "the Word of God" in connection with it. Have you ever wondered why this is so? We all use a great many words every day. Our words are our means of letting other people know what we are thinking and feeling. So really we are within our words. The Lord spoke the Word by means of His prophets. It is divine truth in a form adapted to our understanding. Within it is the Lord Himself. That is why we always have the Word on the altar in the very center of the chancel in our churches, and why the minister opens it at the beginning of the service and closes it at the end. We think of it as the Lord's presence with us.

We know that God is love—perfect, unselfish love—but we know also that He is wisdom—perfect wisdom. That is why the first verse of our chapter says that the Word was in the beginning, that it was with God, and that it was God. It was divine wisdom or truth which was given to the world in the Word. It was divine wisdom which created everything. But within everything divine wisdom does is divine love. If we think a little, we can understand this from our own experience. Whenever you make something, it is your knowledge which plans it and which directs your hands in making it, but behind your knowledge is the desire you have to make it. When John says, "And the Word was made flesh, and dwelt among us," he is telling us that just as divine wisdom or truth came down into the form of human language in the written Word so, when men could no longer understand the written Word (see Matthew 15:1-6), divine wisdom came down into a human body, through which the Lord could show men what the written Word meant and how they ought to live. The Gospels, which became part of the written Word, are the record of His life, preserved so that we can know what He did and said; and, again because they are the Lord speaking to us, He is within them.

The John of whom our chapter speaks is not the apostle John but John the Baptist, of whom we learned so much last year in the Gospel of Mark.

Where did John baptize?
What did he say when he saw Jesus coming?
How was John shown that this was the "Son of God"?

We should know that while Jesus was in the world, He was called the "Son of God," and spoke of God as His Father, but He also said, "I and the Father are one," and, "he that hath seen me hath seen the Father." Read His words to Philip in John 14:7-9. The divine truth which showed itself to the world is called the Son, and the divine love which was within Him and could be seen only by means of divine truth is called the Father. The Philip mentioned in John 14 is the same Philip who is called to follow the Lord in our chapter.

Do you remember how many apostles there were?
Which ones are mentioned in our chapter?

Nathanael is not mentioned by this name in any of the lists of the twelve apostles, but it is generally believed that he was the same person as Bartholomew, who always comes directly after Philip in the lists. *Bartholomew* means "the son of Tolmai"; so he may very well have had a name of his own, too.

Have you noticed how often in this chapter people are told to, "Come and see"? Read verses 9 to 12 to see if you can find out why. Read what the Lord said to Nicodemus in John 3:19-21. These verses help us to understand why some people believed in the Lord and some did not. Those who knew they needed to live better lives and wanted to find out the truth—like those whom the Lord called in our chapter—were eager to "come and see" the Lord and readily accepted what He said. But those who were selfish and self-satisfied did not want to hear or believe Him. The same thing is true today.

―――――――――

Intermediate

A few basic correspondences have been given, but this lesson must be mainly taken up by the effort to explain how the Lord was the "Word made flesh." This is one of our best opportunities to give the young people the doctrine of the Lord. Encourage questions from the class.

We are now studying the life of the Lord as it is recorded in the Gospel of John. We remember that John was one of the first four disciples called by the Lord and one of the three who were allowed to witness the transfiguration of the Lord and who were often singled out from the others for special instruction. The twelve apostles represent all the faculties in us which are called to follow the Lord and meant to be used in the Lord's service. The three most important—Peter, James, and John—represent faith, charity, and the works of charity. John is also said to represent the "good of charity." He was called "the beloved disciple," and in his old age was given the wonderful visions recorded in the book of Revelation.

We know that the Word of God was given through many men and took its literal form from the states of mind and heart in which those men were. John was of a different character from the other disciples, and his Gospel is very different from the other three. We shall find that it contains no declared parables and few miracles in comparison with the others, and that it is mainly concerned with the Lord's ministry in Judea and His instructions to the apostles during the last week of His earthly life.

The difference between John's Gospel and the others appears very clearly in our chapter for today. The first fourteen verses are an account of the Lord's coming into the world, but they tell us nothing about Bethlehem, about Joseph and Mary, or about the shepherds and the Wise Men. Instead we are given teaching concerning the real nature and purpose of the Incarnation. The Lord came as the Word made flesh to be the light of the world. In the New Church we regularly call the inspired Scriptures "the Word." We need to understand why we do this. The practice grows naturally out of the frequent statement in the Prophets, "The word of the Lord came unto me, saying," and out of this chapter of John, but of course there is a reason why this form of expression appears in these places. We are all of us constantly using words, because they are our means of expressing ourselves to others. We are in our words. Likewise the Word is the Lord's expression of HImself to men, and He is in His Word as we are in ours. Every word we speak is an outward form of truth—or falsity. The written Word is an outward form of divine truth. It is our only means of learning what divine truth is and so of knowing the Lord.

The ancient Hebrews alone had the Old Testament Scriptures, and they had been told from time to time to teach them to the Gentiles. [E.g., Psalm 96:3.] But as we have learned in our lessons about Jonah, they despised the Gentiles and preferred to keep the Scriptures for themselves. In the hundreds of years which followed the return from captivity, this selfish arrogance had grown out of all bounds. There were still good people, humble and desirous of learning the truth and obeying it, but most of the people could not read and their teachers, the scribes and Pharisees, had so overlaid the Scriptures with additional laws and regulations of their own that the people did not know what was Scripture and what was not. The Lord shows this when He says to the scribes and Pharisees (Matthew 15:6): "Thus have ye made the commandment of God of none effect by your tradition." So the Lord could no longer reach men through the written Word and He had to give the world His truth in a new form, by clothing Himself with a human body and so living among men and showing them the true way of life: "the Word was made flesh, and dwelt among us." The Lord came not to destroy the Old Testament Scriptures, but to fulfill them. He came as the Word, the divine truth, which was in the beginning with God and was God.

"He came unto his own, and his own received him not." Those

who had the written Word were the ones who rejected the Lord, because they did not want to know what it really taught. But there were a few who did want to know and so received Him. John the Baptist was one of these, and he bore witness fearlessly to the fact that Jesus was the promised Messiah, the "Son of God," which is another expression meaning the divine truth. The sign of the dove which was given to John the Baptist pictures "the Holy of faith," the truths and goods of faith which were all in the Lord.

The rest of our chapter tells of the calling of the first disciples, again in a little different way from the other Gospels. Nathanael does not appear by that name in the lists of the twelve apostles, but it is generally believed that *Nathanael* was the given name of Bartholomew (which means "the son of Tolmai") who appears after Philip in all the lists. He would be called *Nathanael Bartholomew*, just as Peter is called by the Lord in one place (Matthew 16:17) *Simon Barjona*, or Simon, son of Jonas. In John 21:15 the same Greek words are translated "Simon, son of Jonas." We notice that Nathanael was called as he sat under a fig tree. Figs represent goods on the natural plane, which gives us an idea of Nathanael's character. We should remember, as we read this account, that the Lord is saying to all of us, "Come and see," and, "Follow me," just as He said to these men of Galilee long ago.

Basic Correspondences

John	=	the good or works of charity
light	=	truth
baptism	=	purification by the truth
the dove	=	the Holy of faith, or the truths and goods of faith
figs	=	goods on the natural plane

Senior

In the Senior notes the effort has been made to cover the whole chapter in a balanced way. It is a strictly doctrinal lesson, but the Seniors should be studying doctrine seriously.

The Gospel of John is quite different from the other Gospels. John among the apostles represents the good or works of charity. He was the fourth of the apostles to be called, the first three— Peter, Andrew, and James—representing faith, obedience, and charity. This is the order of regeneration. We must first learn and believe the truth, then obey it, then come to love it, and finally reach the state in which we act from charity in the heart instead of in mere obedience to the truth. It is this final state of unselfish love in the heart which is wisdom, and the Lord can flow into it with enlightenment. So John's Gospel is concerned with spiritual realities rather than with externals. Even the three Epistles of John (which do not have an inner meaning) are different from the rest of the Epistles in that they are throughout concerned with love. John was called "the beloved disciple."

Our chapter divides itself into three sections. The first is the spiritual story of the Incarnation, giving us not the external details of the Lord's birth but the statement of just who He was and why He came into the world. He was the Word made flesh, and the Word was in the beginning with God and was God. When we use words, we say we are "expressing ourselves."* We ourselves are in the words—our thoughts, and behind them our feelings. Swedenborg tells us that a person *is* his affections and thoughts. His body with all its activities is merely the form in which he expresses himself in the world. When we wish to communicate something to a friend, we either write to him or speak to him. The inspired Scriptures are the written expression of divine truth—the written Word. The Lord in His Incarnation was the expression of the same divine truth in a physical human form—the Word made flesh. The Lord said He came to fulfill the Law and the Prophets, and He did so by living out divine truth before the eyes of men.

And the Lord came to be the light of the world. The people of the world were living in spiritual darkness because the Old Testa-

---

*The translation of Phillips renders John 1:1, "At the beginning, God expressed himself." —*Ed.*

ment Scriptures, through which alone divine truth could be learned, had been so overlaid by the scribes and Pharisees with their own interpretations and additions that people no longer knew what was Scripture and what was not. The Lord Himself as divine truth had to come into the world to restore the Scriptures to their purity. A few received Him gladly—those who truly wanted to know what was right so that they might do it. The great majority rejected Him because they had no desire to give up their selfish ways. Read John 3:18-21.

The second section of our chapter is concerned with the testimony of John the Baptist. Again the actual baptism of the Lord is not mentioned, but the sign of the dove—which we know was given at the time of the Lord's baptism by John—is included in John's assurance that Jesus is the Son of God. Swedenborg tells us that while the Lord was in the world, His visible humanity was called the Son of God to distinguish it from the Father within, but that in general the Father signifies divine love, the Son the divine wisdom, and the Holy Spirit the divine proceeding or activity. Will, thought, and act in us are analogous to these.

The third section of our chapter tells of the calling of some of the disciples. Here, too, the account differs from those of the other Gospels. We are familiar with the account in the fourth chapter of Matthew of the Lord's calling Peter and Andrew and James and John to leave their nets and follow Him. Here we learn that Andrew had been a disciple of John the Baptist and that he had talked with the Lord and had brought his brother Peter to Him before they were called to follow Him. Regeneration must be preceded by reformation, as the wilderness journey preceded the entrance into the Holy Land. In the Gospels this necessary stage of reformation is represented by the preaching of John the Baptist, whose cry was, "Repent ye, for the kingdom of heaven is at hand." So we can understand why Andrew—who represents obedience—was a disciple of John and was the first of the twelve apostles to recognize the Lord.

Nathanael, whom Philip brought to the Lord, does not appear

by that name in the various lists of the twelve, but he is assumed to be the one called Bartholomew who always comes after Philip in the lists. *Bartholomew* means "son of Tolmai," *Bar* meaning "son." Peter is called *Simon Barjona* in Matthew 16:17, and we find him also called Simon the son of Jona in verse 42 of our chapter. So the disciple next after Philip may well have been Nathanael the son of Tolmai.

We should notice also the last verse of our chapter. You remember Jacob's dream of the ladder (Genesis 28:12) reaching from earth to heaven with the angels of God ascending and descending upon it. This ladder represented the Word as our means of conjunction with the Lord and the angels. Now we find the Lord saying the same thing of Himself. So this verse sums up the teaching of the whole chapter that the Lord was the Word made flesh.

Adult

The teacher will decide which part of this lesson will be most helpful for discussion with his particular class. For adults who are familiar with the doctrine of the Lord, a brief treatment of the first fourteen verses would be sufficient, and time could be given to the rest of the chapter. For young adults and especially for newcomers the first part of the lesson is the essential topic.

The Gospels give us three accounts of the Lord's Advent. Matthew and Luke are concerned principally with the external events which attended it and with its reception. John deals with its nature and significance. John's whole Gospel is of a different character from the others. He could be inspired to write in this way because of his personal turn of mind. We can see his difference from the other apostles if we compare the Epistles of John with those of Peter, for example. John's letters are full of love and are exhortations to love and trust. In making this comparison, however, we should also note how evident is the difference between the books with an inner sense and those without it. John's Epistles are written in the first person throughout. It is John who speaks. But the writer of the Gospel is nowhere apparent as John, and although we do find the first person occasionally in the book of Revelation, it is never to give us John's thoughts, but only by way of attesting the genuineness of the visions recorded.

The letter of the Word gives us a good many facts concerning the life of the apostle John. He was the son of Zebedee and Salome, and with his brother James was called by the Lord from fishing, immediately after the calling of Peter and Andrew. He was one of the three chosen to witness the transfiguration of the Lord and the miracle of the raising of the daughter of Jairus. He was the beloved disciples who leaned on the Lord's breast at the Last Supper, and the one to whom the Lord entrusted the future care of Mary at the time of the crucifixion. Other records tell us that he remained at Jerusalem for some years after the ascension and then went forth as a missionary, his work being particularly centered about Ephesus. In his extreme old age he was banished to the island of Patmos, where he was given the visions recorded in the book of Revelation. He is thought to have been about twenty-five when he was called, and to have lived to the age of ninety-five. He was perhaps the most devoted, zealous, and spiritual of the Lord's followers.

Much is said in the writings about the correspondence of the apostle John. Peter, James, and John represent "faith, charity, and the good of charity" (AC 2135). Elsewhere (AC 6073³) John is said to represent "the goods or works of charity," or (AE 821⁶) "the church as to good works," or simply (AC 3934ᵉ) "good works." But we should note that by "good works" Swedenborg never means mere external benevolences. In AC 10087² the "good of charity" pictured by John is defined as "to do good from willing good," and in AE 45 we are told that John in the highest sense represents "the Lord as to doctrine." Thus it is evident that for works to be "good" they must be prompted by the Lord's love in the heart and directed by His truth in the mind.

The Gospel of John deals with the Lord's life in its divine rather than in its human aspect—with the coming to view in the world of divine love and wisdom in the person of Jesus Christ. It is largely concerned with the Lord's ministry in Judea, which represents the high plane of the will, and it reports in detail the Lord's intimate teaching to His immediate followers, especially during the last week of His earthly life. We note that in John's Gospel the Lord's entry into Jerusalem on Palm Sunday is described in chapter 12, with six chapters between that and the crucifixion story. The Gospel of John records fewer of the miracles than any other and no formal parables, being for the most part a statement of principles applicable particularly to the inner life in its clear recognition of the Lord.

John's account of the Advent is summed up in the statement that "the Word was made flesh, and dwelt among us." In AR 200 Swedenborg says: "All thought, speech, and writing, derives its essence and life from him who thinks, speaks, and writes; the man with his quality is therein; but the Lord alone is in the Word." Our chapter first identifies the Word with God as the creator. This is because divine love creates everything by means of divine wisdom, just as we make and do the things we wish by means of our knowledge and thought. "All things have been created from Divine love by means of Divine wisdom." (DL 1) The Word is spoken of as a person because it is the very form of God, in which divine love is expressed. We can express our love, our desires, only by means of our thoughts, and we know that we *are* our affections and thoughts, and that our bodies are merely the clothing we wear in this world and the means by which we act here.

Next we are told: "In him was life; and the life was the light of men." Divine love is life itself, and divine wisdom is the light of that love, just as the light of the natural world is from the natural sun, which is pure fire. So we are taught that the Lord is the source of all genuine enlightenment, that this light is meant for all, and that if people do not see it, it is only because they do not want to see. In John 3:19 the Lord tells Nicodemus: "And this is the condemnation, that light is come into the world, and men loved darkness rather than light, because their deeds were evil." The scribes and Pharisees had overlaid the Scriptures with a body of regulations calculated to exalt themselves, thus making the commandment of

God of none effect by their tradition (Matthew 15:6). They rejected the Lord because He swept away these traditions and lived and spoke the Word in its purity, condemning their selfishness, arrogance, and hypocrisy. We become "sons of God" when we receive Him, because He then becomes the source of all our affections and thoughts. If we do not receive Him, we live in darkness and are a part of that world which knew Him not although it was made by Him.

Our chapter carries us on to the witness of John the Baptist and the calling of the first disciples, but again in a different way from the other Gospels. The actual baptism of the Lord by John is not mentioned, but the sign of the dove is part of John's testimony to the deity of the Lord. And in connection with this testimony we are given a fact recorded nowhere else—that Andrew was a disciple of John the Baptist and was brought by him to recognize the Lord and that Peter was led to the Lord by Andrew, and this before they were both called from their nets to devote themselves to His service. Peter represents faith and Andrew obedience. John's message of repentance leads to obedience and this in turn to recognition of the Lord and faith in Him.

The name Nathanael does not appear in any of the lists of the twelve apostles, but it is generally believed to have been the given name of Bartholomew—"the son of Tolmai"—who follows Philip in all the lists.

Note how the last verse of our chapter ties in with the first. It is a reminder of Jacob's ladder, which as we recall is a picture of the Word, by means of which we have conjunction with the Lord. Here again the Lord is identified with the Word. Later the Lord said (John 14:6): "I am the way, the truth, and the life: no man cometh unto the Father, but by me." This was just before He told Philip: "Have I been so long time with you, and yet hast thou not known me, Philip? he that hath seen me hath seen the Father; and how sayest thou then, Shew us the Father?"

From the Writings of Swedenborg

Doctrine of the Holy Scripture, n. 100: "Few understand how the Lord is the Word, for they think that the Lord may indeed enlighten and teach men by means of the Word without His being on that account called the Word. Be it known however that every man is his own love, and consequently his own good and his own truth. It is solely from this that a man is a man, and there is nothing else in him that is man. It is from the fact that a man is his own good and his own truth that angels and spirits are men, for all the good and truth that proceeds from the Lord is in its form a man. And as the Lord is Divine good and Divine truth itself, He is *the* Man, from whom every man is a man."

Suggested Questions on the Lesson

J. Who was Jonah? *a prophet of Israel*
J. Why did he try to run away from the Lord? *too proud to warn Nineveh*
P. What happened to him? *swallowed by great fish*
J. What prophecy did he make to the Ninevites? *doom in forty days*
J. Why was it not fulfilled? *people repented*
P. How did Jonah feel about it? *angry*
J. What happened to him which pictured his state of heart and mind? *story of gourd*
J. What lesson did the Lord draw from it for him? *should love all people*
J. When the Lord came into the world, what had the scribes and Pharisees done with the Word? *added their own ideas*
J. Can you repeat the first verse of the Gospel of John?
I. What do we mean when we call the inspired Scriptures the "Word of God"? *the written form of divine truth*
P. Why do we always have the Word on the altar in church and open it at the beginning of the service and close it at the end? *symbol of the Lord's presence*
J. How was the Word made flesh? *in the person of Jesus Christ*
P. In our chapter who testified to the fact that Jesus was the Messiah? *John the Baptist*
P. What sign had he been given? *dove*
J. Which of the apostles are named in this chapter? *Andrew, Peter, Philip, Nathanael*
J. By what other name is Nathanael elsewhere called? *Bartholomew*
I. What is meant by saying that the Lord is the light of the world? *He enlightens men's minds*
S. What is meant by "the Son of God"? *the Lord's visible divine humanity*
S. Why did everyone not receive the Lord? *some loved darkness*

THE MIRACLE AT CANA
John 2:1-11

Because we ought to cover the main facts of the Lord's life each year and the Gospel of John does not give the external story of His birth and the period of His growing up, the teacher should begin with the question, "Who was the Lord?" and then review briefly the incidents of the Lord's birth, the flight into Egypt, the return to Nazareth, the Lord's appearance in the temple at the age of twelve, His baptism, and the forty days of temptation in the wilderness, drawing as much as possible from the pupils' memories. In all classes before taking up today's lesson be sure the class understands what a miracle is and why the Lord performed miracles.

Doctrinal Points

The Lord gradually either put off or made divine everything He received from Mary.

In the Gospels Galilee pictures the external plane of life.

If we are to become spiritual, our natural knowledge of divine truth must be made spiritual by the presence of the Lord in our hearts. We must also be willing to make the effort to give what truth we have to others.

Marriage represents the union of good and truth.

Notes for Parents

As we all know, the Lord was born in Bethlehem, but the home of Mary and Joseph was really in Nazareth, and after the time spent in Egypt—where they were sent to save the infant Jesus from the jealous hatred of king Herod—they returned to Nazareth. There the Lord grew up and remained until He was about thirty years old. Then He came to the Jordan for baptism by John the Baptist and afterwards spent forty days in the wilderness tempted of the devil. During the remaining three years of His earthly life, His active

16

ministry, He made His home at Capernaum on the shore of the Sea of Galilee.

We learn these facts about the Lord's early life principally from the Gospels of Matthew and Luke. John gives us none of them. Some people have wasted a great deal of time trying to imagine what the Lord was doing in all those years, and stories with no truth in them have been written about them. The Gospels tell us all we need to know about the Lord's outward life in the world. We are not meant to dwell too much on it. What we do need to remember is that during those thirty years the Lord was carrying on the great purpose for which He came into the world, meeting day by day all the temptations which men have—which He could not have felt if He had not taken on our selfish humanity through Mary—overcoming them one by one, and so little by little putting off the finite humanity and bringing forth from within Himself a divine humanity to take its place.

That is why at the marriage feast at Cana in our lesson today, when Mary asked Him to exercise the power she knew He had, He said to her: "Woman, what have I to do with thee?" This is more literally translated, "Woman, what [belongs] to me and to thee?" It was not a rebuke to Mary and she did not receive it as one. It was said for us, so that we might understand that the Lord's power did not come from the human nature He had taken on but was in the divine humanity which was from the Father within Him.

This first miracle of the Lord demonstrated His power over nature. As we recently read, "The world was made by Him." The Lord's disciples were simple people. They wanted the truth He came to give and they believed in Him, but of themselves they would find it hard to hold their faith in the face of the arguments of the scribes and Pharisees to whom they had always looked up. The miracles helped to confirm their faith. Today we do not need miracles. We have the testimony of history to prove to our reason, if we choose to use it, that Jesus is God.

But the miracles in the Gospels have great meaning for us nevertheless. Each one teaches us something which the Lord can do for our souls. All of us who want the Lord to come into our lives have "six waterpots of stone," that is, knowledge of the general precepts of the Word waiting to be filled with meaning by study and meditation. To learn more and to think more is the first requirement. Then the Lord says to us, "Draw out now." Use your knowledge of the truth in meeting your daily problems and try to give it to others in need. Try it. It was in the drawing out that the water was turned to wine—the best wine. It is only as we use the truth that it is transformed in our minds and brings us joy and satisfaction.

Primary

The review of the Lord's life should be very simple and brief, covering mainly the Christmas story, the flight into Egypt, the return to Nazareth, and the baptism by John. The first miracle itself is simple and interesting. The children should be told that since the Lord made everything and keeps everything in existence all the time, He of course has control over everything. Be sure they know the details of the miracle.

Do you remember the name of the place where the Lord was born? The Lord did not grow up in Bethlehem. King Herod wanted to kill the Lord because it had been prophesied that He was to be king of the Jews. So Joseph was told in a dream to take Mary and Jesus down into Egypt for a time, where He would be safe. After Herod died, they came back, but they did not go to Bethlehem because that was not their home. They went back to Nazareth, which was the home of Mary and Joseph. Nazareth was in the province of Galilee, farther north in the land than Judea, where Bethlehem and Jerusalem were. The Lord grew up in Nazareth.

When He was twelve years old, He came to Jerusalem for His first Passover feast.

When He was about thirty, He came to John the Baptist to be baptized in Jordan.

What sign was given John at this time?

After His baptism the Lord spent forty days in the wilderness alone struggling with temptations.

Then He was ready for His active ministry.

John and all his disciples had been looking forward eagerly to the Lord's coming, and they received Him with joy. But the religious leaders, just like Herod, did not want the Lord to come, and they tried hard to make the people believe that Jesus was not really the promised savior. Then the Lord began to perform miracles to help the simple good people to overcome the doubts which their leaders put in their minds.

The Lord performed miracles also to strengthen the faith of His disciples.
What is a miracle?
Where was His first miracle performed?
Cana was a town seven miles north of Nazareth.
Why were the Lord and His disciples and Mary at Cana?
Why did Mary ask the Lord to help the people?
How many waterpots did they have?
How much did each of them hold? A *firkin** is about eight gallons.
What did the Lord tell the servants to do?
What happened to the water as it was poured out?

Junior

After reviewing the last lesson, do map work with the children, having them locate Galilee, Samaria, Judea, Capernaum, and Cana. Then with the map in front of them, review the Lord's early life before you go on to the lesson for today.

Each year we should have the facts of the Lord's early life clearly in mind as a preparation for studying His ministry in the world. A Bible map will show you that in the Lord's time the Holy Land had come to be divided into three provinces. Your teacher will help you to find the names of these provinces and also to locate the names of the cities and of the two lakes. You have studied the early life of the Lord in the Gospels of Matthew and Luke. Let us see if you remember the main facts.

Where was the Lord born?
Who was His mother?
Why had Mary and Joseph gone to Bethlehem?

---

*In KJV this translates the Greek *metretes* (measure) and refers to the Hebrew unit called a "bath," about 8-9 gallons. —Ed.

Where was their home?

What danger threatened the Lord after He was born?

Where was He taken until Herod died?

Where did the Lord grow up?

For what feast was He brought to Jerusalem when He was twelve?

What did He do in the temple at that time?

Who had been sent to prepare the people to receive the Lord?

How old was the Lord when He began His ministry?

Why did He first come to John the Baptist?

Where did He spend forty days after His baptism?

What happened to Him there?

Our lesson for today is about the first miracle the Lord performed after He began His ministry. A miracle is a wonderful thing which the Lord does to teach us a spiritual lesson. We have read of several miracles in our study of the Old Testament, such as the parting of the waters of the Red Sea and of the Jordan River, the giving of the manna during the wilderness journey, the bringing of water out of the rock at Horeb, and the healing of Naaman the Syrian. During His life on earth the Lord performed many miracles, and He gave His disciples power to perform them in His name. Some people think that the Lord's followers ought to have this power today, and some individuals even claim that they do have it. So we should know just why the Lord and His immediate followers performed miracles and why it is not orderly for them to be performed today.

We learned last week that when the Lord came into the world only a few simple good people were willling to receive Him. These people had been under the control of the scribes and Pharisees—who did not want the Lord's ministry to prosper—and when the scribes and Pharisees argued against belief in Him, it was hard for the simple people to stand firm. The Lord's miracles gave them something they could point to as proof that He was God, and the same power, which the disciples used in His name, convinced others who wanted to believe but who had not seen the Lord Himself. Today, however, we do not need this kind of proof to strengthen our faith. We can see with our minds that the Lord is God, and we have the testimony of the effect of His coming upon the world and upon men to point to as proof. We know that whenever sickness or affliction comes to us, it is contrary to God's will, but He tolerates it so as not to interfere with our freedom. At the same time He makes such states opportunities for us to gain spiritual strength, if we will. And we know that it is the Lord who heals us or brings us through our affliction when He sees that it is best for us. None of us likes to be sick, but we know that sickness has taught us many lessons.

There is another reason why the Lord performed miracles when He was on earth. His miracles all pictured things He could do for men's souls, and they were recorded in the Gospels to teach us spiritual lessons. For instance, we all can recognize that blindness pictures the inability to see what is true—we say people are "blind" in this way and that they "close their eyes" to things that are perfectly evident, because they don't want to "see" them. So the opening of the eyes of the blind by the Lord teaches us that if we believe in Him, He will make it possible for us to see what is true. Every miracle in the Word has a meaning which you will study when you are older.

Where was the Lord's first miracle performed?
Where was Cana?
Who went to Cana with the Lord?
Why did they go there?
What happened which led Mary to ask the Lord's help?
How many waterpots did the people have?
What did the Lord tell the servants to do?
What happened when the water was poured out?
What did the governor of the feast say about this wine?

Would you like to know a little of what this miracle means? You remember that water is a symbol of truth, and we all learn truth from the Word. But sometimes we just take it into our minds—as the servants filled the waterpots—and it doesn't seem to mean much in our lives. Then the Lord says to us, "Draw out now," and we try to draw out the truth we have learned and apply it to our lives and teach it to others, and suddenly it becomes "wine"—which is truth for our souls.

————————

Intermediate

The lesson for this class is in the correspondence of the details of the miracle. So short a reading gives a good opportunity to show the young people how important and full of meaning every verse is.

We have learned how different the Gospel of John is from the others. After the statement of the coming of the Lord into the world as the Word made flesh it goes directly into the Lord's ministry. For this reason we need at this point to refresh our memories concerning the external facts of the Lord's early life as they are found in the Gospels of Matthew and Luke. Mark's Gospel, you remember, begins with the appearance of John the Baptist and the Lord's baptism.

After the Lord's birth in Bethlehem He was presented at the temple at Jerusalem at the age of eight days according to Old Testament law. It was at that time that the aged Simeon and the prophetess Anna testified to His being the promised Messiah. Later the Wise Men from the East came with their gifts, and it was their visit which informed king Herod that the promised "king of the Jews" had been born in Bethlehem. And because Herod intended to destroy Him, Joseph was warned in a dream to take the young child and Mary to Egypt. When Herod died, they returned to the Holy Land, but not to Bethlehem. They went back to Nazareth in Galilee, which had been their home, and the Lord was brought up in Nazareth. At the age of twelve He was brought to Jerusalem for His first Passover, which was the equivalent of "confirmation" in our church. You remember how during that visit He was found in the temple talking with the learned men there, and that He astonished them with His answers to their questions. He returned to Nazareth with Mary and Joseph and was subject to them and "increased in wisdom and stature, and in favor with God and man." This is all the Gospels tell us about the childhood of the Lord.

We need to know that all through His thirty years of preparation for His ministry the Lord was meeting and overcoming temptations, gradually putting away the selfish human inheritance which He had taken on through Mary and putting forth in its place a divine humanity from within Himself. At about thirty years of age He came down to the Jordan and was baptized by John the Baptist and then went away alone for the forty days in the wilderness. His three temptations by "the devil" during that period picture all the kinds of temptation which He felt and overcame during His earthly life. He answered the devil each time with a quotation from the Word. After our last lesson we should easily understand why this was. Then the Lord left Nazareth and went to make His home at Capernaum on the shore of the Sea of Galilee, from which as a center He went about during the rest of His ministry.

In the time of the Lord the Holy Land was divided into three provinces—Judea, Samaria, and Galilee—representing the three planes of our lives—will, thought, and act. The greater part of the Lord's ministry was in Galilee. The greater part of our lives is spent in trying to serve the Lord and the neighbor in our daily life in the world. The Gospel of John tells us less about this Galilean ministry than the other Gospels, but it gives us the miracle of our lesson for today, the Lord's first miracle, which is recorded in none of the others. This miracle was performed in Cana of Galilee. Cana was a town about seven miles north of Nazareth. Swedenborg tells us that the Lord performed His miracles for two reasons: to strengthen the faith of the simple good people who wanted to believe in Him, and to picture—as part of the Word—the things which He can do in our souls, if we believe in Him and obey Him. We should note that the miracles never convinced anyone who did not already believe in the Lord. His enemies said that His power came from the devil.

Our reading for today is short, but there is a great deal packed into these eleven verses. The scene was in Galilee, symbol of the plane of outward conduct, and the place was Cana. Cana means "reedy." Reeds are the symbol of the simplest and most elementary truths. There was a marriage in Cana of Galilee, and the Lord, His disciples, and Mary were invited. Marriage always pictures the union of good and truth—a time when our desire and our understanding agree as to what we are to do. So this scene pictures a person who wants to do right in his outward life and has learned and obeyed at least the simple precepts of the Word, and who recognizes the Lord and wants His presence. The disciples here picture the means by which the Lord reaches out into the various fields of thought and desire in us, and Mary pictures the church. These were all present at the wedding. And there were six waterpots and plenty of water to fill them all to the brim. The waterpots, like all containers in the Word, picture general doctrines we have in our minds, and six pictures the orderly steps in the development of a good life—we may here go back in our minds to the six days of creation. The water is the truths with which these doctrines may be filled if we apply ourselves to studying them as the Lord commands us to do. The Lord's words to Mary, "Woman, what have I to do with thee?" are not a rebuke or a refusal. A more literal translation of the Greek is "Woman, what [belongs] to me and to thee?" The Lord was merely pointing out that the power He exercised did not come from the heredity He had assumed through Mary.

The Lord gave two commands: "Fill the waterpots with water," and, "Draw out now." We are not to be satisfied with merely knowing our doctrines in a general way; we are to learn all the truth we possibly can "hold." And then we are to use this truth in our lives and to do our best to give it to others. And it is in this drawing out that the "water" is turned into the best "wine"—spiritual truth which will delight our souls more than anything we have tasted before.

Basic Correspondences

Galilee	=	the plane of outward conduct
Samaria	=	the plane of thought
Judea	=	the plane of the will

waterpots = doctrine in the mind

―――――

Senior

The principal lessons to be emphasized are the importance of recognizing the Lord as God, the need of always continuing our study of the Word and the writings, and the fact that only as we use what we learn in service to the Lord and the neighbor can the spiritual be developed in us.

The Gospels of Matthew and Luke give us all we know of the external facts of the Lord's life on earth up to the time when, at the age of about thirty, He began His public ministry. If you are not thoroughly familiar with these facts, you should read chapter 2 of Matthew and chapter 2 of Luke. John, as we said in the last lesson, gives us the inner rather than the outer story of the Advent. John also omits the account of the Lord's baptism and of the forty days in the wilderness which followed it. For these read Matthew 3 and 4:1-11.

The three temptations of the Lord in the wilderness are a symbolic summing up of temptations—on all three planes of life: will, thought, and act—which He met and overcame progressively throughout His life. The Old Testament in its inmost or celestial sense tells the story of these temptations. Through them the Lord little by little put off the finite humanity He had taken on through Mary and put forth in its place the divine humanity from within. This was the process of glorification. By the time when He came forth from Nazareth to make His home at Capernaum after His baptism, this process had reached the point at which He could say to Mary: "Woman, what have I to do with thee?" This was not a rebuke to Mary and she did not receive it as one. Swedenborg gives us a literal translation of the Greek words: "Woman, what [belongs] to me and to thee?" The question points out to us that we need to distinguish between the finite humanity which the Lord assumed and the divine humanity in which He exercises power. We must never think of the Lord merely as the best man who ever lived. We must recognize Him as God, as the Word made flesh. And here we may remember that the Lord answered each of the devil's temptations with a quotation from the Word.

John begins the account of the Lord's ministry with the miracle at Cana. This first miracle of the Lord is recorded only in the Gospel of John. Swedenborg tells us that the Lord performed miracles for two reasons: to strengthen the faith of those who wanted to believe in Him, and to teach us—through their record in the Word— what He wishes to do for our souls and the method of His operation there. As we have learned, the scribes and Pharisees were bitterly opposed to the Lord because He brushed away their convenient traditions and taught the people the Word in its purity. The Lord's disciples were simple people and had been under the direction of the scribes and Pharisees all their lives. They wanted to believe in the Lord, but it was hard for them to maintain their faith in the face of the arguments of their recognized leaders. The miracles confirmed and strengthened their faith. We do not need miracles now. The Lord wants us to choose Him freely and to confirm our faith by reason. For us the miracles of the Gospels are important for their spiritual meaning.

The setting of the miracle of our lesson today is very striking. It was at Cana of Galilee. Galilee represents the plane of our outward life. The word *Cana* means "reedy." Grass and reeds are symbols of the most rudimentary knowledges of truth. Yet the occasion was a marriage feast and marriage represents the union of good and truth, and the Lord and His disciples and Mary were invited guests. And there was plenty of water, although the wine was "wanting." There are many people in the world today in this state, people who wish to live good lives, who want more truth for life than they possess, and who know that the truth is in the Word and seek the Lord and the church, yet who do not have enough knowledge and understanding of the truth to satisfy their spiritual thirst.

We all have "six waterpots of stone"—that is, general doctrines— vessels for receiving truth at all stages of our development. The first essential is that the servants—our faculties and capacities—fill these jars with water "to the brim," that is, that we make use of every opportunity to learn truths from the Word and the writings. Then we must "draw out" this water. Truth in the memory is pictured by the water standing in the jars. As we draw this truth out for use in our daily life and for the help and refreshment of our neighbor, it is turned to wine, "the best wine." Wine represents spiritual truth, truth which satisfies and refreshes the soul.

In the New Church we need to keep this miracle in mind. We cannot rest satisfied with having been brought up in the church and knowing something of its truths. We need constantly to add to our knowledge by our own study and effort, and we need to make these truths our own by living according to them and thinking of them in connection with every problem of our daily lives, and also by trying to present them to others who need them. The miracle will not fail. We shall grow in understanding and grace and find the wine better and better the longer we draw out.

Adult

The lessons suggested for the Seniors are needed by the Adults, too, especially the command to fill our "waterpots" with "water." We have an easygoing tendency to do external good works which our community will applaud rather than to make the effort to grow in understanding of what the Lord means by charity.

The miracle of our lesson is recorded only in the Gospel of John, and John calls it the "beginning of miracles." [KJV] In the other three Gospels we are told that the Lord's active ministry began immediately after His baptism and temptations in the wilderness, and that His baptism was the symbol of His putting off of the evils of the humanity He inherited from Mary. John does not specifically mention His baptism, but he gives more fully and clearly than any of the others the testimony of John the Baptist which was given at that time. And now we find Him, when asked to exert His divine power, first setting Himself apart from Mary. Swedenborg translates the Lord's words in verse 4, "Woman, what [belongs] to me and thee?" [following the Greek literally]. They are not a rebuke

to Mary but a question for consideration, implying that His power
to help the world was in no way derived from or through Mary.
(See the quotation from AC 2649 below.) Mary, as the Lord's
mother, represents the church, by means of which He comes into
the world, and it is in this character that she acts in our story as
the agent between Him and the people at the feast. The finite
humanity which the Lord took on from Mary was merely the instrument by means of which He came in contact with evil and overcame it. The church should perform the same service for us: it
should bring the Lord's truth to view and help us to apply it to
our evils so that, through His power, we may overcome them.

The result of this putting off of the finite humanity through
overcoming its evil tendencies was the gradual union of the Son
with the Father, of divine truth with divine love. It is for this reason
that the first miracle takes place at a marriage feast, for marriage
in its highest sense represents the union of divine love and divine
wisdom. In our study of the divided kingdom we saw the evils
which result when will and understanding are separated, when our
good desires do not seek the truth by means of which they can be
carried out, and our knowledge of the truth is not united with any
desire to act according to it. In the Lord, love and wisdom are
perfectly united. Thus true marriage is the highest possible state
of heavenly happiness, and everything in the world is created with
the desire for union with its complement. Throughout creation,
the things which represent love and truth tend to unite. This is
what makes the distinction between the two sexes and inspires
both with the desire for marriage, men picturing the intellectual
and women the affectional elements. So the highest and deepest
joys of life come from marriage love and the greatest evils and
disasters from its abuse.

The first two verses of our chapter give us a wonderful setting
for the miracle. Three pictures completeness; so "the third day"
suggests the fullness of time, the fact that the Lord had now reached
a state in which He could be in His active ministry. Galilee pictures
the external plane of life, and Cana, which means "reedy," suggests

a mere external understanding, for a reed is the symbol of the ultimate (lowest) sense of the Word, which can be easily bent by the
winds of fancy. The marriage, however, represents some union of
good and truth, Mary's presence the fact that the church is recognized, and the fact that the Lord and His disciples were invited
shows a desire for the presence of the Lord and knowledge of Him.
So all these details together give us a picture of a person living an
external life with a mere external knowledge of the Word, yet
having a genuine desire to live rightly, recognizing the church, and
desiring to know more of the Lord. This is the state of many in
the Christian church today.

What does it lack? The question reminds us of the rich young
man who told the Lord that he had kept the commandments from
his youth up and asked Him: "What lack I yet?" (Matthew 19:20)
What is lacking in this sort of life which the Lord can supply if we
call upon Him and fulfill His conditions?

Mary said, "They have no wine." Water and wine both represent
truth, but water is truth on the natural plane and wine is truth on
the spiritual plane. The commandments, as the rich young man
had kept them, were truths on the natural plane; he had recognized
them as necessary to orderly social life, to the preservation of his
self-respect and of the respect of the community. But when one
sees the commandments not only as necessary external laws but as
the Lord's laws, given through His mercy for the preservation and
development of our souls and to be kept with love and trust in
Him, they become spiritual laws, and the keeping of them brings
spiritual satisfaction. The water has been changed into wine. The
Lord told the rich young man to follow Him. Mary told the servants
at the feast, "Whatsoever he saith unto you, do it." This is following the Lord. "Ye are my friends, if ye do whatsoever I command
you." (John 15:14)

Then the Lord made use of the vessels which were at hand—six
of them, representing the general knowledges essential to the orderly
development of a spiritual life—and bade the servants fill them
with water to the brim. He did not send them out for wine, but

bade them use the water they had. "For this commandment which I command thee this day, it is not hidden from thee, neither is it far off . . . But the word is very nigh unto thee, in thy mouth, and in thy heart, that thou mayest do it." (Deuteronomy 30:11-14) Then He said, "Draw out now, and bear unto the governor of the feast." This is the command to use the truth we have to promote the union of good and truth, which is the Lord's kingdom in the soul. As we do this, the water is changed into wine. We all know that knowledge increases with use. No one realizes this more than a Sunday school teacher. Things become clear to us as we try to give them to a class. When we have made the best preparation we can, and genuinely desire to teach and help our pupils, frequently the right thoughts, the right words seem to come to us by inspiration as we teach. Similarly with all of us when we are facing a difficult problem in our lives, if we use what truth we have, trusting in the Lord, the way opens before us, and what seemed a heavy burden becomes a blessing instead.

In theological terms we are told that influx is in proportion to efflux. (AC 5828[3]) We are also told that the Lord is in everything in its use. If we recognize the Lord and obey Him, His presence will be in every service we perform, turning the water of our natural knowledge into the wine of spiritual truth, and as the water of truth from the letter of the Word cleanses our external lives, the wine of its internal truth will refresh our souls. We often have the experience described in verse 10 also. When we undertake a new service of some kind from merely external motives, our first enthusiasm often wanes and the wine becomes poorer and poorer, but if we are thinking instead of the Lord's service and the upbuilding of His kingdom, the best wine is saved to the last. In the New Church we all have our "six waterpots of stone," our general doctrines. And we must not neglect to fill these to the brim with "water"–to learn more and more truth, all our minds will hold. But the Lord is the vine. The true wine can come only from Him.

From the Writings of Swedenborg

Arcana Coelestia, n. 2649: "As the separation of the first human, which the Lord had from the mother, now follows, and at length the full removal of it, it is to be known that the Lord gradually and continually, even to the last of His life when He was glorified, separated from Himself and put off that which was merely human, namely, that which He derived from the mother, until at length He was no longer her son, but the Son of God, not only as to conception but also as to birth, and thus was one with the Father, and was Jehovah Himself. That He separated from Himself and put off all the human from the mother, so that He was no longer her son, is manifest from His words in John: 'When the wine failed, the mother of Jesus said unto him, They have no wine. Jesus saith unto her, Woman what [belongs] to me and to thee?*' "

Suggested Questions on the Lesson

J. Can you repeat the first verse of the Gospel of John?

J. Why do we call the inspired Scripture the Word of God? *it is God's Word to us*

J. Why does John call Jesus "the Word made flesh"? *He is living truth*

J. What is meant by saying that "in him was life, and the life was the light of men"? *His truth is alive, and enables us to live spiritually*

J. Why did the Lord have to come into the world? *to save us from our sins*

P. Who bore witness to His being the Messiah? *John the Baptist*

P. What sign was given to John the Baptist? *dove*

J. What disciple first met the Lord? *Andrew*

J. What other disciples are mentioned in the first chapter of John? *Peter, Philip, Nathanael (Bartholomew)*

P. Where was the Lord born? *Bethlehem*

J. In what division of the Holy Land was Bethlehem? *Judea*

P. Where did the Lord grow up? *Nazareth*

J. In what division of the land was Nazareth? *Galilee*

J. What division lay between Judea and Galilee? *Samaria*

J. Where did the Lord live during the three years of His ministry? *Capernaum*

J. What is a miracle? *a wonderful thing done by the Lord*

P. Where was the Lord's first miracle performed? *Cana*

P. Why did He go to Cana? *a wedding*

P. What was lacking at the feast? *wine*

P. Who went to the Lord for help? *Mary*

---

*"*Quid mihi et tibi, mulier?*" Also in DL 35. —Ed.

P. What did the Lord first tell the servants to do? *fill waterpots*

P. What happened? *water turned into wine*

P. What did the governor of the feast say about this wine? *it was best*

I. What does marriage represent? *uniting goodness and truth in life*

I. What do (1) water, and (2) wine represent? *(1) literal truth, (2) spiritual truth*

S. Why did the Lord perform miracles? *to strengthen the faith of His followers, and to symbolize the things He can do for our souls*

THE LORD AND NICODEMUS
John 3:1-21

This lesson may be approached through what was said in the lesson on John 1 of the attitude of the religious leaders. Nicodemus was an exception, and yet even he did not quite want to stand openly for the Lord. This is a doctrinal lesson, more important for the older young people and adults but still interesting for young children.

––––––––

Doctrinal Points

The Lord knows our worldly circumstances and makes allowance for our weakness.

The teachings of the Word are given to help and save us, not to make life hard or to condemn.

Disbelief in the Lord comes from unwillingness to live as He would have us live.

We may often recognize evil in our hearts by our efforts to cover up our real feelings.

––––––––

Notes for Parents

We are told in the first verse of our lesson that Nicodemus was a Pharisee and also that he was a "ruler" of the Jews. The latter term means that he was a member of the Sanhedrin, the high religious court, which had seventy members and was presided over by the high priest. This was the court by which the Lord was later tried and condemned. The Pharisees were a sect who prided themselves on their strict observance of all the religious rules, and we know that the Lord called them hypocrites. They opposed the Lord because His teaching undermined their selfish rule over the people.

Nicodemus showed intellectual independence in differing from the opinion of his fellows with regard to the Lord, and he evidently

33

wanted to learn from Him but at the time of our story did not quite have the courage to come to the Lord openly. The Lord did not wait for Nicodemus to ask a question. He knows all that is in our hearts and minds. He knew that Nicodemus, like many who came to him, wanted most of all to know how to get to heaven. So He began immediately to show him that the worldly and selfish attitudes into which we are all born must be changed if we are to become citizens of the kingdom of heaven.

John the Baptist had said, "I indeed baptize you with water unto repentance, but he that cometh after me . . . shall baptize you with the Holy Ghost and with fire." The baptism with water represents reformation—the cleansing of our outward conduct by means of truth from the Word. The baptism with the Holy Ghost (the Holy Spirit) and with fire is the coming into our minds and hearts of the Lord's truth and unselfish love as we try to drive out false thoughts and evil desires. This is regeneration.

Two other very important things the Lord told Nicodemus. One was that He had come into the world not to condemn people but to save them. People who try to bring others to their particular brand of religion by inspiring them with fear of the Lord's judgment should study this verse. The Lord never comes to condemn. If we are condemned, it is by our own choice of self and the world, for selfishness and worldliness are the loves which make hell. There is a kind of "fear of the Lord" which is right and good, but it is not fear of punishment. It is the fear of doing anything against the one who loves us so much.

The other lesson is one which Nicodemus needed and which we all often need. It is found in verses 19 to 21. Whenever we try to cover up our real thoughts and feelings, there is a warning signal. Either our thoughts and feelings are not what they should be, or we are not brave enought to speak the truth openly.

> For every one that doeth evil hateth the light, neither cometh to the light, lest his deeds should be reproved.
> But he that doeth truth cometh to the light, that his deeds may be made manifest, that they are wrought in God.

Primary

First discuss the scribes and Pharisees and the reason for their attitude toward the Lord. Then take up Nicodemus and do what you can with the Lord's instruction to him. The younger children will be more interested in the reason why he came to the Lord by night than in what the Lord told him. You may be able to show them that it is not always the things we see which are most powerful and most important. Verse 8 will help here.

When the Lord came into the world, the most respected among the people were the Pharisees. They were a group who considered themselves more religious than others. They had made up all sorts of rules which were not in the Scriptures and had made the people think that only those who kept all these rules were good. Most of the people did not have the Scriptures themselves and so did not know that the rules of the Pharisees were not part of the law which came from God.

The Lord did not keep the rules of the Pharisees, and He showed the people that the Pharisees were only pretending to be better than other people because they liked to be admired and obeyed. Naturally this made the Pharisees hate the Lord. They tried in every possible way to destroy the people's belief in Him. They could not deny His power to do miracles, but they said His power came from the devil.

But even among the Pharisees there were some men who wanted to do what was right.

One of these was the man in our lesson for today.

What was his name?

He was also a "ruler" of the Jews.

That meant a member of the great council of seventy which ruled the religious affairs of the nation.

What made Nicodemus believe in the Lord?

He was not quite brave enough to come to Him openly.

When did he come to the Lord?

What was the first thing the Lord told him?

Nicodemus could not understand this.

How did the Lord tell him a man must be born in order to enter the kingdom of heaven?

This means that we must learn to think about our souls instead of just about our bodies.

We cannot see our souls any more than we can see the wind.

But our souls are what make our bodies do all that they do.

So our souls are much more important than our bodies.

If our souls are to be healthy, we must learn about the Lord and what He wants us to do.

This was why the Lord came into the world.

He did not come to make life hard for us, but to teach us how to live so that we may be happy both here and in heaven.

Junior

This is a good opportunity to make sure that the Juniors understand who the scribes and Pharisees were and the reason for their attitude toward the Lord. They can also understand why Nicodemus came by night. The more important lessons in the Lord's words to Nicodemus can at least be suggested. There are several helpful Bible references for them to look up.

In Gospel times what two groups were considered the religious leaders?

The scribes were men who made copies of the Scriptures and also interpreted and taught them. The Pharisees were a sect who prided themselves on being more strictly religious than others. The Lord called both the scribes and the Pharisees hypocrites. A hypocrite is a person who pretends to be something he is not.

What had the scribes and Pharisees done to the Scriptures?

In our lesson for today who came to the Lord by night?

What two things do we learn about Nicodemus in the first verse?

A "ruler" of the Jews was a member of the Sanhedrin, the supreme council of seventy members who decided all religious matters. Most of the rulers rejected the claim of Jesus to be the promised Messiah. They wanted and expected a Messiah who would make their nation great again and so increase their own power and glory. When the Lord instead told them they must change their own ways, they tried in every possible way to discredit Him. As they could not deny the fact that He performed miracles, they claimed that His power came from the devil.

But there were at least two members of the Sanhedrin who did not agree with the rest. One was Nicodemus and the other Joseph of Arimathea. Read John 7:45-53 and Luke 23:50-52. Nicodemus was an honest man and could see that the power Jesus exercised must come from God, but he was not quite brave enough to stand openly against the opinions of those with whom he had to associate every day. So he came to the Lord secretly—by night.

Notice that the Lord gave him an answer before he even asked a question. The Lord always knows what is in our minds. Nicodemus was concerned about the way to heaven.

What did the Lord tell him?
What kind of birth did He say was necessary?
Do you remember who baptized with water?
What had John the Baptist said about the Lord's baptism? (John 1:33)

To be "born of water and of the Spirit" means to have both our outward and our inward life—our conduct and our thoughts and feelings—made pure and good by obeying the teachings of the Lord. The Holy Ghost or Holy Spirit is the Lord's Spirit working in us.

The story of the serpent in the wilderness referred to in verses 14 and 15 you will find in Numbers 21:5-9. A serpent, which goes along on the ground, is a symbol of our bodily senses, which are always in contact with the physical world. The Lord showed us what our life in this world is for and how we should use it. He is the example which we should always hold up before us. This is what He means by comparing Himself to the serpent in the wilderness.

The teaching of the Lord in verses 14 to 21 you will understand better when you are older, but you can see a little of its meaning now if you will read John 18:37. The Lord came into the world to teach and to live out the truth so that we may know surely what it is, and be free to do right or wrong by our own choice. Those who reject the Lord do so of their own free will, because they do not want to know and obey the truth. And if we reject the truth and so do wrong, the consequences of our wrong deeds are not from the Lord but of our own making.

The second birth of which the Lord told Nicodemus, which is also called regeneration, is the process of learning the Lord's laws and making ourselves obey them until they have become a part of our very life. Then the love of right can come into our hearts from the Lord, and we can become truly His children.

Nicodemus remained faithful to the Lord all his life. Read John 19:38-42.

———

Intermediate

The important lesson for this class is the meaning of being born again of water and the Spirit. Other lessons are also suggested below.

Nicodemus came to the Lord by night. This was, in the literal sense, undoubtedly because open association with the Lord would have brought upon him ridicule and censure from the other "rulers" with whom he constantly associated. For a "ruler of the Jews" was a member of the Sanhedrin, the supreme council, composed of seventy priests and lawyers. In the spiritual sense the night pictures the ignorance of his mind with regard to spiritual truth.

That Nicodemus was a thoughtful man we know because he did not agree with the vast majority of his fellows, but saw that the power manifested in the Lord must come from God. That he was a good man we know because he came to the Lord to ask the way of life, and also because he remained steadfast in his belief in the face of overwhelming opposition. Read John 7:40-53 and 19:39. This took real courage. At the time of our lesson he had not yet developed this courage. The Lord did not at once rebuke Nicodemus for coming to Him secretly, but in verse 21, after His preliminary instruction, He showed him the right course. The Lord knows all our weaknesses and makes allowance for them, but this should not lead us to excuse ourselves.

The Lord also knows what is in our hearts without our telling Him. He saw immediately just what was the question which was in the mind of Nicodemus, and went at once to the heart of the answer. It was essentially the same answer which He gave to others and which He gives to all who look to Him for the way. To be born again, to be born of water and of the Spirit, is another injunction to repent and follow the teachings of the Lord's truth. You remember that the wilderness journey of the Israelites represented the period of reformation—the putting in order of our outward conduct—and that John's baptism with water also represents this. Now read again John 1:33. Regeneration—the bringing of our inner thoughts and feelings into the Lord's order, which the conquest of the Holy Land represented—is the baptism with the Holy Ghost or Holy Spirit. Regeneration means rebirth.

The same lesson is taught in verses 14 and 15. The serpent pictures the sense life and brass is the symbol of good on the external plane. The brazen serpent which Moses was commanded to raise up on a pole in the wilderness (Numbers 21:5-9) pictures the right use of the sense life, its use to promote the spiritual life. This was exactly the use which the Lord made of the finite humanity which He assumed when He was born into the world. So this reference to the brazen serpent links the Lord's teaching concerning the second birth, or regeneration, with the statement which follows about His purpose in coming into the world. He came as the truth—the Son— to give the world the light by which men might safely walk. The world had lost its way. The Jews alone had the Word and they had so obscured it by their traditions that even Nicodemus did not know what it really taught.

There is a very plain lesson for all of us in verses 19 to 21. When we are bent on having our own way, we do not want to hear the truth: we prefer to walk in darkness. When we really are trying to do right, we seek the truth, the light. In simple terms this means that whenever we find ourselves trying to conceal our real thoughts and feelings, it is time to examine ourselves carefully to see if our thoughts are true and our feelings kind. And whenever we find ourselves resentful of criticism and impatient of advice, it is time to ask ourselves if what we are doing is really right in the Lord's sight. We should always remember that our friends are also instruments of the Lord and that the Lord may be using them as means in His constant effort to help and save us. Read verses 16 and 17 of our chapter.

Basic Correspondences

the serpent	=	the sense life
brass	=	good on the external plane
to be born of water	=	the reformation of the outward conduct
to be born of the Spirit	=	regeneration, the changing of our thoughts and feelings by the Lord's Spirit
night	=	a state of ignorance

Senior

To the lesson suggested for the Intermediates add especially the suggestion made in the Senior notes on the basis of verse 8. Young people need this sort of weapon with which to meet skepticism and materialism, Swedenborg quotes this verse in AC 10240 (where it reads "Spirit" in the first part of the verse where "wind" seems more reasonable, since an analogy is involved). [See, however, AE 130, 183, AR 343 where *ventus* (wind) is used, and also AC 8246, which says "spirit" (or wind)." –Ed.]

In *Divine Providence*, n. 83 Swedenborg tells us: "No one can come into the kingdom of God unless he has been born again, for the reason that man by his inheritance from his parents is born into evils of every kind, but with an ability to become spiritual by the removal of those evils; and unless he becomes spiritual he cannot come into heaven. From being natural to become spiritual is to be born again or regenerated." Elsewhere (*New Jerusalem and Its Heavenly Doctrine*, n. 174): "Man is not born of his parents into spiritual life, but into natural life. Spiritual life consists in loving God above all things, and in loving his neighbor as himself, and this according to the precepts of faith which the Lord has taught in the Word. But natural life consists in loving ourselves and the world more than the neighbor, yea, more than God Himself."

Nicodemus was a good man. His comments and questions show clearly the obscurity into which even the good had fallen when the Lord came into the world. He knew of no other birth than natural birth, and could not understand what the Lord meant when He said one must be born of water and of the spirit. People today are often handicapped in the same way by the materialism of our times. Verse 8 of our chapter suggests a good answer to those who say, "How can I believe in spiritual things which I cannot see?" We cannot see the wind, but we are sure it exists because we see and feel its effects. We can all likewise—if we use our reason—see and feel the effects of spiritual forces.

We can connect the Lord's words with John the Baptist's statement (Matthew 3:11): "I indeed baptize you with water unto repentance: but he that cometh after me is mightier than I, whose shoes I am not worthy to bear: he shall baptize you with the Holy Ghost, and with fire." The baptism with water is the cleansing of the outward life, the baptism with the Holy Ghost (or Holy Spirit) the purification of the thoughts, and the baptism with fire the replacing of self-love by love to the Lord and the neighbor.

The Lord came into the world as divine truth. In the internal sense Father, Son, and Holy Spirit are divine love, divine wisdom, and divine proceeding or operation in the world, a trinity to which will, thought, and act in each of us are analogous. Divine truth is the light of the world. If we recognize and obey it, we walk in the light. If we reject it, we walk in darkness.

The teaching in verses 18 to 21 is very clear and really gives us the whole doctrine concerning judgment. How anyone can read it and believe in predestination is hard to see—or for that matter in punishment as coming from God or in universal salvation or in faith alone.

The Lord as the truth came into the world that men might know the way with certainty. The only reason why men have rejected Him is because they "loved darkness rather than light, because their deeds were evil." There are no rational grounds for rejecting the Lord—only selfish grounds. It is wholly a matter of our free choice. From the beginning the Lord has always given men light for their way if they were willing to use it. Jeremiah wrote: "And the Lord hath sent unto you all his servants the prophets, rising early and sending them; but ye have not hearkened, nor inclined your ear to hear."

There is a lesson for us, too, in the fact that Nicodemus came to the Lord by night. It was, of course, a symbol of his ignorance, but it also showed his unwillingness to face the consequences of showing his real opinion in public. Whenever we feel ourselves unwilling to be "open" in our dealing, it is time to take stock of ourselves. We may, like Nicodemus, be thinking rightly but ashamed to stand up for what we think. Or we may be selfish in our thoughts and feelings and trying to pretend that we are not. In either case something needs correction. The Lord knows our weaknesses and deals with us very kindly, trying to lead us to face ourselves honestly. Notice that although he did not charge Nicodemus with his cowardice, His instruction led finally to the statement in verse 21, which clearly pointed out his fault. Read John 7:45-53, which shows that Nicodemus at least made an effort to support the Lord after this, and also John 19:39, which shows us that Nicodemus remained a faithful follower of the Lord.

Adult

There are several good discussion topics here: the reason why people accept or reject the Lord, the meaning of reformation and regeneration and the necessity for them, the purpose of the Lord's coming, and the reason why people are saved or condemned.

Nicodemus was a Pharisee and a ruler of the Jews, yet he believed that the Lord came from God, and he came to Him for instruction. The Pharisees were a sect who adhered very strictly to the literal observance of the religious laws. We know from the Lord's own words that they were for the most part hypocrites (Matthew 23:25-28), keeping the law only externally and caring nothing for its spirit. Nicodemus was evidently altogether ignorant of the meaning of the Scriptures, for he did not understand what the Lord is talking about; yet he wanted to learn. His coming by night pictures his state of ignorance, as well as his fear of the judgment of his worldly associates. His recognition of the Lord's authority was based not upon any understanding of the Lord's character but upon the miracles He had performed. The Lord did not immediately call his attention to his cowardice in coming by night, but explained to him with divine patience just what his state was and what was needful if he was to attain the kingdom of heaven. We should note, however, that His instruction led up to the statement in verse 21, which must have shown Nicodemus his weakness. The Lord did not advise Nicodemus, as He did the rich young man, to leave his wealth and position and follow Him, but He pointed out the necessity of a change in his inner attitudes.

That Nicodemus remained true to the Lord is attested by his attempt to defend Him later (John 7:50) and by the fact that he was one of the two rich men who cared for the Lord's body after the crucifixion (John 19:39). The Lord always recognizes our outward circumstances and the limitations they impose on us. Recall the permission given to Naaman the Syrian by Elisha (II Kings 5:18-19) and the Lord's prayer for His disciples: "I pray not that thou shouldest take them out of the world, but that thou shouldest keep them from the evil." (John 17:15)

We know that throughout the Word natural birth and development are analogous to regeneration, but the Jews had no such knowledge, although more ancient people had had it (AC 4904²). Regeneration, which means rebirth, does not take place suddenly and all at once, but gradually and progressively, like natural conception, birth, and growth. Nothing could be clearer than Swedenborg's explanation of the Lord's teaching in our lesson: "No one can come into the kingdom of God unless he has been born again, for the reason that man by inheritance from his parents is born into evils of every kind, but with an ability to become spiritual by the removal of those evils; and unless he becomes spiritual, he cannot come into heaven. From being natural to become spiritual is to be born again or regenerated." (DP 83) "Man is not born of his parents into spiritual life, but into natural life. Spiritual life consists in loving God above all things, and in loving his neighbor as himself, and this according to the precepts of faith, which the Lord has taught in the Word. But natural life consists in loving ourselves and the world more than the neighbor, yea, more than God Himself." (NJHD 174) See also NJHD 179 below. A detailed explanation of verses 5 to 8 of our chapter is given in AC 10240.

We are familiar with the teaching concerning reformation and regeneration, for we had it in the stories of the wilderness wanderings and the conquest of the Holy Land. Reformation is the first part, our first duty, the setting in order of our outward lives in accordance with the truths of the Word. Regeneration begins when we begin to try to recognize and fight our inner foes, the evils and falsities in our hearts and minds, enabling the Lord's spirit to enter as we drive out the things which oppose it. This inflow of the Lord's spirit is compared to the wind. We do not see it but we are conscious of its effects. It may be noted that it is the same word in the Greek which is translated "spirit" in most of the chapter and "wind" in verse 8, the context suggesting the change in translation. The Greek word has both meanings. The same lesson is taught in the brief parable in Mark 4:26-29. Reformation and regeneration are also described in the work of John the Baptist and that of the Lord, and John the Baptist uses words similar to those in our chapter in Matthew 3:11. That only the Lord's spirit has power to raise men into heaven is taught in verses 11 to 15. The brazen serpent lifted up in the wilderness for the healing of the people was a symbol of the Lord's sensual nature which He lifted up by conquering all its temptations, thus showing us the way to heaven. The human which He took on in the world was in the inverted order described above, but in His life in the world He progressively glorified it, that we might see what the true order is and form our lives according to it. By the second birth, the birth of a new character from the Lord's spirit working within us, we become children of our heavenly Father. "But as many as received him, to them gave he power to become the sons of God, even to them that believe on his name: Which were born, not of blood, nor of the will of the flesh, nor of the will of man, but of God."

Naturally we think of those teachings of the Word which oppose our selfish impulses as hard. The Lord seems to condemn. Yet we have intelligence enough to see that this is not so. In Deuteronomy 6:24 we are told that the Lord commands us to keep His statutes and to fear Him "for our good always." The Lord came into the world in a human which He calls His Son to show us the nature of His love, to show us that He is always ready to give us His love if we will only open the way for it in our souls by putting aside the evils which shut Him out. He wants us to be happy, and He knows that happiness can never come through self-seeking. He teaches us this by every means in His power, by plain instruction, by parable, by miracle, by personal experience, by His own life in the world. If we believe in Him—really believe in Him so that we take His advice—we shall without fail be happy; we shall have "everlasting life." But if we do not believe in Him, we are "condemned," not by Him but by our own choice of worldliness and self-seeking, which are bound to lead us to unhappiness.

To believe in the Lord's "name" is to believe in His character, to believe that the love, humility, meekness, and gentleness which He manifested are truly divine characteristics, virtues to be cultivated. If we do not believe this, we are, as He says, "condemned already." For the love of self and the world which we cultivate instead of His virtues is in itself the fire of hell. Verses 19 to 21 are easily understood. We know that when we are bent upon having our own way, we will not listen to advice; we do not want the light of truth to show us that our way is wrong. This is the fundamental reason for disbelief in the Lord—unwillingness to recognize our evils and to correct our lives according to His teachings. Whenever we are anxious to cover up our deeds, or our thoughts, or our feelings, we may recognize it as a danger signal, for "he that doeth truth cometh to the light, that his deeds may be made manifest, that they are wrought in God."

From the Writings of Swedenborg

The New Jerusalem and Its Heavenly Doctrine, n. 179: "Every one has an internal man and an external man; the internal is what is called the spiritual man, and the external is what is called the natural man, and each is to be regenerated, that the man may be regenerated. With the man who is not regenerated, the external or natural man rules, and the internal serves; but with the man who is regenerated, the internal or spiritual man rules, and the external serves. Whence it is manifest that the order of life is inverted with man from his birth, namely, that serves which ought to rule, and that rules which ought to serve. In order that man may be saved, this order must be inverted; and this inversion can by no means exist, but by regeneration from the Lord."

Suggested Questions on the Lesson

J. Who were the (1) scribes, and (2) Pharisees? *(1) men who copied the Scriptures, (2) a strict religious sect*

J. What had they done to the Scriptures? *added many of their own ideas*

J. What did the Lord call them? *hypocrites*

J. Why were they opposed to the Lord? *he exposed their hypocrisy*

P. What is the name of the man in our lesson for today? *Nicodemus*

J. What was he besides being a Pharisee? *a ruler (member of Sanhedrin)*

P. Why did he come to the Lord by night? *afraid of ridicule*

J. Why did he believe in the Lord? *miracles*

J. What did the Lord see he wanted to ask? *way to heaven*

P. What did the Lord tell him? *you must be born again*

I. What did the Lord mean by being "born again"? *repent, follow His teachings*

J. What did the Lord say about the brazen serpent in the wilderness? *. . . so must Son of man be lifted up*

J. Why did the Lord say He came into the world? *to save it*

J. Why does He say some people are condemned? *will not believe*

J. Why should we stop to think every time we find ourselves trying to cover up our thoughts or feelings or actions? *probably means we just want our own way*

I. What does it mean to be "born of water"? *outer life cleansed*

S. What does it mean to be "born of the Spirit"? *inner life purified*

S. How is this related to the work of (1) John the Baptist, and (2) the Lord? *(1) cleansing outer life (2) purifying thoughts, replacing self-love with love of the Lord and the neighbor*

THE LORD AT JACOB'S WELL
John 4:1-42

This story ties in with several of our earlier lessons, especially the deaths of Jacob and Joseph and the lesson on the conquest of Israel by Assyria. The teachers should read for background Genesis 33:18-20; 48:21-22; 50:24-26; Exodus 13:19; Joshua 24:32; and II Kings 17:24-41. These links connecting our chapter with the Old Testament story should be touched on in all classes but not at such length as to leave insufficient time to develop the lesson of the chapter.

Doctrinal Points
The more we learn about the Lord's life and teaching the more we will become convinced that He is God with us.

The Word is our well of living water.

Charity needs faith or truth to maintain it.

Likewise faith needs charity to maintain it. Each perishes when separated from the other.

Notes for Parents
After the first miracle at Cana the Lord with His disciples went down to Jerusalem to celebrate the feast of the Passover. Our story today is about something that happened on their journey back to Galilee.

Between Judea in the south and Galilee in the north lay the province of Samaria. It was so called from the city of Samaria, which had been the capital of the kingdom of Israel before it was conquered by Assyria. The foreigners who were sent in by the king of Assyria to take the place of the people of Israel kept Samaria as their chief city and came to be called the Samaritans. And in our lesson we find that their descendants were still despised and shunned even after seven hundred years, and in spite of the fact that from the first they had accepted the God of the Jews as an object of worship and had learned much from their sacred Scriptures.

The Samaritans were Gentiles, but our story shows us that they were well-disposed and open-minded, for they believed the Lord much more readily than did most of the Jews. The Lord told the woman of Samaria plainly that He was the promised Messiah, and when she and her people had listened to His teaching, they accepted Him as the Christ, the savior of the world.

It is this acceptance which can turn the water of truth which everyone to some extent draws from the Word of God—Jacob's well—into living water springing up into everlasting life. It is only as we see and acknowledge that Jesus Christ was indeed "God with us," the "Word made flesh," that we begin to find the real truth in the Word and to love it. Sometimes people—people who honestly think they are looking for truth in the Scriptures—say that of course Jesus was limited by the ideas and conditions of His times, and that if He had lived in our country and our times, He would have said different things. They are thinking of Jesus as merely the best man who ever lived and setting their own opinions up as more valid than His. Their ideas are like the pitcher of the woman of Samaria, which could draw only a little water from the deep well. But when we believe that Jesus was God Himself, living for a time in a finite human like ours, we know that He always spoke the eternal truth and that only as we receive His teachings and try to form our lives according to them can His Spirit enter our souls with the life of heaven. As He had told Nicodemus in Jerusalem just before the time of our story for today, "Ye must be born again," and, "Except a man be born of water and of the Spirit, he cannot enter into the kingdom of God."

———

Primary

The history of the parcel of ground may be used to bring back to the children's minds the names *Abraham*, *Isaac*, *Jacob*, *Joseph*, and *Moses*. Then tell them who the Samaritans were and why they were despised, so that they will understand the woman's words in verse 9 when you read the story. If they show any curiosity about the Lord's words, tell them simply that the living water is truth about the Lord and heaven, which our souls need just as our bodies need water. Stress the fact that the Samaritans readily believed the Lord.

After the wedding in Cana, where the Lord turned water into wine, He went down to Jerusalem to the Passover feast. On His way back to Galilee He was going through the part of the land called Samaria, and He stopped to rest at Jacob's well.

Do you remember who Jacob was? He was Isaac's son and Abraham's grandson. Long, long before the time of our story he had bought a piece of ground near the center of the land and had dug a well there. And when he died, he left this particular piece of land to his son Joseph. Perhaps you remember, too, that when Joseph died in Egypt, he commanded his people not to bury him in Egypt but to preserve his body and take it back with them when they went home. So they embalmed his body and put it in a coffin, and when Moses led them out of Egypt, they took Joseph's body with them. They carried it all through the journey in the wilderness and, after they conquered the Holy Land, finally buried it in this very piece of land which Joseph had received from his father. So Jacob's well was a very fitting place for the Lord to rest.

But the people who lived in the neighborhood at this time were not Jews. They were called Samaritans. They were descended from the foreigners whom the Assyrians had sent in to take the place of the people of Israel when their kingdom was overthrown by Assyria. So now, even after hundreds of years, the Jews still despised the Samaritans, although the Samaritans to some extent had accepted the religion of the Jews. We need to know this to understand our story for today.

What did the Lord ask of the Samaritan woman?
What did the Lord tell the woman she ought to ask of Him?
She did not understand what He was talking about.
"Living" water means truth from the Lord, for which our souls ought to be thirsty.
The Samaritans had learned about the Jewish religion and accepted part of it.
What question did the woman ask which showed this?
What did the Lord tell her?

The woman believed Him, and she went and brought other Samaritans to hear Him.

He stayed with them two days teaching them, and they believed what He said.

Junior

After the review have the class look up the Bible references. They will be interested in the story from II Kings 17. The more we can tie the Old Testament and the New together in their minds the better. The Juniors should also be able to get something of the correspondence of the two kinds of water.

Into what parts was the Holy Land divided in the Lord's time?
In which part were Jerusalem and Bethlehem?
In which part were Nazareth and Cana?
In what city in Galilee did the Lord live during His ministry?

The last part of chapter 2 tells us that not long after the wedding at Cana the Lord went down to Jerusalem for the feast of the Passover. The events of chapter 3 took place there. Then the Lord started back to Galilee.

What part of the land lay between Judea and Galilee?
Where did the Lord stop to rest?
Who came to the well to draw water?
What did the Lord ask of her?
Why was the woman surprised?

To understand this chapter we need to look up some passages in the Old Testament. First read Genesis 33:18-20; 48:21-22; 50:24-26; Exodus 13:19; and Joshua 24:32. You see that this particular piece of ground had a great deal of history behind it. Yet it was now part of the district belonging to the Samaritans. This was because it had been part of the kingdom of Israel, and when Israel was conquered by Assyria, all its people were carried away captive and never came back. Foreigners were brought in to settle the land in their place. The Samaritans were the descendants of these foreigners. Now you can see why the Jews had no dealings with the Samaritans. They despised them because they were not Jews.

Yet you find in our story that the Samaritan woman was aware that the Messiah was to come and was willing to believe the Lord, although the Samaritans did not go to Jerusalem to worship. There is an interesting story which tells us how the Samaritans came to accept part of the Jewish faith but not all of it. Read this story in II Kings 17:24-33.

What did the Lord say the woman should have asked of Him?
What did He say about this "living" water?
What did He tell the woman about herself?
What question did she ask Him?
What did He tell her about God?
What did He tell her about the Messiah?
What did He tell His disciples about His food?

The Samaritans believed the Lord much more readily than the Jews did. They were like the Gentile people of Nineveh who believed Jonah and repented. This was because they were not full of pride in themselves and their own wisdom. You know that when a person "thinks he knows it all," it is very hard to teach him anything.

Now let us think a little about what the Lord meant by "living" water. You know that water is the symbol of truth. We sometimes say a person has a "thirst for knowledge." Our minds need knowledge just as our bodies need water. And we need knowledge about the Lord and heaven and about what is right and wrong. This is the water of Jacob's well—the knowledge we get from the Word of God. We are constantly having to learn more of this kind of knowledge. But people may have a great deal of knowledge about the letter of the Word and yet not be good people. This was the case with the scribes and Pharisees. They were proud of their knowledge, but did not use it to correct their own evils. They did not take it to heart. Those who received the Lord, however, wanted truth from Him so that they could live according to it. They came to Him for truth for their souls. This is the living water, because we receive it constantly from the Lord and make it our own by obeying it.

===

Intermediate

The lesson in its Old Testament background involves some review, in which the correspondence will be interesting and helpful, and the meaning of the lesson itself is important. Stress the necessity of recognizing the Lord as God and seeing that all genuine truth and goodness are from Him.

The Lord and His disciples had been to Jerusalem for the feast of the Passover and were returning to Galilee. One of the first things to notice in our lesson today is the statement in verse 4 that "he must needs go through Samaria." We have learned that the three divisions of the Holy Land in Gospel days—Judea, Samaria, and Galilee—represent the three planes in our lives—will, thought, and act. The Lord made this journey between Judea and Galilee in one direction or the other many times. In either direction He had to pass through Samaria. Spiritually this is true in our lives. When we have a desire of some kind, in order to carry it out in act we must think about it. And before the circumstances of our outward life and conduct can have any effect on our will or motives, we must think about them. Our minds are the connecting link between our motives and our conduct.

This part of the land was inhabited by the Samaritans. You remember that they were descendants of the foreigners who were brought in to settle the land when the kingdom of Israel was conquered by Assyria and its people were carried away captive never to return. This explains why the Jews had no dealings with the Samaritans. They were not of their nation. However, the Samaritans to some extent practiced their religion, although they did not go to Jerusalem to worship. In II Kings 17 we are told that when the foreigners first came into the land, they were plagued by lions and thought that it was because they did not know how to worship the gods of this land. So the king of Assyria sent back one of the captured priests to teach them, and they added the worship of Jehovah to the worship of the various gods of their native lands. Verse 41 of II Kings 17 says: "So these nations feared the Lord, and served their graven images, both their children, and their children's children: as did their fathers, so do they unto this day." Some of the statements of the woman of Samaria in our chapter are explained by this.

There is also an internal meaning for us in this condition. We all grow up in the world. Our minds have in them some knowledge of the truths of the Word, but this knowledge is mixed up with all sorts of worldly ideas, many of them accepted because they favor our natural selfishness—our native land. Yet we do have a center which we recognize as the source of genuine truth to which we go regularly when we feel the need, as the woman of Samaria went to Jacob's well. You may remember from our Old Testament lessons that Jacob represents the natural plane of our lives in its relation to the Lord, and a well represents the Word. In Genesis 33:19 we learn that Jacob had bought this "parcel of ground" from Hamor, who was a Hivite—the Hivites were one of the good remnants of the Ancient Church. It was this field which Jacob on his death bed gave to his son Joseph as an extra portion (Genesis 48:22), and it was here that the Israelites, after they reconquered the Holy Land, buried the bones of Joseph, which they had brought back with them from Egypt (Joshua 24:32) in accordance with Joseph's last request (Genesis 50:25-26).

The village of Sychar was in the same general locality as the old sites of Shechem and Shiloh. Shechem was the place where Abraham erected his first altar when he came into the land of Canaan from Ur of the Chaldees, and Shiloh was the place where Joshua set up the tabernacle after the conquest, with Mount Ebal to the north and Mount Gerizim to the south. The importance of this small section of the Holy Land appears clearly from all these references, and now it is finally the scene of the Lord's simple, literal statement that He was the promised Messiah (verse 26). Try to remember this chapter and verse, for you will hear people who do not want to accept Jesus Christ as God actually say that He never claimed to be the Messiah.

Our minds, then, are symbolized by the district of Samaria. Ideally, in the center of our minds we have the Word, to which we go for truth as we need it. If we are in the state represented by the woman of Samaria—wanting to know the truth and yet very much mixed up in our minds because of false ideas there—we have to go again and again, drawing only a little "water" (that is, truth) at a time and then thirsting again. Then suddenly one day we come to the well and find the Lord sitting there. We are faced with the necessity of making up our own minds about Jesus Christ instead of just getting along on what we have been taught. It is not until we have reached this point that we can find the *living* water—that the truths of the Word come to be a vital part of our lives, "a well of water springing up into everlasting life," because we see that they come from divine wisdom itself, the Lord Jesus Christ.

The woman questioned the Lord, as we have to question. It takes time to come into understanding. You remember that in general a woman represents affections and a man thoughts. What the Lord told the woman about herself in verse 18 pictures the state of one who wants to be good and tries one system of belief after another hoping it is the right one, yet is never really satisfied. There are many people in that state today. The fact that the Lord could tell her the truth about her condition immediately convinced the woman that He was a prophet, and as she went on talking with Him, she believed more and more and finally brought others to believe in Him. It will be the same with us if we continue to learn of the Lord.

The little incident concerning the disciples balances the story. They already believed in the Lord. They had faith in Him. But they still did not quite understand about charity. Food, in general— in contrast to drink—represents goodness. The disciples had bought food. This pictures the fact that they thought goodness or charity was something they could acquire by their own efforts and so think of as their own. But the Lord would not accept this food. He showed them that true goodness cannot be bought for a price. It comes from the Lord alone. "My meat is to do the will of him that sent me, and to finish his work." This teaches us the lesson that of ourselves we have no goodness and that true charity is to do as well as we can whatever work the Lord gives us to do in the world, looking to Him for the strength to do it and giving Him credit for all good that comes of it.

Basic Correspondences

"this" water = natural truth
"living" water = the truth when we recognize
the Lord's presence in it.

Senior

The lesson for this class may well be centered on the Samaritan state in our minds. Young people take into their minds in school and through their friends many things which they are not prepared to evaluate. If they know this, they will find it less difficult to hold their faith until understanding comes to them with maturity.

Our chapter for today really carries one step further the lesson of the miracle at Cana. Between that miracle and the story of the Lord at Jacob's well, the Lord had been to Jerusalem to celebrate the Passover and there had given Nicodemus the teaching concerning the necessity of rebirth or regeneration. Of the three divisions of the land in the time of the Lord, Judea represents the plane of will or motive, Samaria the plane of thought, and Galilee the plane of outward life or conduct. In the miracle at Cana in Galilee the Lord teaches us that only as we use the truth in our daily lives can we come to enjoy right living. In His instruction to Nicodemus in Judea (chapter 3) He points out that our motives must be made heavenly instead of selfish. Now in returning to Galilee he "must needs go through Samaria" and His lesson there has to do with our thoughts.

Our minds—at least during the early years of our lives—are a sort of "no man's land." We have in them knowledges of right and wrong given us from the Word by our parents and teachers, the "parcel of ground that Jacob gave to his son Joseph." And we also have in our minds "Jacob's well," the Word in its letter. But the land is in the possession of the Samaritans, who were Gentiles although they knew and accepted many of the precepts of Judaism. The Samaritans were descendants of the foreigners whom the king of Assyria sent in to take the place of the ten tribes of Israel who were carried away and never returned. In II Kings 17 you will find the story which explains the religious confusion in which the Samaritans were. The Jews despised them and would have no dealings with them, but throughout the Gospels they are represented as well-disposed people and more open to instruction by the Lord than were the Jews. Swedenborg tells us that every new religious dispensation, while it begins among the good remnant of the former dispensation, has its real growth among the Gentiles. This was true of the First Christian Church and it will be true of the New Church.* Right now the New Church is growing much faster in Asia and Africa than in the so-called Christian countries.

There is also a Gentile state in many people living in Christian countries. Many people all around us are well-disposed but in complete confusion as to their religious belief. The Lord said of the Samaritan woman, "Thou hast had five husbands; and he whom thou now hast is not thy husband." We remember that in general a woman represents affections and a man thoughts. The Samaritan woman had never found the right husband. So good people today may drift from one denomination to another without ever finding a doctrine in which they can really believe. It is just such people that we of the New Church organization should recognize as the fields "white already to harvest." Because, like the disciples, we have accepted the Lord and have the knowledge these Christian Gentiles are seeking.

The contrast in our chapter between the Lord's words to the Samaritan woman and His words to His disciples is very striking. The Samaritan woman came to Jacob's well to draw water. Good intentions or charity must seek truth. The disciples, who had accepted the Lord as the truth, had "gone away unto the city to buy meat." Here the disciples stand for those who seek goodness, but think they can obtain it by their own efforts apart from the Lord. Faith must be united to charity, but often those who have

---

*Although some statements in Swedenborg give this impression (e.g., AE 49, 52), there is considerable reason to doubt that this is his final position. See, for instance, AR 547, which strongly implies that the New Church will grow from "the former church" once falsities are removed. —Ed.

faith look to themselves as the source of goodness and to the world about them for direction in exercising it. The Lord did not accept the food which the disciples brought Him. He told them, "My meat is to do the will of him that sent me, and to finish his work." True charity is not in obvious external benefactions, but in humble obedience to the Lord in whatever work He gives us to do.

One of the most striking passages in our chapter if found in verses 13 and 14. "Whosoever drinketh of this water shall thirst again . . ." We get truth from the letter of the Word as we go to it to draw for ourselves, but we can get only a little at a time and with much effort. The well is deep and our own "pitcher" is very limited in capacity. But when we accept the Lord Jesus Christ as our one God, the source of all truth and goodness, the truth in the Word becomes living from His presence in it. The Word then becomes in our minds "a well of water springing up into everlasting life."

One more thing in this chapter we need to note carefully. You will meet people who wish to think that Jesus Christ was merely the best man who ever lived, and such people will sometimes tell you that Jesus Himself never claimed to be the Messiah. Then remember that in verse 26 of chapter 4 of the Gospel of John He told the woman of Samaria without hesitation or circumlocution that He was the Messiah.

――――――

Adult

There are two especially important discussion topics for the Adults in this chapter: the necessity of recognizing the sole deity of Jesus Christ if we are to find the living water in the Word, and the receptiveness of the Samaritans in contrast to the closed minds of those of the established church. Both points have an immediate bearing upon our thought of our own church and of our responsibility in our relations with people of other churches.

When the kingdom of Israel was conquered by Assyria, all its people were carried away captive, never to return. To take their place in the land the king of Assyria sent in people from the East.

We read this story in II Kings 17, which tells also how, when these foreigners were troubled by lions and believed it was because they did not know the manner of worship of the gods of this new land, a priest of Israel was sent back to teach them, after which they worshiped Jehovah, but continued also to worship their own gods. Now we read in John 4 that after seven hundred years their descendants were still regarded as aliens and shunned with Pharisaic fanaticism. Yet Samaria was the central one of the three great divisions of the Holy Land, the link between Judea and Galilee. Judea pictures the inmost plane of our life—the will or motive—and Galilee the outmost—the conduct. Between these two is Samaria, the thought plane. When the Lord went from Judea to Galilee, "he must needs go through Samaria." Before we can carry out our desires in external conduct, we must think about them. We know how far astray we often go through trying to carry out our desires without thought. When we think of the Holy Land as picturing the church in us, Judea pictures the celestial church, worship of the Lord in the heart; Samaria the spiritual church, worship of the Lord in the mind; and Galilee the external church, worship of the Lord in the outward life. The spiritual church is the church which is in the affection of truth, and its associated good is the good of charity toward the neighbor (AC 2702[5]; AE 375[42]). When Israel was carried away captive, spiritual truth was lost, and the people who replaced the Israelites remained Gentiles, ignorant of the truth, although they had some knowledge of the letter of the Scriptures.

In the Lord's time the Samaritans were symbols of "the gentiles who were in the good of charity toward the neighbor" (AE 375[42]). The parable of the Good Samaritan embodies this significance. So, too, the woman in our lesson today had been married five times and was now living with one not her husband. This pictures one who wishes to do good and who has tried one religious faith after another, and whose idea of truth still is not adequate to her desire. Her water jar pictures her limited doctrine. It is evident from the story that the Samaritans heard the Lord gladly and accepted Him as the Messiah; so they picture all Gentiles "that were to receive

Divine truths from Him" (AE 483[12]). Because of their humility and desire to be instructed they received the Lord much more readily than the Jews, and we know that the Christian Church grew up among the Gentiles, although it was begun among the Jews. The Lord told the woman of Samaria that the Jews had the knowledge which was necessary to salvation, but He also told her that worship at Jerusalem as well as worship on the mountain in Samaria would shortly be superseded by a different and more spiritual type of worship. Swedenborg tells us that every new dispensation, although it begins with the good remnant of the former one, develops principally among the well-disposed Gentiles, and he says that this will be true of the New Church.*

The region around Sychar was hallowed ground. It was the "parcel" bought by Jacob from Hamor the Hivite, the father of Shechem, and given to Joseph as an extra portion (Genesis 48:22). Joseph's bones, brought up out of Egypt at the time of the Exodus, were buried there. Jacob's well, the "fountain of Jacob," is also mentioned in Deuteronomy 33:28. Jacob's well is a picture of the Word (AC 2702[5]). The Samaritans possessed and used this well, picturing those who possess and use the Scriptures. But the well was deep. The fact that they drew their water from the well in small quantities and with great effort symbolizes the way many draw their truth from the Word. And, as the Lord said, "Whosoever drinketh of this water shall thirst again." Mere external knowledge, even of the Scriptures, does not satisfy. The Lord must "sit on the well" and give us "living" water. The truth must be made living by our consciousness of His loving presence in the Word. So long as we see only the external sense of the Word, its harsh commands, its condemnation of evil, its stories of wars and destruction, we draw refreshing truth from it only in small amounts and with great labor. But when we see the Lord within it, showing us the hideousness and destructiveness of evil only so that we may avoid it, and accommodating His truth to us in all our states, however far away

---

*See footnote to Senior notes. —Ed.

from Him we have willfully gone, so that we may be led back to the way of peace, then the truth becomes to us "a well of water springing up into everlasting life," satisfying us at every turn with knowledge of the Lord's loving purpose and guidance and of His providence over us.

In Revelation 22:17 the Lord's invitation to the woman of Samaria is given to all: "And whosoever will, let him take the water of life freely." The Christian Church, springing from the Lord's living presence with men, was to be an internal church, observing the external forms of worship not as religion itself, but as symbolic expressions of the true worship in the heart and mind. God is Spirit, dwelling within the good works of those who look to Him for guidance and power. He is with us just as really today as He was with the woman of Samaria, ready to give us living water if we ask Him.

It is interesting to consider the fact that, while the Lord talked of water to the Samaritan woman, who pictures goodness desiring truth, He talked to His disciples, who picture those instructed in truth, of living food. The food which they went away to the city to buy and which they offered Him on their return is a symbol of natural goodness, just as the water the woman drew for herself from Jacob's well was the symbol of natural truth. The Lord contrasted it with His food, just as He contrasted natural water with living water. The woman had charity and needed faith. The disciples had faith and needed charity. The Lord's food, the food which nourished His real life, was "to do the will of him that sent me, and to finish his work." To do the Lord's will instead of our own is what nourishes and strengthens our spiritual bodies, our heavenly character. To forget self in doing the Lord's work is what brings happiness. The same lesson is taught in verses 35 to 38. In AE 911[16] Swedenborg tells us that these verses treat of the establishment of a new church, and that the one who labors is the Lord, and we enter into His labors. He, as we learn from the familiar parable, is the Lord, and we enter into His labors. He, as we learn from the familiar parable, is the sower.

Then, as if to give us a concrete example of the working of His

Spirit, we are told how the Samaritans came to Him and urged Him to stay with them, and how they accepted Him as the Christ, the savior of the world. At first they believed because of the testimony of the woman, but afterward because they had heard Him themselves. Our first acceptance of the Lord should be from an impulse of the heart, but this must be followed by acceptance by the reason. Verse 26 of our chapter is an important one for us to remember, for people who do not wish to acknowledge the Lord as God sometimes claim that He never Himself said He was the Messiah. Only recognition of the Lord as the one God of heaven and earth harmonizes all the Scripture and enables us to go to the Word with confidence for guidance and strength and to receive it with joy.

From the Writings of Swedenborg

Apocalypse Explained, n. 1074[2]: "As the Divine truth, in passing from the Lord Himself through the three heavens down to men in the world, is recorded and becomes the Word in each heaven, so the Word is a bond of union of the heavens with each other, and a bond of union of the heavens with the church in the world. For the Word is the same everywhere, differing only in perfection of glory and wisdom according to the degrees in which the heavens are; consequently the holy Divine from the Lord flows in through the heavens into the man in the world *who acknowledges the Lord's Divine and the holiness of the Word whenever he reads the Word*; and so far as such a man loves wisdom, he can be instructed and can imbibe wisdom from the Word as from the Lord Himself, or from heaven itself, and can thus be nourished with the food with which the angels themselves are nourished, and in which there is life; according to these words of the Lord:

> The words that I speak unto you are spirit and are life. (John 6:63)
> The water that I will give you shall become . . . a fountain of water springing up unto eternal life. (John 4:14)"

Suggested Questions on the Lesson

J. What were the three divisions of the Holy Land in the Lord's time?
Galilee, Samaria, Judea
J. Which was the middle one? *Samaria*

J. Who were the Samaritans? *foreigners brought in by Assyria*

J. What journey was the Lord making at the time of our lesson for today? *Judea to Galilee*

P. Where did He stop to rest? *Jacob's well*

J. What can you tell about the parcel of ground where Jacob's well was? *Jacob had bought, and later gave to Joseph*

P. Who came to the well as the Lord sat there? *a Samaritan woman*

J. Why was she surprised when the Lord asked her to give Him a drink? *Jews didn't talk to Samaritans*

J. What did the Lord tell her? *you should have asked me . . .*

J. What did He tell her about herself which showed her He was a prophet? *five husbands*

J. What did He tell her about Himself? *I am Christ*

J. What did He tell the disciples about His food? *to do God's will*

J. What made the Samaritans believe in the Lord? *His words*

I. What does Jacob's well represent? *the Word*

S. What is "living" water? *divine truth lived*

THE POOL OF BETHESDA
John 5:1-16

The teachers should read the account of the Lord's second miracle in Galilee in John 4:43-54 and tell the classes about it after the review of the last lesson. There is a suggestion in John 2:23 that the Lord may have performed miracles in Jerusalem when He went down for the Passover, and this is borne out by John 4:45. John also tells of a cleansing of the temple in that first visit (John 2:13-16). These first chapters of John show us that the Lord went back and forth between Judea and Galilee frequently.

Doctrinal Points

The Lord works in us through the knowledge of the Word in our minds.

The knowledge of the Word which we gain in childhood is our "pool of Bethesda."

This knowledge is stirred up in our minds whenever we really recognize one of our faults and sincerely want to correct it.

When one fault is cured, we must go on to fight others. As we go on, we discover deeper and deeper evils in our hearts, but this should not discourage us. It means that we are making spiritual progress.

Notes for Parents

The Lord had gone to Jerusalem for another of the great feasts. About sixty years ago men making repairs in one of the ancient Christian churches in Jerusalem, a church located near what was known as the "sheep gate," found under the crypt a pool. Further excavation discovered a five-arched portico, on the walls of which were faded frescoes portraying the miracle of our chapter. So evidently this pool was known in the early Christian Church to be the pool of Bethesda.

The story is told only in the Gospel of John. This is the third lesson we have had in this Gospel involving water, which we know is one of the symbols of truth. Water gathered into a pool represents truth gathered in the memory. The pool of Bethesda near the sheep gate in Jerusalem symbolizes knowledge of the Lord and of what is true and right—knowledge which is lying in our memories as a result of the teaching we received in our innocent childhood. We may perhaps think of the five porches as our five senses through which that knowledge has come to us and been impressed upon us.

Who are the sick people who lie around this pool waiting to be healed? Are we not all sick—spiritually—in various ways? We know that we all have faults and that there is always some particular fault of which we are immediately conscious. If we really want to get rid of this fault, the angel of the Lord—the spirit of the Lord working through our conscience—comes down and "troubles" the water in the pool. The truth in our memory is stirred up, and if we are quick to see and apply it, our fault can be cured.

But we all have deeper evils within us, too. We recognize and acknowledge them, but we are likely to think they are too strong for us. We say, "I can't help it; I was born that way." This is the impotent man who had had his infirmity for thirty-eight years and who was never quick enough to get into the pool when it was troubled. We need to see that the Lord is standing beside us looking into our hearts. And what does He say?

First He asks, "Wilt thou be made whole?" Do you really want to be a thoroughly good person? Then if you do, "Rise, take up your bed, and walk." Do not just lie there thinking how helpless you are. You know enough of what is right to overcome this evil if you have the will to do it. Later when the Lord met the man in the temple, He said to him: "Behold, thou art made whole: sin no more, lest a worse thing come unto thee." We must never let ourselves think that because we have conquered one temptation, we are perfect. As long as we are in this world, we are to go on seeing and fighting deeper and deeper evils within ourselves. This is the way we grow spiritually. It is the purpose of our whole life and our daily challenge. But the Lord is always there to help us.

―――――――

Primary

Mention the second miracle to the children and then read the lesson for the day, which needs no long introduction. This is a lesson from which a spiritual meaning may be drawn even for little children. They can understand that when they are naughty, it shows that there is something wrong with their souls which needs to be cured. Stress our part in the healing of both our bodies and our souls—the necessity of really wanting to be well and of making an effort ourselves.

Our lesson finds the Lord again in Jerusalem. He had been back to Galilee and had performed another miracle there, healing the son of a rich nobleman. Then He returned to Jerusalem for another of the feasts.

What pool was near the sheep gate in Jerusalem?
How many porches did it have?
Who were gathered around this pool?
What happened to the pool every once in a while?
What happened to the sick person who first stepped in after the water was troubled?

You know that when you are sick, you are likely to feel very sorry for yourself. You want to be waited on all the time and you keep calling your mother from her work to do things for you—often things you do not really need at all. People who have had a long sickness sometimes enjoy the attention they get so much that they stay in bed long after they could get up and take care of themselves.

How long had one man been sick?
What did the Lord ask him?
Why did the man say he had never been healed?
What did the Lord tell him to do?
What happened?
What did the religious leaders say to him?
What did he answer?

The man to whom the Lord spoke had not been really trying. He expected someone else to do the work for him. So the Lord first asked him if he really wanted to be well, and then told him to get up and make an effort himself.

Later the Lord said to him, "Sin no more, lest a worse thing come unto thee." Our faults are sicknesses in our souls, and sometimes we are just as slow to make the effort to give them up as we are to help ourselves to be well. When our parents tell us we must do differently, we say, "I can't," just as the man in our story did. So the Lord is speaking to us, too, in this story, and telling us that we must first make up our minds that we really want to be good and then try hard to overcome our faults. If we do this, He is always near at hand to help us.

Junior

The spiritual lesson of this miracle can be easily understood by Juniors. In connection with verse 14, be sure to review with the children the reasons why the Lord performed miracles. These were given in the Junior notes of the lesson on "The Miracle at Cana," John 2.

Through which division of the land did the Lord have to pass in going from Judea to Galilee?
Where did the Lord stop to rest?
Who came to the well for water?
Why did the Jews despise the Samaritans?
What kind of water did the Lord tell the woman He could give her?
What is "living" water?
What did He tell her about herself?
Whom did He declare Himself to be?
Of what "food" did He speak to His disciples?
What did the Samaritans think of Him?

The Lord went on into Galilee and there performed a second miracle. Then He returned to Jerusalem for another of the religious feasts, and our story for today takes place there. For many years there was uncertainty among scholars as to which of several pools in Jerusalem was the pool of our story, but there seems to be no longer much doubt. Harper's Bible Dictionary says it is now believed to be "the pool found during repairs in 1888 near St. Anne's Church in the Bezetha Quarter of Jerusalem not far from the

Sheep's Gate and Tower of Antonia. It is below the slippery-stepped crypt of a ruined 4th century Church of St. Mary Probatica, and has a five-arched portico with faded frescoes of the miracle of Christ's healing (John 5:2 f.)."

Again we remember that water is the symbol of truth. Any gathering together of waters, like the sea or a lake or a pool, pictures truth gathered in our memories. The pool in Jerusalem pictures truth about the Lord and about what He tells us is the right way to live. We all have some of this truth in our memories. So we all have our pool of Bethesda. Sheep picture innocence and gentleness. The Lord's truth is stored up in our memories especially at times when we are in innocent and gentle states, because then we like to hear it.

Who were gathered around the pool of Bethesda?
What were they waiting for?
Do you remember what the word *angel* means?
What happened to the first sick person who stepped in after the water was troubled?

Did you ever, when you were about to do something wrong, have a little voice inside of you say, "Don't do it; you know it's wrong"? That voice is an angel or messenger from the Lord stirring up the truth in your memory. If you listen to that voice and obey it at once, you are like those who were quick to step into the pool and be healed. All our faults are spiritual diseases and infirmities.

How long had one man at the pool been sick?
What did the Lord ask him?
What was his answer?

Sometimes we think our faults are too strong for us. Then we don't really try to overcome them, and no one else can do it for us.

What did the Lord tell the man to do?
What happened when he tried?

We must first really want to be good, and then if we make a sincere and active effort to correct our faults, remembering that the Lord is present to help us, the Lord can give us strength to overcome them.

On what day of the week was this miracle performed?
Why were the Jews angry?

Can you repeat the commandment about the sabbath? We can see that the work we are not to do is the kind of work we have to do all the rest of the week, the kind of work which is necessary to our life in the world. We are to keep the sabbath "holy." This means that we are to use it for worship of the Lord, for learning about Him and how He wants us to live, and for doing kind things for other people for which we do not have time during the week. Look up Luke 4:16. This teaches us that the Lord always went to the synagogue on the sabbath day. He also performed many miracles on the sabbath. And He said, "It is lawful to do well on the sabbath days." (Matthew 12:12)

What did the Lord say to the man when He met him again in the temple?

He did not heal the man just to make his body well, but to help him to do right. If a person is bad, he can do more harm in a well body than in a sick one. We do not overcome all our faults at once, but one at a time. As soon as we get rid of one, we should be on the watch for another one to fight.

=====

Intermediate

A study of the correspondences in the story will introduce the important subject of how we overcome our faults—both the superficial and the deeper ones. The command, "Rise, take up thy bed, and walk" should be impressed upon young people as a constant challenge.

After His two days in Samaria the Lord went on into Galilee. John records a second miracle performed there (John 4:43-54) and says that the Galileans also received Him, "having seen all the things that he did at Jerusalem at the feast: for they also went unto the feast." This suggests that He may have performed miracles in Jerusalem also on His first visit there after the beginning of His ministry. The Galileans referred to were probably Jews, since they went to the feast at Jerusalem. Most of the Galileans were Gentiles. Galilee was called "Galilee of the Gentiles." We might note also that John tells of a cleansing of the temple in that first visit (John 2:13-16). The other three Gospels place the story of the cleansing of the temple at the time of the Lord's entry into Jerusalem at the beginning of the last week of His earthly life. There may have been more than one cleansing, but such differences in order in the Gospel accounts need not trouble us, for we know that the historical sequence of events is not important, but the sequence as recorded in the Word is. That is, there is always a reason in the internal sense why the events in any chapter come in the order in which they do come.

In our chapter for today the Lord has again gone down to Jerusalem for one of the great feasts. There were three of these: the Passover, the feast of the first fruits, and the feast of the ingathering or harvest, which was also called the feast of tabernacles. The pool of Bethesda in Jerusalem has been almost certainly identified by the discovery in 1888 of a pool under the crypt of a fourth-century Christian Church in Jerusalem. This pool has a five-arched portico decorated with faded frescoes of the miracle of our lesson, and it is near what was known as the sheep's gate. You notice that in your Bible (KJV) the word *market* in verse 2 is in italics, which means that it is not in the original Greek text. The text says only "near that of the sheep"; so *gate* is as reasonable an assumption as *market*. In the correspondence it is the word *sheep* which is important.

In the Word all diseases and afflictions of the physical body picture diseased conditions of the soul, and in our lesson today we have a vivid picture of the condition of the church in the Lord's time—which Jerusalem represents—where, around the pool of Bethesda lay "a great multitude of impotent folk, of blind, halt, withered, waiting for the moving of the water."

The pool of Bethesda, "at Jerusalem by the sheep," pictures the knowledges of God and of the way of life stored up in our memories from the day of our innocent childhood. This pool had five porches. Throughout the Word five is the number which signifies "few." But it is also often associated in our thoughts with the number ten which signifies "remains." *Remains* [*reliquiae*] is the word Swedenborg uses for the states of goodness and the knowledges of truth acquired in our early childhood, which the Lord stores up deep within us to draw upon for our help in later life. The five porches which lead to this pool are on the one hand our five senses through which all knowledges enter our minds in the first place and on the other hand they picture the fact that some of the people still had a few remains through which they could be reached. Each of us, too, has this pool with the five porches.

All our faults and weaknesses are pictured by the sick people who were lying around the pool. We read that "an angel went down at a certain season into the pool, and troubled the water." From time to time in our own experience an "angel" or messenger of the Lord stirs up our memory of the truth. We call this "angel" conscience. The sick person most alert and eager to get to the water was healed. In the same way, the particular fault of which we are most conscious and which we are most eager to overcome is corrected.

But we all have more serious and crippling faults which are harder to fight. We may recognize them, but they seem so much a part of us that we feel that it is of no use even to try to overcome them. This is the impotent man of our story. The Lord says to us, as He said to the man, "Wilt thou be made whole?" Do we really want to get rid of our evils? And when we excuse ourselves, He says: "Rise, take up thy bed, and walk." Put in other words: "Lift up your thoughts to the Lord, remember the religious principles in which you have been brought up, and do right instead of wrong." With the Lord's help we can do this.

"And on the same day was the sabbath." The sabbath day represents the state of peace and rest which comes after a victory over temptation has been won. The Lord often healed on the sabbath day. The religious leaders had made the day one of rigid external observance and had forgotten its origin and purpose. The Lord stripped off their tradition and restored the sabbath as a day to be kept holy, a day to worship the Lord and to serve the neighbor.

We have many problems connected with Sunday keeping. In
Matthew 12:12 the Lord tells us "it is lawful to do well on the
sabbath days." He Himself always went to the synagogue on the
sabbath and then went about doing good. We should follow His
example. Young people who differ from their parents as to what
should or should not be done on Sunday might remember that
they do not "do well" when they disobey their parents. Sunday
should be a day for worshiping the Lord, learning of Him, and
doing things which help others and which advance our spiritual
progress.

Basic Correspondences

a pool = truth gathered in the memory
five = a few "remains" of good states
a bed = the doctrine which we have accepted

Senior

Our will to be made whole by the Lord is the question to be placed squarely
before this age group. They find excuses easily, and their own individual
responsibility for their spiritual development is a thought we should keep
constantly in their minds.

As we have learned, the Lord often went back and forth between
Judea and Galilee in the years of His ministry. This is more evident
in the Gospel of John than in the other three Gospels because the
story of the greater part of His three years' ministry is compressed
into the first half of the Gospel to make room for the fuller development of His teaching during the last week of His life. So in our
chapter for today we find Him again going to Jerusalem for one of
the feasts. We might note, too, that again our lesson is concerned
with water—this time with water in the city of Jerusalem itself.
This is an interesting development, for our lesson on the miracle
at Cana concerned truth applied to the outward conduct, and the
teaching at Jacob's well concerned truth in the mind, and now we
have a lesson which emphasizes the application of truth to the will.
The pool of Bethesda "at Jerusalem by the sheep market" with

its five porches filled with "impotent folk" waiting for the troubling of the water is a wonderful picture of the state of the church at the time of the Lord's Advent. The pool near the sheep market—or sheep's gate—stands for knowledge of the truth remaining from an earlier state of innocence and trust. "Five" signifies "a little but enough." The scribes and Pharisees had left the people very little access to the genuine truth of the Word. This is illustrated in their attitude toward the sabbath. And the body of the church was full of disease—"blind, halt, withered." Yet the people gathered around the pool at every possible approach, waiting for the occasional touch of the Lord's spirit which might bring healing to someone.

All of us who make up the church today are also like these people. We recognize that we have faults, and we know that we must try to correct them one by one. As we see and acknowledge each one, we—spiritually speaking—go to the pool of Bethesda at Jerusalem by the sheep's gate (the truths of the Word which we have learned in our innocent childhood), and the Lord stirs the pool for us and shows us just the truth to apply for the correction of that particular fault.

But our story is principally concerned with one man who had had his infirmity for thirty-eight years and did not believe he could ever get to the pool in time. We have deep-seated evils within us which seem so much a part of us that we are likely to say of them, "I was born that way; I can't be expected to change my nature." In any dark state of the world or of the individual soul the worst disease is discouragement, which paralyzes all effort to improve. This is pictured in the story by the fact that the man felt that he could not get to the pool in time because he had no one to help him. But a new day had dawned for this man with the appearance of the Lord at the pool. Swedenborg tells us that *thirty* pictures "something of combat" and also "a full state of remains." The man was not beyond hope of reform, and he actually possessed enough knowledge to correct his condition if he had the will to correct it. The first question the Lord asked him was, "Wilt thou be made whole?" *Eight*, because the eighth day is the beginning of a new week, pictures "every beginning."

So now the Lord says to him, "Rise, take up thy bed, and walk." Rising always pictures the elevation of our thoughts above the natural level; a bed—on which we rest—pictures the doctrine we have accepted as the basis of our life; and to walk is to move forward. If we look to the Lord for strength, remember the Christian principles which we have been taught, and exert ourselves to go forward with them, there is no sin or weakness which the Lord will not give us strength to overcome. Recall how Joshua, after the defeat at Ai, "rent his clothes, and fell to the earth upon his face before the ark," and said, "Alas, O Lord"; and the Lord said to him, "Get thee up; wherefore liest thou upon thy face?" All of us need at times to remind ourselves that discouragement is from hell and that to give in to it is a sin. Many of our troubles come from the weakness of our will to overcome them.

We need also to take to heart the Lord's later words to the same man in the temple: "Behold, thou art made whole: sin no more, lest a worse thing come upon thee." When we have been "made whole," we need to examine our former state to see the evils in ourselves which brought it about so that we may avoid them in the future. The sabbath is the state of rest and peace after victory, but we do not remain in the sabbath state while we are in this world. There is always a new work week beginning, with new problems to solve and weaknesses to recognize and fight. The sabbath is the time to look to the Lord with gratitude for the past help, and also a time for self-examination and new resolutions.

Adult

By way of introduction the Adults may be interested in the presumed identification of the Pool of Bethesda given most fully in the Junior notes, and in the difference between the KJV translation and the original in verse 2. (The Revised Standard Version says "sheep gate.") There are several obvious discussion topics in the lesson—notably the recognition of discouragement as a personal evil to be overcome. Verse 14 is also important for Adults. Read here *Divine Providence*, n. 231 on the seventh kind of profanation.

Again we have a lesson about water, but this time it is about water gathered into a pool, truth gathered in the memory, our knowledge of the Word. This pool of Bethesda is in Jerusalem near the sheep market, or sheep's gate. Spiritually, it is in the holy city of our minds and associated with our affections for innocence. Is not this true of our knowledge of the Word, stored up throughout our childhood when our minds are in innocent and open states? The same is suggested by the five "porches," five being the number which signifies both "a little" and "remains." Divine providence provides that every mind shall have such a "pool," such a body of truth from the Word, even though such knowledge may not have come by direct contact with the Word itself.

In these porches—at every point of access to the pool—lay a great multitude of impotent folk. How clearly this pictures the spiritual state of each one of us: a multitude of diseased affections and thoughts, blind, lame, and helpless, gathered around the little pool of truth which the Lord has stored up deep within us for their healing. For, we are told, "an angel went down at a certain season into the pool, and troubled the water." Most of the time the pool of divine truth lies quiet in our minds, but now and then, when our state and circumstances make it profitable for us, an angel, a messenger of the Lord, the Lord's spirit working in us for our regeneration, comes down and stirs the pool, quickening our consciousness of the truth. Swedenborg tells us that the troubling of the waters represents "vivification through acknowledgment and faith, thus also purification through truths" (AC 10083[4]).

Then some one fault in us may be healed. The invalid who was most alert, who was watching most keenly for the moving of the waters, was the fortunate one; that is, the fault of which we are most keenly conscious and which we are most anxious to correct is the one which will be touched and healed by our quickened understanding of the truth. We cannot fight all our faults at once. The writings tell us that genuine repentance must go further than a general confession that we are sinners: it must single out one particular sin after another and fight it (TCR 525). Our regeneration advances step by step. For "precept must be upon precept, precept upon precept; line upon line, line upon line; here a little, and there a little" (Isaiah 28:10).

But there was one man at the pool who had been helpless for thirty-eight years and who had never been able to get to the water in time. He pictures some deeper evil in us which we feel helpless to fight. Each one of us has some such deep evil which we attack only halfheartedly, feeling that it is so much a part of us that we can never get rid of it. "I can't help it; I was born that way," we say. The thirty-eighth year suggests that we have enough remains of good and truth to overcome this evil if we will—represented by *thirty*—and that it is time for a new state to begin in us—represented by *eight*. It is at this point that the Lord Himself comes to us and says, "Wilt thou be made whole?" Do we really wish to get rid of our deeper evils? Do we wish to make a thorough job of our regeneration? Or are we content to attack the more obvious, superficial faults and to let our really serious shortcomings remain, excusing ourselves by pleading helplessness?

The Lord answered the man's excuses with a challenge: "Rise, take up thy bed, and walk." Does not this remind us of the Lord's words to Joshua, after his defeat at Ai: "Get thee up; wherefore liest thou thus upon thy face?" From the writings we learn that "to rise" signifies elevation, as from evil to good or from ignorance to intelligence (AC 2401; 4481). We must lift up our hearts and minds out of the obscurity of worldly fears and doubts, and trust in the Lord's promises and power. Then we must raise what we know of the truth—the bed on which we lie—and take it with us actively in our effort to overcome our evils, just as David, confident that the Lord was on his side, used one smooth stone from the brook to slay Goliath. The Lord said to the disciples, when they asked why they could not cast out a certain devil: "Because of your unbelief; for verily I say unto you, If ye have faith as a grain of mustard seed, ye shall say unto this mountain, Remove hence to yonder place; and it shall remove; and nothing shall be impossible unto you." The mountain in this passage pictures our satisfaction with ourselves as we are, with our own qualities and our own ideas. We are often even secretly pleased with our deeper faults because we think of them as part of ourselves, as making us different from other people. This self-satisfaction is a great mountain in the way of our spiritual progress. So we must first be sure that we sincerely want to be made "whole," and then, looking confidently to the Lord for help, go forward actively with all the truth we have.

In this miracle we have one of the numerous instances in which the religious leaders found fault with the Lord for His use of the sabbath. They had added to the commandment in regard to the sabbath many traditions, which they had come to consider binding. The Lord disregarded these traditions and went about teaching and healing on the sabbath. In one argument with the scribes and Pharisees on the subject the Lord told them, "The sabbath was made for man, and not man for the sabbath: Therefore the Son of man is Lord also of the sabbath." (Mark 2:27-28) The sabbath was indeed made for man. Men who do not observe the sabbath inevitably sink into a state of absorption in self and the world, which is the death promised to the sabbath-breaker, the death of all spiritual life. While we are in this world, the greater part of our time must necessarily be spent in taking care of ourselves and our families. We need one day in seven when we lay aside our concern with worldly affairs and think about the Lord and His kingdom. This is the purpose of the sabbath. The Lord performed so many miracles on the sabbath as a picture of the fact that the sabbath is a day peculiarly set aside for the healing of our souls.

The practical question of what we should or should not do on Sunday is a perennial one, everywhere complicated by custom and tradition. Every nation, every community, every family has its own ideas on the subject. When we adhere to these traditional ideas to the hindering of the Lord's work in our souls or in the souls of others we are doing as the people in Gospel days did. On the other hand, we must not use the Lord's statements about the sabbath as an excuse for doing anything we happen to want to do on Sunday. Nothing in the Lord's example gives us warrant for laziness, for selfish indulgence, for neglect of worship. "As his custom was, he went into the synagogue on the sabbath day" (Luke 4:16). The sabbath should be a day of rest from worldly thoughts and activities, and a day of active approach to the Lord. We should welcome it as an opportunity to think and to learn of Him, to take stock of our souls, to cultivate our affections for the neighbor, and to strengthen our good resolutions in preparing for the coming week. It is the day of all days to "take up our bed and walk" spiritually.

From the Writings of Swedenborg

Arcana Coelestia, n. 10360[8]: "When the Lord was in the world, and united His Human to the Divine Itself, He abrogated the sabbath in respect to representative worship, or in respect to its worship such as was with the Israelitish people; and made the sabbath day a day of instruction in the doctrine of faith and of love. This is involved in what is written in John . . . by the 'healing of the sick' is signified the purifying of man from evils and the falsities of evil; by a 'bed' is signified doctrine; and by 'walking' is signified life."

Suggested Questions on the Lesson

J. Where was Samaria? *middle of land*
J. Who were the Samaritans? *foreigners*
P. Where did the Lord stop to rest on His way from Jerusalem to Galilee? *Jacob's well*
J. Why was the Samaritan woman surprised when He asked her to give Him a drink? *Jews didn't talk to Samaritans*
J. What did He tell her about water? *you should have asked . . .*
J. What did He tell her about Himself? *I am Christ*
J. What did He tell His disciples about His "food"? *to do God's will*
P. How did the Samaritans receive Him? *many believed*
J. Where was the pool of Bethesda? *Jerusalem*
P. How many porches did it have? *five*
P. Who waited in the porches? *sick people*
P. What were they waiting for? *"troubling" of water*
P. What happened whenever the water was troubled? *first to step in was healed*

J. How long had one man at the pool been sick? *thirty-eight years*

J. What did the Lord first ask him? *do you want to be healed?*

P. What did he answer? *no one to help me*

P. What did the Lord tell him to do? *rise, take bed, walk*

P. What happened when he tried? *he was healed*

J. What did the religious leaders tell him? *he was breaking the sabbath*

J. When the Lord met him again, what did He say to him? *sin no more*

J. What did the leaders try to do when they learned who had healed the man? *kill Jesus*

I. What is the pool of Bethesda in us? *knowledge of God's way, stored in memory*

S. What is meant by the words, "Rise, take up thy bed, and walk"? *elevate your thoughts, take the doctrine on which you base your life, and move forward*

THE MAN BORN BLIND

John 9

In this lesson not only the miracle itself but the argument to which it led give us important instruction. The teacher should read all the notes and try to give his pupils as much as possible and to impress the chapter as a whole upon their minds.

Doctrinal Points

Afflictions are not punishments for sins. They can, however, be opportunities for the development of character.

To be born blind, spiritually, means to have been deprived by outer circumstance of the opportunity to learn and understand divine truth.

There are no defective souls.

Notes for Parents

You know that there are some Christian churches whose doctrines teach that because Adam sinned, all his descendants are born sinners and will go to hell unless their sin is removed by baptism, and some churches also teach that all sickness and misfortune is inflicted upon man by the Lord as a punishment for sin. But this is not at all what Christ Himself taught.

Our chapter for today answers our natural questions about why apparently good people should have afflictions to bear. The Lord here tells us that it is in order that "the works of God should be made manifest" in them, and in John 6:29 He tells us what the works of God are: "This is the work of God, that ye believe on him whom he hath sent." Read the story of the blind man in our chapter for today and you will see how this came true for him.

There is a much more serious kind of blindness than physical blindness. Even though a good person may have to go through this earthly life without seeing the beauties of nature or the faces of

loved ones, we can be sure that as soon as such a person puts off
the physical body, he will be able to see, because his soul has
always been able to see. Our souls see when we understand and
accept the truth. We say to a naughty child, "Can't you see how
much happier you would be if you would only try to be good?"
And the only reason the child does not see it is because he does
not want to. This is the lesson which the conduct of the Pharisees
in our chapter teaches us. They refused to see the truth because it
was contrary to their selfish pride and ambition.

But the blind man was humble and anxious to know what was
right so that he could do it. When we read that the Lord saw him,
we know that He saw his heart and his thoughts. So the Lord
could give him sight. He did give him physical sight, but He gave
him the more important sight also. See how the man's understanding of the Lord grew as he was led to think about his experience.
First he knew Him only as "a man that is called Jesus"; then as he
had to answer the questions of the Pharisees, he came to see that
He must be a prophet, and then that such power could come only
from God; and finally he was ready to see that Jesus was actually
the Son of God, the promised Messiah who was God Himself in
the flesh, and worshiped Him. The Lord must rise in this way in
our minds if the works of God are to be made manifest in us. Outward affliction may be the means of bringing us in touch with the
Lord, because it can make us humble and eager for the help which
He always stands ready to give to those who will trust in Him.
Affliction is not a punishment for sin, and neither does the Lord
hold anyone responsible for ignorance for which he is not to blame.

Primary

Even little children can form an idea of what blindness represents and can
understand the meaning of the story if it is carefully explained. Discuss the
meaning of the Lord's words in verse 41.

Do you remember the story about the man at the pool of Bethesda, who had been sick for thirty-eight years and did not think he

could help himself to become well? The Lord told him to try, and then healed him when he obeyed.

Today we have a story about a man who really could not help himself.

What was this man's trouble?
How long had he been blind?
What did the disciples ask the Lord?
What did He tell them?
How did He heal the man?
The Pharisees again objected to the healing.
At first they refused to believe that the man had been healed.
Then they tried to tell him that Jesus was a sinner.
But the man felt sure that only God could have such power.
So the Pharisees put him out of the synagogue.
Then Jesus came to him again and told him who He was.
The man believed Him and worshiped Him.
See if you can think what verse 41 means.

This miracle, like many of the Lord's miracles, was performed on the sabbath day, and so the Pharisees found fault. They were always looking for faults in the Lord because they did not want people to follow Him.

When your mother asks you to do something, you often say, "Why?" Then when she explains why, sometimes you say, "I see," and do what she asks. But sometimes, if it is something you don't want to do, you pretend you don't see why, even if you really do. That is what the Lord is showing us in this story. Our minds, as well as our eyes, see. The Lord makes it possible for our minds to see what we ought to do, and so when we don't do it, we are to blame.

═══════

Junior

This is a good lesson through which to teach the Juniors the importance of being honest with themselves and recognizing the folly of the "know-it-all" attitude into which children of this age so often begin to slip. The open mind and the humble heart and the sincere effort to learn more and more all the time about what is right should be presented as essential virtues.

In our lesson for today the Lord had come to Jerusalem again, this time for the feast of tabernacles, the harvest feast. He had been teaching in the temple and arguing with His enemies and, as usual, the argument ended by their trying to destroy Him, this time by casting stones at Him. But, as on several other occasions, they had no power to injure Him because His work in the world was not finished. The last verse of chapter 8 says: "Jesus hid himself, and went out of the temple, going through the midst of them, and so passed by."

As He passed by, whom did He see?
What did His disciples ask?
What did He answer?

There is a very important lesson for us here. Some people think that all sicknesses and misfortunes are the direct result of sin. Here the Lord teaches us that this is not necessarily true. Sometimes they are. For example, when we overeat, we may be sick as a direct result. But many good people have sicknesses for which neither they nor their parents are to blame. The Lord tells us the reason: "that the works of God should be made manifest." No sickness or misfortune is ever permitted by the Lord to come to a person unless the Lord sees that it can be the means of leading to good for him and for others. Many people have become great through their efforts to rise above physical handicaps, people who might otherwise have settled down into very ordinary lives. An invalid who is patient and cheerful and interested in other people's problems often becomes the friend and counselor of many well people.

In the case of the man in our chapter, the Lord used his affliction to teach the world deep lessons, which we all need. He healed this man, as He healed many others, and when you are older you will study the spiritual meaning of the details of this particular miracle. But some of the lessons which resulted from the healing you can understand now.

On what day of the week did this healing take place?
What did the Pharisees decide from this?
Whom did they ask to confirm the miracle?

Why were the man's parents afraid to speak up for the Lord?
Why was the man himself not afraid?
What argument did he use?
What did they do to him?
What did the Lord tell him about Himself?
What did the man do then?

The last three verses of our chapter help us to understand what was behind this argument between the man and the Pharisees, and also what is meant by blindness. This is one of the places in the Bible where the internal or spiritual sense comes out into the letter. In fact we should know from our common speech that blindness pictures ignorance of the truth, for we often say a person is blind when we are not talking about physical sight at all, and we all say "I see," when we mean "I understand."

The scribes and Pharisees, were proud of their possession of the Scriptures. They claimed to understand them and to be the only ones who could tell others what the Scriptures taught. But when the Lord faced them with things in the Scriptures which they did not want to obey, they refused to look at the truth. The Lord always spoke the truth of the Scriptures because, as we have seen, He was the Word made flesh. So all His life and teaching came as a judgment, "that they which see not might see; and that they which see might be made blind." Those whose sight He opened to see the truth were people like the blind man in our story, who were willing to accept and obey the truth when it was shown them. And those who were made blind by His coming were those who pretended to understand more than others but who closed their minds against any truth which condemned their selfish ways.

We should remember this lesson whenever we are listening to advice or correction. We, too, often try to close our eyes to unwelcome truth about ourselves.

=====

Intermediate

Center the lesson on the correspondences in the miracle itself, and be sure the meaning of the miracle is clear before you go on to the other lessons of the chapter. Point out that the crucial difference between the blind man and the Pharisees was in the matter of willingness to accept the Lord.

The Gospel of John contains the account of only eight miracles of the Lord as against more than twice as many in each of the other Gospels. But only two of the eight—the feeding of the five thousand and the Lord's walking on the sea—are found in any of the other Gospels. And, as we should expect, the six which are unique with John are of deep importance. We are studying four of them.

The one we have for today gives us many things to think about. Even people who know nothing of the heavenly doctrines know that blindness pictures ignorance, because the word is so used in our common speech. When something happens unexpectedly which we immediately realize we ought to have foreseen, we say: "How blind I have been!" The man in our chapter had been blind from his birth; that is, his condition pictures ignorance which comes from the circumstances in which we are born and brought up. We can easily see that people brought up, for instance, in the interior of Australia might never even have heard of the Lord or the Word. But we do not have to go so far from home as that. There are people all around us who are ignorant of the Word because no one has ever tried to teach them, and there are many more who are blind to its real meaning because they have been brought up in false ideas of it. This was true of the people of the Lord's time.

When we read that the Lord "saw" anyone, we know that it means not just that He saw the person sitting there before Him, but that He saw all that was in his heart. The heart of this blind beggar was humble and good, and his mind contained some knowledge of the letter of the Word although, because he had been taught false ideas about it, he was blind to its real meaning. The ground upon which he sat pictures the church in man's heart, the goodness in a person founded on belief in the letter of the Scriptures as coming from God, whatever its meaning might be. The saliva which proceeded from the Lord's own mouth represents genuine truth from the letter of the Word, and the clay which was formed out of soil by means of it represents goodness in the man's heart reshaped by this bit of genuine truth. When this was applied to the man's eyes, he was told to go and wash in the pool of Siloam. A pool represents truth gathered in the memory. When he washed, he came seeing.

What does this mean in actual life? Let us think of a person brought up with a knowledge of the Bible but with false ideas of its meaning. He is a good person and tries to live as well as he knows how, in spite of his ignorance. Then one day something comes to him which he immediately feels to be new and really true. It may be something said to him by a friend (each of us can be this kind of missionary) or it may be a new thought growing out of something that has happened. He goes to his Bible to see if this new thought will help him to understand things there which have been dark to him, and he finds that he suddenly sees what they mean.

This is the meaning of the miracle itself. But there are many other lessons connected with it in our chapter. The question asked by the disciples in verse 2 is a very common question in people's minds. Are sickness, handicaps of various sorts, and misfortunes punishments for sin in the person who suffers or in others close to him? We know, of course, that some sicknesses and reverses are directly due to our own misdeeds; we can almost always recognize the source of these. But the Lord says this is by no means true of all our trials. In the case of the person who is doing wrong, the Lord often has to permit his wrongdoing to result in unpleasant consequences in order to stop him short and make him think about the nature of what he is doing. And in the case of a good person, trials of various sorts are permitted to come when the Lord sees that meeting them will strengthen and deepen his character. Few of us can stand uninterrupted good fortune without becoming lazy and self-satisfied. In either case it is true that affliction is sometimes permitted to come to a person "that the works of God should be made manifest in him."

The way in which the man's neighbors received the miracle shows us the difference in people. Some believed it and some did not. No one is ever convinced by a miracle against his will. And the rest of the chapter tells us—through the dealings of the Pharisees with the man—to what lengths a person who is selfish and satisfied with himself will go to discredit facts which do not agree with his own opinions and way of life. Keep this chapter in mind, for as you grow older you will find it illustrated again and again in the arguments and conduct of those who do not want to believe in the Lord. They completely brush aside the experience of the thousands whom the Lord has enabled to see, finally calling them fools and refusing to associate with them.

But fortunately those who have once recognized the Lord and come to see Him as the Word made flesh have reached a security and a firm standing ground which cannot be shaken. And truth is the final judge. Those who acknowledge their own ignorance and look to the Lord for light receive more and more from Him, but those who reject the Lord and consider themselves wise really become blind, and their blindness is their own doing. This is what is meant by the last three verses of our chapter. The Pharisees condemned themselves. Read John 3:18-21.

Basic Correspondences

blindness = ignorance

the Lord's saliva = truth from the letter of the Word

Senior

This can be made a very important lesson for the Seniors if it helps them to recognize and reject the tendency to "brush off" truth which they do not want to obey. It will also help them to understand some of the trends in the world they are about to enter.

One of the things Swedenborg tells us about the Word is that it is like a man clothed, but with his face and hands bare [SS 55]. This means that although for the most part the letter of the Word conceals rather than reveals the internal meaning, there are enough places in it where the internal clearly appears so that anyone approaching it with a genuine desire for the Lord's instruction will see its quality and find in it strength and help. Our chapter for today is one of the "bare" passages. This does not mean that there are not depths of meaning in it which cannot be seen on the surface, but it does mean that no one who reads it with an open mind can fail to see some of its spiritual application.

The key to this spiritual meaning is found in the last three verses of the chapter, which show us clearly that the blindness with which the Lord is really concerned is not physical but spiritual blindness, blindness to divine truth. If we study the chapter with this in mind, we shall find several deep and important lessons in it.

The man in the story had been blind from birth. He represents those who for one reason or another have never had an opportunity to learn and understand divine truth. The question of the disciples and the Lord's answer in verses 2 to 5 help our thinking about all the trials and handicaps which come to good people. The Christian Church over the centuries developed some terrible doctrines which are here plainly shown to be false: the doctrine of "original sin," for example, which declares that the sin of Adam is imputed to all his descendants and can be removed only by the sacrament of baptism, so that all infants who die without being baptized as well as all people in the world of other than the Christian faith are condemned to hell after death. The Lord said that no blame attached to the man because of his blindness.

The Lord's method of giving the man his sight is explained in the passage from the writings at the end of this lesson. You will understand it if you think of the attitude of the man after his healing in comparison with the attitude of his neighbors, his parents, other people, and finally the Pharisees. The man himself knew what had happened to him and was honest enough to face the facts squarely and brave enough to stand by his new knowledge whatever the consequences to himself might be. It is only such people who can be shown divine truth—who can really see it. Follow the man through the chapter and see how his understanding

grew and deepened. First he said, "I am he." He realized that this
thing had really happened to him, that he was the same person
who had so short a time before been blind and hopeless. Then he
said, "a man named Jesus" had healed him. He knew only the
Lord's name and thought of Him as merely a stranger passing by.
Then, as the questioning set him thinking of the nature of what
had happened to him, he realized that this was no ordinary man,
and he said, "He is a prophet." Goaded further, he became confirmed in the belief that the power could have come only from
God, and he dared to use the very teachings of the Scriptures to
contradict the judgment of the Pharisees (verses 30-33). So they
put him out of the synagogue—excommunicated him—and then,
freed from the last vestige of control by the falsities in which he
had been brought up, he found himself again in the presence of
the Lord, the Lord told him who He really was, and the man said,
"Lord, I believe." And he worshiped him. Here, you see, was a
Jew to whom the Lord was able to make the same clear declaration
of His deity which He had made to the Gentile Samaritan woman.
But the man had to break with the synagogue first. Read here
Matthew 9:16-17.

With this history in mind go back to the Lord's answer to the
disciples in verse 3: "Neither hath this man sinned, nor his parents:
but that the works of God should be made manifest in him"; then
note something which the Lord had previously said to the people
when they asked Him: "What shall we do, that we might work the
works of God?" His answer was, "This is the work of God, that ye
believe on him whom he hath sent." All the trials and afflictions
which come to good people are permitted by the Lord because He
sees that meeting them will bring these particular individuals into
states of humility and trust which not only will enable Him to
help them but will also enable them to believe in Him more deeply
and intelligently.

Now consider the states of the others in this story. Even some
of the man's neighbors who had seen him daily preferred to imagine
that this man who could see must be someone else. His own parents,

who could not deny his identity or the facts in the case, were afraid to face these facts and reshape their lives according to them. And the others, when they found that they could not deny the facts, chose to attribute the Lord's power to the devil, just as they had once before (Matthew 12:24).

So the lesson of the chapter is summed up at the end. The judgment which the coming of the Lord brought to the world was not a judgment imposed on men by Him. It was a new revelation of divine truth on the most external level, so that anyone who really wanted the truth could see it. Those who did not want any truth which they found inconvenient to accept were free to reject it, but in rejecting it they rejected the Lord and condemned themselves. Read John 3:19. As you face your life in the adult world, this is the choice which is offered you. The Lord has given us the truth and has shown us plainly the consequences of both choices. Each of us has to decide for himself whether to believe the Lord or to believe only what suits one's own selfish convenience.

———

Adult

The teacher will probably have to choose which of the topics covered in this chapter will be most helpful to his particular class for discussion. They are all vital questions: the spiritual meaning of blindness, the cause of afflictions, the necessity of belief in the Lord, and our responsibility for our choice.

The fact that this miracle and its consequences are described in so much detail suggests that the lessons it teaches are complex and far-reaching. We realize the truth of this even in reading the first three verses of the chapter. Here was a man born blind. Why? People are always asking why afflictions are permitted, especially to those apparently innocent. Many, contemplating the evils and the sorrows of the world, are tempted to deny the existence of a loving God. Others, like the disciples in the story, believing in God, can find no other explanation for afflictions than that they are the direct or indirect punishment for sin; they are merely in doubt as to whether the blame belongs to the individual or to his environment. But the Lord tells us: "Neither hath this man sinned, nor his parents: but that the works of God should be made manifest in him." In the letter this points to the fact that the history of this man, as of all the people of that day, had been so guided by divine providence that the account of his healing might serve as a lesson to all future generations. But there is a deeper and more universal meaning than this. No one is held responsible for the evil tendencies which he inherits or for the falsities in which he is brought up. The conditions in which he is born, the circumstances by which he is surrounded are but the setting of his life work. Afflictions, like any other circumstances, are opportunities for the development of character—"that the works of God should be made manifest." We are individually responsible for what we do with the opportunities given us, for acknowledging and struggling against the evil tendencies in our hearts and for accepting the truth and following it as fast as we see it.

The character of the man of our story appears clearly to us as we read the chapter, but the Lord knew it before He performed the miracle. The very first verse reads, "And as Jesus passed by, he saw a man which was blind from his birth." Whenever we read that the Lord "saw," we know that it means that He saw the heart and mind as well as the outward condition. He saw in the blind man the humility and goodness and the desire for truth which would make it possible for him to see. His affliction had made him humble and gentle instead of proud and stiff-necked like the Pharisees. In John 6:29 we read: "This is the work of God, that ye believe on him whom he hath sent." The heart of the blind man was in a state open to belief; so the "works of God" could be made manifest in him. This is the object of everything which the Lord permits to come into our lives. Divine providence watches over us at every turn, seeking to check us when we are going in the wrong way, to show us our evils and our weakness, and to open our hearts and minds to Christ's way as the only way of happiness.

Blindness represents ignorance. We use the word in this way today—it is one of the simplest correspondences to illustrate. For example, we say "I see," when we mean, "I understand." We say "How blind I have been!" when we have been ignorant of the course of events leading up to a given circumstance. We call a person "short-sighted" when he is ignorant of the consequences which are likely to follow a particular course of action. The man of our story had been blind from birth. This makes him a picture of one ignorant of spiritual truth, not from any unwillingness or laziness of his own, but because he has never had an opportunity to learn. In performing this miracle the Lord made use of three things: clay representing good—the "good ground" of the parable of the sower— which the Lord saw in the man's heart; saliva, water from the Lord's own mouth, representing a divine truth expressed in a form adapted to the external states of men, "truths from the sense of the letter of the Word" (AE 239[19]); and the pool of Siloam in which the man washed off the clay representing the removal of false ideas by means of truth from the letter of the Word. This pool, like the pool of Bethesda, pictures the knowledge of the letter of the Word which we have stored up in our minds. It was at that time pure, fresh spring water and part of the water supply of Jerusalem, a symbol of the knowledge of the letter of the Word cleansing and satisfying the Holy City of the soul. Such knowledge, as we have seen before, is stored up by the Lord in each one of us, but one who has not had true spiritual instruction may not recognize its use and value; he may think of it as mere man-made morality and not connect it with the Lord and heaven. Until we make a living contact with the Lord and begin to set our lives in order according to the Word because He commands it, we remain spiritually blind. But once we begin to see, our experience leads to certainty.

The rest of the story shows in a wonderful way this development of belief. In the first place nothing that the Pharisees could say could outweigh the man's experience. They sought first to deny the fact of the miracle. Then they tried to discredit the means by which it was performed. And finally they called the man an ignorant sinner, and cast him out. The modern Pharisee is equally impervious to truth. When he comes in contact with one who has had a deep spiritual experience, he first tries to disprove it, then to "explain" it by natural or by unworthy causes, and finally he dismisses it altogether by calling the person a fool. He refuses to see the truth simply because he does not want to see it. But the man in our story was not to be shaken. He had his experience. He knew what he had been and what he was now: "One thing I know, that, whereas I was blind, now I see." When one's eyes have been opened by experience to see spiritual truth, one knows its reality, and this knowledge gives him the power to penetrate the shallowness of the arguments which would reduce his experience to a mere natural occurrence.

Moreover, opposition served to clarify the man's own understanding of his experience and finally led him to recognize its true source. We find that he first spoke of the Lord as "a man that is called Jesus." But the questions of the Pharisees made him consider seriously who this man was, and presently he said of Him, "He is a prophet." Then as the Pharisees tried to discredit the Lord, the man saw more and more clearly that He was from heaven, and finally, when He again appeared, the man needed only His own assurance that He was the Son of God, "And he said, Lord, I believe. And he worshipped him."

The same can be true with us, once we have had a real experience of the illuminating power of the Word. Opposition—whether from other people or from worldly reasonings in our own minds, which are also "Pharisees"—merely serves to stimulate and to clarify our thought about our experiences, and ultimately we accept the Lord as God with us. People today often start with the idea that Jesus was a man like other men, but if they continue to study His teachings with a desire to learn how to live, they are inevitably led to recognize Him first as a prophet, then as in some way divine, and finally as God Himself. Men today who, like the Pharisees, are unwilling at heart to recognize any authority higher than themselves treat the record of the Lord's life and teachings just as the Pharisees themselves treated the Lord and His work, although many of them claim to be followers of truth, just as the Pharisees claimed to be disciples of Moses. Of all such professed followers of the truth who reject the Lord from pride and self-will He says: "If ye were blind, ye should have no sin: but now ye say, We see; therefore your sin remaineth."

From the Writings of Swedenborg

Apocalypse Explained, n. 239[19]: "Why the Lord did this no one understands unless he knows the internal or spiritual sense of the Word; in that sense, by 'a man blind from birth' those are meant who are born outside of the church and who therefore could not know anything about the Lord, or be taught out of the Word. 'The clay that the Lord made from spittle on the ground' signifies reformation by means of truths from the sense of the letter of the Word; 'the ground' is the church where the Word is; 'clay' is the ultimate Divine forming; 'anointing the eyes of the blind with it' is to give thereby the understanding of truth; 'the pool of Siloam' also signifies the Word in the letter; 'to be washed there' is to be purified from falsities and evils."

Suggested Questions on the Lesson

J. Where was the pool of Bethesda? *Jerusalem*
P. How many porches did it have? *five*
P. Who lay in the porches? *sick people*
P. Why did they lie there? *hoping to be healed*
J. How long had one man been sick? *thirty-eight years*
P. What did the Lord ask him? *do you want to be well?*
J. What did he answer? *no one helps me*
P. What did the Lord tell him to do? *rise, take bed, walk*
P. What happened when he obeyed? *healed*
J. What did the Lord tell the man later? *sin no more*
P. In our story today how long had the man been blind? *since birth*
J. What did the disciples ask the Lord about him? *who sinned?*
J. What did the Lord tell them? *no one*
P. How was the man's sight restored? *clay, washing in pool*
P. What was the first objection to the miracle? *done on the sabbath*
J. What did their questions first lead the man to decide about the one who had healed him? *a prophet*
J. Why were the man's parents afraid to praise the Lord openly? *fear of being cast out*

J. When they could not deny the facts, what did his enemies say about the Lord? *he is a sinner*

J. What did the man answer? *"Never since the world began . . ."*

P. How was he punished? *cast out*

J. What did the Lord then tell him? *He was Son of God*

P. How did the man respond? *worshiped Him*

J. Why did the Lord say He came into the world? *for judgment*

J. What did the Pharisees ask? *are we blind?*

J. What did He tell them? *if you were . . . no guilt*

I. What does blindness represent? *ignorance*

S. What vital choice in life must each one of us make? *whether to believe the Lord or not*

THE GOOD SHEPHERD
John 10

All but the youngest classes are probably already familiar with this story. But even the best-known parts of the Word are inexhaustible in their meaning and yield new thoughts every time they are read.

Doctrinal Points

In order to hear the Lord we need to keep our hearts and minds humble and trustful.

Anyone who puts his own ideas or the ideas of other men above the teachings of the Lord is stealing from the Lord.

Notes for Parents

Everyone seems to know and love the twenty-third Psalm. It appeals to people universally because deep down in every person the Lord has stored up states of innocence and trust which that person experienced in infancy. These "remains" of our early states are referred to symbolically as the Lord's "lambs." We sometimes instinctively call a little baby a "lamb." By the same token, the Lord's "sheep" are the virtues which we have allowed to grow up out of these remains: humble recognition of our ignorance and weakness, trust in the Lord, kindly feelings toward all His other children, etc.

The modern world does not seem to think too much of these humble, childlike states, advising us instead to be self-confident and self-assertive. But in our Bible chapter the Lord teaches us that our only hope of safety and of heaven is in keeping our hearts and minds humble and trustful so that we shall hear His voice and follow him.

Many today who profess to be Christians are like the hirelings of whom the Lord speaks. They do right because of what they hope to get out of it (reputation in the community and honor from men), not because they really love goodness. Whenever doing right seems to threaten them with personal loss, their principles break down. This is why the Lord tells us that all who came before Him are thieves and robbers. All who put their own ideas or the ideas of other men before the teachings of the Lord are stealing from the Lord. The Lord is the door. Only obedience to the truth which He gives us in His Word leads us to safety and happiness.

All whose minds are open to hear the Lord's voice and whose hearts are willing to follow Him are His sheep, whether they belong to the Christian fold in this world or not. There are many good people in the world who have never learned about the Lord. They can, however, be taught about Him when they come into the other world. But those who, like the Pharisees in the Gospels, let their own self-importance and self-will close their ears to what they might learn here cannot be taught in the other world either. The Lord says of them, "You will not believe because you are not my sheep." When, a moment later, the Lord said, "The Father and I are one," these same people refused to consider His statement and merely accused Him of blasphemy and threatened to stone Him. This is exactly the same attitude that some people today have toward the Lord's words.

Primary

The correspondence of sheep is one which can be explained and illustrated even at this age level. This lesson offers a good opportunity to introduce the children to the thought that Bible animals represent traits of character with which they are familiar. The *main* objective of the teacher, however, should be to put into their minds thoughts about the Lord's tender love and care, and of our need of trustful obedience to Him. Read the lesson from the Word with them, giving them time to think of what each verse may mean.

Most of you have seen sheep. If not you have probably seen pictures of them; you may even have seen a picture of the Good Shepherd and a lamb. Sheep are gentle, useful animals. Their flesh is good to eat and their wool is very useful to us in another way.

Every winter their wooly coat grows very thick to protect them from the cold; in the spring, when it is warm again, their owners can cut the wool off and sell it to make cloth for clothing and blankets to keep people warm.

In some countries today sheep are still cared for very much as they were in the Holy Land long ago when the Lord was on earth. The shepherds lead the sheep out into the pastures in the spring and live there with them, guarding them in the daytime from wild animals and at night leading them into enclosures or folds where they can be safe from attack while the shepherds sleep. The shepherds love their sheep and call them by name, and the sheep know the voice of their own shepherd and follow wherever he leads them.

Did you ever hear someone call a baby a "little lamb"? It is a natural phrase to use because babies are gentle and innocent and like little lambs. The Lord called His followers His sheep. Let us read what He said about them. [Read John 10:1-14.]

Sheep and lambs picture innocence, the quality which leads us to trust in the Lord instead of ourselves. Shepherds, who lead and guard sheep, picture those who care for and protect this quality. The shepherds at Bethlehem who were told of the Lord's birth had this same meaning, representing this beautiful and important quality.

The Lord knows and loves each one of us just as a shepherd knows and loves his sheep. We should listen when He speaks to us in His Word, and learn to love Him and follow Him willingly wherever He leads us. One especially lovely part of the Old Testament tells us this, too. Let us read together the twenty-third Psalm, which is sometimes called the "Shepherd Psalm." It is probably known by heart by more people than any other part of the Bible except the Lord's Prayer.

Do you remember a much earlier part of the Bible, the time when the Israelites were first commanded to celebrate the Passover?
What was the reason for the first Passover?
What did they eat for Passover?

There was a reason why the meat to be eaten was lamb. When we eat, the food eventually becomes part of us, doesn't it? The things we take into our minds and hearts become part of us, too. Everything which the Lord commanded the people to do in Bible days pictured something necessary for us, when understood spiritually, if our souls are to become healthy and strong. In the Word, different animals represent different traits of character. Everyone knows, for instance, what we mean when we call a person a pig. It may not be so obvious to us, though, that sheep and lambs picture innocence.

Who do you think are the Lord's sheep?

The Lord knows and loves each one of us as a shepherd does his sheep. We should listen to the Lord's voice as He speaks to us in His Word, and follow Him wherever He leads us. Then He can feed our souls and keep us safe. No one else can be trusted to lead us safely. This is part of what He means when He says, "I am the door." Think of this when you join in the closing benediction in Sunday school: "The Lord keep our going out and our coming in, from this time forth, and even for evermore."

―――――

Junior

The correspondence of sheep and their relation to the shepherd can be given in some detail to this class, as well as the meaning of the Lord's being the "door" of the sheep. This is a good lesson in which to impress on them the responsibility that goes with our freedom of choice.

What kind of meat was eaten at the Passover?
What was David doing when he was called by Samuel to be anointed as king?
Who were the first to be told of the Lord's birth at Bethlehem?
How does Psalm 23 begin?

In John Worcester's book *Animals of the Bible* we read:

The shepherds of the East give a name to each member of their flocks, which the sheep soon learn, and to which they instantly respond. In the dry season many shepherds with their flocks meet at regular times around the wells. The flocks mingle at the troughs, drinking. But when all are satisfied, the shepherds move off in different directions, calling their sheep, which immediately follow, every one its own shepherd, with scarcely the possibility of a mistake . . . It is a peculiarity of sheep that while they are so easily *led* by one whom they know, they are *driven* with difficulty. They huddle together as if frightened and the more they are pressed, the more frightened they seem; but if the leaders start forward, the flock follows. Affection for their shepherd is stronger than their mutual love. Him they will follow away from their friends.

The sheepfold mentioned in the first verse of John 10 refers to an enclosure into which the sheep could be led for safety. In those days there were evidently thieves and robbers to be guarded against as well as wolves and other wild animals.

Although the Lord spoke of natural things familiar to His hearers then, He was also talking about and to people in all times. His words are meant for us as well as for the people who listened to Him long ago. Let us learn some of this timeless language. For instance, we may hear someone call a baby a "little lamb." This is not just a casual expression. A human infant shows characteristics that correspond to those of a lamb, being innocent and trustful, looking to someone wiser for care and protection, and having no desire to harm anyone. Babies soon grow out of this state, however, and begin to want their own way and to try to get it even if it leads to injury of others. It is easy to see that these later traits are not good and beautiful like the first ones.

In our chapter the Lord is saying that innocence and trust are qualities He wants us to keep, and that if we will trust and follow Him, as the sheep trust and follow their shepherd, He will "feed us in green pastures," as the twenty-third Psalm says, and care for us and protect us always. It is only when we refuse to listen for His voice in order to follow him that we wander away from safety and fall prey to the "wolves" of selfish and cruel feelings.

What does the Lord call Himself in verse 9?
What does He call those who do *not* enter by the door?
What other kind of person is mentioned (verse 12)?
What does this person do when a wolf appears?

If you think a little you will see what this means spiritually. Thieves and robbers are those who try to steal sheep away from their true shepherd. This means that when anyone refuses to accept the Lord as God or to be obedient to Him, but tries some other way to enter a heavenly state, that person is acting like a robber, trying to steal from the Lord what is his and to lead the Lord's sheep astray. In the same way, a hireling means a person who claims to be working for the Lord, but who is really only interested in the good reputation of the Lord's followers. Whenever obeying the Lord threatens to be a disadvantage to such a person, he turns his back on his duty.

The last part of John 10 relates a conversation the Lord had with some of His enemies as he walked in the portico of Solomon, the colonnade on the east side of the temple.

What did they ask Him to tell them?
Why did the Lord say they wouldn't believe Him?
What did He finally tell them (verse 30)?
Then what did they try to do?
Why did they say they wanted to stone the Lord?

This shows us what the Lord meant by His sheep and by calling Himself the "door" of the sheepfold. You are old enough to understand that the Lord has given each one of us the freedom to choose whether to will to be good or bad. First He tells us what is good, and then He tells us that only those who are good can ever be happy. If we choose to believe Him and try to do what He tells us is right, we can become His sheep and follow Him in safety and peace. But if we choose not to believe Him, we shall never know what safety and peace are. We may be able to get *some* things we think we want, but we shall soon tire of them and want other things. Such people will never be satisfied or happy either in this world or the next.

―――――

Intermediate

The meaning of innocence and charity should be impressed upon this class through the correspondence of lambs and sheep. It is at this age that young people often develop the most obvious and disagreeable form of self-assurance, and the teacher can help the parents by leading the class to see that this trait is not admirable but is a "wolf" come to steal away their good qualities.

Did you ever stop to think how many familiar passages in the Bible involve sheep and shepherds? We might begin with the story of Cain and Abel, in which Abel was a keeper of sheep and his offering of the firstlings of his flock was accepted by the Lord. Then in the story of Abraham's trying to sacrifice Isaac, the Lord provided a ram as a substitute. When Jacob fled from Esau and came to the well at Haran, he fell in love with Rachel when he saw her coming with her father's sheep to the well. The meat commanded for the Passover feast was lamb, and many of the sacrifices specified in the laws at Sinai used sheep and lambs. When Samuel was sent to anoint David, David was called from tending his father's sheep. And the twenty-third Psalm, which next to the Lord's Prayer is probably the best-known passage in the Bible, begins: "The Lord is my shepherd." In the New Testament we think at once of the shepherds at Bethlehem watching over their flocks by night, to whom the angels announced the Lord's birth. Then there is the parable of the lost sheep; the instance of the Lord's telling Peter, "Feed my sheep . . . feed my lambs"; and the statement of John the Baptist when he saw the Lord coming: "Behold the Lamb of God, which taketh away the sin of the world." (John 1:29) Finally, in the book of Revelation the Lord is many times called "the Lamb."

But why should the Lord be called the lamb and also the shepherd? It is because the quality which sheep and lambs represent is the inmost quality of the Lord and also the quality which He is always seeking to develop and preserve in each one of us, His children. It is the quality of charity or genuine goodness—represented by sheep—which develops out of the quality of innocence—represented by lambs. The word *innocence* literally means "not harming," but this is a result of the quality called innocence rather than the quality itself. Swedenborg tells us that innocence and also charity are inmostly the acknowledgment that we are not either good or wise in ourselves, but that all goodness and wisdom are in and from the Lord. This is the quality which makes a person always ready to hear and obey the voice of the Lord and always careful to do nothing which may tend to harm another. If we have this quality we follow the Lord just as sheep in the eastern countries follow their shepherd. And if we do this, the Lord can watch over us and keep our souls safe from selfish and cruel impulses which, like wolves, are lurking in all of us ready to spring out when we are "off our guard."

A sheepfold is a picture of heaven, and the Lord Jesus Christ is its only door. He alone is a safe guide, because He alone loves us with pure, unselfish love which is divine love. All other guides we may choose to follow are either thieves and robbers, trying to steal us away from the Lord and heaven, or to some extent at least "hirelings," claiming that they are serving goodness and truth but really doing so for the sake of their own reputation and comfort, and not to be trusted if their own interests are threatened.

But there are many people in the world who have the quality of innocence—who sincerely want to be good—who, for one reason or another, have never come to recognize Jesus Christ as the true shepherd. These are the "other sheep" the Lord speaks of in verse 16. Swedenborg tells us that such people can be instructed in the truth after they come into the other world, because their hearts and minds are open. (We should know that in this verse 16 in KJV there is an error in translation. The word correctly translated "fold" in the first part of the verse is not the same word used in the last part, which should be translated "there shall be one flock, one shepherd," as in several more recent translations.) There are many different societies in heaven—many folds—but all are the Lord's sheep, recognizing Him alone as their shepherd.

In the last part of John 10 the difference between those who are the Lord's sheep and those who are not is made clear by the Lord's conversation in the temple. The people asked Him about Himself not because they wanted to learn the truth but that they might find an excuse to condemn Him. They thought themselves wise and considered themselves good; they were not innocent. The Lord told them plainly, "Ye believe not, because ye are not of my sheep." Their pride in their own wisdom and goodness had closed their minds and hearts. Such people cannot be taught the truth either in this world or in the next.

Basic Correspondences

shepherd = one who leads and teaches and protects those who are in good

wolf = the evil that is opposite to innocence and goodness and seeks to destroy them

---

Senior

This is a good opportunity to point out to Seniors the shallowness of a worldly attitude, and also the weakness of the belief in Christ in many Christian groups today. They need clear sight and a firm hold on the Lord and His own teaching to safeguard them as they go out into the world.

There are two lessons in our chapter for today about which we should think very seriously. One centers about the Lord's statement that His sheep hear His voice and follow Him, and the other about His statement that He is the door.

Lambs and sheep represent innocence and the genuine goodness and charity which develop from innocence. The ground of both innocence and charity is humility. In our modern civilization this is not a popular virtue; in fact, it is scarcely considered to be a virtue at all. The emphasis in politics, in business, and in professional life is on self-confidence and self-assertion. When a modern man says people are like sheep, he is not meaning to compliment them. He means that they are easily led to do what "everybody" is doing, and much of our modern advertising is geared to this fact.

Our chapter for today gives us a very different thought about sheep. They are indeed prone to follow rather than to lead, and without the true shepherd they are easily stolen by thieves or destroyed by wolves. But they also recognize the voice of the true shepherd when they hear it, and follow Him willingly and trustfully. This means that those who have humility can be led to the heavenly fold. Here read the quotation at the end of the notes for Adults.

Those who believe in their own wisdom and goodness close their ears to the shepherd's voice and go their own way to destruction. The Lord told a group of the people, "Ye believe not, because ye are not my sheep." Confidence in self may achieve fame and fortune for a time in this world, but even here its achievements are not lasting. The great people of history have not been of this kind.

Once a person has the basis of innocence and goodness in the heart there is only one great need, and that is to find the true shepherd. Read Jeremiah 23:1-4. (*Pastor* is another word for shepherd.) The false shepherds of whom Jeremiah speaks are the thieves and robbers mentioned in our chapter, and also the "hirelings." A hireling is one who professes to be serving the Lord, but is really concerned chiefly with his own importance and welfare. The Lord alone is the true shepherd, and we hear His voice when we read the Word in an affirmative spirit, accepting what He says as true because He says it, and trying our best to understand and obey.

This is why the Lord calls Himself the door of the sheep. You will be surprised, as you go out into the world and mingle with Christian people not of your own church and attend their services and meetings, to find how much of their teaching they draw from what others have said about Christ and how little they attend to what Christ said about Himself. Remember always that as New Churchmen you believe that Jesus Christ is the door by which we must enter heaven, that He knew what He was saying and spoke the simple truth when He said (verse 30), "I and my Father are one," and when later (John 14:9) He said to Philip, "Have I been so long time with you, and yet hast thou not known me, Philip? he that hath seen me hath seen the Father."

We have to make up our minds as early as possible whether we are going to devote our lives to getting what we can of this world's goods and honors, closing our minds to the consideration of what lasts to eternity, or whether we are going to develop the deeper and higher possibilities which the Lord offers to each one of us. The people around us may not understand what we are trying to become. They may even think that we are foolish. But the Lord knows each of us through and through. He says: "I am the good shepherd, and know my sheep."

———————

Adult

The teacher of this class should read also the Senior notes, for many adults are prone to be over-impressed with modern worldly reasoning and with Bible studies based on disbelief in the divine inspiration of the Word. The quotation on innocence at the end of the lesson notes may also be used as discussion material.

In the writings sheep are variously interpreted as "celestial things," "those in charity and thence in faith," "the good of the will," or simply "those in good." Lambs picture especially the good of innocence, that inmost affection which must be in everyone who enters heaven, and which especially reigns with the angels in the celestial heavens (AE 314; HH 276-283), the tender, gentle, loving spirit which does not trust in self but looks to the Lord alone for guidance. It has no selfish wish, and because this is the inmost quality of the Lord's love, He is so often called a lamb (John 1:29, 36; Isaiah 53:7; Revelation 5:6, 7:17). Because we must never forget that this quality is an essential part of true worship of the Lord, the people in Old Testament days were commanded to offer every day "two lambs of the first year without spot," one in the morning and one in the evening (Numbers 28:3-4). we keep this statute in spirit when we pray morning and evening, "Deliver us from evil," desiring to be kept from thinking or acting in any way which would injure the Lord or the neighbor. It is this love that saves us from bondage to evil and falsity; it was for the same reason that lamb was the meat of the feast of the Passover (Exodus 12:3-10). Because infants are the external embodiment of this love, a lamb was the appropriate offering for the birth of a child (Leviticus 12:6).

Those who guard and cherish this innocent love are called shepherds. The Lord is primarily the Good Shepherd, as we learn in our chapter for today, and in many other places in the Word He is called a shepherd (Psalm 23; Isaiah 40:11). We likewise know that the beautiful parable in Luke 15:3-7 teaches of His loving care. He sent the apostles forth as lambs among wolves (Luke 10:3), but we are promised that a time shall come when the wolf shall dwell with the lamb (Isaiah 11:6; 65:25), picturing the time when our evil affections will be completely restrained by the power of the Lord's love in our hearts. When we read of the Lord asking Peter if he loved Him, telling him three times to feed His sheep and His lambs (John 21:15-17), it is a solemn reminder that if we do not cherish tender and gentle affections in ourselves and others, we do not truly love the Lord. When He came into the world, those to whom His advent was first made known were shepherds keeping their flocks by night around Bethlehem. This means that those who in the midst of ignorance and evil guard and cherish the good of innocence are prepared to recognize the Lord. Another interesting story in the Word is the coming of Joseph's brethren before Pharaoh, when they concealed their true calling of shepherds and said their trade had been keepers of cattle, because "every shepherd is an abomination to the Egyptians" (Genesis 56:34). This pictures the fact that the natural mind can recognize value in affections for useful work—represented by cattle—but has no use for the inner qualities of the heart. Throughout the Word the Lord's providence is pictured as feeding and cherishing the inmost affections for goodness, and as protecting and leading those in whom these affections are found.

In Jeremiah 23:1-4 we read a condemnation of false pastors or shepherds who neglect their duty and destroy and scatter the Lord's sheep, and we have there the promise of the Lord's coming to gather the sheep again into their folds. In our chapter for today the Lord presents Himself as the fulfillment of this prophecy. We have seen that He is the lamb, in that His inmost love is innocence. Now we find that He is also the Good Shepherd and the door of the sheepfold. He is the Good Shepherd in that He cares for and feeds the things that are His own in us; and He is the door in that He is the truth by which alone we can find the way into His fold, which is heaven. Those who seek to enter heaven without recognizing the Lord are thieves and robbers, claiming as their own what belongs solely to the Lord. His sheep hear His voice; those whose hearts are innocent recognize the Lord as God and obey Him. And "he calleth his own sheep by name"; i.e., He recognizes the true quality of each one. " 'To call the sheep by name' means to teach and to lead every one who is in the good of charity according to the state of his love and wisdom." (DP 230) "By me if any man enter in, he shall be saved, and shall go in and out, and find pasture." This means to draw close to the Lord in our hearts and to follow Him in our outward life; it reminds us of the familiar benediction: "The Lord keep our going out and our coming in from this time forth, and even forevermore." Those who would be true shepherds are, like the Lord, ready to give their life for the sheep, to sacrifice selfish desires when they threaten heavenly innocence. But the hireling, he who does good only for what he can get out of it, deserts the sheep in time of danger, cares for them only while it is obviously to his advantage to do so. The "other sheep . . . which are not of this fold" refer to those whose minds must be satisfied, who are pictured in the advent stories by the Wise Men from the East who saw the star (AC 3969). This whole chapter, like the twenty-third Psalm, is one of the most universally known and loved in the Word, because, whether we understand it or not, it appeals to the innocent states which the Lord has stored up in everyone from infancy, and which are the first to recognize Him.

The Pharisees were not of the Lord's sheep. They were evil shepherds and hirelings. When they questioned Him, it was not for the sake of learning the truth, but to draw from Him statements which they could condemn. So He often answered them in such a way as to point out their insincerity and if possible to make them judge their own conduct and motives. In one conversation He asked them to study and judge the works which He had done, and challenged them to find fault with His works. But He also declared plainly His oneness with the Father. Although this is exactly what they had asked Him to say, they immediately accused

Him of blasphemy "because that thou, being a man, makest thyself God." People today who do not wish to accept the Lord's teachings as divine truth pretend to investigate His claim, but like the Pharisees they have their minds made up to start with, and as soon as they come upon a direct statement of His deity they say, "Impossible; no man could make such a claim; this must be a fiction of the apostles." They refuse, as the Pharisees did, to consider His works as evidence of the source of His power. They are not of His sheep; that is, they do not have in their hearts the humility and the innocent and trustful affection which open the mind to His voice. Here again we have the lesson that belief is primarily of the will. "My sheep hear my voice." Those who really desire the Lord's guidance can find ample proof of His claim, but those who wish to guide themselves cannot be convinced by any type of proof.

From the Writings of Swedenborg

Heaven and Hell, nn. 276-280: "What innocence is and its nature few in the world know, and those who are in evil know nothing about it. It is, indeed, visible to the eyes, as seen in the face, speech, and movements, particularly of children; and yet what innocence is, and especially that it is that in which heaven is stored up in man is unknown. In making this known let us proceed in order, and consider first the innocence of childhood, then the innocence of wisdom, and lastly the state of heaven in regard to innocence. The innocence of childhood or of children is not genuine innocence, for it is innocence not in internal form but only in external form. Nevertheless one may learn from it what innocence is, since it shines forth from the face of children and from some of their movements and from their first speech, and affects those about them. . . . I have been told from heaven that children are especially under the Lord's auspices, and that they receive influx from the inmost heaven, where there is a state of innocence; that this influx passes through their interiors, and that in its passing through, their interiors are affected solely by the innocence; and for this reason innocence is shown in their faces and in some of their movements and becomes evident... The innocence of wisdom is genuine innocence, because it is internal, for it belongs to the mind itself, that is, to the will itself and from that to the understanding. This is why it is said in heaven that innocence has its abode in wisdom, and that an angel has just so much of innocence as he has of wisdom. This is confirmed by the fact that those who are in a state of innocence attribute nothing of good to themselves, but regard all things as received and ascribe them to the Lord; that they wish to be led by Him and not by themselves; that they love everything that is good and find delight in everything that is true, because they know and perceive that loving what is good, that is, willing and doing it, is loving the Lord, and loving truth is loving the neighbor; that they live contented with their own, whether it be little or much, because they know that they receive just as much as is good for them . . . Neither are they anxious about the future . . . As innocence consists in being led by the Lord and not by self, so all who are in heaven are in innocence; for all who are there love to be led by the Lord, knowing that to lead themselves is to be led by what is their own, and what is one's own is loving oneself."

Suggested Questions on the Lesson

P. What does the Lord call Himself in this lesson? *Good Shepherd*

P. What does He say a true shepherd does? *calls his sheep by name*

P. What does He say about the sheep? *they know His voice*

J. What does He say about those who came before Him? *thieves and robbers*

P. What else does He call Himself, besides Shepherd? *door of fold*

J. How is He the door? *through Him we enter heaven*

J. What does He say about the hireling? *cares nothing for the sheep*

J. What does He say about other sheep He has? *not of this fold*

J. What did some of the Jews ask Him to tell them? *are you the Christ?*

J. What did He point to as witness that He came from God? *His works*

J. Why did He say they would not believe Him? *not His sheep*

J. What did He say about Himself and the Father? *I and Father are one*

J. What did they then accuse Him of? *blasphemy*

P. What other very familiar Bible passage calls the Lord a Shepherd? *twenty-third Psalm*

I. What do (1) lambs, and (2) sheep represent? *(1) the quality of innocence out of which grows (2) the quality of genuine goodness in the life*

S. What is innocence, spiritually understood? *the acknowledgment that all goodness and wisdom are from the Lord; thus the willingness to be led by the Lord (literally, harmlessness)*

THE RAISING OF LAZARUS
John 11:1-46

For all classes this story offers one of our best opportunities to give the doctrine of the future life. In our chapter the Lord shows clearly that He raised Lazarus in order to teach that we never die and that it is He alone who determines when our consciousness should be transferred from this world to the spiritual world.

―――――――

Doctrinal Points

Death is a kind of "sleep" leading to resurrection.

The only "death" we need fear is the death of goodness in our hearts.

Unless we try to obey the Lord, believing in His Word, we are in danger of letting selfish and worldly desires kill any hope that we may become spiritual people.

―――――――

Notes for Parents

Our story for today tells us many things which will help us all through our lives, if only we are willing to believe them. One thing it shows us is that belief is a matter of our free choice. Sometimes we hear people say, "I wish I could believe that death is not the end." They could believe if they were really willing. Mary and Martha and Lazarus were willing; the chief priests and the Pharisees were not. Belief involves changing our lives and we tend to put off making such an important decision.

The Lord tells us plainly that all are raised up after death, not on some distant judgment day but immediately. He told His disciples first, "Our friend Lazarus sleepeth" and then "Lazarus is dead." Both statements were true. For death is nothing more than going to sleep in this world and waking up in a much more beautiful and happy one.

110

You notice that when the Lord was first told that His dear friend Lazarus was sick, He said: "This sickness is not unto death, but for the glory of God." He knew that the work of Lazarus in this world was not finished, and that He would reawaken him here. This life is our school. We all have work to do here—work for others and also the work of forming our own souls into the image and likeness of God. It is right that we should hope for a long life here, so that we may do all the good and make all the progress we can. But still this is just our beginning, and we should trust the Lord to decide when it will be best for us to be transferred to our eternal homes, and we should look forward to that time. Death is always a blessing for the person who dies, however we may feel the loss here. The only death we should fear is the death of goodness in our hearts. This is the death which is meant in verse 26 of our chapter. If we do not make up our minds here to believe in the Lord and try to obey Him, we are in danger of letting our own selfish and worldly desires kill out in us all possibility of becoming the kind of people who live in heaven.

Primary

Introduce the characters in the story and then read the lesson from the Word. Talk about what death really is and about the beautiful world which is prepared for us; do not fail to emphasize that we must learn here to be heavenly people if we are to live in heaven when we die. The teacher should try to find out what the children know of death, and let that lead into a discussion of what death really is, the spiritual world, and the purpose of our life here.

Often when the Lord went to Jerusalem for any of the great feasts, He did not sleep in Jerusalem, but at night went out to Bethany, a little town about two miles from Jerusalem, and stayed with some dear friends He had there. These friends were a man named Lazarus and his two sisters, Martha and Mary. They are mentioned several times in the Gospels. Our story today is about something that happened to them and a miracle which the Lord performed.

What had happened to Lazarus?
Why did the Lord wait to go to Bethany until after Lazarus had died?
Who went out to meet Him?
What did Martha say when she met the Lord?
What did she think about the resurrection of the dead?
What did the Lord tell her?
When they came to the grave, what did the Lord tell them to do?
What did the Lord say when they took away the stone?
What happened?

When anyone we love dies, we feel very sad because we know how much we shall miss him and what a change in our lives his going will make. This is a natural feeling and not wrong, but we must be sure that we do not let ourselves feel that the Lord ought not to have let our friend die. The Lord always does what is best for every one of us.

The Lord raised Lazarus from the dead to teach us two things which we must always remember. One is that, as verse 25 of our chapter tells us, He is the "resurrection and the life." All life comes from the Lord. The other is that no one ever really dies. When a person is said to die, it just means that he is waking up in the spiritual world instead of here on earth. And the spiritual world is much more beautiful and happy than this one. We live here on earth for just a few years to learn to be the kind of people the Lord wants us to be, and then the Lord can let us wake up in the other world and find the homes where we shall live always—very beautiful homes if we have been good.

Junior

The principal lessons to be impressed on the Juniors are that our life here is given us as a time of free choice of God or self, that death is not to be feared, that the Lord decides when it is best for us to leave this world, and that no one can be convinced by miracles who does not want to obey the Lord.

Our lesson today is about another miracle—perhaps the most striking one of all. The story is told only in the Gospel of John. It happened very near the end of the Lord's life on earth, for at the end of the chapter we are told that the Passover feast was at hand, and in the beginning of chapter 12 we have the story of the Lord's entry into Jerusalem on Palm Sunday.

Where did Lazarus live?
Who were his sisters?
To whom did they send when Lazarus became sick?

Bethany was a little town about two miles from Jerusalem, and it was at the home of Mary and Martha and Lazarus that the Lord was in the habit of lodging when He went to Jerusalem. In our lessons from Luke we had a story about Mary and Martha. If you have forgotten it, read it in Luke 10:38-42. Read also John 12:1-8, which explains verse 2 of our chapter.

Did the Lord go at once to Bethany when He heard that Lazarus was sick?
What did He first say to His disciples about Lazarus?

When we die, we do merely go to sleep in this world and wake up in the spiritual world, which we know is our real home and a much more beautiful and happy world than this one. We live in this world for a few years to learn how to live and to make our free choice of the kind of people we want to be. It is right that we should want to stay here as long as we can in the effort to become better and better ourselves and more and more useful to other people. But we should never be afraid of death. In fact we should all, if we are trying to do right, look forward to the day when the Lord can say to us, as He said to the man in the parable (Matthew 25:21): "Well done, thou good and faithful servant . . . enter thou into the joy of thy lord." For it is always the Lord who decides just when it is best for us to leave this world.

In the case of Lazarus the Lord knew that this time had not really come. We learn this from verse 4 of our chapter. Lazarus did die, but the Lord planned to wake him again in this world instead of in the other.

What reason does the Lord give in verse 4?
When the Lord reached Bethany, how long had Lazarus been in the tomb?
What did Martha say when she met the Lord?
What did the Lord tell her?

When did Martha think Lazarus would rise?
What did the Lord say?
What did Mary say when she came to the Lord?

Both Martha and Mary believed firmly that Jesus was the Messiah and they knew He had performed many miracles. He had twice before brought back to life someone who had been pronounced dead. We have studied one of these stories (Luke 7:11-15). The other is told in Matthew, Mark, and Luke. Read it in Luke 8:41-42, 49-56. Martha and Mary may have known of these miracles, but both had been performed very soon after the death of the person. It never occurred to the two sisters that the Lord could restore their brother to them after he had been buried for four days. Martha's words in verse 39 of our chapter show what their thought was.

How did Lazarus appear when he came out of the tomb?
What did the Lord tell the people to do?
What effect did the miracle have on many who saw it?

You should read the next few verses (47-53) to see the different effect of this miracle on the chief priests and Pharisees. You can see that they knew that the story was true, but their only thought was of how to preserve their own power with the people and the favor of the Roman governor. Miracles never convince anyone who does not want to obey the Lord.

Intermediate

The young people should be shown how clearly the Lord teaches that the death of the body does not interrupt the life of a person, and that He is always in control. Include the correspondences presented in the Easter lesson and show how they apply here. Call attention to the attitude of the chief priests and Pharisees and show how this lesson leads into the crucifixion of the Lord.

The miracle of our lesson for today was performed near the end of the Lord's life on earth. In verse 55 of our chapter we read, "And the Jews' passover was nigh at hand," and the next chapter tells of the Lord's coming to Jerusalem for this Passover and entering the city as a king, welcomed by the multitude—our Palm Sunday lesson. In that chapter (chapter 12) we are also told that many of the multitude had come more to see Lazarus than to see the Lord. We can well imagine how widely the miracle was discussed.

The scene of the miracle was Bethany, a little town about two miles from Jerusalem. You may remember this from the story of Mary and Martha (Luke 10:38-42). The Lord was in the habit of lodging at their house when He came to Jerusalem for the feasts, and it was there that He lodged during the last week of His life also. Mary and Martha and their brother Lazarus all believed the Lord to be the Messiah. They knew of His miracles of healing, and it was natural that they should send word to Him when Lazarus was taken sick. As we see from our chapter, both the sisters felt sure that the Lord would have healed Lazarus if only He had come in time, but neither of them imagined that He had power to restore their brother to life after he had lain four days in the tomb. They had the same material thoughts that everyone else had, and supposed that life was in the physical body, and that after their brother's body had begun to decay, he could not live again until all men's physical bodies should be raised to life again at the "last day." You will find that, in spite of the Lord's teaching, many people still believe this today.

The Lord tells us that He purposely waited before going to Bethany (verses 14-15). Twice before He had raised someone from the dead (Luke 7:11-15; 8:41-42, 49-56), but in one of these cases the miracle was performed almost immediately after death and in the other so soon after that the body was not yet buried. The raising of Lazarus was to carry a step further the disciples' understanding of the Lord's power over life. It should have prepared them to expect His own resurrection, but we know that it did not, and this is one of the things which teaches us how hard it is for anyone who has let himself become absorbed in the things of the material world to be brought to understand and believe in spiritual things, which are after all the real things.

Jesus told Martha: "I am the resurrection and the life." The Lord alone is life, as we learned in the first chapter of John (1:4).

and all our life, and all the apparent life of the physical world comes from Him moment by moment. Before He went to Bethany He said to His disciples: "Our friend Lazarus sleepeth; but I go that I may awake him out of sleep"; then He said: "Lazarus is dead." What we call death is really only a short sleep from which we wake to consciousness in the spiritual world instead of in this. None of us should fear it. The Lord knows when each one of us has made all the preparation for eternal life that he is willing and able to make. Every once in a while we read in the papers of someone who has apparently died and then, by massage of the heart or some such treatment, has been restored to life. And we know that often people who have apparently drowned are resuscitated. In all such cases we may think that the Lord is saying, as He said of Lazarus in verse 4: "This sickness is not unto death, but for the glory of God." The person resuscitated and also those around him have something to learn from the experience.

The Easter lesson contains all the correspondences we need know for our study of the meaning of this miracle: the tomb, the stone, and the graveclothes. Whenever we are faced with the death of someone we love, we should remember that in the Word death and burial signify resurrection, and we should try to "think as angels think, and feel as angels feel"; that is, think of the person waking to fuller and more beautiful life and rejoice with him, even while we naturally grieve that we ourselves shall not see him for a while.

Read carefully verses 4, 15, 41, and 42 to see how plainly the Word shows us that the Lord stands guard over all the experiences that come to us and wishes us to learn from them.

But we do not learn if our minds are full of self and of our success in the world. Read verses 47 to 53 to see how the Pharisees took the news of the raising of Lazarus, and read verses 10 and 11 of chapter 12 to see how far their self-interest led them. The Lord has given every human being two great gifts: freedom and rationality.* Each one of us, if he is to be what he is created to be, must

---

*Rationality is the ability to distinguish between right and wrong; freedom

first decide freely to believe the Lord and obey Him instead of letting selfishness rule his life, and then he must study the Word and
think about all he reads there, and in this new age he must also
study what the Lord in His Second Coming has taught us concerning its true meaning.

Basic Correspondences

stoning	=	(in a good sense) truths used resolutely to condemn evil
	=	(in an evil sense) denial and perversion of truth
Lazarus	=	charity and openness toward the Lord
raising Lazarus	=	restoring these qualities in the church
death	=	the "sleep" of resurrection

Senior

It is very important that young people form as early as possible the right
habit of looking at death. A clear understanding and firm faith will enable
them to decide more easily many problems and also to help those who have
not had the same spiritual opportunities which they have had.

Recall the story of the Lord's healing of the man blind from
birth, the effect this miracle had on the man himself and the quite
different effect it had on the religious leaders around him. Our
story today gives us a still more striking example of the same lesson.
It happened very near the end of the Lord's life on earth. In the
letter it is closely associated with the Palm Sunday lesson (chapter
12:9), and in its significance with the Easter lesson. It also gives us
(verses 47-53) the final reason why the chief priests and Pharisees
determined that they must destroy the Lord.

As you grow older, if you continue to read the Gospels over and
over again, you will be struck with the way in which the Lord's

---

(or liberty) is the ability to make our own choices between right and wrong as
we are confronted by good and evil day by day. —*Ed.*

power as well as His consciousness of His divine nature increased with His overcoming of the successive temptations which came to Him through His assumed human. You remember perhaps that when He was twelve years old, He said to Mary and Joseph when they found Him tarrying with the doctors in the temple: "Wist ye not that I must be about my Father's business?" (Luke 2:49). Now, just before the final scenes of His earthly life, He can say to Martha: "I am the resurrection and the life," and presently (John 14:9) to Philip: "He that hath seen me hath seen the Father."

Yet we can also see in our chapter that something of the assumed humanity still remained with Him, for He wept and also groaned, and weeping and groaning, although they are often produced by love, are not characteristics of infinity. We learn from this chapter that the Lord permitted Himself to do and say many things because of their effect on those around Him. With this in mind read verses 4, 6, 11-15, 41-42.

The Lord had twice before raised someone from the dead (Luke 7:11-15; 8:49-56), but in neither case had the person been buried. In the minds of the people this would make a great difference in the effect of the miracle, for the people of that day, as we know, were wholly external in their ideas, and believed that life was in the body and could not exist apart from it. Even Martha and Mary—who were friends of the Lord, knew of His miracles, and believed Him to be the Messiah—could not imagine that any power could restore life to a body which had begun to decay. The raising of Lazarus ought to have made the disciples realize that the Lord Himself could not be subject to extinction by death, but we know that it did not. Only His own resurrection finally opened their eyes.

The lesson for us in this story is simple and clear. The Lord spoke the truth equally when He said, "Our friend Lazarus sleepeth," and when He said, "Lazarus is dead." When we die, we merely go to sleep in this world, just as we go to sleep every night, and we wake up refreshed and rested and ready for another day—only instead of waking in this world to go on trying to cope with our earthly problems and fighting temptations, we wake in a far more beautiful and happy world, with our problems and temptations behind us. Death is always a blessing for the one who dies.

The time had not come when the Lord thought best to take Lazarus to his eternal home. There was still work for him to do and progress for him to make in this world. Read verse 4, which teaches this plainly. Our times are in the Lord's hand (Psalm 31:15). This does not mean, as some people think, that a particular moment for our death is set in advance and that nothing we can do makes any difference. Every choice we make from day to day and also the choices which other people make play a part in determining the time when the Lord sees that it is better for us and for others that we wake in the spiritual world instead of in this. And the death of someone we love always presents us with a new series of choices. We can lament and rebel against what has happened, or we can let it draw us closer to heaven and the Lord. This life is our time of choice and preparation. It is right that we should want it to be long. But we should also trust the Lord to do what is best. We should always think of death as a natural and good step in our lives, for it is only the end of our stay in "kindergarten." In Psalm 90 we read: "So teach us to number our days, that we may apply our hearts unto wisdom . . . O satisfy us early with thy mercy; that we may rejoice and be glad all our days."

Adult

The Adult notes suggest several common questions which this story helps us to answer. These make good discussion topics. The teacher should also call attention to the connection of the story with the events which immediately followed it, especially in its bearing upon the attitude of the multitude on Palm Sunday and upon the determination of the chief priests to dispose of the Lord. Help will be found here in the Senior notes.

Three instances of the Lord's power to raise the dead are recorded in the Gospels: the raising of the widow's son at Nain (Luke 7:11-16); the raising of the daughter of Jairus (Matthew 9:18-26; Mark 5:22-43; Luke 8:41-56); and the raising of Lazarus, which is recorded only in John. The first two were performed in Galilee, and picture the Lord's power to restore to life the dead thoughts and affections of the external plane of our lives. But Lazarus lived in Bethany, close to Jerusalem, and was a beloved friend of the Lord, the brother of Mary and Martha, at whose house the Lord was often entertained, and this miracle pictures a more internal and spiritual work. In our reading of the story we should note that the scene is laid close to Jerusalem, that the time is near the end of the Lord's earthly life, that those concerned are believers and close friends of the Lord, and that throughout the story the Lord discloses to us the purpose governing the events. We should also note that, although many believed because of this miracle, those who opposed the Lord became even more violent against Him as a result of it. This illustrates the truth of Abraham's statement to the rich man in hell (Luke 16:31): "If they hear not Moses and the prophets, neither will they be persuaded, though one rose from the dead." The same parable is further linked to our story by the fact that the beggar is called Lazarus, and Swedenborg tells us that the Lord chose the name for the beggar in the parable because of the Lazarus of our story, whom He loved (AC 9231[3]; AE 137[2]; SS 40[3]).

Throughout the story it is evident that the miracle was performed not in order that Lazarus might enjoy a few more years in this world, but that the disciples might see the Lord's power over death. This is the most obvious and external lesson which we may draw from the miracle. It is a fact that all life is from the Lord, that our times are in His hand (Psalm 31:15), that not a sparrow falls to the ground without our Father (Matthew 10:29). But the life of the body is of relative unimportance in relation to the life of the soul. In fact, the life of the soul scarcely becomes apparent until after the death of the body. So the angels, reading the Word, understand resurrection where we read "death," and death in a good sense always signifies resurrection. There is another kind of death, which is sometimes called in the Word the "second death." This is spiritual death, death to goodness and truth, resulting when evil in the will becomes conjoined to falsity in the understanding. From this death also the Lord wishes to raise us, and has power to raise us if we will believe in Him and obey Him. "For I have no pleasure in the death of him that dieth, saith the Lord God: wherefore turn yourselves, and live ye." (Ezekiel 18:32)

When the Lord came into the world, His truth had been so perverted by the religious leaders that even those who wished to do right were threatened with this spiritual death, because they could not find the truth by which to live. This state is pictured in our story. Martha and Mary represent the desire to serve the Lord—Martha an external type and Mary a more internal, spiritual type of affection. Their brother Lazarus pictures such truth as they had, and the fact that he fell sick and died means that even that truth failed and was lost. They sent for the Lord, but He tarried until they thought Lazarus was gone beyond recall. There are many people today brought up in beliefs so mingled with falsity that their beliefs cannot survive the questions of their adult minds. When these people see their faith threatened, they often pray that it may not be taken from them, and feel that somehow the Lord might save it for them if He would, as Martha and Mary both cried, "Lord, if thou hadst been here, my brother had not died." But the Lord tarries purposely. He knows our condition, but He waits the fullness of time, until we are convinced that our old beliefs have no life in them. Then, if we continue to look to Him and believe in Him, as Martha and Mary did, He can perform the greater miracle of raising up our faith to new life and freeing it from the prejudices and habits of thought—the grave clothes—which had bound it in the sepulcher. Swedenborg tells us (AC 2916[4]) that the raising of Lazarus "involves the raising up of a new church from the Gentiles." The ancient Jewish Church era had to be consummated before the first Christian Church could be raised up. The first Christian dispensation had to consummated before the New Church could be raised up. Each new church has developed among those who realized the deadness of the old but still believed in the Lord and turned to Him with trust and obedience.

In connection with the story of Lazarus we are taught why the Lord often does not answer our petitions immediately. It is because He has higher things in store for us than the particular thing we want. He said to the disciples, "And I am glad for your sakes that I was not there, to the intent ye may believe." The disciples, as well as Martha and Mary, felt that the Lord could have kept Lazarus from dying, but the Lord wanted to show them that He had even greater power. We must all learn to "rest in the Lord, and wait patiently for him" (Psalm 37:7), and we must learn that there is no bitterness of loss or depth of despair in which He cannot teach us and save us if we will let Him.

Then we have the Lord's answer to those who believe that all are to remain in their graves until some final resurrection day. For He told Martha, "I am the resurrection, and the life: he that believeth in me, though he were dead, yet shall he live: And whosoever liveth and believeth in me shall never die." We know that this does not refer to the death of the body, for everyone must lay aside the material body before he can become really conscious of the life of heaven, but that it refers to spiritual death, the shutting out from the soul of the Lord's life, that life which alone can give eternal happiness. Those who live and believe in the Lord, whose hearts and minds are ordered according to His laws, are conscious of no interruption of that heavenly life when they lay aside the material body. For "this is life eternal, that they might know thee, the only true God, and Jesus Christ whom thou hast sent." (John 17:3)

Again, our story suggests the answer to the question, "If Jesus was God, why did He pray to the Father, and why did He appear to suffer?" Our story tells us that Jesus "groaned in the spirit, and was troubled," and that "Jesus wept," and in verse 41 we are told that he "lifted up his eyes, and said, Father, I thank thee that thou hast heard me." But He goes on immediately: "And I knew that thou hearest me always: but because of the people which stand by I said it, that they may believe that thou hast sent me." We know that the Lord, while He was in the world, was clothed with a finite humanity like ours. Bruce* suggests that such manifestations as His groaning and weeping were the natural reactions of the finite humanity to the working of the Divine within, just as our efforts to live according to what we know of divine love and truth produce struggle and grief in our lower, selfish natures. The Lord, while He was in the world, did humanly grieve over the waywardness and faithlessness and blindness of those He sought to save—this was one of His most severe temptations—and in this story we are allowed to see it outwardly manifested, because we need to understand and recognize that the Lord underwent such a temptation and overcame it, refusing to tamper with the free will which His wisdom had implanted in man. We sometimes feel this temptation to bring people to our way of thinking by force. The Lord shows us His struggle and then immediately the victory and its source by His thanksgiving to the Father.

From the Writings of Swedenborg

Arcana Coelestia, n. 2343: "That all regeneration or new life, thus salvation, is from the Lord alone, is indeed known in the church, but is believed by few, for the reason that men are not in the good of charity. It is as impossible for those who are not in the good of charity to have this belief, as it is for a camel to go through the eye of a needle; for the good of charity is the very ground for the seeds of faith. Truth and good agree, but truth and evil never: they are of a contrary nature, and are averse one to another. For this reason, so far as a man is in good, so far he can be in truth; or so far as he is in charity, so far he can be in faith; especially in this chief point of faith, that all salvation is from the Lord . . . But that they who are in evil, that is, in a life of evil, cannot possibly believe that all salvation is from the Lord, has been made evident to me from those who had come into the other life from the Christian world; and also from those who in the life of the body had confessed with the mouth, and had even taught, according to the doctrinal tenet of faith, that without the Lord there is no salvation, and yet had led a life of evil. These, when the Lord was merely named, forthwith filled the sphere with endless difficulties (for in the other life that which spirits merely think is perceived,

---

*Rev. William Bruce, *Commentary on the Gospel of John*, pp. 264-265. —Ed.

and diffuses from itself a sphere, in which it becomes manifest in what kind of faith they are)."

―――――

Suggested Questions on the Lesson

P. Who was Lazarus? *a friend of Jesus*

P. Who were his sisters? *Martha and Mary*

P. Where did they live? *Bethany*

J. When did the miracle of our chapter take place? *near the end of Jesus' life*

P. When Lazarus became sick, did the Lord go to Bethany at once? *no*

P. When He arrived, how long had Lazarus been in the grave? *four days*

P. What did Martha say when she met the Lord? *"If you had been here . . ."*

J. How did the Lord answer? *". . . will rise again."*

J. What was Martha's idea of the resurrection of the dead? *at the "last" day*

J. What did the Lord tell her? *I am the resurrection*

P. Can you tell about the raising of Lazarus? *took stone away, called loudly, Lazarus come forth*

J. What did the chief priests and Pharisees think about it? *plotted to kill Him*

I. Why did the Lord wait so long to go to Bethany? *to show His power over death*

S. Why did He first say Lazarus slept and afterward that he was dead? *death is a sort of sleep, with reawakening in the spiritual world*

PALM SUNDAY
John 12:12-50

The familiar Palm Sunday story is told very briefly in John. We should be sure all the classes are familiar with it and then go on to the rest of our chapter, which teaches more general spiritual lessons. All the teachers should read the Junior, Intermediate, and Senior notes for today, as a different portion of the chapter has been singled out for development in each, although the general lessons are the same.

Doctrinal Points

Using Christ as our example, we must conquer the temptation to think of ourselves first.

We should regard our bodies as mere tools, and our life in the world as our opportunity to form our souls into a heavenly pattern.

Evil has no real power over goodness.

Notes for Parents

As we enter upon the week which in the church is called Holy Week, and read the story of the Lord's triumphal entry into Jerusalem on the first Palm Sunday, two questions naturally arise in our minds: (1) How could that great crowd of people welcome the Lord on Sunday and crucify Him on Friday? and (2) Why did the Lord allow His enemies to crucify Him? The Lord Himself answers both these questions for us in this chapter from the Gospel of John.

The people who welcomed Him did so because they had heard of His miracles, especially of His raising Lazarus from the dead. They—like many people today—thought of death as the ultimate misfortune, because their minds were concerned only with their health and prosperity in this world. They had no thought of the promised Messiah except as one who would come as an earthly king to overthrow the power of Rome and make their nation great once more. Even the Lord's closest disciples, we are told, contended

among themselves which of them should be greatest, and when the
Lord was crucified, they all "forsook him and fled." Our chapter
tells us that even those leaders who believed the Lord's claim were
afraid to support Him lest they should be put out of the synagogue,
"For they loved the praise of men more than the praise of God."
This is the reason why the people so soon turned against the Lord,
and it is the reason for moral and spiritual cowardice in all times.

The answer to our second question grows out of this answer to
the first. The kingdom of heaven is made up of people who love
the Lord and the neighbor instead of just themselves. "He that
loveth his life shall lose it; and he that hateth his life in this world,
shall keep it unto life eternal." This was the lesson which the Lord
came to teach us. It is not what happens to our bodies that is
important, but what is going on in our souls. The Lord took on
from Mary a human nature like ours, in which He could feel all
our temptations. Even to the end of His life in the world He had
to fight this fundamental temptation to think of self first. We see
this in our chapter when He says: "Now is my soul troubled; and
what shall I say? Father, save me from this hour: but for this cause
came I unto this hour." He always conquered the temptation, and
in conquering set us an example and showed us how to conquer
it. He had to pass through death to show us that death is only a
necessary incident in our continuing life. He had to put off the
physical body so that the divine man within might be seen. He had
to let His enemies do their worst to teach us that evil has no real
or lasting power over goodness. As Psalm 118:6 puts it, "The Lord
is on my side; I will not fear: what can man do unto me?"

To be a Christian is to take the Lord Jesus Christ as our king, to
learn His teachings and obey them, to set Him up as our ideal and
hold His example steadily before us day by day. "And I, if I be
lifted up, will draw all men unto me." "If any man serve me, let
him follow me: and where I am, there shall also my servant be."

Primary

This is a good lesson in which to give the younger children an idea of the purpose of the Lord's life on earth, and the reason why some people loved Him and others hated Him. The contrast between His triumphal entry into Jerusalem and what He knew was to come can be shown. Draw as much as possible from the children themselves.

This week is a very special week in the church, for in it we are thinking of the last week of the Lord's life on earth. God Himself long ago came into the world as our Lord Jesus to show us how we ought to live. He let Himself be born as a little baby in Bethlehem and grow up just as we do and finally die as we all do and then rise again from death, as we all do. And we know that, if we try, by studying His life and trying to live as He taught us to live, we can become more and more the kind of people He wants us to be, and that He is always near us and ready to help us.

You know that the Lord had many enemies when He was in the world, because He always told the truth, and people who want their own way do not like anyone who tells them that their way is wrong. Are you ever like that? The scribes and Pharisees hated the Lord so much that they finally had Him put to death.

Because the Lord was God, He knew that this was going to happen. He came to Jerusalem on Sunday, at the beginning of His last week, knowing that on Friday He would be crucified. His disciples did not know it, and neither did the people who welcomed Him. Let us read the story of how He entered Jerusalem and of some of the things He told His disciples at that time. [Read John 12:12-24.]

The feast to which our chapter refers was the Passover.

How did the people receive the Lord?

Why do we call this Palm Sunday?

What kind of animal did the Lord ride into Jerusalem?

The Gospel of John says the crowd went to meet Him because they had heard that he had raised Lazarus from death.

What did the Lord say about a grain, or kernel, of wheat?

What He meant was that His death would teach us something we could not have learned without it.

On Easter Sunday we shall see what that something is.

Junior

We have centered the lesson for this age group on verse 24 as an explanation of the nature and purpose of the Lord's life on earth and the reason for His death, with a secondary application to our own lives. Be sure the class looks up and reads the prophecies of the Advent, as suggested in their notes, and as each one is read, point out that it is God Himself who is promised.

Since our lessons for this Sunday and next are about the last week of the Lord's life on earth, let us make sure that we know the general facts concerning that life up to this point.

Where was the Lord born?
What two groups of people were told of His birth?
Where was He taken to save Him from the wrath of Herod?
Where did He grow up?
Where did He go when He was twelve years old, and why?
How old was He when He began His ministry?
Who was sent to prepare the people to receive Him?
Where did He make His home during His ministry?
Who was the Lord Jesus Christ?
What does the first chapter of John say about Him?
What did He tell the woman of Samaria about Himself?
What kind of people believed in Him?
Why did the scribes and Pharisees hate Him?

We are all familiar with the Palm Sunday story, which is told in all four Gospels. We know that today we commemorate the Lord's entry into Jerusalem at the beginning of the last week of His earthly life.

What kind of animal did He ride?
How did the people receive Him?
What did they carry in their hands?
What did they shout?

Hosanna means "save now." All those people who greeted the Lord in this way on Palm Sunday were acknowledging with their minds and lips that Jesus was the promised Messiah or Christ come to be their king and savior. Look up and read some of the things their prophets had told them about Him: Isaiah 9:6, 25:9; Jeremiah 23:6; Micah 5:2; Malachi 3:1. If they accepted Him, they should have known that He was God Himself. But even these people who accepted Him were most of them really thinking of themselves. They wanted to be saved from their worldly troubles rather than from their sins. They were expecting a king who would overthrow the power of Rome and make them the leading nation in the world. We say we know better. But we are often very much like the people who hailed the Lord as their king on Palm Sunday and crucified Him before the week was over. We call ourselves Christians, but what we really expect the Lord to save us from is suffering in this world; and when suffering comes to us or disappointment of any kind, we sometimes blame the Lord and say, "What is the use of worshiping the Lord if He won't do for me what I want Him to do?" Whenever we do this it shows that we really want to rule God—not to let God rule us.

The Lord knew all that was in the hearts and minds of the people, and He knew—as He always knows—the future. He knew when He rode into Jerusalem in triumph on Palm Sunday that He would be crucified the next Friday. The Gospel of John gives us more of His teaching on this occasion than the other Gospels do. Read carefully verses 23 to 33.

Verse 24 gives us in one little parable the reason why the Lord allowed Himself to be crucified. The important part of a grain of wheat is the inner kernel, and the outer parts of the seed are of value only because they protect, nourish, and foster the living wheat germ within. They are necessary for these purposes until the germ has attained its full development. Then they have to be put off, as they are when the seed is planted in the ground. In any person the living kernel is the soul, and the physical body is only the outer husk. So we all have to pass through death and put off that outer husk. Our life in this world is the time when we are developing the special kind of kernel we want to be. While we are here, we are choosing whether we want to be good and useful plants or weeds and poisonous plants. The kernel cannot be changed after the husk is put off.

The Lord's soul was God Himself. While He was on earth, He

was making Himself a divine human nature by choosing always to do right in spite of all the temptations which came to Him from day to day. When this divine human was fully formed, He had to put off the outer husk by passing through physical death just as we do. As long as He was seen only in the physical body He had taken on through Mary, people could form only imperfect ideas of what was within. What was accomplished by His death is our lesson for Easter Sunday.

Intermediate

The correspondence of the Palm Sunday story and of the incident of the Greeks and Philip and Andrew introduces the general teaching of our need for putting the welfare of our souls above that of our bodies. Since this was the avowed example which the Lord set, it should be one of the distinguishing marks of every Christian.

The actual story of the Lord's entry into Jerusalem on Palm Sunday takes only four verses in the Gospel of John. It is told in much more detail in the other Gospels. However, we need to remind ourselves of the facts and of their meaning. At the beginning of the last week of His earthly life the Lord entered Jerusalem as its king, in fulfillment of the prophecy in Zechariah 9:9. He rode upon a young ass, or an ass's colt, the symbol of natural truth, to picture the fact that He had completely mastered the inclination of the assumed human nature to judge things by their outward appearance and to make decisions on the basis of results in this world.

The palm branches which the people carried correspond to "Divine truth in ultimates" or "Divine truth of the sense of the letter" of the Word. The Jews had the Scriptures. They knew from the literal prophecy that the Messiah was to enter Jerusalem in this way as king of Israel. So they hailed Him as king. But their idea of a king was a wholly worldly one. They took it for granted that the Messiah, when He came, would overthrow the power of Rome and restore their nation to first place in the world. It was because the Lord immediately showed by His words and acts that He had no such purpose that the very people who had hailed Him as king on

Palm Sunday shouted for His crucifixion on the next Friday. We should always remember that the Lord's concern is with our souls. If in the case of any particular individual He sees that constant health and prosperity are possible without "spoiling" him spiritually, then He is happy to permit these worldly blessings—and He also often permits them to such selfish people as He sees could not be benefited by adversity—but often people need adversities either to check them in wrongdoing or to stimulate the development in them of understanding and sympathy and spiritual strength. Then adversities come. If we take the attitude that the Lord ought to keep all His professed followers from any earthly suffering, we are like those who welcomed the Lord and then crucified Him.

John's account of Palm Sunday is concerned principally with the Lord's teaching on that day. Perhaps we think it strange that in the letter this teaching is prompted by the request of "certain Greeks" to see Jesus, a request which in the letter is apparently ignored by the Lord. The Greeks of that day were Gentiles and, like the Samaritans, picture those in good states who do not have the truth they need to guide them, and the Greeks characteristically were of a higher degree of intelligence than the Samaritans. Swedenborg does not give us the correspondence of Philip, but, though a Jew, he had a Greek name, a name which means "lover of horses," and horses picture our higher reasoning faculty. So Philip may be thought of as representing intelligence in a person of the church. That he was of an inquiring mind we may gather from the other incidents in the Gospel of John in which he figures (1:43-46; 6:5-7; 14:6-11). Andrew, we are told, represents obedience. These two qualities are necessary if we are to "see" the Lord. And the Lord's answer is really the answer the Gentiles were seeking. They were not looking for an earthly king, but for a teacher who would make clear to their minds the true way of life so that they might walk in it.

So Jesus said, "The hour is come, that the Son of man should be glorified." Then He showed them why He must pass through death. It was because men must be brought to see that it is not what happens to their bodies that is important, but what kind of soul they are developing within them. This is beautifully taught in verses 24 to 26 of our chapter, verses which we should all read and think about again and again. We should all begin as early in life as we can to think of our bodies as mere tools, and of our life in the world as our opportunity to form our souls into a heavenly pattern by resisting our selfish impulses and learning to serve the Lord and the neighbor.

We should notice also verses 42 and 43. How often we are afraid to stand up for what we know to be true and right! The Lord came into the world to be its light, to show us how to live so that we may be happy forever. He came to save us from ourselves. Some people think of the Lord as a stern judge, condemning those who do not accept Him. He tells us in this chapter, as well as in other places in the Word, that He does not judge and condemn. He seeks only to save. But we condemn ourselves by choosing to live for self and the world after He has shown us the better way.

Basic Correspondences

an ass's colt	=	natural truth
Philip	=	intelligence
Andrew	=	obedience

Senior

The two questions suggested in the first paragraph below form a good basis for the development of the lesson, since the young people will have to face these questions in their own minds and from the lips of others.

Today is Palm Sunday, the beginning of the week which the Christian Church calls "Holy Week" because it commemorates the last week of the Lord's earthly life. The week begins with His entry into Jerusalem as the "King of Israel" and ends in His resurrection, but in between lies the dark episode of His rejection, condemnation, and crucifixion. Our Palm Sunday lesson, therefore, should answer the questions which this contrast naturally raises in our minds: How could the people hail the Lord as king on Sunday and shout for His crucifixion the next Friday? and, Why did the Lord permit Himself to be put to death by His enemies?

In this chapter of the Gospel of John both these questions are answered for us by the Lord Himself. We should note first that the Lord rode into Jerusalem on a young ass to signify His complete subjugation of the natural reason, which judges according to the appearance in the world, and that the palm branches that the people carried signify divine truth as it is found in the sense of the letter of the Word.

Because of the Lord's reported miracles the people were prepared to believe that Jesus was the promised Messiah, and when they saw Him riding on an ass's colt, in fulfillment of the prophecy in Zechariah 9:9, they acclaimed Him. But their idea of the Messiah, based on their strictly literal understanding of Scripture, was of an earthly king who would exalt their nation once more to world power. As verse 40 tells us, "He hath blinded their eyes, and hardened their heart; that they should not see with their eyes, nor understand with their heart, and be converted, and I should heal them." Their question in verse 34 shows their lack of thought of any other life than that in this world. Even many who were disposed to listen to the Lord's teaching were afraid to support Him openly "lest they should be put out of the synagogue: For they loved the praise of men, more than the praise of God" (verses 42 and 43). We should keep this verse in mind, for we often lack the courage to stand up for what we know to be right. There is nothing praiseworthy about spiritual cowardice.

The two classes of people—those who did not want to believe and those who believed but were afraid to stand against the others—are described in verse 29 by those who, hearing the voice from heaven attest the divinity of the Lord, said, "it thundered," and those who said, "An angel spake to him." In the same way, our minds either refuse or welcome spiritual truth.

The reason the Lord permitted Himself to be put to death by His enemies is clearly stated in verses 23 to 28. His death on the cross was foreseen from the beginning and recognized as necessary to His purpose: "for this cause came I unto this hour." His enemies had to be allowed to do their worst that we might see that evil has no real power over goodness. Men had to be shown that the death of the body is only a necessary step in the endless life of the soul, and that the real power is in the soul. The Lord does not condemn the evil; they condemn themselves. If we reject the Lord's teaching, we reject God Himself; and if we reject God, we condemn ourselves to walk in darkness not only in this world but after death to eternity.

We may think of the Lord's riding into Jerusalem on a young ass as the symbolic embodiment of the teaching of the whole chapter. The Lord enters our lives as our king when we recognize that the soul is more important than the body and resolve steadily to obey the laws of the Lord at whatever cost in terms of comfort or pleasure or position in this world. To be a Christian means to be one who follows the teaching and example of Christ, and nothing in the teaching or example of the Lord gives us any excuse for worldliness or self-seeking. "If any man serve me, let him follow me; and where I am, there shall also my servant be." "And I, if I be lifted up, will draw all men unto me." We may think that the verse which follows this one is a mere literal statement: "This he said, signifying what death he should die." But *death* in this verse does not mean merely the death of the body. The death He died was the death of all the selfish promptings of the assumed humanity. This is also what is meant for us in verse 25.

Adult

What is involved in being a Christian is perhaps the chief topic which this chapter presents to the Adults—what is meant by receiving the Lord as king, and our individual responsibility in the decisions which follow.

The Lord's triumphal entry into Jerusalem is recorded in all four Gospels, some giving more detail than others. John links it closely with the miracle of the raising of Lazarus, saying that many people hailed the Lord as the Messiah because He had performed this miracle. When we realize the Lord's power to bring us back from spiritual death, we are prepared to welcome Him into the "holy city" of our minds as king and savior. He comes riding upon a young ass as a symbol of His subordination of natural reason, which the ass represents, and is greeted with joy. Palm branches picture divine truth in the sense of the letter of the Word, and the waving of the palm branches suggests the joy which comes from the realization that the Lord's truth does bring life and happiness (AC 8369; AR 367). *Hosanna* means "save now."

The people, even the disciples, were still thinking of the Lord as a temporal king, one who would save them from their enemies and lead them to victory. Our first recognition of the Lord's power is often of this character. We are thinking of our own welfare, our own salvation. The Lord's entry into Jerusalem was "the beginning of the end." Our first full acceptance of the Lord is followed immediately by temptations more severe than any we have known before. This is because we must be purified of natural thoughts and selfish motives. The first three Gospels emphasize the more external consequences of the entry into Jerusalem, the cleansing of the temple, which pictures the examination of our thoughts for selfish and worldly things which may be polluting them, the incident of the barren fig tree, which points to the necessity of bringing forth fruit, and the Lord's weeping over Jerusalem, the realization of the extent of our departure from the Lord, which comes to us as soon as we begin genuinely to try to bring ourselves under His rule. But John characteristically teaches us the depth of the change which must take place in us if we are really to follow the Lord.

First we have the reaction of the Pharisees (verse 19), the immediate stirring up of the Pharisee in us—our vanity and self-satisfaction—against this new, deep allegiance to the Lord. The good Gentiles always represent our good impulses which have no truth to guide them, and the Greeks perhaps especially intellectual need for the truth, for a rational understanding of the Lord. They appealed first to Philip, the Jew with the Greek name which means "lover of horses," thus representing the quality of intelligence, and sought introduction to the Lord through him, with the help of Andrew, who represents obedience. It requires both intelligence and obedience to bring us into a state in which the Lord can really teach us concerning Himself and the requirements of true discipleship. The Lord's discourse from verse 23 on is an answer to this desire to understand rationally the earthly life of the Lord.

There can be no simpler explanation of the Lord's whole life and purpose than the parable of the "grain of wheat." The living kernel in each of us is the soul. Until the soul is developed, it needs the external coverings of mind and body which envelop it in this world, but these are of value only as they minister to its proper growth. It cannot produce its final fruits until the material wrappings have been cast off, as they are by the death of the body. With the Lord the inner living kernel was the Divine Itself, the outer wrappings the finite humanity. This finite had to be put off completely before His divine humanity could exercise its full power. So the Lord had to pass through death. But death is only the last act in the putting off of the outer coverings. As we have seen before, the Lord throughout His life was putting off the finite through temptations, and replacing it with the Divine.

We can perform a similar work with His help. So far as we persistently subordinate worldly considerations to spiritual ones, by doing the Lord's will instead of our own, we become spiritual men and women instead of natural ones even while we are living in this world. The life which we are to hate is the selfish nature into which we are born. The life which we should seek to keep "unto life eternal" is the regenerate life which we receive from the Lord as we learn and do His will. In every situation which we face from day to day we feel the pull of both natures, the lower or worldly and the higher or heavenly; we are free to yield to either, but so far as we choose either we reject the other. That the Lord, to the very end, felt these two appeals just as we do is evidenced in our chapter, for He says: "Now is my soul troubled; and what shall I say? Father, save me from this hour; but for this cause came I unto this hour. Father, glorify thy name." The first alternative came from His finite nature, the second from His divine nature, and His soul was troubled because of the conflict. The fact that our choice is free and not enforced by any authority or fate is shown in the rest of the chapter, in which it is evident that some believed and others did not. Those who wished to follow the Lord found conviction in His miracles and in His teachings: they believed in the light. But those who did not wish to follow Him were blind to the truth, and were permitted to remain blind because if they had acknowledged His divinity and then had not followed Him, their sin would have been greater.

In verses 47 and 48 the Lord shows us plainly that the responsibility rests with us. He came into the world that all men who wished the truth might have it and be saved. The Lord condemns no one. His love and truth are free to all. "He maketh his sun to rise on the evil and on the good, and sendeth rain on the just and on the unjust." (Matthew 5:45) Those who choose to open their hearts to His love also see His truth when it is presented to them. "He that is of God heareth God's words." (John 8:47) Thus the truth, the Lord's Word, is our judge, for if we do not hear and obey it, it is only because we voluntarily choose self-love, which is the life of the hells. That is, our choice of the Lord or of self while we are in this world builds our souls into forms of heaven or hell, and when the outer covering of this world is laid off at death, the form which we ourselves have made determines our final home.

So the entry of the Lord into Jerusalem, our recognition of the Lord as the true king of our souls, ushers in the real conflict between heaven and the world in our hearts and minds, which is a conflict to the death, the death of heaven or the death of the world, as we choose.

―――――――

From the Writings of Swedenborg

Apocalypse Explained, n. 899[14]: "As men rise again after death, therefore the Lord willed to undergo death and to rise again the third day, but to the end that He might put off every thing human that He had from the mother and might put on the Divine Human; for every thing human that the Lord took from the mother He rejected from Himself by temptations, and finally by death; and by putting on a Human from the Divine Itself that was in Him He glorified Himself, that is, made His Human Divine; therefore in heaven His death and burial do not mean death and burial, but the purification of His Human, and glorification. That this is so the Lord taught by this comparison with wheat falling into the earth, which must die that it may bear fruit."

Suggested Questions on the Lesson

J. How long was the Lord's ministry? *about three years*

J. Why did He frequently go down to Jerusalem? *for the feast days*

P. Why did He go there at the beginning of the last week of His life on earth? *Passover*

P. What kind of animal did He ride into Jerusalem on that day? *an ass*

J. Why did most of the people welcome Him? *thought He would become king*

P. What did they carry in their hands? *palm branches*

P. What did they cry? *Hosanna*

J. What does *Hosanna* mean? *save now*

I. Why did the Lord ride on a young ass? *sign of royalty, to fulfill prophecy (Zechariah 9:9)*

J. Who were angry at His coming? *scribes and Pharisees*

J. What Gentiles were anxious to see Him? *Greeks*

J. Which apostles were asked to introduce them to Him? *Philip and Andrew*

J. How did the Lord explain the necessity of His death? *parable of grain of wheat*

J. What did He say we must do to save our spiritual lives? *lose our selfish life*

J. Why did He say the scribes and Pharisees could not see the truth? *didn't want to*

J. Why did some who did believe Him not support Him openly? *loved praises of men . . .*

I. What is it that judges us? *divine truth*

S. What is represented by the Lord's riding on a young ass? *His mastery of inclination to judge by worldly reasoning or outward appearance*

S. What is represented by the palm branches? *the divine truth of the letter of the Word*

THE PARABLE OF THE VINE
John 15

It will be helpful in all classes to link this lesson with the miracle at Cana. Even the youngest classes can be told that we bear fruit when we do good. And all classes should get the lesson that all life and all goodness are from the Lord alone.

––––––

Doctrinal Points
All life and all goodness are from the Lord alone.
Only as we follow the Lord's example can we hope to produce "good fruit."

––––––

Notes for Parents
The twelve chosen disciples of the Lord had been with Him throughout His ministry, traveling about the country with Him, seeing all His miracles, and listening while He taught the people. He had also given them much special instruction. Several times we are told how, after the multitude dispersed, He took His disciples aside and explained to them more fully the meaning of what He had been saying. A good example of this is found in the story of the parable of the sower in Matthew 13:1-23. During the last few days of His earthly life—between Palm Sunday and the crucifixion—the Lord gave the disciples more direct and deep instruction than He had ever given before, much of which we find recorded only in the Gospel of John.

Our lesson today was spoken by the Lord in the upper room in Jerusalem after they had partaken of the Last Supper and after Judas had gone out to make his final arrangements for the betrayal of his Master.

All through the Word the church on earth is described by the symbol of a vineyard. Read Isaiah 5:1-7, where under the figure of a vineyard the prophet tells what the church had done to the

139

divine truth entrusted to it. The "wild grapes," as we can easily see, were the false requirements which the scribes and Pharisees had substituted for the life of true charity commanded by the Scriptures.

Now, at the close of His life on earth, the Lord is charging His disciples not to repeat this sin as they go out to found a new church. He tells them that He is the true vine and that they cannot bear good fruit unless they are careful to remain true to His teachings. For, just as in the parable of the sower the seed represents the Word of God, so the Lord, who was the Word made flesh, is divine truth, the only source of our knowledge of the good or heavenly life. The grapes we are to bring forth are works of charity, but these must not be merely external benefactions, for such things may be done without any real thought of God in them. If we give ourselves credit for the good we do, it is not inwardly good at all. The Lord says to us, as He said to His disciples in that last solemn charge: "This is my commandment, That ye love one another, as I have loved you." To know just how the Lord loved us we must study His life and words, for only by trying to follow His example can we produce good fruit.

Primary

Talk about the vine and the grapes. The miracle at Cana may be recalled in some detail as a basis for showing that all life is from the Lord. This class can be given the idea of the difference between good done from self and good done from the Lord.

You have all eaten grapes. You know that they come in bunches and are very sweet and juicy and refreshing. Perhaps some of you have been in places where grapes are grown, and have seen the grape vines twining upon the trellises built to support them. We not only eat grapes, but their juice is used to make the wine which is served at the Lord's table in the Holy Communion, which you will share when you are old enough to be confirmed.

Wine was served at the Passover feast when the Lord was on earth, and at other feasts, too.

Do you remember how the Lord turned water into wine at the wedding feast at Cana?

There were no grapes in that story, were there?

The Lord did not need the grapes in order to produce wine.

From our lesson today can you tell why?

All the power to produce anything comes from the Lord.

Without Him we can do nothing, just as verse 5 of our chapter says.

The "fruit" the Lord wants us to produce is good deeds.

But goodness can come only from Him.

If we praise ourselves instead of the Lord for our good deeds, they are not really good at all.

They are like artificial fruit, which looks pretty but cannot be eaten.

When we think our goodness is our own, we are cutting ourselves off from the vine.

We must learn what the Lord wants us to do, and ask Him to help us do it.

Every time you say the Lord's Prayer remember that you are asking the Lord to help you to be His branches and to bring forth the good fruit which He expects of you.

Junior

The Juniors can understand a good deal of the correspondence of this lesson, and it offers a good opportunity to teach them the principle of correspondence and to familiarize them with the word "correspondence" as it is used in the New Church. The immediate practical lesson for them is suggested in the last paragraph of their notes.

Notice that in the Gospel of John there are five whole chapters between the account of the Lord's entry into Jerusalem on Palm Sunday and chapter 18, which tells of His betrayal by Judas on the Thursday night of that same week. This is because John gives us less about the external facts of the Lord's life on earth and more of His teachings, and some of the deepest of these teachings were given to His disciples during the last week of His life. Our lesson for today is an example of this deeper instruction.

When we had our lesson on the Lord's first miracle at Cana, you may have wondered how the Lord could turn water into wine without any grapes. Here we have a clear answer. "I am the true vine." This has a deeper meaning which you will study when you are a little older, but you can see something about it now. The Lord is the creator of everything in the natural world, and it is His life flowing in which gives everything the power to continue to exist and to bear fruit. We must always try to remember this, for to us, while we live in this world, material things seem to exist of themselves. When the Lord was living in the world in a finite body, He could exercise His power directly and immediately, and this is the explanation of His many miracles.

Because the Lord has created everything, each thing in nature is an outward expression of something in the Lord. As the teachings of the New Church say, each thing in nature "corresponds" to something spiritual and divine which is its cause. As you grow older, you will learn more and more about these correspondences; you already know some of them, such as the correspondence of fire to love and of light to truth. Most of you know the parable of the sower. If you do not remember it, you will find it in Matthew 18:3-9. And in verses 18-23 of that chapter the Lord explains the parable to His disciples, showing us that seed corresponds to truth from the Word and the fruit which is produced from the seed to the good which is developed in our lives, as we obey what we learn of the truth.

In the vegetable kingdom there are three fruits which are mentioned again and again in the Word: the olive, the grape, and the fig. These three correspond to good in the three planes of our life: our will, our thoughts, and our acts. Now read Isaiah 5:1-7. This means that the Lord gave the Word of the Old Testament so that people might know the truth and do good in the world by means of it. But instead, this "vineyard" brought forth "wild grapes." The scribes and Pharisees used the Scriptures to make themselves powerful instead of to help and guide those who wanted to know how to be good. They were branches that did not abide in the vine.

What does the Lord say happens to those who do *not* abide in Him?
How can we abide in Him?
What special commandment does the Lord give us in this chapter?

Read carefully verse 16. This shows us just what our lives are for. Sometimes people think they are better than others because they have joined the church and do things which their community recognizes as good. If they think in this way, they are not better— often they are worse—because they are taking credit to themselves for goodness instead of recognizing that all goodness is the Lord's. Did you ever try to bite into a piece of artificial fruit? No deeds of ours—however good they may appear to be—are really good unless the life of the Lord, life from the true vine, is in them. Try to learn never, even in your thoughts, to praise yourself for being good.

====

Intermediate

Use this lesson to lead the young people to a desire to serve as "branches" of the Lord in the world, and then stress the condition of such service and the importance of looking to the Word for guidance instead of to self or to one's associates.

Our lesson for today is part of the last instruction which the Lord gave to the apostles after they had partaken of the Passover feast on the night before His crucifixion. Judas had already gone out to arrange for his betrayal of the Lord. The eleven who remained were the ones who were to begin the work of founding the Christian Church.

In the Word the vine is mentioned many times. In its highest sense it represents the Lord as to divine truth. So He says, "I am the true vine." In our lives it represents charity, which is what Swedenborg calls "the good of truth." Charity, as we have learned before, is the heartfelt recognition that we of ourselves are neither good nor wise, that all goodness and wisdom are in the Lord, and that we can do good to our neighbor only as we try to learn from the Lord what is good and to obey His commandments. As we do this we serve as branches of the true vine and can produce genuine works of charity—represented by grapes.

From this you can see why there is so much in this chapter about abiding in the Lord and about obeying His commandments.

We should not, for instance, join the church and then think, "Now I am good; as long as I go to church sometimes and am kind to my neighbors and don't do anything most people consider wrong, I don't have to do any more studying or thinking about my religion." You would be surprised to find how many people do think just that way. But one may do all these things and not really be a Christian at all. He may very soon have fallen into the state of those we learned about in our Palm Sunday lesson who "loved the praise of men more than the praise of God" (John 12:43). He may be looking to other people instead of to the Lord for guidance. So he becomes a branch that is cast off and is withered.

A branch is an extension of the vine. The apostles were to carry out into the world the truth the Lord gave them. He was warning them never to substitute their own ideas for His truth. Read verse 16. This means that the Lord can be with us and make our efforts to do good successful only as we try to do His will and not our own. We must not think ourselves better than other people. The Lord wants each one of us to be an "apostle"—one sent out—one of His branches. He has put each one of us in a particular place and time in the world to do work for Him which no one else can do. If we faithfully keep on studying His Word and trying to understand it and to obey His commandments, His life and love can be in what we do and make it good fruit.

And He promises something to us, too. He says, "These things have I spoken unto you, that my joy might remain in you, and that your joy might be full." Are you ever really happy when you are doing something you know is wrong? You may think you are having fun, but down underneath, you are uncomfortable. When we are young, being good looks hard because we haven't tried being good long enough to find out how much happier it can make us than having our own way.

The Lord does not tell us that we shall have an easy time. He told His apostles that the world would hate them just as it had hated Him. We may often be made fun of by our associates when we stand up for our principles. But if we are doing what the Lord tells us to do, He can give us courage and a happiness that is deep down inside, so that what other people say will not disturb us.

The lesson of our chapter for us is that, whatever other people may think or do, we know that the Lord is the only one who can really tell us what we ought to think and how we ought to feel and behave, the only one who can keep us from spiritual harm, enable us to do the things which will really be for the good of our neighbor, and bring us into heavenly happiness here and in the world to come.

Basic Correspondences

the vine = the Lord as to divine truth

grapes = works of charity

Senior

The quotation from the writings found at the end of this lesson leads easily into a discussion of the cause of the fall of each of the four churches which preceded the New Church, and makes the teaching of our chapter a very solemn charge to our young people just starting out in the church.

The passage quoted at the end of this lesson occurs in the writings in connection with the explanation of Genesis 9:20: "And Noah . . . planted a vineyard." This is the first of a great number of passages in the Word in which the vineyard, the vine, and grapes figure. The Most Ancient Church, described by Adam and Eve and their descendants, was a "celestial" church; that is, in the beginning it was in love to the Lord, and the Lord could enlighten and direct its people by influx into their wills. But after the will of these people became selfish, the influx from the Lord was turned by their wills from truth into falsity, and the Most Ancient Church came to its end in a great flood of falsity and evil. Then the Lord separated the will and the understanding in men so that they no longer had to think just as they felt, and the Ancient Church, pictured by Noah, was raised up. This was a "spiritual" church, in which men first received the truth into their minds and then by obeying it could be given a new will. This is why it is said that

Noah planted a vineyard, for a vineyard represents the spiritual church, the vine being spiritual truth and the grapes spiritual good. But verse 21 of Genesis 9 tells us that Noah "drank of the wine, and was drunken," which means that the people of that church soon began to use the wonderful truth that was given them to exalt themselves, and we remember that this tendency ended in the tower of Babel and the dispersion and vastation of the Ancient Church.

This story about Noah has a very close connection with our chapter for today. At the end of the Ancient Church the Lord had given a new Word to the world through the Israelitish nation, who through it became not a true church but the correspondential representative of a true spiritual church. This church again is pictured as a vineyard. Read Isaiah 5:1-7. The traditions with which the scribes and Pharisees had overlaid the Scriptures were the "wild grapes" which that church had produced instead of its true fruit.

Now the Israelitish Church was at its end and the Lord was providing for the beginning of a new spiritual church in the world through His apostles. The teaching of our chapter was given to the eleven after they had partaken of the Last Supper on the eve of the crucifixion—Judas had already gone out to arrange for the betrayal of the Lord. And what the Lord was really saying to the eleven was: "Do not do as the earlier churches did; do not pervert the truth I have given you by imagining it is produced by your own minds and mixing it with your own ideas." Over and over again He said to them, "Abide in me." The vine in its highest sense represents "the Lord as to Divine truth." In the first chapter of John we learned that the Lord came into the world as the Word made flesh. And now in the same Gospel He says, "I am the true vine." Unless we study what the Lord Himself tells us and look to Him alone for guidance, there is no life in any of the apparent good we do; we cannot bear fruit.

The apostles were faithful to the Lord's charge, but we know that afterward the first Christian Church, like all that had preceded it, began to pervert and confuse the Lord's teachings—to separate itself from the vine. The Lord foresaw that this would happen and described it for us in the visions given to John at Patmos. As you go out into the world and attend other churches besides the New Church, you will find that some base their preaching and teaching for the most part upon what Paul and later men said rather than upon what the Lord Himself said. Their basic doctrines stem from the decisions made by men at the Council of Nicea in A.D. 325.

The Lord has had to come again to clear away these traditions and restore to us divine truth, enabling us to read the Word with understanding. You may know the motto of the New Church: "Nunc licet"—"now it is permitted" to enter intellectually into the mysteries of faith. [See TCR 508³.] But this does not mean that we may now twist divine truth this way and that to suit our convenience. The Lord says to us today, as He said to the eleven at the Last Supper: "If a man abide not in me, he is cast forth as a branch, and is withered." And He says to us also: "Ye have not chosen me, but I have chosen you, and ordained you, that ye should go and bring forth fruit, and that your fruit should remain. It is divine providence which has cast your lot in the New Church. The Lord has a work for you to do which no one else can do. But if you do not abide in Him, your fruit will not remain. And He says, "If ye keep my commandments, ye shall abide in my love."

Adult

In preparation for this lesson the teacher should read carefully the Senior as well as the Adult notes, as his particular class may be much interested in a discussion of the departure from the Lord's teaching and the turning to human intelligence instead which has caused the downfall of each succeeding church on earth, including the first Christian Church.

Recall the Lord's miracle at Cana, when He turned water into wine. There the wine, in contrast to the water, signified spiritual truth, truth about the Lord and our relation to Him, truth effective for our regeneration, the rebirth of which the Lord told Nicodemus. Now the Lord calls Himself the true vine, the source of all spiritual truth, apart from which we can do no genuine good.

In discussing the meaning of the vineyard and the vine Swedenborg tells us that we cannot understand it unless we know that
there is a celestial church and a spiritual church, the one made up
of those who receive the Lord primarily in their wills, and the
other of those who receive Him primarily in their understandings;
the olive yard is the symbol of the one, the vineyard of the other.
The Most Ancient Church was of the celestial type and the Ancient
Church of the spiritual. That is why it is said that Noah, the symbolic founder of the Ancient Church, "planted a vineyard" (Genesis 9:20). We remember also that *Israel*, the name given to Jacob
after he returned to the Holy Land from Haran, is used in the
Word to signify the spiritual church, of which the Jewish Church
was representative. So throughout the Old Testament the vineyard
and the vine are mentioned in connection with the name *Israel*
(Jeremiah 2:14, 21; Hosea 10:1). The Lord came as the truth,
"a light to lighten the Gentiles, and the glory of thy people Israel"
(Luke 2:32). He came to restore to the world knowledge of spiritual truth, because Israel had become indeed an "empty vine."
The perversion of the truth which had been entrusted to them
is described in Isaiah 5:1-7 under the symbolism of a carefully
prepared and planted vineyard which brought forth wild grapes
instead of its intended fruit, and the character of those who were
responsible for this perversion is pictured in verses 20 to 23 of
the same chapter. In Psalm 80 the figure of a vineyard is again
used to describe the state of the good and innocent and their need
of a savior.

So the Word made flesh, divine truth clothed in a form adapted
to the comprehension of men, is indeed the true vine. The New
Testament treats of the spiritual church in the beautiful parables
of the vineyard (Matthew 20:1-16, 21:33-45; Mark 12:1-12; Luke
20:9-16), as well as in Revelation 14:17-20, where judgment is
described as the harvesting of the fruit of the vine. The vineyard,
the vine, the grapes, the wine are so frequently mentioned throughout the Word that there are many references to them in the writings
(see particularly AC 1069, 5113, and 9139). In our lesson the Lord

speaks of Himself as the vine and of the Father as the husbandman. It is "the Father," divine love, which plants, sustains, and tends the vineyard, but "the Son," divine truth, is the vine by whose means the grapes and wine are produced. If we are to produce any good fruit we must be branches of this vine, we must draw spiritual truth from the life and teaching of the Lord, our minds must be formed according to the truth which He gives us—not according to any ideas of our own or of other men.

But there is more to abiding in the vine than merely to know the Lord's teachings. In verse 10 the Lord tells us what it is to abide in Him: "If ye keep my commandments, ye shall abide in my love." Swedenborg explains the "mechanics" of this statement in TCR 70, as follows: "From the Divine omnipresence man is in God to the extent that he lives in accordance with order, for the reason that God is omnipresent; and where God is in His Divine order, there He is in Himself, because He is order, as has been shown above. Since, then, man was created a form of Divine order, God is in him—fully in him to the extent that he is living in accordance with Divine order. Nevertheless, God is in him if he is not living in accordance with Divine order, but only in the highest regions in him, thereby giving him the ability to understand what is true and to will what is good; that is, giving him the faculty of understanding and the inclination to love. But so far as man lives contrary to order he shuts up the lower regions of his mind or spirit, and thus prevents God's descending and filling those lower regions with His presence; consequently, while God is in him, he is not in God." So the Lord says, "He that abideth in me, and I in him, the same bringeth forth much fruit." No matter how much we may know of the Lord's teachings, if we do not live according to them, we are spiritually barren branches, our souls wither, and our evils cut us off from the Lord and consume us. "If a man abide not in me, he is cast forth as a branch, and is withered; and men gather them, and cast them into the fire, and they are burned." It is only when we act according to the truth which we receive from the Lord that we bring forth spiritual fruit. And this bearing of fruit is the whole purpose of our life in this world: "Ye have not chosen me, but I have chosen you, and ordained you, that ye should go and bring forth fruit, and that your fruit should remain."

However, as we have noticed in other lessons, the Lord does not permit us to imagine that a mere external keeping of the law is sufficient. He says, "This is my commandment, That ye love one another, as I have loved you." "Greater love hath no man than this, that a man lay down his life for his friends." The Lord literally laid down His life for us at the crucifixion, but this was only the symbol of the work which He had been doing all along, laying down every selfish impulse and thought day by day: "Every branch in me that beareth not fruit he [the Father, divine love] taketh away; and every branch that beareth fruit, he purgeth it, that it may bring forth more fruit." When He tells us to love one another as He loved us, He is telling us to lay down our life, our selfish desires and ambitions, day by day. So we become His friends by understanding His loving ways, instead of servants who merely obey from fear or from a sense of duty. It is by obeying His commandments inwardly as well as outwardly that we can overcome the world, even as He overcame it. He does not tell us that our way will be easy, but that the victory is sure. "In the world ye shall have tribulation: but be of good cheer; I have overcome the world."

The lesson should be emphasized that nothing is genuinely good which does not include recognition of the Lord and obedience to Him within it. We are to abide in the vine. It is the Lord's truth we are to seek, the Lord's commandments we are to follow, not the standards of the world or our own ideas of what is right. We hear people praising themselves for their kindness to others; we all do it inwardly at least part of the time; and when we do, we may be sure that our kindness is to some extent inwardly selfish and not done from the Lord. Even charity done in the name of the church is not free from this taint. The Lord says: "Many will say to me in that day, Lord, Lord, have we not prophesied in thy name? and in thy name have we not cast out devils? and in thy name done many wonderful works? And then will I profess unto them, I never knew you: depart from me, ye that work iniquity." How can one who goes to church, keeps the laws, is honest and industrious, and kind and generous to his neighbors "work iniquity"? He may be doing all these things for the sake of self, for his reputation and his self-satisfaction. Good works must be inwardly good. In DP 215 Swedenborg compares good works done for worldly ends with the same works done from love to the Lord and the neighbor: "One is like artificial fruit, which in external form appears like fruit from a tree, although it is colored wax containing within it dust or bitumen; while the other is like excellent fruit, pleasing in taste and smell, and containing seeds within."

From the Writings of Swedenborg

Arcana Coelestia, n. 1069[5]: "Since the 'vine' signifies the spiritual church, and the primary thing of the spiritual church is charity, in which the Lord is present, and by means of which He conjoins Himself with man, and Himself alone works every good, therefore the Lord compares Himself to a vine, and describes the man of the church, or the spiritual church, in these words in John . . . (15:1-5, 12); from these words it is evident what the spiritual church is."

Suggested Questions on the Lesson

J. When did the Lord give His disciples the teaching of our lesson for today? *the night before the crucifixion*

P. What does He call Himself in this chapter? *the vine*

P. What does He call His disciples? *branches*

P. What does He say they must do in order to bring forth fruit? *abide in Him*

P. What happens to those who do not abide in the Lord? *cast out*

J. How do men abide in the Lord? *obey Him*

J. Why does the Lord say He tells us these things? *so we may share His joy*

P. What does He say in His commandment? *love one another*

J. Does He promise His disciples an easy life in this world? *no*

J. What does He promise them? *to be hated and persecuted by the world*

I. What does the vine represent? *divine truth*

S. What do the grapes represent? *spiritual goodness*

THE RESURRECTION
John 20

The distinctive incidents in the Easter story in the Gospel of John are Mary's recognition of the risen Lord and Thomas' doubt and its resolution. But the teachers should be sure that all the classes have a knowledge of the general Easter story, as well as of its background in the states of the disciples.

———

Doctrinal Points

When we die we go on living in a spiritual body.
The Lord glorified His humanity, uniting it with the divinity which had begotten it.
Our idea of God is the most important idea we have.

———

Notes for Parents

On the first Easter Sunday the Lord rose from the sepulcher in which His body had been placed after the crucifixion and showed Himself to several of His followers, and during the next forty days, He appeared to the same people many times and to others also. We need have no doubt of the facts here—all history was changed by them. The Lord's resurrection not only restored the faith of His disciples but gave them courage to go out through the world and found Christian churches in many places.

For us as individuals the Easter lesson means the certainty that our life continues after the death of the body. But it means a great deal more than that. When Mary Magdalene recognized the Lord as He spoke her name, He said to her: "Touch me not; for I am not yet ascended to my Father." Mary was not to think of the Lord as merely the friend and master she had known and loved in the world. He had to rise in her thoughts and be recognized as the heavenly Father Himself. Jesus had once said to Philip, when Philip had asked Him to show them the Father: "Have I been so long time with you, and yet hast thou not known me, Philip? he that hath seen me hath seen the Father." We must learn to think of Jesus not as a man who lived in this world many centuries ago, but as the one God of heaven and earth, who loved us so much that He was willing to take on a human nature like ours in order to show us how to meet and overcome our temptations, and who then put it off to show us that He really is our heavenly Father and that He is not far away but present with us in all our struggles and disappointments, even though we do not see Him with our physical eyes.

Mary and the disciples did not see the risen Lord with their physical eyes. He opened their spiritual sight, as He could open ours if He found it needful for us. The body in which He rose was His divine body, with which He had been gradually replacing the finite physical body He had put on through Mary. He appeared to the disciples without coming through doors. He appeared to each one as that one was prepared to recognize Him. This teaches us a very important lesson. We see the Lord only as we prepare our minds to see Him by learning all we can about Him and obeying His teaching. If we are faithful, He will rise in our minds and will become to us "the way, the truth, and the life."

Primary

Get as much of the background from the children as possible. Use the attitude of the disciples to show how foolish it is to think that spiritual things are not real.

When the Lord rode into Jerusalem on Palm Sunday, He knew that the very people who were welcoming Him as their king would turn against Him in just a few days and shout, "Crucify him!" just as loudly as they had shouted "Hosanna!" The disciples did not know this. He had told them what was to happen, but they had not believed it or even remembered it.

When on the very next Thursday night the Lord was seized by His enemies, even His closest followers who loved Him "forsook

Him and fled." They were not quite brave enough then to risk their own lives for Him. They still thought of life in this world as the most precious thing and of death as the end of everything. So when on Friday He was put to death, they thought all their hopes had come to nothing and that they would never see Him again.

But some of the women who had loved the Lord thought of one last thing they could do for Him.

It was their custom to use certain spices in preparing bodies for burial.

So on Sunday morning the women took these spices to the tomb where the Lord's body had been laid.

The first one to reach the tomb was Mary Magdalene.

What did she find?

What did Peter and another disciple do when she told them?

After they had gone home, what did Mary see in the tomb?

Who then came and spoke to her?

How did the Lord appear to the disciples that same day?

Thomas was not with them, and he would not believe.

How did the Lord convince him?

The disciples knew then that death was not the end of life.

Do you wonder that after this none of the disciples was ever afraid of death again? And we need never be afraid of it either.

—————

Junior

Do more in this class with the events of Holy Week before you go on to the lesson proper. At this age especially children need to be impressed with the facts of the Lord's life and with the assurance of His continued presence in the world.

What kind of animal did the Lord ride to enter Jerusalem the last Sunday of His earthly life?

How did the people receive Him?

What did they carry in their hands?

What did they shout?

What did they think the Messiah would do?

What did the Lord know would happen?

What parable did He tell to explain why He had to die?

You would think, wouldn't you, that the Lord's disciples would have understood Him? But the ideas of life and death which were

in their minds were very much like those of the rest of the people.
When we are born, we do not have any knowledge of the Lord or
of heaven, and unless we are taught these things when we are children, we grow up thinking that this life is all there is and that
death is the end of everything for us. And after we are grown up,
it is very hard for us to change our habits of thought. Even if we
come to see that there must be a God and a future life, it is hard
for us to think of either as real, because the things of this earth
seem to us the only real things. So, although the Lord had told His
disciples that He would be put to death and would rise again on
the third day, it seemed so impossible to them that they scarcely
even remembered it.

You may remember that the Lord spent the first two days of
His last week teaching in the temple, and at night went out to
Bethany and lodged at the home of Mary and Martha and their
brother Lazarus, whom He had raised from the dead. By Tuesday
night the opposition to Him in Jerusalem had become so great that
He remained at Bethany and did not enter Jerusalem again until
He came for the Passover feast on Thursday evening. At that feast
He instituted the Holy Supper, and after it He went outside the
city to the Garden of Gethsemane to pray. There Judas betrayed
Him into the hands of the officers whom the chief priests had sent
to arrest Him.

When He was arrested, all His disciples forsook Him and fled,
and on Friday, after He was crucified, they were completely discouraged. Their hopes had centered in Him, and when He did not
save Himself from death at the hands of His enemies, they felt that
they must have been mistaken in their belief in Him. They were
very unhappy about it, but they had no hope. As the two disciples
on the way to Emmaus said (Luke 24:20), "We trusted that it had
been he which should have redeemed Israel." You see even the disciples had been thinking of the Lord as an earthly king.

But the women who had followed the Lord had loved Him for
Himself. They had not been so concerned with earthly greatness.
They, too, did not expect to see Him again, but they thought of

Him instead of themselves and wanted to do the last thing they could for Him, which was to prepare His body properly for burial according to their customs. That was why they came to the tomb with their spices early on Sunday morning. They could not come before, because it was not considered lawful to do such things on the sabbath.

The first one to reach the tomb on that first Easter morning was a woman out of whom the Lord had cast seven devils (Mark 16:9, Luke 8:2).

Who was this woman?
What did she find?
Whom did she tell?
What did Peter find in the tomb?
What did Mary afterward see in the tomb?
Who came and spoke to her?
Whom did she at first think He was?
When did she recognize Him?
What did He tell her?
When did he appear to all the disciples?
Which one was not present?
Why would he not believe the others?
How did the Lord convince him?
What did the Lord tell Thomas, which also applies to us?

We should notice that although there was nothing of the Lord's physical body left in the tomb, and although He appeared to Thomas with the nail holes in His hands and the wound in His side, still Mary at first did not recognize Him, and He appeared suddenly among the disciples in spite of the fact that the doors were closed. We know that death is no more the end of us than it was the end of the Lord. We go right on living in the spiritual world in our spiritual bodies—just as much ourselves as ever. But there is a difference between the Lord and us. We leave our physical bodies behind us when we die, and we no longer have any conscious contact with this world except when the Lord permits us to feel our nearness to the people we love here or to others whom we can help. The Lord also put off the physical body He had taken on from Mary, but He replaced it with a divine body. So He is present in this world everywhere and sees and knows all that goes on here. We do not see Him unless He wishes us to, and when He does appear to anyone, He takes on the form in which the particular person can recognize Him.

These two special lessons we learn from Easter: death is only a step in life, and the Lord is always here with us.

Intermediate

There are a number of correspondences here around which to build the lesson for this class. The principal thought to stress is the necessity of rising above earthly ideas. Carry this out in its application to our thoughts of death, if the young people are at all uncertain about this.

At the end of the nineteenth chapter of John we are told that after the crucifixion two members of the high court of the Jews, Joseph of Arimathea and Nicodemus (see Luke 23:50 and John 3:1), with the consent of Pilate, the Roman governor, took the body of Jesus and wrapped it in linen cloths with spices [cf. Mark 16:1, Luke 24:1], according to their burial custom, and laid it in a new tomb. Matthew 27:60 tells us that the tomb belonged to Joseph of Arimathea and that after the burial he rolled a great stone in front of the door. We learn still more about this stone from Matthew 27:62-66.

In our Palm Sunday lesson we learned something of the reason why the Lord had to pass through death. In the Word, burial and a tomb, in the case of a good person, represent resurrection and regeneration. We can understand this most easily if we try to put ourselves in the place of the angels who welcome people into the spiritual world, who see the person awaking there just about the time when his grave in this world is being closed. The ideas which we in this world have about the person who has left us are pictured by the linen cloths in which Joseph and Nicodemus wrapped the body of Jesus before they laid it in the tomb. The spices represent truth also, but more interior truth which comes from goodness in the heart. Both Joseph and Nicodemus believed in the Lord and were trying to do right, although their thought of Him was entirely of His earthly life, which now seemed at an end.

In all four Gospels we learn that it was the women who first discovered that the stone had been rolled away from the entrance to the tomb and that the Lord's body was no longer there. Women represent affections. A stone, in a good sense, represents truth in its basic or lowest form. In this case it represents the truth which had been wrongly used by the Lord's enemies to make sure that He would "stay buried." They had falsified the letter of Scripture by making it mean what they wanted it to mean. In Matthew 28:2 we are told that there was a great earthquake and that the angel of the Lord rolled back the stone from the door. All the thinking of the world was upset eventually by the resurrection of the Lord. The women first discovered it because it is love in the heart which makes it possible for the Lord to show anyone the real truth. The women then told the men—just as our affections, if they are good, enable our minds to see.

When we die, we go on living in a spiritual body. The body we lived in here in the material world we leave behind us, but it lasts— at least in part—a good many years after we have left it, although it no longer has any life. We rise from death only in the spiritual world. But the Lord continued to be in contact with this world. He was seen and recognized by the women, by the disciples, and later by many others. And there was no material body left in the tomb. Yet Mary at first did not recognize Him; He appeared to the disciples suddenly although the doors were closed; and we remember from one of our lessons from Luke that the two disciples who walked with Him to Emmaus did not recognize Him until they began to eat with Him. All through His life in the world the Lord had been putting forth from the Divine within Himself a human nature to replace the finite nature which He took on from Mary. As He overcame each temptation, He put off that bit of the finite and replaced it with the Divine. Someone long ago compared this process with drawing out one thread at a time in a piece of cloth and in its place weaving in a thread of gold, until finally the whole piece would be gold instead of cloth. So when the Lord rose, there was nothing left of the human He had assumed—even of the material body—but He had a divine humanity in its place in which He could always be present in the natural world. His last words in the Gospel of Matthew are: "Lo, I am with you always, to the close of the age." The Lord, unlike spirits and angels, sees and knows everything that goes on in this world because He is present in it in His divine humanity.

The only things that were left in the tomb were the linen cloths and the napkin, which had been about His head. The linen cloths represent the truths about the Lord which we find in the literal sense of the Word, and the napkin the memory of His external life on earth as it is recorded in the Gospels. These are what are left to us to pick up and examine as evidence of the truth. Read verse 31.

We should all study and remember the little incident about Thomas in verses 24 to 29 of our chapter. The kind of person today who likes to say, "Well, you'll have to show me" is sometimes called a "doubting Thomas." The Lord did "show" Thomas by appearing to him just as Thomas wanted to see Him, but He did not praise Thomas for his very earthly idea. The Lord "appears" to every good person just as the person has learned to think of Him, but He does not want us to confine our thoughts of Him to material ideas. This is what is meant by His words to Mary in verse 17 as well as by His final words to Thomas in verse 29. As we learn more and more of the Lord from the Word, our idea of Him should rise higher and higher, lifting us above the level of earthly thoughts and ambitions.

Basic Correspondences

women	=	affections
burial	=	resurrection and, in the case of a good person, regeneration
linen	=	truth of the natural man
spices	=	interior natural truth from good

a napkin = the memory of the natural man

─────────────

Senior

The Senior notes have been devoted principally to the question of the importance of having a true idea of God. This lesson is the one to stress, but the teacher may feel that his particular class will be helped also by some of the other points which he will find in the notes for the other classes.

We usually think of the Easter lesson as given to teach us that our life goes on uninterrupted after death and that we should therefore think of death, whenever and however it occurs, not as a tragedy but as merely the beginning of a new and fuller life for the person who has died. This is true, and it is the most obvious lesson to be drawn from the story of the Lord's resurrection. But there are also deeper and more far-reaching lessons in this story.

When the Lord was on earth, even the good people had no thought about goodness except in terms of this world. Even the apostles, who had lived with the Lord for three years and listened to His teaching, still thought of His kingdom as an earthly kingdom and felt, when He was put to death, that all their hopes were over. We see this same belief in our lesson today in the experience of Mary Magdalene. She was a woman out of whom the Lord had cast seven devils. She believed in Him and loved Him. She was not, as the disciples were, concerned about her own future now that He was gone, but the only service she could think of which she could still render Him was the proper care of His body. She was a simple woman. But there was no higher idea than this in the minds of those of the Lord's followers who had education and worldly position, as we see from the deed of the two counselors, Joseph of Arimathea and Nicodemus, in verses 38 to 42 of the preceding chapter. The linen cloths in which they wrapped the Lord's body represent their natural ideas of Him, and the spices the quality added to these same ideas by the goodness in their hearts. Spices represent "interior natural truth from good." Truth which we love to learn affects us more deeply than truth we learn because we have to. The people of those days knew the truths of the letter of the Word, but only a few of them loved them. The stone which sealed the tomb was the truth of the letter of the Word falsified by the interpretation of it by the religious leaders.

The Lord's resurrection was first discovered by the women, who represent affections, and they made it known to the men. Unless our hearts are loving, we can never be given any spiritual insight. Mary Magdalene was the first actually to see the Lord after His resurrection, although she did not immediately recognize Him. She knew Him when He pronounced her name. In the Word a name represents the whole quality of a person. Only the Lord knows the quality of each one of us. Then the Lord said to Mary: "Touch me not; for I am not yet ascended to my Father: but go to my brethren, and say unto them, I ascend unto my Father, and to your Father; and to my God, and your God." Here again the Lord was pointing out to His followers by means of one who truly loved Him that their thoughts of Him must be lifted above the level of the worldly ideas they had had, until they could identify Him with God rather than with man.

All our thinking as we go through life really depends upon our idea of God. If, as many do, we think of God as merely the sum total of the forces of the natural world, then all our ideals and aspirations will be for worldly success, and even if we mean to be good and useful people, helping people physically will be the best we can do. If, as the people of the Gospel did and as some sects do today, we think of God as a stern ruler and judge who wants our worship and sacrifices and takes revenge upon us and punishes us if we do not give them, then in our dealings with fellow men we shall think these same things justifiable. If we think of God as merely the first cause, someone or something which created the first material cell and left it to develop according to certain laws, we shall think that every man must determine for himself what he should believe and do and that one man's idea is as valid as another's—that there is no such thing as fixed truth. We are in this same position if we think that there is a God active in the universe but that we can know nothing about Him.

Then among Christians there is the problem of what to believe about Christ. Many Christians—people who accept Christ as their example—still think of Him only as the best man who ever lived. This leaves them free to take what they like of His teaching and say of what they don't like, "He was of course limited by His nation and His times; if He were living here and now, He would speak differently." But Christ was the Word made flesh, God Himself come into the world to live out the truth and to give us an ideal of which we might be sure, to show us that this life of ours in the world is only the beginning of our life and is important only as we use it to give our souls the truest form we can. So our thoughts of Christ must rise above the thought of Him as a man who lived a long time ago, and must be lifted up until we think of Him as God, our heavenly Father Himself. As He had told His disciples (John 16:28): "I came forth from the Father, and am come into the world: again, I leave the world, and go to the Father." He always adapts Himself to our ability to see Him, just as He did with Thomas in our chapter, but if we study the Word and try to increase our capacity to see and understand, he rises in our minds.

And in this new age in which we live He has come again in the opening of the inner meaning of the Word, giving us the means to a rational understanding of His teachings, so that our questions may be answered. If we make use of this means, our vision of the Lord will become clearer and more wonderful all the time, the things of self and of this world will fall into their proper places, and we shall come to live—even while we are still in this world—in the light of heaven.

Adult

The Adults will doubtless be familiar with the usual lessons drawn from the resurrection story. These should of course be touched upon, and the summary of the post-resurrection appearances of the Lord should be mentioned. A good discussion topic is found in the last two verses of the chapter. Even New Church people are sometimes fascinated and confused by stories and moving pictures which add imagined detail to the Bible story. Another good discussion topic is the effect of false ideas of the Lord as compared with that of a true idea. Suggestions on this topic will be found in the Senior notes.

In our study of the Easter lesson from the Gospel of Luke, we considered especially the effect of the resurrection upon the apostles, and through them upon the world. This should be recalled, because we all need to feel the force of the external evidence of the access of divine power which came into the world with the resurrection. But the Gospel of John characteristically suggests rather the deep personal application of the story of the resurrection to the regenerating individual.

Many Christians cling to the finite humanity of the Lord, trying to picture Him as He was in the world, stimulating their imaginations with the study of the racial and historical and geographical background of His finite humanity, believing that in this way they are drawing closer to Him and understanding Him better. This effort is unconsciously epitomized in the phrase "Back to Jesus," as if the real Jesus were somewhere in the past. They feel that the historic Christ is the whole Christ. The apostles were in this belief. In spite of all that the Lord had told them, they felt that they had lost Him when His material body was laid in the tomb. In the resurrection He taught them that they were wrong, and He wishes us to see that we are wrong when we confine Him in our thoughts to the humanity which He put off.

Early in the morning, while it was yet dark, Mary Magdalene came to the tomb and discovered that the stone had been removed from the entrance. Morning always pictures the dawn of a new state, but the ignorance still in her mind is represented by the fact that it was yet dark. Mary, out of whom seven devils had been cast (Luke 8:2), represents the heart which has been deeply purified through temptations. It is a deep and loving desire for the Lord which first discovers that He cannot be confined to the sepulcher, the mere letter of the Word; but it is the faculties of the mind— pictured by Peter and John (who was almost certainly the other disciple in our chapter)—which explore the sepulcher. They saw the linen cloths which were left in the sepulcher, the truths concerning the Lord in the letter, but it was Mary again, the loving heart, who perceived the angels, the living truths within the letter. Also it was Mary who first saw the Lord Himself after His resurrection. It is the loving heart which can first be given to feel the reality of the ever-present savior, even though it does not at first recognize Him. The Lord must rise in our hearts and minds. We begin our discipleship by studying His life in the world and trying to follow His example, but if we are faithful, the time will come when we shall no longer think of Him as someone who lived nearly twenty centuries ago, but as someone who is present in the world today, walking with us and speaking to us in the Word.

The Lord rose differently from any finite man. We leave something behind us when we die; we rise as spirits with full consciousness in the spiritual world, but we have left behind us the instruments by which we saw and heard in this world. The Lord glorified even His sensuous, replacing the material substance with divine substance,* so that He left nothing in the tomb, but rose a complete man even to ultimates. "For a spirit hath not flesh and bones, as ye see me have." (Luke 24:39) (AC 10252[7], 6135; HH 316) Through the divine humanity He sees and hears in this world, and could even eat with His disciples and be handled by them. His humanity, being divine, is infinite; so He is present with all men at all times instead of being confined in a finite body which is subject to the limitations of space and time. But His presence is not imaginary; it is the most real fact there is: "Lo, I am with you always, to the close of the age."

The Gospels record several appearances of the Lord after the resurrection. The first was to Mary Magdalene, and Matthew records that He was also seen by the other women at the tomb. That same afternoon He appeared to the two on the way to Emmaus, as recorded in Luke and mentioned in Mark. An appearance to

---

*Cf., however, *Ath. Creed*, nn. 161-162 (London, 1954 ed.) or AE, Vol. 6, p. 519 (New York, Standard Edition, 1949). —*Ed.*

Peter is also mentioned in Luke (24:34). Mark, Luke, and John all record the appearance to the apostles as they sat at meat on the evening of the first day, and John tells us that although Thomas was not present on that occasion, the Lord appeared to them eight days later when Thomas was present. Matthew tells of an appearance in Galilee upon a mountain where the Lord had told them to meet Him, and John gives the story of the meeting by the sea of Tiberias (or Galilee) (John 21). In Acts 1:3 we learn that the Lord was seen over a period of forty days after the resurrection, and Paul says (I Corinthians 15:6-7) that He appeared to five hundred brethren, and also to James. Evidently the Lord provided that there should be ample evidence of His living presence in the world after the crucifixion, and that the testimony of many should be recorded. But He told Thomas, "Blessed are they that have not seen, and yet have believed." There is a higher sight than that of the eye, and a deeper hearing than that of the ear. If our minds accept the Lord's truth and our hearts receive His life, we have a far deeper conviction of His presence than if we were to see Him with the physical eye. Most of those who saw Him in the flesh rejected Him. Many things which we see and hear in the world make little impression on us because we are not interested in them. Those who do not wish to recognize and obey the Lord simply refuse to believe the testimony of those who saw Him after the resurrection. If they had a vision of Him themselves, they would soon explain it away. Belief is of the will. We are free to choose the Lord or self.

John tells us (20:30-31) that the testimony which he has just recorded is not the only evidence of the Lord's deity, but that He did many other signs, and in the last verse of his Gospel (21:25) he says that if all the acts of the Lord were written, the world itself would not contain the books.

The Lord's earthly life was one of constant active service. We are told that He went about all Galilee teaching and preaching in the synagogues and healing the sick. Only a very few of His words and deeds are recorded, but these few are so chosen through divine providence that, in the letter, they illustrate all phases of His work, and in the spirit they contain the fullness of divine life. We should be willing to accept the wisdom of divine providence in this selection. In the early part of our lesson we spoke of the tendency to cling to the finite humanity of the Lord as the whole Christ. It is this tendency which causes many to waste time and effort—however sincere and reverent the intention—in trying to reconstruct by means of imagination plus historical studies, portions of the Lord's life which are not recorded in the letter; for example, to picture the Lord as a boy among other boys in Nazareth or as a young man working in Joseph's carpenter shop. Had there been any spiritual value in such thoughts of the Lord, the facts would have been recorded in the Word. Let us rather learn the facts which the Lord Himself considered it necessary for us to know about His earthly life, and not confuse His own picture of Himself with human imaginings, which tend to tie Him down in our minds to the plane of finite humanity. Then the Lord will gradually rise in our minds until we come to see Him as our living, present savior, God with us.

From the Writings of Swedenborg

Apocalypse Explained, n. 687[18]: "Angels were seen in the tomb, sitting one at the head, and the other at the feet (John 20:12; Mark 16:5). These things seen were representative of the Lord's glorification, and of introduction into heaven by Him; for the 'stone' that was placed before the sepulchre, and that was rolled away by the angel, signifies Divine truth, thus the Word, which was closed up by the Jews, but opened by the Lord. . . . And as a 'sepulchre,' and pre-eminently the sepulchre where the Lord was, signifies in the spiritual sense resurrection and also regeneration, and 'angels' signify in the Word Divine truth, therefore angels were seen sitting one at the head and the other at the feet; 'the angel at the head' signifying Divine truth in things first, and 'the angel at the feet' Divine truth in ultimates, both proceeding from the Lord; and when Divine truth is received regeneration is effected, and there is resurrection."

Suggested Questions on the Lesson

P. What kind of animal did the Lord ride into Jerusalem on Palm Sunday?
an ass

P. What did the people shout? *Hosanna*

J. What did they think the Lord had come to do? *overthrow Rome*

J. What happened when they found that He had not come to be an earthly king? *rejected Him*

P. On what day was He put to death? *Friday*

J. What was done with His body when it was taken down from the cross?
put in new tomb

J. What two men performed this service? *Joseph of Arimathea, Nicodemus*

P. Who first came to the sepulcher on Sunday morning? *Mary Magdalene*

P. Why did she come? *to anoint body*

P. What did she find? *stone rolled away*

J. What did Peter and the other disciple see in the tomb? *linen cloths*

P. What did Mary see there? *two angels*

P. When the Lord appeared to her, how did He make Himself known?
spoke her name

J. Why did He tell her not to touch Him? *not yet ascended*

J. How did He appear to the disciples? *through closed doors*

J. Which disciple was not present? *Thomas*

J. What did Thomas say would be necessary to convince him that the Lord was alive? *"Unless I see . . . and touch . . ."*

J. How did the Lord convince him? *appeared again*

J. What did the Lord afterward say to Thomas? *"Blessed . . . not seen and believed"*

J. What does John say about things not recorded in the Gospel? *too much to record*

I. What does burial represent? *resurrection*

S. What is represented by the stone which closed the sepulcher? *false idea of God*

S. What is represented by the linen cloths? *ideas of disciples as to who the Lord was*

JOHN'S VISION
Revelation 1

With all the older classes the historical connection with the Gospels should be made. In A.D. 70, some forty years after the resurrections and ascension of the Lord, Jerusalem and the temple were finally destroyed by the Romans under Titus, and the Christians were dispersed and driven into Asia Minor and beyond. So the early churches developed in Asia Minor. Be sure the children make the distinction between John the Baptist and the Apostle John. Also call their attention to the other name for the book of Revelation—the Apocalypse, the Greek word meaning unveiling or revelation—as they will hear it used frequently.

———

Doctrinal Points
The risen and glorified Lord is the one God of heaven and earth.
The vision in chapter 1 gives us a complete picture of the Lord to hold in our minds when we pray to Him.
The book of Revelation is the "charter" of the New Church.

———

Notes for Parents
The book of Revelation has always been a challenge to the Christian Church. Even people who scoff at everything supernatural cannot quite deny its power. For it does not read like something anyone would or could "make up."

It is recognized as prophecy, and many attempts have been made to connect one or another war or disaster or other great historical event with some one of its striking pictures. In the first verse of the book John tells us that it speaks of the things "which must shortly come to pass," and in verse 19 of the first chapter he is told: "Write the things which thou hast seen, and the things which are, and the things which shall be hereafter."

John was "in the spirit." His spiritual eyes were opened to see the hearts and minds of the people of the Christian Church as they would appear in the searching light of divine love and wisdom. What he saw was like a great moving picture portraying in marvelous symbols the process of judgment.

And first he saw the Lord, the same master he had followed in the world and had seen transfigured once long before. But now the glory is so great that John falls at His feet as dead. And now the Lord can tell him plainly, "I am the first and the last." Jesus Christ risen and glorified is God Almighty. There is no other God.

We see many paintings of Christ, but we know that they are all merely the artists' ideas of what He may have looked like. No likeness painted when He was on earth or by one who saw Him then has come down to us. Why? Because we are not intended to dwell on the thought of Him as one who walked the roads of Palestine centuries ago. We are to think of our living, present Lord. The Lord's last words to His disciples in the Gospel of Matthew were: "Lo, I am with you always, even to the close of the age."

And we can see Him with our minds. People sometimes ask, "How ought I to think of God when I pray to Him?" The Lord Himself gives us the answer in this first chapter of Revelation. We may think at first that it is a strange picture which is given us, but it is just what we should expect: one "like unto the Son of man," one whom we can imagine walking among us doing and saying the things we find in the Gospels, and yet glorified, surrounded by light, with stars in His hand and a sharp, two-edged sword of absolute divine truth coming from His mouth. The sword destroys what is evil and false, but it defends and protects all that is pure and good.

Primary

Speak of John, the apostle whom the Lord loved best, and tell the children how, when John was a very old man and had been driven away from his church and sent to a lonely island, the Lord Jesus whom he loved appeared to him one Sunday in a beautiful vision. The children should distinguish between the two Johns and be told the relation in time of the book of Revelation to the Gospel story which we have been studying. Make the connection between

John's vision of the Lord and the story of the transfiguration. Have them notice how everything in this vision is a form of brightness and tell them that light is a picture of the Lord's truth which shows us the way in our lives. Read them verses 12 through 16 and suggest that this forms a beautiful thought about the Lord to keep in their minds when they pray.

Not long ago we had a story about how the Lord took His three closest disciples up on a high mountain and let them see a wonderful vision. Do you remember about it? One of those three disciples was John—not John the Baptist, but the John through whom the Lord wrote the Gospel of John.

Do you remember how the Lord looked to the three disciples at the transfiguration?
What three disciples saw Him transfigured?
Many years later the same John had a similar vision.

John was probably the youngest of the twelve apostles, and he lived on for a great many years after the Lord's death and resurrection. He was faithful to the Lord and went about telling people the good news about Him. Many people believed what he told them and were baptized, and Christian churches were started in several places. When John was an old man, he had charge of seven of these churches in Asia Minor, which was north of the Holy Land.

The rulers at the time of our story, like the scribes and Pharisees, were trying to destroy the Christian faith.
John was now an old man, and had been banished by his enemies to the island of Patmos.
On what day of the week did John have the vision recorded in the book of Revelation?
John was "in the spirit."
This means that his spiritual eyes and ears were opened.
What did he hear first?
Then whom did he see?
Can you describe how the Lord looked?
What did John see around the Lord?
What did the Lord have in His right hand?
What did He say about Himself?
What did He tell John the stars and the candlesticks meant?
For whom did He give John messages?
He also told John to write down all he saw and heard.

What he wrote this time is the last book of our Bible, which is called
Revelation. This means a revealing of hidden things. It is often also
called the Apocalypse, which is the Greek word meaning the same
thing.

———

Junior

Tell this class more about how the apostles, after the Lord left them, obeyed
His command and went out into the world to found the Christian Church.
Tell them something about the persecution of the early Christians and how
much John needed the encouragement of this vision. Remind them of the
correspondence of light, and tell them that every detail of the vision has a
beautiful correspondence which they will study when they are a little older.
Impress upon them also that this vision is for us, too, and that we should
think of the Lord in this way.

What three disciples had seen the Lord transfigured?

Many years later John had another wonderful vision of the Lord.
It was nearly sixty years after the Lord's crucifixion, resurrection,
and ascension. John was the only one of the twelve apostles still
living, and he was a very old man. Jerusalem and the temple had
been destroyed by the Romans some years before and the Christians had been scattered through Asia Minor and even farther
away. The first Christian churches had been organized in Asia
Minor. John was the leader of the church at Ephesus, and probably
had supervision over the other churches in that area.

But now the Christians were being persecuted, and John had
been banished to the little island of Patmos out in the Aegean Sea
twenty-four miles west of the coast of Asia Minor. One Bible dictionary tells us that the island is divided into two parts and says:
"On the hill to the south, crowning a commanding height is the
celebrated monastery which bears the name of 'John the Divine.'
Halfway up the ascent is the cave or grotto where tradition says
that St. John received the Revelation."

On what day of the week was the vision given to John?

John was "in the spirit." That is, his spiritual eyes and ears were opened to see and hear things in the spiritual world. He was prepared for the vision by hearing a great voice "as of a trumpet," which seemed to come from behind him so that he had to turn toward the voice. We have to turn toward the Lord with our minds before He can instruct us.

What was the first thing the voice said to John?

Alpha and omega are the first and last letters of the Greek alphabet. We often see these letters on chancel furniture in churches. They look like this:

$$A \; \Omega$$

The vision showed John immediately that the person he had known as Jesus Christ was really God Himself. Swedenborg tells us that no one can enter the heavens who does not recognize Jesus Christ as the only God of heaven and earth, but that good people who have not learned this before they die can be instructed in the other world. It is much better for us, of course, to know it now, because so we can base our lives on the real truth about God.

What was John told to do with the vision?
What did he see around the Lord?
How was the Lord dressed?
What was His voice like?
What did He hold in His right hand?
What went out of His mouth?
What did the seven lampstands picture?
What did the seven stars picture?

Every true church is like a lampstand upholding the truth which gives light to the world. You remember the word *angel* means "messenger." John was given messages for the seven churches in Asia Minor. He had already been the Lord's messenger in bringing to the people there the good news—or Gospel—of the Lord's coming as their savior. Each one of us can be a messenger of the Lord, if we try to learn all we can from Him and live as He wants us to live. If we are His messengers here, we shall be angels when we go into the other world.

Intermediate

The general correspondence of the vision, particularly as to the recurrence of light in all its details, should be stressed. The young people should be urged to read this chapter often and to learn to think about the Lord as He is pictured in it. Call their attention to the fact that, although John recognized Him as the same person who had been his master and his friend in the world, he now saw Him as a glorious being, the alpha and omega, God reigning in heaven.

The apostle John was called "the beloved disciple." To him was given to write not only the Gospel of John but also three letters and the book of Revelation. He outlived all the others. Forty days after the resurrection the disciples saw the Lord ascend into heaven. This is told in Luke 24:50-53. After the ascension the apostles went out, as the Lord had commanded them, to preach the Gospel to all the world. Their dispersion was hastened by the destruction of Jerusalem and the temple at the hands of the Romans in A.D. 70. Asia Minor then became their principal field of activity, and there groups of Christians were formed into churches. John seems to have been leader of the church at Ephesus, and in his old age, as the only survivor of the twelve, was doubtless looked upon as the head of the Christian Church. In one of the persecutions of the Christians he was banished to the island of Patmos in the Aegean Sea, where he had the vision recorded in the book of Revelation. This book is also called the *Apocalypse*, the Greek word for "revelation."

The Old Testament is composed of the Law and the Prophets. So is the New Testament, the Gospels constituting the Law and the book of Revelation the Prophets. The other books of the New Testament, like the books of the Old which were included as Sacred Writings, are not part of the Word (not having an inner sense), but are valuable and interesting as history.

John was "in the spirit." His spiritual sight was opened to see "the things which are, and the things which shall be hereafter." The vision was like a mighty symbolic moving picture enacted before his eyes. Swedenborg tells us that the substance of the spiritual world is not inert like material substance, but is immediately responsive to spiritual forces, so that everything there takes on at once an outward form corresponding to the affections and thoughts of the angels or spirits or devils.

John's vision began with an appearance of the Lord to him. He recognized the master he had known in the world; yet the accompaniments were those of deity, and John fell at His feet as dead. And the words spoken left no doubt that this was the creator Himself as well as the master whom John had known. In the New Church we accept this as our vision of the Lord. We do not look beyond Jesus to some more powerful and more terrible God. The Lord says to us, as to John, "Fear not; I am the first and the last."

John's vision gives us a picture to hold in our minds when we think about the Lord and when we pray to Him. The predominant feature of the picture is brightness—the golden lampstands, the stars, the eyes as a flame of fire, the feet like fine brass, and the countenance "as the sun shineth in his strength." We get the impression of a human form, but so bright that we can scarcely bear to look at it and cannot do more than glimpse its details. The correspondence throughout is to divine truth, except that the golden girdle or belt pictures divine love which binds all together, and the golden lampstands the love of divine truth which makes people of our age into a church. The two-edged sword is a picture of divine truth defending good and destroying evil.

The succeeding visions in the book of Revelation are concerned first with the condition of the church in the world and in men's minds and hearts—conditions which beset it and which eventually destroyed it in the final judgment. Their second concern is the way in which the Lord would build up a new church. The book of Revelation has been called the "charter of the New Church." But we must remember that everything that is said in the Word about the church in general has an application to our own individual lives also, and that each of us has within himself the evils which are pictured, and must fight them and try to grow into a true church.

Basic Correspondences

golden candlesticks or lampstands = divine truth loved

a two-edged sword = truth defending good and
destroying evil

a golden girdle or belt = the divine love

―――――――

Senior

The special lesson for the Seniors is the importance of the book of Revelation for the New Church, and of this opening vision of the Lord for our concept of Him. Use the details of the vision, in their spiritual sense, to clarify this concept and to stimulate thought about the Lord.

The book of Revelation has been called "the charter of the New Church." It is the strictly prophetic part of the New Testament and treats in all its details of the final dispensation of the Lord's truth which accomplishes the Last Judgment and establishes the Lord's true church, symbolized by the holy city New Jerusalem, coming down from God out of heaven.

The book of Revelation could not be understood in the light given to the first Christian Church era. All sorts of strange and conflicting interpretations of it were given. Only the opening of the Word in the Second Coming of the Lord has made it intelligible. In the light of the doctrine of correspondence it becomes a marvelous study.

It begins with John's vision of the Lord, and the picture given in our lesson for today is as near as we can come to a true picture of the Lord which we may hold before our minds when we worship. He is, as John saw Him to be, in the human form, the Christ of the Gospels, and yet so resplendent in glory that there can be no lingering thought of Him as a mere historic name, a finite man like ourselves. We see Him as God, the alpha and omega, the I AM.

The foundation of every church is its doctrine of the Lord. All its other doctrines grow out of this and the quality of life depends upon it. In the New Church *the Lord* means to us Jesus Christ always. Swedenborg tells us that "throughout all heaven no other than the Lord alone is acknowledged as the God of heaven" (HH 2). The Old Testament prophesied that Jehovah Himself would come into the world, and the Lord, when He was in the world, said: "He that hath seen me hath seen the Father." Now He declared it to John in the words, "I am the first and the last." While the Lord was in the world it was necessary, in order that He might meet and overcome temptations, for Him much of the time to feel Himself to be a man like other men, and thus to look to the Divine as above Him, as His Father rather than as His own indwelling soul, for had He always felt Himself to be God, temptation could not have touched Him. The language of the trinity—Father, Son, and Holy Spirit—was necessitated by this fact. It has confused the men of the church, although even the letter of the Gospel should have shown them that the separation was only an apparent and temporary one, and that the Father, the Son, and the Holy Spirit are but three aspects of one and the same person. Every New Churchman should think this problem through for himself and be sure he understands it, for only in this way can he present his belief to others clearly.

Jesus Christ is God in the flesh, Jehovah come into the world to show us how this life of ours should and can be lived, and to disclose Himself to us as our friend and companion as well as our Father and our God. It is as if a king, finding himself misrepresented by his ministers and misjudged by his people, should put on the clothes of a workman and live for a time incognito among his subjects so that they might really come to know and understand him. This is not by any means all the purpose and work of the incarnation, but it is perhaps its simplest aspect. We can really know God only if we know Him as Jesus Christ. John's vision assures us that His return to the Father meant simply returning to His own eternal glory by putting off the finite clothing which had been necessary to His work on earth. In the vision John saw Him reigning in the heavens, but recognized Him as the master and friend whom he had known on earth.

The correspondence of the details of the vision as recorded in the Word shows us the various aspects of divine love and wisdom. We can go far, with the help of the writings, in studying each detail. Yet we need frequently to imagine for ourselves the vision as a whole, to think of ourselves as falling at the Lord's feet with John, and hearing the Lord's voice "as the sound of many waters" saying to us: "Fear not; I am the first and the last." We need to realize that we are of His church, with a golden lampstand to uphold which draws its light from one of the stars in His right hand. His messages to the seven churches are spoken to us. The sealed book of which we read in the fifth chapter is the very Word which He has given us, and the judgment which, in the rest of the book of Revelation, follows the opening of the seals goes on in us as we accept or reject its inner truths. It is for us to say whether we shall be cast into the lake of fire or lifted up to enter the gates of the Holy City.

This vision is not just something which one man saw centuries ago. It is something eternally real and present, to be seen by our spiritual eyes today so that we may examine ourselves in its light and take our stand on the side of the angels in the affairs of our everyday life. The great voice "as of a trumpet" is calling us to turn and listen.

Adult

The outline of the general content of the book of Revelation will be helpful to the Adults. It is hard to see the outline for oneself amid the multiplicity of details. The opening vision should be discussed as teaching the primary doctrine on which the New Church is founded.

Under divine providence the apostle John was permitted to live out a long life, and in his old age the wonderful vision recorded in the book of Revelation was given through him to the world. It was given on the island of Patmos, to which John had been exiled— possibly during the persecution of the Christians under Emperor Domitian in A.D. 95, John being about ninety years old at that time. We are told plainly in the first chapter that it is a vision seen in the spiritual world—"I was in the spirit on the Lord's day"—and that it is a vision of the state of the church and of what was to come in the future. Swedenborg says (AE 5) that it treats of the state of the church "in the last times" just before the Last Judgment rather than of the history of the church from its beginning.

Although theologians and others throughout the history of the Christian Church have attempted to interpret and to explain and to apply these visions, the law of correspondence revealed through Swedenborg is the only key to a consistent interpretation. Reverent readers of the Word have always felt their power, and young children love to hear them read, but no one before the Second Coming was able to make any intelligent use of them. We should clearly recognize and be thankful for the fact that "now it is permitted to enter intellectually into the mysteries of faith." We may think of these visions of John, as of those of the Old Testament prophets, as dramas, vast symbolic living pictures enacted in the spiritual world for the instruction and enlightenment of angels and men. The particular prophet is a chosen witness by means of whom the essential features of the drama may be recorded and transmitted to men on earth and preserved in the ultimates of earthly language. The literal details of these visions are powerful and striking, and when we attempt to visualize them for ourselves, they deeply affect the mind. But their ultimate value is in their symbolic meaning. And the Lord in these latter days has made it possible for us to know surely that meaning.

The book of Revelation is a picture of the spiritual forces which were at work even from the beginning of the Christian Church, of the conflict between good and evil, truth and falsity, angels and devils, of the Lord's permission of the evil until its consequences should be plainly seen—as the tares in the parable were allowed to grow along with the wheat until the harvest—and of the final triumph of good and truth and the descent of the holy city New Jerusalem upon the earth. After the opening vision we have the messages to the seven churches in Asia Minor, of which John was doubtless the recognized head. Under the names of these churches all types of acceptance and rejection of the Lord's truth are described, the specific rewards of each type of acceptance shown, and the specific dangers of each type of rejection. Then under the symbols of the throne, the sealed book, and the Lamb, we are shown how the Lord's providence directs the spiritual course of the world through the Word, at first closed and then gradually opened. Then we see how the opening of the Word searches the hearts and minds of men, revealing deeper and deeper evils, how the forces of falsity and evil—under the representation of the dragon and the beast—war against the Lord and the angels for the possession of men's souls, how they are permitted to appear to triumph, but how the good, who in the Lord's strength fight against and overcome their temptations, are preserved, and the New Church, which is born in the midst of the conflict, is saved, and the Lord's kingdom finally prevails throughout the earth.

The book of Revelation has been called "the charter of the New Church" because it prophesies its establishment. Coming to it, as we do, at the close of our study of the whole course of the Word, we should be able to recognize it as the crown of the Word, the culmination of human history, the final act in the great drama of man's spiritual development both as a race and as an individual. Very little can be done with it in the time allotted to it in our course. We can study it for ourselves with the help of Swedenborg's *Apocalypse Revealed* and *Apocalypse Explained* and draw more and more illumination and inspiration from it.

This first chapter gives us the wonderful picture of the Lord Jesus Christ reigning. John recognizes Him as the "Son of man," the master he knew in the world, and the Lord declares Himself to be "he that liveth and was dead," but also says plainly, "I am the first and the last." Thus the book opens with the identification of the Lord Jesus Christ as the eternal God of heaven and earth.

Many before John had had visions of the Lord beginning, we recall, with Moses and the seventy elders (Exodus 24:9-10). All these visions are characterized by the appearance of brightness or fire and usually by the specific mention of the human form of the

Lord (Ezekiel 1:26-28). The fire and the brightness are symbols of divine love and wisdom. The Lord has always made it clear that we are to think of Him as a divine man. Swedenborg says He is actually the only man, that He is "Very Man" [*ipse homo*]. But it was not until after the Lord's life on earth that, because He had ultimated His divine human, a vision could be granted whose details could be recorded more specifically. This is the picture of the Lord which He wishes us to hold in our minds. We should study and think about this picture instead of any of the imaginary and strictly finite representations which the artists of various periods have conceived. People often say, "How shall I think of the Lord? What picture of Him shall I have in my mind when I pray to Him?" John's vision is the Lord's answer to this question. If we have any less definite picture, He will not seem to us a real person; if we have any more ordinary picture we shall have no feeling of His glory and power.

The very fact that there are some details in the picture which we find it difficult to imagine and which would be impossible to put on canvas helps to lift our thought of the Lord above His finite humanity to the glorified divine humanity. To understand the meaning of the vision each of us must study it for himself, recalling correspondences already familiar: garments symbolize truth, gold love, the head the directing intelligence which extends to the hairs, its outmost applications; white signifies purity, the eyes understanding, fire love, the feet the outward conduct, brass or bronze natural good, the voice like the sound of many waters "the Divine truth in ultimates" or divine truth as it comes to us, the stars knowledges of spiritual things, the two-edged sword divine truth attacking evil and falsity and defending goodness, the countenance the expression of the interior character, the sun divine love and wisdom, the lampstands the church on earth, whose office it is to receive and transmit divine truth to mankind. Swedenborg in both the *Apocalypse Explained* and the *Apocalypse Revealed* gives pages to the interpretation of these few verses. Yet the vision itself may be read in a minute and memorized in a short time, and one will then have in his mind a true concept of the Lord, given by the

Lord Himself, which will direct and enlighten all His thought about the Lord and fill his everyday life with meaning and purpose.

From the Writings of Swedenborg

Apocalypse Explained (Introduction to chapter 1): "Many have expounded this prophetical book called the Apocalypse, but none of them understood the internal or spiritual sense of the Word. They have therefore applied the particular things in the book to the successive states of the church, which they have learned from histories; many things, moreover, they have applied to civil affairs. For this reason these expositions are for the most part conjectures, which can never appear in such light that they can be affirmed as truths. As soon, therefore, as they are read, they are put aside as speculations. The expositions of the Apocalypse now extant are of this character, because, as has been said, their authors had no knowledge of the internal or spiritual sense of the Word."

Apocalypse Revealed (preliminary *Contents* of chapter 1): "Ver. 12. 'And I turned to see the voice which was speaking with me,' signifies the inversion of the state of those who are in the good of life as to the perception of truth in the Word, when they turn themselves to the Lord. 'And having turned I saw seven golden lampstands,' signifies the New Church which will be in enlightenment from the Lord out of the Word. Ver. 13. 'And in the midst of the seven lampstands One like unto the Son of Man,' signifies the Lord as to the Word, from whom is that church. 'Clothed with a garment down to the foot,' signifies the proceeding Divine, which is the Divine truth. 'And girded at the paps with a golden girdle,' signifies the Divine love of the Divine wisdom in firsts and in ultimates. 'And His eyes as a flame of fire,' signifies the Divine love. Ver. 15. 'And his feet like unto fine brass, as if glowing in a furnace,' signifies the Divine good natural. 'And his voice as the voice of many waters,' signifies the Divine truth natural. Ver. 16. 'And having in His right hand seven stars,' signifies all the knowledges of good and truth in the Word from Him. 'And out of His mouth sharp two-edged sword going forth,' signifies the dispersion of falsities by the Lord through the Word and through doctrine therefrom. 'And his face was as the sun shining in power,' signifies the Divine love and the Divine wisdom, which are Himself, and proceed from Him."

Suggested Questions on the Lesson

J. Of what two Johns do we read in the Gospels? *John the Baptist, apostle John*

J. Through which one was the Gospel of John written? *the apostle*

J. What happened to Jerusalem after the Lord's death? *it was destroyed*

J. Where were the first Christian churches started? *Asia Minor*

J. What other books in the Bible were written through John? *three letters, Revelation*

J. Where was John when the Revelation was given him? *Isle of Patmos*

P. What did John hear first? *great voice like a trumpet*

P. What did he first see when he turned? *seven gold lampstands*

P. Who stood in the midst of the seven golden lampstands? *the risen Lord*

P. How did the Lord appear? *dressed in long robe, . . .*

P. What did He have in His right hand? *seven stars*

J. What did the Lord say about Himself? *I am alpha and omega*

J. What did He say the seven lampstands and the seven stars were? *churches/angels*

J. What did He tell John to do? *write down the vision*

I. Why are there so many mentions of light in this vision? *to show power of divine truth*

I. What does the golden girdle or belt represent? *divine love binding all together*

S. What does this vision teach us? *how we should "picture," i.e., think of, the Lord*

THE MESSAGES TO THE CHURCHES
Revelation 2; 3

There are some general facts concerning John's messages to the seven churches which can be presented to all but the youngest children. These have to do with the similarities of all the messages: (1) Each picks out a particular feature of the vision of the Lord; (2) Each commends the church for what it is doing that is good; (3) Each rebukes the church for its particular evil and shows what the resulting punishment will be if the evil persists; (4) Each offers a special promise if the evil is put away; (5) Each closes with the words, "He that hath an ear, etc.," leaving the church free to choose whether it will obey or not.

═══════

Doctrinal Points

We can see the rightness and wrongness in our lives to the extent that we are "in charity and faith."

The church in itself is one, but various according to reception.

The Lord is always standing at the door knocking. It is up to us to open it to Him.

═══════

Notes for Parents

We remember that the Lord told John that the seven golden lampstands among which He stood were "the seven churches" and that the seven stars in His right hand were "the angels of the seven churches." The word *angel*, we recall, means "messenger." Now He gives John a special message for each of the churches.

The seven churches mentioned were actual churches. They had been founded in Asia Minor by the early Christians, and had developed especially after the destruction of Jerusalem by the Romans in A.D. 70, when the remaining apostles and their followers were dispersed. The messages sent to them by the Lord

183

through John show us plainly that the early Christians were much like ourselves, prone to differences of opinion, to worldliness, and to spiritual laziness. We have already seen how little even the twelve apostles understood of the Lord's teachings, and how easily they were induced to save themselves rather than to remain faithful. Although the resurrection gave them new faith and courage and some of them afterward suffered martyrdom for their faith, they did not suddenly become perfect and infallible. The Christian Church almost from its beginning went astray because it looked to men for its teaching rather than to the Lord, relying on the Epistles rather than on the Gospels, and in later times basing its whole structure on decisions arrived at by men at the Council of Nicea three hundred years after the time of the Lord. We need to go to the four Gospels and the book of Revelation for our knowledge of what the Lord actually teaches.

But the messages to the seven churches are of more than mere historical interest to us. The seven churches show us seven types of people. Each one of us has his own special qualities and abilities and also his own special weaknesses and faults. The Lord sees both, and in these messages He says to us, "Hold fast the good which has developed in you, but recognize also the evil and repent and change your ways, lest you lose the place prepared for you in heaven." Each one of the churches was given a special promise if it was faithful, as each one of us has a special heavenly character which it is possible for him to attain. And we might notice that the church of Laodicea, which received the most severe condemnation because it was "lukewarm," was promised the greatest reward for overcoming its fault. This is because their fault was the hardest to overcome. Is not this same "lukewarmness" in spiritual things the besetting sin of most of us? We acknowledge what we ought to do but we excuse ourselves for not doing it. We take the easy way. The Lord is always standing at the door of our souls. We often hear His knock. But how often we are too busy with our own affairs to open the door!

The Lord has a special message for each one of us. He tells us plainly that if we go our own way, we shall find only unhappiness in the end, and that if we follow His way, it will lead us to eternal joy; but He leaves us free to make our own choice. He says to each one of us, as He said to each of the seven churches, "He that hath an ear, let him hear what the Spirit saith unto the churches."

Primary

Spend a little time recalling to the children's minds John's vision of the Lord, ending with the explanation given in the letter of the stars and lampstands. Then tell them that there really were seven churches and that the Lord gave John a different message for each one. Read them the following verses, stopping at each to make the connection with John's vision: 2:1, 8, 12, 18 and 3:1, 7, 14. Then tell them that the closed door is the little door which we close in our minds when we are naughty and do not want to hear what is right, and make the connection between this and the memory verse. Also call attention to the five similarities in all the messages, and illustrate by reading the messages to the churches in Philadelphia and Laodicea (3:7-22).

The book we are studying now is about a wonderful vision which was given to the apostle John when he was an old man.

Where was John at this time?
What was the first thing he saw?
What did the Lord say about Himself?
To how many churches was John given messages?

They were the seven Christian churches which had been founded in Asia Minor, over which John was the head.

Our lesson today is about messages which the Lord gave to John for these seven churches—a different message for each church.

The Lord sees what is in the heart of every one of us—what is bad and what is good—and does His best to lead every one of us to heaven. We all have good things in us but we also have bad ones, and we cannot get to heaven unless we are willing to be told when we are doing wrong and to admit it and try to change. So the Lord told each of the seven churches what its good qualities were and also what its bad ones were and what it must do to be truly heavenly.

Finally He made each church, if it would be faithful, a special beautiful promise.

Like the seven churches, each one of us does some good things and some bad ones.

So the Lord has a special message for each of us, and we need to listen and obey.

And for each of us He has some special beautiful thing in store, if we are faithful.

What two doors are mentioned in our lesson? (verses 8 and 20 of chapter 3) The open door is the door of heaven.

The closed door is the one we close in our minds when we do not want to hear what the Lord is trying to tell us.

Verse 20 of chapter 3 is a very important one, for each one of us has to choose whether he will just do as he pleases—in which case he cannot possibly get to heaven—or take the right way, the Lord's way, which is harder but which leads to true happiness. The Lord is always standing near us ready to come into our minds and hearts if we will just open the door to Him.

Junior

The Juniors are old enough to understand that the messages are to us as well as to the churches of long ago, although they will be interested in looking at a map which shows the location of those churches and the relative position of Asia Minor and the Holy Land. Be sure to point out Patmos. Something of the spiritual meaning can be given simply by pointing out that we are all different and that the Lord treats each of us in a special way, that we all have some good things in us which the Lord tries to encourage and some bad ones which He points out to us so that we can fight them, and that the choice of what we become must be our own.

Where was the vision recorded in the book of Revelation given?
To whom was it given and when?
What was the beginning of the vision?
What was John commanded to do?
What were the seven stars said to be?
What were the seven lampstands?

Find these seven cities on a map. John was in charge of the church at Ephesus, but he was probably head of all seven. Find the island to which he had been banished when he received his vision.

The business of every church on earth is to uphold the truth the

Lord has given it, so that it will give light to men's minds. So each church is like a lampstand. And also each church has a special spiritual character, a living spirit which connects it with heaven and the Lord; this is its "angel"—its "messenger." It was to this living spirit in each church that John's message was given.

The seven churches were different from each other just as the churches of today are, and just as individual Christians are. Each had some virtues and some faults, and the Lord commended the virtues and pointed out the faults, and to each church He gave a special promise if it would overcome its faults. Philadelphia was described as the most faithful of them all, though there were some in it who were hypocrites. The door of heaven was said to be open to the people of this church and it was told only to hold fast its truth and goodness. Notice that those who did hold fast were to take the name "New Jerusalem."

Laodicea, on the other hand, was severely rebuked because it was "lukewarm." We are lukewarm Christians when we slide along through life not trying very hard to learn what the Lord would have us do, but always taking the way that seems to us easiest at the moment. It is to such people that the Lord says, "Behold, I stand at the door, and knock," because they are keeping the doors of their minds closed to the truths which they need. But if they will open the door and change their ways, He makes them one of the best of the promises. This is because it is very hard to overcome the temptation to take the easy way, and victory over that temptation brings a high reward. If you will stop to think, you will realize that it is the people who are willing to work hard and to stand firmly for what is right who become great.

Now read verse 13. We all have ears, haven't we? But do we always hear what is said to us? Did you ever try to hear—for instance when your mother wanted you to stop playing and do something for her? All people who really want to be good must listen and obey.

Intermediate

Develop in some detail, with illustrations from any one of the seven messages, the general outline suggested, and emphasize the fact that we are all different and that the Lord expects each of us to do his best to develop his individual capacities and to fight his particular temptations. Encourage the young people to read the two chapters carefully at home for themselves.

Everything in the Word has, in addition to its literal sense, three major inner meanings, one within the other, relating (1) to the spiritual history of the human race, (2) to the development of our own individual souls, and (3) to the life of the Lord. This is just as true of the book of Revelation as of the Old Testament and the Gospels.

In the first sense, which is called the internal historical sense, the seven churches in Asia Minor picture various types of Christian organizations which developed as a result of the spread of the Gospel by the apostles and early Christian leaders and the various types which will exist in every age. In the second sense, which is called the spiritual sense, they picture the various states in which each one of us may find himself at one time or another as to his religious life. In the third sense, which is called the celestial sense, they picture the Lord's dealing with churches or individuals in these various states, the accommodation of His love and wisdom to meet all human needs and to lead all men to the highest states which they will freely choose to attain.

In general we can see that the Lord is telling each of us in what ways he is right and in what ways wrong. This rightness or wrongness depends on how far we are "in charity and faith"; that is, how far we have the Lord's unselfish love in our hearts and the truths of His word in our minds. And these must go hand in hand. If we have more love than truth or if we have more truth than love, we fall into certain temptations and need to repent and restore the true balance. And if we recognize and fight our temptations, we prepare ourselves for the very place in heaven which will give us the greatest happiness.

Notice that in each of the messages the Lord describes Himself in a slightly different way. All the attributes He mentions are details of John's original vision of Him, but in each He stresses just the divine qualities which will most appeal to the people in the state described by that particular church. For example, to the church of Philadelphia—which, Swedenborg tells us, pictures those "who are in truths from good from the Lord"—the things mentioned (3:7) all have to do with truth, and it said of these people that the "door" is open before them. But the church of Laodicea, which pictures those who "alternately believe from themselves, and from the Word, and so profane holy things," is reminded that the Lord is the source of all things and told to open the doors of their minds to Him. The temptation to trust in our own wisdom instead of in the Lord's truth is the deepest of all temptations, but if we overcome it, the Lord will guide all things for our eternal welfare. This is what is meant by the promise, "To him that overcometh will I give to sit with me in my throne."

Just as the Lord presents Himself in a different way to each type of person—each of the seven churches—so the promise of reward for victory is a different promise for each. Each of us has his own possibilities, his own weaknesses, and his own temptations; no two people are ever just alike. The Lord knows each one of us through and through and deals with each in a little different way, to give each the best chance of attaining the stature and place for which he was created. And He says to each one of us: "He that hath ears to hear, let him hear."

Basic Correspondences

Ephesus	=	those who regard truths of doctrine, not good of life
Smyrna	=	in good of life but falsities as to doctrine
Pergamos	=	place everything in good works, nothing in truths
Thyatira	=	both faith from charity and faith separate from charity
Sardis	=	dead worship

Philadelphia = in truths from good

Laodicea = those who profane holy things

———————

Senior

Study with the class the meaning of each of the seven churches as stated in the quotation in their notes, discussing different types of churches in the world today and different types of minds, in the effort to help the young people to see themselves and other people more clearly. Study the message to Laodicea in more detail, showing them what is meant by "lukewarm" in their religion.

In the *Apocalypse Revealed* Swedenborg says of the opening chapter of the book of Revelation: "This Revelation is from the Lord alone; and it is received by those who will be in His New Church, which is the New Jerusalem, and who acknowledge the Lord as the God of heaven and earth."

And he tells us there briefly, as well as in detail elsewhere, that the messages to the seven churches are messages to the churches in the Christian world: "To those there who primarily regard truths of doctrine, and not goods of life, who are meant by the Ephesian Church. To those who are in goods as to life, and in falsities as to doctrine; who are meant by the church of Smyrna. To those there who place all of the church in good works, and not anything in truths; who are meant by the church in Pergamos. And to those who are in faith from charity, as also to them that are in faith separated from charity; who are meant by the church in Thyatira. All these are called to the New Church, which is the New Jerusalem. . . . They in the Christian world who are in dead worship, which is without charity and faith, who are described by the church in Sardis. They who are in truths from good from the Lord; who are described by the church in Philadelphia. They who alternately believe from themselves, and from the Word, and so profane holy things; who are described by the church in Laodicea. All these likewise are called to the New Church of the Lord." The general meaning of the messages and their application to us could not be stated more briefly and clearly than this.

With this quotation at hand each of us can study the messages in detail for himself. In making this study note that in each case the Lord identifies Himself by signs which, by correspondence, would touch a responsive chord in the minds of people of that particular character; that He calls attention to the special good qualities and the special temptations of each; and that in return for fidelity He promises a reward exactly suited to the highest desire of those of that type. Swedenborg tells us that the heavens are divided into many societies, each society being made up of congenial people and each society performing a particular use to the whole heaven which no other could perform. No two societies are alike, yet all work together in harmony because all accept the Lord alone as their God and desire above everything else to do His will.

Further we need to remember that each one of us is, as Paul said, "a temple," or as Swedenborg says, "a church in its least form." The messages are not only to groups associated into churches but to each individual who desires to be good or who in any way recognizes the necessity of religion. So as we study these two chapters, we are studying ourselves, our particular virtues and weaknesses, the particular aspect of the Lord we need to dwell on, and the particular goal of character toward which we should strive. Each one of us is a child of God and has a direct personal relationship to Him, a special set of faculties and possibilities, and a special place to fill both in this world and in heaven. Our highest happiness will be in the attainment of this place and use.

But we must also realize that the Lord has left it to our own free choice whether or not we shall strive for and attain this place. Our freedom of choice is the thing which the Lord has given us as the essential human quality, which distinguishes man from the animals, and in everything He does He guards this freedom of choice for us. It is an inner freedom—we know that many thing prevent our carrying out in external life all our desires. But each of us is free to desire and to think as he pleases and to try to accomplish his own desires. Our fundamental choice is between self and the Lord. If we choose to put self first, we shall reject belief in the

Lord and in His Word, so closing our ears to His warning voice. If we choose to believe in the Lord, we shall study the Word to find the way of life, and we shall find it. So each of the seven messages ends with the words, "He that hath ears to hear, let him hear what the Spirit saith unto the churches."

Adult

This is a lesson in which the teacher may well use the passages from the writings quoted in the Adult notes as the basis for discussion. Call attention to the fact that, although the seven types are discussed with reference to the beginning and mission of the New Church, they already existed before the end of the first century A.D. To find the truth for the Christian Church we must go to the Gospels, not to the decisions of later church leaders.

In the first chapter of Revelation we are given the clue to the meaning of our lesson for today: "The seven stars are the angels of the seven churches: and the seven candlesticks which thou sawest are the seven churches." In numbers 65 and 66 of the *Apocalypse Revealed* Swedenborg says: "*The seven stars are the angels of the seven churches*, signifies the New Church in the heavens, which is the New Heaven. The church is in the heavens equally as on the earth; for the Word is in the heavens equally as it is on the earth, and there are doctrines from it, and preachings from it . . . In the spiritual world there appears an expanse full of stars, as in the natural world, and this appearance is from the angelic societies in heaven. Each society there shines like a star before those who are below; hence they know in what situation the angelic societies are . . . by 'angels of the seven churches,' is meant the entire church in the heavens, consequently the New Heaven in the aggregate. *And the seven lampstands which thou sawest are the seven churches*, signifies the New Church on earth, which is the New Jerusalem descending from the Lord out of the New Heaven . . . by 'the seven lampstands' are not meant seven churches, but the church in the aggregate, which in itself is one, but various according to reception. Those varieties may be compared to the various jewels in the crown of a king; and they may also be compared to the various members and organs in a perfect body, which yet make one. The perfection of every form exists from various things being suitably arranged in their order. Hence it is, that the whole New Church is described as to its varieties by 'the seven churches.' "

This is the ideal picture, and we note that although the church is one, there are varieties within it which are distinct, as are the societies in the heaven with which they are associated. We should keep this in mind today when we are considering the ecumenical movement. Also we should note that it is not said that the churches on earth were ideal in themselves, for the messages actually point out how far each had fallen from the ideal. And although it was undoubtedly true that the Christian organizations which by the end of the first century after the Advent had developed in the seven cities of Asia Minor were actually in the various states described in the letter of the Word, in the internal historical sense our attention is directed to the states existing in the various branches of the first Christian Church as it was at the time of the Second Coming and the conditions on which the people of these branches might be expected to respond to the invitation to the New Church. And in the spiritual sense we are to think of the various types of Christians today to whom the message of the New Church is offered and to the same types as we find them also in the organized New Church.

We should note the similarity in pattern of all seven messages: (1) the presentation of the Lord in the particular aspect which would appeal most strongly to the type of person addressed; (2) the Lord's commendation of the good characteristics of that type; (3) the pointing out of the evils to which that type is most subject, and the command to recognize these and repent; (4) the promise to each of that particular "place in the sun" which it is possible for him to attain if he does repent and regenerate; (5) the reminder that our reception or rejection of the message will be of our own free choice: "He that hath ears to hear, let him hear what the Spirit saith unto the churches."

Swedenborg's own words—from the contents at the beginning

of chapters 2 and 3 of the *Apocalypse Revealed*—are the clearest and briefest possible statement of the distinct meaning of the seven churches: "To the churches in the Christian world: To those there who primarily regard truths of doctrine and not good of life, who are meant by the church of Ephesus. To those there who are in goods as to life and in falsities as to the doctrine, who are meant by the church of Smyrna. To those there who place the all of the church in good works, and not anything in truths, who are meant by the church in Pergamos. To those there who are in faith from charity, as also to those who are in faith separated from charity, who are meant by the church in Thyatira. . . . (Chapter 3) This chapter treats of those in the Christian world who are in dead worship, which is without charity and faith; who are described by the church in Sardis. Those who are in truths from good from the Lord; who are described by the church in Philadelphia. Those who alternately believe from themselves, and from the Word, and thus profane holy things; who are described by the church in Laodicea. All of these likewise are called to the New Church of the Lord."

The last sentence points to the fact that each of the seven emphases can be useful in the New Church, indeed is necessary to the perfection of the church. It is only when one aspect is emphasized at the expense of the others that condemnation is pronounced. It is useful to any church to have within it some whose primary interest is in doctrine, some who emphasize good will, some who insist on good works, some who wish to define the relation between faith and charity, some who love the ritual of the church, some who are well-balanced Christians, and some whose shortcomings keep the church reminded of the necessity of self-dedication and sincere, steady devotion. But if the church is to work together in harmony and perform its full use each of these types must recognize and applaud the contribution of all the others. None must assume that his own emphasis is sufficient in itself. One of the most noticeable characteristics of both the Word and the writings is the constant insistence on the balanced life. For example, the parable of the Good Samaritan (Luke 10:30-37), which can so easily be interpreted to mean that external good works are the all-important thing, is immediately followed in the Word by the incident of Mary and Martha (Luke 10:38-42) in which Martha, who was "cumbered about much serving," is told that Mary, in sitting at the Lord's feet hearing His words, has chosen "the better part." And in the writings statements on the importance of truth and those on the importance of good works are so constantly alternated that one cannot exalt one at the expense of the other except by lifting sentences or parts of sentences entirely out of their context.

The most scathing condemnation of all is meted out to the church of Laodicea which is "lukewarm." And yet to him who overcometh in Laodicea is promised the highest reward of all, "to sit with me in my throne." Does not this point to the fact that the most universal and persistent of our temptations and the most difficult to overcome is the temptation to take the easy way, to refuse to take up wholeheartedly and courageously the Lord's cause, to see how little responsibility we can assume instead of how much, how small a contribution we can "get by with" instead of how much we can give, to travel the path of religion with our ear to the ground! It is to this church that the Lord says, "Behold, I stand at the door, and knock." To look for the easy and popular way closes the door against the Lord's truth. Read what Jeremiah says of Moab (Jeremiah 48:11). The heavenly character is not attained by "settling on our lees," by taking the easy way. The Lord gives each of us special abilities, particular opportunities, an individual use to serve, and a particular crown to attain—if we will. He has for each one of us a direct, personal message, searching and challenging—if we have ears to hear.

From the Writings of Swedenborg

Apocalypse Revealed, nn. 202-204 (concerning the church in Laodicea): "*That thou art neither cold nor hot,* signifies that they who are such, sometimes deny that the Word is Divine and holy, and at other times acknowledge it. . . . They are also such concerning God, at one time they deny, and at another time acknowledge Him; in like manner as to all things of the church;

for which reason they are sometimes with those who are in hell, and at other times with those who are in heaven. They fly as it were between both, up and down, and wherever they fly, thither they turn the face. They become such who have confirmed with themselves the belief in the existence of God, of heaven and hell, and of life eternal, and afterwards recede from it. When the first confirmation returns, they acknowledge, but when it does not return, they deny. They recede because they afterwards think only of themselves and the world, continually aspiring to pre-eminence, and thereby they immerse themselves in their proprium; thus hell swallows them up. I would thou wert cold or hot, signifies that it is better for them either from the heart to deny the holy things of the Word and the church, or from the heart to acknowledge them. . . . The reason is, because they have mixed truths with falsities, and goods with evils, thus holy things with profane, even so that they cannot be separated. And since man cannot then be prepared, either to be in heaven or in hell, the whole of his rational life is destroyed, and the ultimates of life alone remain, which, when separated from the interiors of life, are mere phantasies.''

Suggested Questions on the Lesson

P. Who saw the vision described in the book of Revelation? *the apostle John*

J. Where was John when he saw it? *Patmos*

P. At the beginning of the vision whom did he see? *the risen Lord*

P. Can you describe how the Lord looked? *[see Chap. 1]*

P. What did John see around the Lord? *seven lampstands*

J. What did the Lord tell John the seven lampstands were? *churches*

J. Where were these seven churches? *Asia Minor*

J. What is our lesson today about? *messages to those churches*

J. How were all the messages alike? *praised good, condemned faults, made promise*

J. How were they different? *different faults and rewards*

J. Which church is described as the most faithful of all? *Philadelphia*

P. In the message to Philadelphia what is said about a door? *open*

J. What was wrong with the church of Laodicea? *lukewarm*

P. What did the Lord say to that church about a door? *closed*

J. With what words does each of the seven messages close? *He that hath an ear . . .*

J. What do these words mean? *obey, if you are willing*

I. How do these two chapters apply to us? *we are free to open or close "door"*

S. Why is the condemnation of Laodicea's "lukewarmness" so severe? *hardest fault to overcome*

JOHN'S VISION OF THE THRONE
Revelation 4

Review briefly what is known about the apostle John and his situation at the time the visions of the book of Revelation were given.

─────────

Doctrinal Points
Spiritual warfare is going on all the time in this world.
Divine providence, by means of the truths of the Word, protects
*   the good and separates them from the evil.*
The Lord is the only judge.

─────────

Notes for Parents
The book of Revelation is the final book of the Word of God. It is also sometimes called the Apocalypse, which is just the Greek work for revelation. It is the record of a long and wonderful vision which was given to the apostle John when he was a very old man, probably ninety years old. Tradition says that he was the only one of the apostles—except Judas, who hanged himself from remorse—who did not die a martyr's death, because both the leaders of Judaism and the Roman government were afraid of the growing Christian Church and tried to stamp it out. John was not put to death, but he was exiled to the little island of Patmos off the coast of Asia Minor, where the vision was given him.

The word *revelation* means an "unveiling." John says that when this vision was given him, he was "in the spirit," and he was told to write "the things which thou hast seen, and the things which are, and the things which shall be hereafter." So this book is first of all a description of spiritual conditions, states which exist in the hearts and minds of men, and it is a prophecy of what these states will inevitably lead to.

It is such a strange and powerful vision that it has always captured the imaginations of men and led them to try to think what it can mean, and many things in it have been applied at one time or another to events which have been taking place in the world, especially to great wars and battles, for all through the book conflicts are described. But we should realize that all these things are given us as symbolic pictures of a spiritual conflict which goes on all the time, the conflict between good and evil in our hearts and between truth and falsity in our minds. It is a picture of judgment given to show us the inevitable results of evil and falsity and to help us choose what is good and true.

The chapter the children have for today sets the stage for this great conflict, for it shows us that in heaven it is the Lord who reigns and that everyone and everything there loves to acknowledge and worship Him.

Primary

The children will be interested in John and in the vision itself; so the reading of the chapter should come early in the lesson. They may remember the word *cherubim* in our study of Ezekiel and should be reminded of it. Tell them the colors of the precious stones mentioned and connect verse 8 with its use in the church service.

The Lord when He was on earth chose twelve of His disciples to receive special instructions and powers from Him so that after He left them they could go out all over the world and preach the Gospel—the "good news"—that He had overcome evil and would give to all who would learn of Him and obey Him the power to overcome their temptations and become heavenly people. These twelve men were called the apostles, which means men "sent out." The three apostles who were closest to the Lord were Peter, James, and John. All the apostles except Judas were faithful, and did the work the Lord had given them to do.

The apostle who apparently lived longest was John. He is believed to have lived to be nearly ninety and he was in charge of

several of the early churches. Before He died He was given a wonderful vision of what would happen to this new church which was
called Christian. We have been studying this vision as described in
the book of Revelation, the last book in the Bible.

First John saw the Lord as He may be seen in the heavens, and he recognized
Him as the same Lord he had known and followed on earth.

Then he was shown how everyone is judged according to the truth which is in
the Word.

Our lesson today is the beginning of this vision of the judgment.

Read the chapter and then see how many of the details of the vision you can
remember.

Do you remember our lesson about Ezekiel's vision?

Nearly seven hundred years before John, Ezekiel had seen some of the same
things.

The "beasts" [KJV] in our chapter are the same "living creatures" seen by
Ezekiel.

They are also called *cherubim*.

We can easily see that the Lord himself was the king sitting on
the throne, whom everyone and everything in heaven worships. Do
you go to church with your parents? If you do, listen carefully to
the singing, and you may hear some of the very words that John
heard in heaven. This is because when we are in church, we are
worshiping the Lord with the angels.

Junior

After your introduction, in connection with which you should use a map,
have the class look up the Bible references and compare the various visions,
picking out the similarities. Stress the fact that everyone in heaven worships
the Lord.

Between the Gospels and the book of Revelation we find in our
Bibles twenty-two books. The first—the only one of any length—
is called the Acts of the Apostles, and is an account of the first
beginnings of the Christian Church and also many things about
what the apostles themselves thought. If we read these books
attentively, we shall find that the apostles and others who went
out to preach the Gospel did not always agree as to just what the

Lord meant people to do. So we cannot take our instruction from them, although they said many fine and helpful things. We must study the Word itself. And after the Acts and the Epistles there comes one more book of the Word, the book of Revelation.

The book of Revelation, as we have already noted, is the record of the visions given to the apostle John when he was a very old man. Tradition says that he was the youngest of the apostles and outlived all of them. Judas, we remember, hanged himself before the crucifixion, and again tradition says that all the others except John were martyred sooner or later. This was because the Christian Church grew so fast that the Roman government was afraid of its power and tried to stamp it out.

John was no doubt protected by the Lord so that he might be the instrument through whom the final book of the Word might be given. But he, as we learned from Revelation 1:9, was finally exiled to the island of Patmos off the coast of Asia Minor. You can find this island on a map of the area, as well as the part of the world covered in the journeys of the apostles and the location of the seven churches in Asia Minor over which John himself had supervision. That these churches were quite different—people are bound to differ in their opinions and likes—we have learned from the messages which the Lord gave John for them (Revelation 2, 3) praising them for their good characteristics but also pointing out certain evils into which they had already fallen, and warning them to correct these evils.

John was first given a wonderful vision of the Lord as He is seen in the heavens, and yet John could recognize Him as the same master he had followed in the world (Revelation 1:13). Then followed the messages to the seven churches in Asia Minor, and then a long and detailed vision of the spiritual course which the Christian Church would take, the war within it between the forces of the Lord and the forces of evil, the judgment which would be executed upon it, and the final coming of a new church. We may think of this amazing vision as a sort of tremendous moving picture acted out before John's spiritual eyes to teach him and us deep spiritual lessons. John says he was in the spirit (Revelation 1:10, 4:2) when he saw these things. Our chapter for today is the beginning of the picture of the judgment.

What was the first thing John saw after the door was opened in heaven?
Who do you think was the one who sat upon the throne?
What men were around the throne?
How were they dressed?
What other creatures were about the throne?

Do you remember one of our lessons from Ezekiel? Ezekiel, nearly seven hundred years before John, saw a very similar vision. If you have forgotten, read Ezekiel 1:4-18 to see how many things were similar, and then read Ezekiel 10:1 to see what the four living creatures were called. We should know that the Greek word translated "beasts" [KJV] in our chapter for today might better be translated "living creatures" as the Hebrew word is in the first chapter of Ezekiel. In our church service some of us use the words which the living creatures spoke (verse 8), and also we may be familiar with verse 11 because it is sung in some of our responsive services.

We may think of the whole chapter as picturing the fact that the Lord Jesus Christ reigns in heaven and that everyone in heaven worships Him and is governed by Him.

Intermediate

Take up the outline of the correspondence, enlarging on it as the young people show interest. Stress the fact that judgment is according to truth, as this will be good preparation for later lessons.

In Mark 16:19 we are told of the Lord's ascension. This took place forty days after the resurrection and is most fully described in Acts 1:1-12. The book of Acts—the Acts of the Apostles—tells the story of the beginnings of the Christian Church. This book and the twenty-one Epistles—letters written by the apostles and others to the groups of Christians which they organized—do not have an inner sense and so we do not study them in Sunday school, but they are very valuable historical books and interesting to all Christians. The apostles did go out all over the then-known world and preach the Gospel. Everywhere they went they found some people who were hungry for the good news they had to give of the life of the Lord and the salvation He had made possible. And the Christian Church grew so fast that the Roman government soon began to be suspicious of it and tried to stamp it out. Tradition says that all the apostles except John died martyrs' deaths.

Tradition also says that John was the youngest of the apostles and lived to be about ninety. Near the end of his life he was exiled by the Romans to the little island of Patmos off the coast of Asia Minor. John had been in charge of seven of the Christian churches which had been organized in Asia Minor. At Patmos he was given the vision which is recorded in the book of Revelation, the last book in our Bible and the final book of the Word. We are told in Revelation 1:19 and in the first verse of our chapter for today that it is a book of prophecy. As we have seen, it begins (chapter 1) with a vision of the Lord—whom John recognized as the same master he had followed in the world—reigning in heaven. Then (chapters 2 and 3) John was given messages to his seven churches in Asia which show us what their inner states were. They were all different; they had good characteristics and bad ones, and they were warned to repent and correct their faults if they wished to remain true representatives of the Lord in the world.

In the Acts and Epistles we learn that very soon after the Lord left them the apostles began to come into differences of opinion as to how His teachings were to be applied to life. They remembered His words but interpreted them differently. We can understand from this why there are so many Christian sects today. The Lord does not force any one of us to think in one way or another, and we are all different; so we draw different ideas from the Lord's teaching. Still we should all be studying the Word and doing our best to understand and obey it. If we are, the Lord can lead us to heaven, even though we may sometimes misunderstand what we read. But if, instead of this, we are forming our opinions according to our own desires and then trying to find in the Word only what confirms our own chosen opinions, we are not open to the truth in it and the Lord cannot lead us. In the Christian Church—in all Christian churches—there have always been true followers of the Lord and others who only pretended to follow Him. And we know that in each one of us there are tendencies both to good and to evil. The Lord and the angels are working to protect the good and to control the evil both in the individual and in the church. So there is a spiritual war going on all the time, and when we come into the other world there is a time of judgment when the good and the evil are separated. It is this war and the resulting judgment which were shown to John in a series of wonderful living pictures of which the first is our chapter for today.

This vision is very much like one which the prophet Ezekiel had had long before. Read Ezekiel 1:26-28. Read also Exodus 19:16 and 24:10. A trumpet always means the power of the Lord's truth speaking, and a throne is the picture of judgment. It is of course the Lord who sits upon the throne, executing judgment by means of the truth. The precious stones picture the way in which the truth appears to those who love it, showing many different beauties, like the different colors, but always clear and shining, and the sea of glass pictures the clear atmosphere in which even the people of the natural heaven live. The rainbow which Ezekiel saw appeared to John, too. A rainbow is formed by the rays of the sun reflected from raindrops. For us the truths we learn from the Word are spiritual raindrops, and when we realize that the Lord is speaking to us in them, they become shining and beautiful and many-colored.

Now read Ezekiel 1:5-14. The "living creatures" Ezekiel saw are the same "beasts" which John saw. In fact the Greek word translated "beasts" [KJV] would be better translated "living creatures." See if you can remember from our lesson on Ezekiel what the lion, the calf, the man, and the eagle picture. These living creatures are not actual, even in the spiritual world: they are "cherubim," symbolic figures representing the protecting power which divine providence exercises through the letter of the Word. That is why they are said to be "full of eyes before and behind," because the Lord sees everything, past, present, and future. Their wings picture the power of the Word to lift out thoughts above the earth.

The twenty-four elders in white garments represent all the good people who have made their thoughts clean by learning the truth, and the crowns of gold show that they have overcome their temptations by means of unselfish love. "Elders" is a name given to people in churches who are looked up to as wiser than others. If we live rightly, we all may grow to be "elders" in this sense, because we become wiser with every year. But if we do not live rightly, we do not become wise with age.

The chapter closes with the worship of the Lord by the creatures and the elders. So John was assured at the beginning of his vision that the Lord rules everything in heaven. He was to see some terrible dangers, and he needed to be sure from the start that the Lord would win the victory. We need to be sure of this, too. The book is written for us.

Basic Correspondences

a trumpet	=	the power of truth speaking
a throne	=	judgment
a lion	=	power of good or evil
a calf	=	natural affection
a man	=	wisdom
an eagle	=	understanding

Senior

This class will be interested in the fact that differences in belief and practice began early in the Christian Church, and also in the way in which the letter of the Word serves as a guard to the genuine truth within. They should learn that the whole book of Revelation is a prophecy of the end of the first Christian dispensation and the beginning of the New Church era.

The book of Revelation is also called the *Apocalypse*, which is a Greek word meaning "revelation." The Jews think of the Old Testament as composed of the Law and the Prophets. In the New

Testament the four Gospels may be thought of as the Law and the book of Revelation as the Prophets. For the "new covenant" for the Christian Church is given in the Gospel record of the Lord's life and teaching, and the book of Revelation is a prophecy of what would happen to the first Christian Church, founded on a literal interpretation of this new law, and a prophecy of the final coming of a new Christian Church when the true spiritual interpretation could be revealed to men.

The beginning of the external history of the first Christian Church is given us in the book of Acts and the twenty-one Epistles which, although they are books which lack the inner sense, are very valuable to all Christians not only as history but because they give us some idea of what the apostles themselves thought about the Lord's teaching. We do not study them in Sunday school because we should draw our instruction from the Word rather than from the thoughts of men, but you should become familiar with them because they contain many fine statements and much useful information and because they are regarded as authoritative by other Christians who do not have our doctrine of the Word.

John, as we learn from Revelation 1:9, was in exile on the island of Patmos. He was the last of the apostles. The Roman government had tried to suppress the Christian Church from the beginning, and tradition has it that all the apostles except John died a martyr's death. If this is true, no doubt John was providentially protected so that he might be the instrument through whom the Lord could give this final prophecy.

John's mind was led step by step into the prophetic details of his vision. First (chapter 1) he was given to see that the master whom he had followed in the world was indeed the almighty God. Then (chapters 2 and 3) by the messages to the seven churches under his care he was shown the inner condition of the groups of Christians which already existed and their relation to the future of the church.

Then, in the first verse of our chapter for today, we read that he saw a door opened in heaven and heard the trumpet-like voice telling him to come up and see there a vision of things to come. And the first thing he saw was again the Lord, this time seated on His throne, the Lord executing judgment by means of the truth.

Every detail of the vision has to do with the beauty and power of truth: the throne itself, which represents judgment; the precious stones, which represent truths made clear and brilliant by love of them; the rainbow, truth as it is reflected in the knowledges of the letter of the Word which we receive in our minds; the white raiment of the elders, truth expressed in life, "the righteousness of saints" (Revelation 19:8); the sea of glass, the clear atmosphere of the ultimates of heaven; and the four "beasts" or cherubim, which picture the Lord's protection of inner truth by means of the letter of the Word.

The chapter should be compared with Ezekiel's vision (Ezekiel 1 and 10), Isaiah's (Isaiah 6:1-3), Daniel's (Daniel 7:9-10); and with the vision granted to Moses and the elders of Israel at Sinai (Exodus 24:10).

John needed this vision of the glory and power of the truth he was to proclaim. He was to see terrible things portrayed, but he knew from the beginning that the armies of evil would inevitably fail.

We need this reassurance also. Our world today is shaken by fear of the future. Evil forces seem to be abroad, and the voices which speak for love and peace seem weak. But the Lord is with those who proclaim His truth. They may have great tribulation, but they will conquer in the end. "For there is no restraint to the Lord to save by many or by few." (I Samuel 14:6) Each of us can do a great deal of good in our world today by speaking and living without fear, believing in the Lord's Word with its laws and its promises, and putting our whole trust in Him. We can worship every Sunday with the very words of this vision: "Holy, holy, holy, Lord God Almighty, which was, and is, and is to come." So we help to establish the Lord's kingdom on earth. We cannot establish it by looking to men for wisdom.

Adult

The relation of the Acts and Epistles to the Word is important for all adults because we hear so much emphasis placed on the Epistles by non-New Church people. Many interesting points are suggested in the sections from the *Apocalypse Revealed*, which may be read and discussed one by one.

In our study of the Gospel we saw how little the apostles, devoted though they were, understood the Lord's teaching, and how prone they were to forget things that He told them, and also at the end how weak was the flesh, however willing the spirit may have been. Only their contact with Him after the resurrection and their witness of His ascension (Mark 16:19) could have inspired in them the courage and perseverance with which they afterward accomplished their assigned task of preaching the Gospel to all the world (Mark 16:15). The record of their accomplishment is preserved for us in the book of the Acts of the Apostles, which is the basis of our knowledge of the beginnings of the Christian Church. Although the book of Acts—written by Luke—does not have an inner sense, and for this reason we do not study it in Sunday school, it gives us a certain background for our approach to the book of Revelation. It shows the bitterness of the opposition to the early Christians both by the Jews and by the Romans, and it also shows that the apostles did not always agree as to just what the teachings of the Lord were and how they should be applied in the daily life. The Epistles are further evidence of this, and while they contain many fine and helpful statements and much valuable information, we must still for our doctrine go to the Word itself.*

Tradition says that all of the eleven apostles except John were martyred. John, the youngest of them, was the only one who lived to very old age. No doubt he was providentially protected that he might be the instrument through whom the great prophetic vision might be recorded which concludes our Word. This vision is thought to have been given him in the year A.D. 95, when he was about ninety years of age. Although he was living in exile on the island

---

*But several New Church doctrines are succinctly *stated* in the Epistles. —*Ed.*

of Patmos, he was still looked to as the head of seven churches in Asia Minor. From the messages given him for these churches (chapters 2 and 3) we learn that even at that early date the different groups of Christians had developed different characteristics and ideas. Although we recognize these messages as applying in their inner meaning to the different types of Christian discipleship in all times, still they should show us how foolish it is for anyone to imagine that unanimity of belief and practice is possible today. One of the lessons of our chapter for today is that the Lord provides in the letter of the Word a guard over its inner truths for the very purpose of permitting differences of interpretation. In AR 239 Swedenborg says: "The sense of the letter of the Word serves as a guard for the genuine truths which lie within; and the guard consists in this, that the literal sense can be turned hither and thither, that is, can be explained according to everyone's apprehension, without its internal being hurt or violated; for no harm ensues from the literal sense being understood differently by different people; but it does harm when the Divine truths which are within are perverted, for it is by this that the Word suffers violence. To prevent this, the literal sense guards, and it guards with those who are in falsities from religion, but yet do not confirm them, for from these the Word suffers no violence. This guard is signified by 'cherubim,' and is also described by them in the Word."

The whole vision is a vision of judgment, a picture of how divine providence by means of the truths of the Word protects the good and separates them from the evil. This judgment goes on in each individual, but we know that the book of Revelation particularly describes the judgment which was to take place at the end of the first Christian dispensation, and the beginning of a new dispensation through the opening of the Word. Chapter 4, Swedenborg says, "treats of the arrangement and preparation of all things in heaven for the judgment, to be executed from the Word, and according to it; likewise concerning the acknowledgment that the Lord is the only judge" (AR introduction to chapter 4).

In studying this chapter we should begin by comparing it with earlier visions of very similar nature: Exodus 19:16, 24:9-10; Ezekiel 1 and 10; Isaiah 6:1-3; and Daniel 7:9-10. If we wish to study it in greater detail we should go to the *Apocalypse Explained*, but we shall find a condensed explanation, including a very brief summary interpretation, in the *Apocalypse Revealed*. Here we shall note that the voice of the trumpet always pictures the power of truth speaking, the throne judgment, and the four "beasts" or cherubim the guard the Lord provides against profanation.

In AR 233 we read: "He who does not know the spiritual sense of the Word, and at the same time the genuine truths of the church, may believe, that when the Last Judgment shall come, the Lord will sit upon a throne, and that there will be other judges also upon thrones around Him. But he who knows the spiritual sense of the Word, and at the same time the genuine truths of the church, knows that the Lord will not then sit upon a throne, and that neither will there be other judges about Him; and further, that neither will the Lord judge anyone to hell, but that the Word will judge every one, the Lord moderating that all things may be done according to justice . . . 'Twelve' signifies all, and is predicated of the truths and goods of heaven and the church (n. 348); the same is signified by 'twenty-four'; therefore 'the twelve apostles' and the 'twenty-four elders' signify all things of the church; and 'twelve,' as also 'twenty-four thrones,' signify the all of judgment."

We are told in AR 237 that by the seven lamps are signified "the New Church in heaven and on earth from the Lord through the Divine truth proceeding from Him," just as by the seven stars and the seven lampstands in Revelation 1:20, and in AR 238 that "*Before the throne there was a sea of glass like unto crystal*, signifies the New Heaven from Christians who are in general truths from the literal sense of the Word." The New Heaven referred to in the last quotation is the heaven which was formed at the time of the Second Coming from all the good souls of the first Christian Church who are described in Revelation 6:9-11.

We recognize in verse 8 one of the familiar responses which is sung in some of our churches, and another in verse 11 which appears

in some of our responsive services. When we sing these, it will be
helpful to remember that they are sung in heaven also and especially
that if we sing them with sincere hearts, the Lord can make them
a bulwark for us against many temptations.

═══════

From the Writings of Swedenborg

Apocalypse Revealed, n. 231: "'A stone,' in the Word, signifies truth in ultimates, and 'a precious stone,' truth transparent from good (n. 915). There are
two colors fundamental of the rest in the spiritual world, the color white and
the color red. The color white derives its origin from the light of the sun in
heaven, thus from spiritual light, which is shining white; and the color red
derives its origin from the fire of the sun there, thus from celestial light, which
is flamy . . . This is the reason why precious stones, in the Word, signify such
things as are of the truth of wisdom, or of the good of love, and that 'the
jasper,' because it is shining white, signifies the things which are of the truth
of wisdom; and 'the sardius,' because it is red, the things which are of the
good of love."

Apocalypse Revealed, n. 232: "In the spiritual world there appear rainbows
of many kinds, they appear of various colors as upon the earth, and they
appear of one color; here of one color, because it is said 'like unto an emerald.'
. . . The Divine sphere which surrounds the Lord is from His Divine love, and
at the same time from His Divine wisdom, which, when it is represented in
the heavens, appears in the celestial kingdom red like a ruby, in the spiritual
kingdom blue like the lapis lazuli, in the natural kingdom green like the emerald; everywhere with ineffable splendor and radiance."

Apocalypse Revealed, n. 238: "*And before the throne there was a sea of glass
like unto crystal*, signifies the New Heaven from Christians who are in general
truths from the literal sense of the Word. In the spiritual world there appear
atmosphere, and also waters, like as in our world; the atmospheres, in which
the angels of the highest heaven dwell, are as it were ethereal; the atmospheres,
in which the angels of the middle heaven dwell, are as it were aerial; and the
atmospheres, in which the angels of the lowest heaven dwell, are as it were
aqueous; and these last appear as seas at the boundaries of heaven, where they
dwell who are in general truths from the literal sense of the Word. . . . by 'the
sea of glass' which was before the throne, is meant the church among those
who are at the boundaries . . . It is called 'a sea of glass like unto crystal,'
from the pellucidity of the Divine truth proceeding from the Lord."

═══════

Suggested Questions on the Lesson

J. What books in the Bible tell about the beginnings of the Christian Church?
Acts, Epistles

J. Why do we not study these books in Sunday school? *they do not have an inner sense*

P. What book are we now studying? *Revelation*

J. By what other name is this book called? *Apocalypse*

J. What is it about? *visions*

P. To whom were these visions given? *the apostle John*

J. Where was John and why? *Patmos, exiled*

P. What did John see first? *the risen Lord*

J. What messages were given him? *letters to seven churches*

P. In our chapter for today what did he see? *a throne*

J. Can you describe the throne? *[see verses 2-5]*

J. How many elders were there? *twenty-four*

P. How many creatures were there? *four*

P. What faces did they have? *lion, calf, man, eagle*

J. Where have we learned of beasts like these before? *Ezekiel 1*

J. By what other name do we know them? *cherubim*

J. What did they cry before the Lord? *Holy, holy, holy*

J. Where have we heard these words before? *a familiar hymn, the Sanctus, the Trisagion*

I. What does a throne represent? *judgment*

S. What do the four beasts represent? *protecting power of divine providence:*
    lion   = power for good
    calf   = natural affections
    man   = wisdom
    eagle = understanding

THE SEALED BOOK
Revelation 5

As the vision in this chapter goes right on from that of our last lesson, simple questions on the review are the best possible introduction.

Doctrinal Points
The New Church is founded upon the opened Word.
The Lord opened the seals of the book by revealing to Swedenborg the inner meanings of the Word.

Notes for Parents
The book seen in vision in the Lord's hand is the book we have been studying all year, the Word of God, and if the Lord had not fulfilled this vision, we could not have had the teaching we have had this year. There would be no new understanding of the Word in the world, and no New Church.

For the New Church is founded on the opened Word. Six hundred years before the time of John's vision the Lord had said to the prophet Daniel: "But thou, O Daniel, shut up the words, and seal the book, even to the time of the end: many shall run to and fro, and knowledge shall be increased." And when the Lord was in the world, He said to His disciples: "I have yet many things to say unto you, but ye cannot bear them now." Many centuries had to pass after John's time before men's knowledge had increased to the point where the Lord could finally open the sealed book and show us the things which are hidden within it. But He did do this nearly two hundred years ago.

In John's prophetic vision the seven seals were opened one after another, and strange and dreadful things happened with the opening of each seal. You know how it is with a truth from the Word, such a truth, for example, as "Thou shalt not steal." You learned

it when you were a little child and at first it was just words. But
you were taught that you must not take toys or candy or money
that belongs to someone else, and that you have to make yourself
remember and obey. Then someday you realized that saying bad
things about someone else is stealing, too—stealing his reputation—
and you have had to learn to control your temptation to idle gossip.
Then you were perhaps tempted to take credit for some good
work which someone else had actually done, and it came home to
you that that is stealing, too. Finally it may have been pointed out
to you that since the Lord alone is good and wise and everything
comes to us from Him, taking credit to ourselves for any goodness
or knowledge we may seem to have is really stealing from the
Lord. And that gives us the hardest struggle of all. So one by one
the seals which closed those four words—"Thou shalt not steal"—
have been opened, and with each opening came a deeper temptation
and a more severe conflict. But the rewards of victory, as we shall
see, are greater each time.

Primary

Even the young children should be able to picture the throne with the Lord
sitting upon it, the elders, and the living creatures. Be sure they know that the
one on the throne was the Lord, that the book was the Word, and that the
Lord really has opened the Word for us now so that we can understand its
true meaning. Verse 14 offers a good opportunity to be sure that the children
know what we mean when we say "Amen."

Do you remember how John saw the Lord sitting on a beautiful
throne in heaven, with twenty-four elders and four cherubim bowing down before Him? Our chapter for today goes right on from
there.

What do you suppose the Lord had in His hand? Let us read our
chapter for today. [Read Revelation 5.] The scroll or book was
the Word of God. You know that there are some things in the Bible
which everyone can understand—like the ten commandments, for
example. But there are a great many things in it which no one can

really understand without the Lord's help. There are of course a great many things which grown people can understand although little children like you cannot. But even grown people always have more that they need to learn from the Lord, because He is the only one who knows everything.

Do you remember what a parable is?

If we could not understand the inside meaning of a parable, we might say it was sealed.

The whole Word is really a parable because it has an inner meaning.

Its inner meaning was sealed for hundreds and hundreds of years.

But John's vision showed him that someday the Lord would open the seals.

And many years after the time of John the Lord did open the Word.

He showed the inner meaning to a man named Emanuel Swedenborg.

And He told Swedenborg to write what he learned in books and publish them.

Swedenborg obeyed; so now we may all learn about this inner meaning.

In our chapter the Lord is also called the Lamb.

He is a Lion because He is strong and powerful.

He is a Lamb because He is gentle and innocent.

In verse 14 what did the creatures say?

Amen means "So be it."

When we say "Amen" at the end of a prayer, it means that we will do all we can to help the Lord make the prayer come true.

The Lord does not explain things to us until we are ready to understand and to try to live according to what He tells us. Let us read what the Lord said to the prophet Daniel long, long before the time of John. [Read Daniel 12:4.] The book was sealed because people did not want to obey its teachings. You have learned already in your lessons this year that the whole of the Word of God is a parable, a story with another meaning inside of it.

The time finally came when there were people in the world who were ready and willing to understand this inside meaning. Then the Lord could open the sealed book. This is what the Lord was showing John in his vision. As you grow older, if you are good children and really want to learn from the Lord, He will help you to learn more and more of what the Bible really means.

Junior

The details of the vision should be impressed on this class with as much explanation as they are able to understand. Have them look up Daniel 12:4 and tell them why the book was sealed. Then tell them how this vision of the opening of the book was fulfilled in the Second Coming and what a privilege we have today in being able to study the inner meaning of the Word.

You remember that a throne is a picture of judgment. John was to be shown a symbol picture of the way in which people on earth would receive or reject the Lord, and of how they would be judged and what their eternal life would be. For the Lord tells all of us about Himself and about how we should live, and the way in which we use this knowledge determines our lives, not only in this world but in the other world forever.

When a case is brought into court in this world, the first thing that must be done is to try to find out the facts. But our lives are made up not only of the things we do which everyone can see, but also of our hidden thoughts and feelings. These are not easy to find out. Sometimes we don't even know them ourselves. But the Lord does, and in the other world they all come into view.

So in John's vision the beginning of the judgment was the opening of the book of life. The scroll or book which John saw in the Lord's hand was the Word. In the Bible as we have it the Lord's thoughts and feelings are clothed in thoughts and words which we can understand—which even evil people can understand. There are things in the letter of the Word which appeal to the good and things which strike home to the evil. Each one sees in it what meets his own needs.

We can get some idea of how the Word is written if we remember that sometimes we cannot say to someone—a child, for instance—just what we mean, and yet our real meaning is within what we say, and an older person hearing us will understand the real meaning. In the same way, the Word is a book with an outside and an inside meaning, and the inside cannot be opened except to people who can understand it. And since the inside meaning of the Word is full of love and truth from the Lord, the things which make people unable to understand it are selfishness and worldliness. So as people became more and more evil, the Word had to be sealed. Read Daniel 12:4. But when the Lord came into the world, a new upward trend among men began, and this in time made it possible for the Word to be opened again. Then the Lord made His Second Coming, and the New Church is founded on the opened Word.

In our chapter for today John is shown in vision how the Word is to be opened.

Why did John weep?
What did the angel tell him?

It is the Lord who is called the Lion of the tribe of Judah, and He is called a lion because of His power. He also appears to John as a "Lamb as it had been slain" to picture that the Lord was perfect innocence although He was put to death by men, as we recently learned.

What was peculiar about the Lamb?
This means that the Lord is all-powerful and all-seeing.
What did the creatures and elders have?
What are the golden vials full of odors said to be?
What was the new song they sang?

We repeat these same words and also the ones later in the chapter in some of our responsive services in church. When we take our service from the letter of the Word, we may know that we are using words which have an inner meaning and which have been given us by the Lord Himself.

In verse 14, what do the creatures say? *Amen* means "So be it." Whenever we say "Amen" at the end of a prayer or sing it at the end of a hymn, we should remember that we are giving our solemn consent to the words we have just been saying.

———

Intermediate

Explain the correspondence of the details of the vision, stressing the fact that only the Lord could open the Word. Relate this to the New Church belief in regard to Swedenborg's function as the instrument of the Second Coming.

Our chapter for today continues the vision which begins in chapter 4. We remember that a throne is a symbol of judgment; so we recognize that what John was to see was a judgment which would take place on the people of the Christian Church. You can see that it is quite fitting that this vision should come directly after the messages of rebuke and warning which John had been given for his seven churches in Asia Minor. In the New Church we accept Swedenborg's statement that the great judgment here prophesied, which is called the Last Judgment, actually took place in Swedenborg's day. He says that all the men and women from the first Christian Church who passed from this world from the time of the Lord's ascension to the time of this judgment had been allowed to live in "imaginary heavens" until the "fullness of time" when the judgment could take place. The fullness of time was the time when men had reached such a stage of development that the inner meaning of the Word could safely be opened to them.

The judgment was brought about, just as our chapter for today pictures it, by the Lord's opening the sealed scroll or book. The book is the Word. It is written "within and on the backside." That is, it has an obvious surface meaning and an inner meaning. The inner meaning was sealed, except for the glimpses which the Lord gave His disciples when He was in the world, and occasional verses in which it is allowed to come to the surface. Such a verse is verse 8 of our chapter for today, in which we are told plainly what the "vials full of odors" picture. The twelfth chapter of Daniel tells about the sealing of the book and the reason for it.

In John's vision the sealed book is in the right hand of the Lord as He sits on the throne of judgment. Sooner or later our lives must be judged as to whether or not we have lived according to the teachings of the Word. Read also chapter 20, verses 11 and 12. The more deeply we can see into the Word, the more clearly our real motives and thoughts come to view. So our chapter is followed by others telling of things that happen as the seals are opened, one after another, until finally all who are at heart opposed to the unselfish love which is the inmost of the Word have turned from its light and found their places in the hells, and all who are in harmony with it have been prepared to enter the gates of the holy city.

The Lord on the throne is the Lord as He is in Himself above our power of comprehension. The lion of the tribe of Judah is the Lord in the power of His love, reaching down to teach us the way of life. The lamb "as it had been slain" is the Lord as He came into the world and died for us, leaving us free to choose the believe in Him or not.

The Lord alone could open the seals. Swedenborg tells us again and again that what he was allowed to write down of the inner meaning of the Word did not come from his own mind, but was revealed through him by the Lord, and that this opening of the Word to his understanding and through him to ours was actually the promised Second Coming of the Lord. At the same time that the book was unsealed in this world, it could be unsealed in the spiritual world; so the Last Judgment took place there. From that time on, everyone who has passed from this world into the spiritual world has been free to make his choice there, which is his judgment, because the necessary truth is open and available, but he makes it according to the kind of life he has learned to love while he was in this world.

In addition to the "golden vials full of odors, which are the prayers of saints"—we may think too of the golden altar of incense in the holy place—we should know that harps picture "confession of the Lord from spiritual truths." Earlier in this course we spoke of different kinds of musical instruments mentioned in the Word, and you will perhaps remember that stringed instruments symbolize our expressions of truth and wind instruments expressions of love.

We should notice also the passages in verses 12 and 13 which we use in some of our responsive services.

Basic Correspondences

a lamb = innocence
golden vials full of odors = the prayers of saints or worship from spiritual good

a harp = confession of the Lord
from spiritual truth

_____

Senior

The opened Word as the basis of the New Church is the important lesson for
the young people. They need to see this clearly and to gain a sense of the
privilege and responsibility of being New Churchmen.

A throne is always a symbol of judgment, and this vision and
the chapters following it picture the judgment which was to be
made on the first Christian Church, the judgment which Swedenborg says actually took place in his day at the time of the Second
Coming. For the Second Coming was the opening of the seals,
and with it the opening of the inner life of motive and thought
necessary to the establishment of a truly Christian Church.

Without a knowledge of the spiritual sense of the Word one
might think that in this chapter the one who sat on the throne and
the lion of the tribe of Judah and the lamb were three different
persons. But they are three aspects of the divine being. The one
who sat on the throne—of whom we are given no definite description—is God as He is in Himself, the Infinite beyond our comprehension. The lion of the tribe of Judah is the Lord as to the power
of His divine love. The lamb is the divine humanity, in which God
manifested Himself to us, and continues to manifest Himself. The
words "as it had been slain" refer not only to the crucifixion, but
to the way in which the Christian Church finally destroyed all true
understanding of the divine humanity by the separation of God
into three different persons and the doctrine of the vicarious atonement—the doctrine that Christ died to satisfy the wrath of an
angry God and pay the penalty for our sins in our place. The lamb
had seven horns and seven eyes to picture the omnipotence and
the omniscience of the Lord in His divine humanity.

The explanation of the "golden vials full of odors" in verse 8
as "the prayers of saints" is one of the places where the inner
meaning of the letter is clearly stated in the letter itself. It is a good

passage to remember, and we should think of it in connection with the golden altar of incense in the holy place of the tabernacle and with all the laws for the offering of incense. In verse 11 Swedenborg says that *myriad* (translated "ten thousand") stands for truths and *thousand* for goods because "a myriad is the greater number, and a thousand a less, and truths are manifold, but goods are simple." So the multitude of angels picture the hosts of heaven—all those who worship the Lord from the good of love or from the truth of faith.

This whole chapter should impress upon us the fact that the Lord alone could have opened the Word; hence, that what we are told in the writings of Swedenborg is from the Lord, and is merely transmitted by Swedenborg as a human agent, "servant of the Lord Jesus Christ," as he calls himself. Our church is a small organization from a worldly standpoint, and sometimes when you go out into the world—especially if you live away from your own church—you may begin to wonder if it really has the truth, and if other churches are not just as good. When such doubts come into your mind, remember this chapter of Revelation and remember that only the New Church acknowledges the opening of the Word and has access to its inner meaning in any consistent way. This knowledge is available to everyone in the writings of Swedenborg, but accepting it means accepting the fact that Swedenborg was the human instrument of the Second Coming of the Lord, and very few people will even consider such a possibility. What Swedenborg calls "the pride of self-intelligence" is very strong in the world. Once one has really seen for himself, however, how wonderful the inner meaning of the Word is and how it helps us to understand the meaning of life and ourselves and our relation to the Lord, and how it helps us to see what is right and to do it, there is no room left for doubt.

Later we shall carry on our thought from this chapter into our study of the last part of the twentieth chapter which brings the judgment home to each of us individually. Actually we are judging ourselves from day to day as we choose either to live for self, closing our minds to the truth when it comes to us, or as we seek to learn more and more of the truth and examine ourselves more and more deeply in the effort to write the Word of the Lord "on our hearts," so that when we come into the other world and are given to see ourselves clearly "inside out," we shall find that our books tally with the book of life.

Adult

The reason for the sealing of the Word and for the time chosen by the Lord for its opening should be discussed, and also the reason why it is often so difficult and even impossible to interest others in the truths which mean so much to us.

At the beginning of the explanation of this chapter in the *Apocalypse Revealed* Swedenborg says that its general meaning is "that the Lord in the Divine Human will execute judgment from the Word and according to it, because He Himself is the Word; and that this is acknowledged by all in the three heavens."

The Word itself contains many references to a "book of life." There are also statements as to the actual writing of the Word in its letter, such as Deuteronomy 31:9 and Jeremiah 36:1-4. Nor is our chapter for today the only place where we are told that the Word has been a sealed book. Isaiah 29:9-12 is a clear picture of the inability of men to understand the Word by means of their own unenlightened reason. And Daniel (12:4) is told to "shut up the words, and seal the book, even to the time of the end." That the prophets themselves did not understand the meaning of the words which were given them to write appears from the same chapter of Daniel (12:8-9): "And I heard, but I understood not: then said I, O my Lord, what shall be the end of these things? And he said, go thy way, Daniel: for the words are closed up and sealed till the time of the end." It is evidence from these verses in the letter that the Word was purposely sealed by the Lord, and that it could not be opened except by the Lord, and not until men had reached a particular stage of development. From the very letter of Scripture, therefore, we should see that there is something written within the Word which can never be read without some divinely revealed key. Our chapter for today gives us this truth in unmistakable terms.

The New Church is the church of the opened Word. It believes that the inspired portions of the Scriptures are divine truth spoken by the Lord but necessarily—in order to reach men—clothed with corresponding forms of angelic and earthly thought and expression, just as light, coming to earth from the sun, is modified by the atmosphere and broken up and reflected in various ways by the natural forms which receive and transmit it. The letter of the Word is the outmost expression of divine truth. Being given through the minds of men in both good and evil states, it shows the truth as it appears both to the good and to the evil. Thus often the real truth takes on a directly opposite expression. That is why, for example, the Lord is sometimes spoken of as being angry, jealous, and vengeful, and as punishing and destroying. We can easily understand this if we will think how arbitrary and hard our parents' loving admonitions seemed to us as children, when we were bent on disobeying. Or we may hear critics of the Word find fault with the commandments because they are in the negative form; but we may answer that to be told not to steal, for instance, is no hardship except to one who wants to steal. Truth inevitably seems hard to those whose desires are evil, and the only way in which the Lord can reach them is by showing the consequences of their evils, just as genuine love of parents for their children must express itself in checking their evils as well as in encouraging their good deeds. The letter of the Word is written for all sorts and conditions of men in all times, and there is enough genuine truth in the surface meaning to show any sincere person the way to salvation.

And the letter of the Word is absolutely necessary. As Swedenborg says in the *Doctrine of the Sacred Scripture*, n. 30, the sense of the letter of the Word "is the basis, the containant, and the support of the spiritual sense and of its celestial sense." Without the letter of the Word divine truth would be dissipated just as the contents of a pitcher is spilled and wasted if the pitcher is broken.

The book was "sealed." But it was promised that it should be opened at "the time of the end" and it was said, "many shall run to and fro, and knowledge shall be increased." (Daniel 12:4). The New Church believes that "the time of the end" when the book should be opened came in the middle of the eighteenth century, when people had mentally "run to and fro" and had increased in worldly knowledge to the point where good people with a sincere desire to know the Lord could no longer believe all the letter of the Word to be literal fact. At that time, through the prepared mind of Emanuel Swedenborg, the Lord Himself opened the Scriptures, by revealing once more the knowledge of correspondences. This involved not only verse-by-verse explanations of portions of the Word, but the revelation of detailed realities of the spiritual world and its relation to this world, and also doctrines which, drawn from the letter of the Word itself, enable us to read it with enlightenment and to understand the Lord and His purposes and our relation to Him. This was the promised Second Coming of the Lord, a coming not in the flesh, but in His Word—in the "clouds of heaven"—opening its inner meaning and so fulfilling His promise to His disciples: "I have yet many things to say unto you, but ye cannot bear them now." (John 16:12)

Our chapter tells us that "no man in heaven, nor in earth, neither under the earth, was able to open the book," and Swedenborg claims no credit to himself: he says that the spiritual sense was revealed to him by the Lord alone as he read the Word (TCR 779-780). In SS 25-26 he tells us that no one can see the spiritual sense "except from the Lord alone, nor unless from Him he is in genuine truths," and he also tells us that "for a long time the spiritual sense will not be recognized, and that this is entirely owing to those who are in falsities of doctrine, especially concerning the Lord, and who therefore do not admit truths," and that the conflicts described in the book of Revelation picture the opposition in the world to the spiritual sense. All those who have received with delight the teachings of the New Church with regard to the Word and have endeavored to share this delight with relatives and friends attached to the doctrines of other churches have had personal experience of this opposition. Both Ezekiel (2:9-10; 3:1-3) and John (Revelation 10:8-10) in vision were told to eat a little book, and both found it sweet as honey in the mouth. But as the angel told John and he proved by experience, "It shall make thy belly bitter." Our first taste of the opened Word is full of delight and promise, but if we "eat it up," if we sincerely try to live it out, we must be prepared to take the bitter with the sweet. This is the challenge to our sincerity and courage. And most people shrink from anything which promises to make drastic changes in their ways of thought and life.

Our chapter presents a beautiful picture of the power of the Lord through the Word and of the worship of the Lord in the heavens. The "Lion of the tribe of Juda, the Root of David" pictures the Lord as to the power of His love. "A Lamb as it had been slain" is "the Lord as to His Human, not acknowledged in the church to be Divine" (AR 269). The seven horns picture His omnipotence and the seven eyes His omniscience. The harps in the hands of the beasts and elders represent "confession of the Lord's Divine Human from spiritual goods" (AR 277). The new song "signifies the acknowledgment and glorification of the Lord, that He alone is Judge, Redeemer, and Saviour, thus the God of heaven and earth" (AR 279). "And the four beasts said, Amen" signifies "Divine confirmation from the Word" (AR 292). We recall that the beasts or cherubim picture the Lord's protection of inner truth by the letter of the Word and the twenty-four elders all who are in the Lord's church in the heavens and on earth.

─────

From the Writings of Swedenborg

Apocalypse Revealed, n. 276: "*Having every one of them harps*, signifies confession of the Lord's Divine Human from spiritual truths. It is known that confessions of Jehovah were made in the temple at Jerusalem by singing, and at the same time by instruments of music which corresponded; the instruments were principally trumpets and timbrels, and psalteries and harps; the trumpets and timbrels corresponded to celestial goods and truths, and the psalteries and harps to spiritual goods and truths; the correspondences were with their sounds."

Apocalypse Revealed, n. 277: "*And golden vials full of incense*, signifies confession of the Lord's Divine Human from spiritual good. The reason why 'incense' signifies worship from spiritual goods, but in this instance confession from such goods, is because the principal worship in the Jewish and Israelitish Church consisted in sacrifices and incense; wherefore there were two altars, one for sacrifices and the other for incense; the latter altar was within the tabernacle, and was called the golden altar, but the former was without the tabernacle, and was called the altar of burnt offering; the reason was, because there are two kinds of goods, from which all worship exists, celestial good and spiritual good: celestial good is the good of love to the Lord, and spiritual good is the good of love towards the neighbor. Worship by sacrifices was worship from celestial good, and worship by incense was worship from spiritual good. . . . Likewise in Matthew 2:11, 'The wise men from the east opened their treasures, and offered to the Lord recently born, gold, frankincense, and myrrh.' The reason why they offered these three was, because 'gold' signified celestial good, 'frankincense' spiritual good, and 'myrrh' natural good, and from these three goods all worship is made."

Suggested Questions on the Lesson

P. What did John see when a door was opened in heaven? *a throne*

P. Who sat on the throne? *the Lord*

J. How many elders were there? *twenty-four*

P. How many creatures were there? *four*

J. What faces did they have? *lion, calf, man, eagle*

J. What is another name for these creatures? *cherubim*

J. What did they say when they worshiped the Lord? *Holy, holy, holy*

P. In our lesson for today what did the Lord have in His right hand? *scroll or book*

P. Why did John weep? *no one worthy to open seals*

P. Who could open the book? *Lion of Judah*

J. Can you describe the Lamb that John saw? *as though slain, seven horns, seven eyes*

J. What did the elders and the beasts have in their hands? *lamps, incense*

J. How many angels were singing? *myriads*

J. What can you tell about the new song they sang? *"Worthy is the Lamb . . ."*

P. What did the four creatures say after the song? *Amen*

P. What does *Amen* mean?   *So be it*

I. What is John's vision in the rest of this book about?   *judgment of all*

S. What does the New Church believe about the opening of the book?
   that the Lord has opened the book, making inner meaning available

THE FOUR HORSEMEN
Revelation 6

In all the classes the teacher should summarize briefly the first five chapters, stressing the throne, the four beasts, the sealed book, and the lamb, as a preparation for the visions which followed.

―――――

Doctrinal Points
All the prophecies in the Word relate to things which affect the souls of people.

The effects of the prophetic Word differ according to the states of mind and heart of people.

No one can understand the Word without doctrine.

―――――

Notes for Parents
Ever since the book of Revelation was written—about A.D. 90—the Christian world has been busy trying to interpret it. It is the prophetical part of the New Testament and, unlike the books of the Old Testament prophets, there is no possibility of associating any of it except the first three chapters with events of John's own time. It obviously foretells things to come.

Many attempts have been made to connect various wars and battles which have taken place during Christian history with some of these visions of John, and such attempts are still being made. The four horsemen in our chapter for today have especially intrigued men's imagination and even—not too many years ago—furnished the material for a best seller.

We ought to realize, however, that the Bible is given to teach us spiritual lessons and that all the prophecies in the Bible are pictures not of worldly happenings but of things which happen in people's souls under certain conditions. You may remember in our lesson about Jesus on the road to Emmaus, how the Lord "opened the understanding" of the apostles to understand the things concerning

Himself in all the Scriptures. The "seals" which are opened in our chapter for today are seals with which the Lord closes these inner things in the Bible until He finds people ready to make some good use of what is there. People who do not want to live according to the Lord's laws are better off without the knowledge, for sin is doing what we know to be wrong.

This is what the Lord is trying to impress upon us in our chapter. The opening of the seals affects people differently according to the states of mind and heart in which they are, and the four horses and their riders are pictures of different ways in which people receive the truth about their souls as it is presented to them in the Word of God. (1) Some people welcome all the truth they can learn and use it to discover and correct their faults and to help them live as the Lord would have them live. This kind of reception is symbolized by the white horse. (2) Some people like to learn the truth only in order to condemn other people, without applying it to themselves at all. This is pictured by the red horse. (3) Some are not interested in learning anything from the Bible about their souls, but like to pick out a verse here and there and haggle over its literal meaning, as if that was all there was to the Bible. This attitude is represented by the black horse. (4) And then there are those who reject the Bible altogether because they have no intention of doing anything except get all they can for themselves in this world; so the Lord cannot reach their souls at all: they are spiritually dead. This state of mind is portrayed by the pale horse.

The Lord has given the Bible to all of us and the truth is there, deeper and deeper truth as we study it and try to live it out. Each of us is free to choose between the Lord and self, and when we go into the other world, the judgment is according to our own choice. This is what the rest of our chapter teaches us.

Primary

Center the lesson around the apostle John, reminding the children of the stories they have had in which he figured, and making clear that he was John the apostle, not John the Baptist. Then try to impress the children with the wonder of what the Lord let John see. Tell them the first visions and then read the lesson, trying to have them remember the colors of the horses in order. Deal with the place of the book of Revelation in the Bible. In reviewing the first five chapters, stress the fact that the sealed book is the Word and that the lamb is another name for the Lord. Try to make the children feel an eagerness for the understanding of these visions which they will have when they are older.

Do you remember how many men the Lord chose to be His apostles? There were twelve. The first four He chose were two sets of brothers, Peter and Andrew, and James and John. They were all fishermen, and the Lord told them that if they would follow Him, He would make them fishers of men. So they left their nets and followed Him.

John is the one we want to think about this morning. He was probably the youngest of the twelve, and is called "the beloved disciple." It was he together with his brother James and Peter who saw the Lord transfigured. After the Lord ascended to heaven, John was one of the four men chosen to write down an inspired account of the Lord's life. The other three were Matthew, Mark, and Luke. Do you know what we call these accounts?

But John was chosen for another great work when he was a very old man. He had been faithful to the task which the Lord had given to the apostles and had helped to spread the good news about the Lord through all the country called Asia Minor. Seven Christian churches had been formed there, and they all looked up to John as their leader.

But there were always people who hated the Christians, just as the scribes and Pharisees had hated Christ Himself. They did not put John to death, but they took him away from his people and put him out on an island, the island of Patmos, to live.

John was a very old man when he was given this revelation.
He was head of seven Christian churches which had been established in Asia Minor.
The first chapter of Revelation tells how the Lord appeared to John in Patmos.
His appearance was even more shining and wonderful than when John, with Peter and James, had seen Him transfigured.

But John recognized Him as the same Lord he had known so well.

First He gave John messages for the seven churches in Asia Minor.

Then He gave him a vision of a great throne with twenty-four elders sitting on seats around it.

And there were also four "beasts" or living creatures, which were cherubim, one like a lion, one like a calf, one like a man, and one like a flying eagle.

In the hand of the one who sat on the throne John saw a book sealed with seven seals, which only the Lord could open.

We have learned that this book was the Word.

Today our story is about the opening of some of the seals by the Lord, who is here called the lamb.

What did John see when the first seal was opened?

What did he see as each of the next three was opened?

When you are older, you will be able to learn what these four horses mean.

Junior

A review of the story of the first five chapters of Revelation should precede the actual lesson. Give the children a chance to tell anything they remember from other years. Then take up the four horses in some detail, finishing with a suggestion of their general meaning, and of the meaning of the rest of the chapter.

Which Gospel follows the Gospel of Luke?

Who was John?

John was probably the youngest of the apostles and he lived the longest. Several times in the Gospels he is called "the disciple whom Jesus loved." There are many traditions concerning his later life and his work as an apostle, and it seems fairly well established that he finally made his home at Ephesus and was regarded as the head of the seven Christian churches which had been established in Asia Minor. Find the names of these seven cities on a map of the New Testament world.

See also if you can find on the map the island of Patmos. For many years the Christians were feared and hated by the rulers of the countries where they lived, just as the Lord Himself had been feared and hated by the chief priests and by the scribes and Pharisees. John is thought to have been about ninety years old when he was banished to the island of Patmos. He tells us the reason for his exile in Revelation 1:9. It was in Patmos that the Lord appeared to him in a glorious form (Revelation 1:12-16) and told him to write down all he saw and heard. Then He gave John messages for the seven churches and then a long and wonderful vision, which was a prophecy of what would happen in the souls of the people of the Christian Church as the centuries rolled on. What John wrote down we have in the last book of our Bible, the book of Revelation.

The first chapter is a vision of the risen and glorified Lord. Chapters 2 and 3 contain the messages to the seven churches. We learn from them that each of these churches was different from all the others and that each had its good points, but also that each had developed certain faults which the Lord wanted to point out to its people so that they might be corrected. He gave each church a warning, and made each one a special promise if it would repent and be faithful. In chapter 4 we have the vision of the great throne (which was a picture of judgment) with the twenty-four elders sitting on seats around it, and the four "beasts" or cherubim, the first like a lion, the second like a calf, the third like a man, and the fourth like a flying eagle. And they were all praising the one who sat on the throne. Finally in chapter 5 is the vision of the book sealed with seven seals, which was in the right hand of the one who sat on the throne, and the promise that the "Lion of the tribe of Juda," who also appeared as a lamb, would loose the seals and open the book. The book was the Word and the Lamb was the Lord Himself.

In our chapter for today we have the vision of the opening, one after another, of the first six seals, and what John saw each time.
What did John see when the first seal was opened?
What weapon did the horse's rider have?
What else was given him?
What was he to do?
What did John see when the second seal was opened?
What weapon did his rider have?
What power was given him?

What did John see when the third seal was opened?
What did his rider have in his hand?
What was he weighing?
What was he told not to do?
What did John see when the fourth seal was opened?
What was the name of his rider?
What power was given him?

You want to remember as much as you can about these four
horses, for ever since the book of Revelation was written people
have been wondering what they meant, and many guesses have
been made about it. You will even find books written about these
guesses. But the Lord has revealed through Swedenborg what the
four horses represent, and when you are older, you will be able
to study the meaning of every least part of this strange vision.
Perhaps you can remember now that the horses picture the different ways in which people understand the Word of God and the
effect that these different kinds of understanding have on the lives
of the people themselves and on the world. And you can remember
that the white horse pictures a true understanding. Read Revelation
19:11-13.

Do you remember how the Lord "opened the scriptures" to the
two disciples on the way to Emmaus, and that they said that as
they listened, their hearts burned within them? The opening of
the fifth seal tells us how good people feel when the Word is opened
so that its real meaning is seen. And the opening of the sixth seal
tells how this same revelation affects the bad people who do not
want the Lord's truth because it shows up the evils in their lives.

Intermediate

The correspondence of the opening of the seals one after another and of the
effect as pictured by the four horses and their riders is the major lesson for
this class. The teacher should study the details of the vision as given in the
Adult notes and be able to add to the general correspondence wherever the
young people show interest.

The book of Revelation, the last book in our Bible, is a wonder-

ful series of visions describing the inner states which would develop
in the people of the Christian Church as the years went on. You
may recall from earlier studies that these visions were given to the
apostle John when, as a very old man, he was living in exile on the
island of Patmos, off the coast of Asia Minor. John, of course, had
been among the apostles on the night of Resurrection day, when
the Lord appeared to them and opened their understanding that
they might understand the Scriptures. In his vision on Patmos he
was given to see how the truth in the Word, as it had been revealed
to men by the Lord's life on earth, would gradually uncover deeper
and deeper evils in men's hearts, and how some would choose to
obey the truth and fight their evils, and how others would choose
to deny the truth or to falsify it in one way or another so that
they might continue in their evils.

John first saw the wonderful vision of the Lord standing in the
midst of the seven lampstands, and was given messages of judgment and warning to the seven churches in Asia Minor over which
he had charge, and then he saw the vision of the great throne of
judgment and the twenty-four elders and the four creatures, and
then the vision of the book sealed with seven seals, which the lamb
was to open. Today we begin the vision of the opening of the seals.

The Bible is given us by the Lord to teach us how to live. He
promises that if we live according to its teachings, we shall be
happy both in this world and in heaven. Our common sense tells
us that this must be true. Then why don't we always want to learn
more and more of the truth and obey it? It is because we are selfish, and the Bible tells us that we must be unselfish. The more we
understand about the Bible, the deeper we have to look into our
own minds and hearts to find the selfishness and root it out.

So the opening of the seals in John's vision revealed greater and
greater evils. As the first four seals were opened, John saw a series
of horses with their riders. Horses in the Word picture intelligence,
or our higher reasoning powers. Our reasoning power is one of
our most useful faculties, isn't it? But sometimes we use it in the
wrong way—for instance, to help us get what we want even though

we know it is bad for us to have it. We can do this even with what we know of the Bible. So the different horses picture the ways in which different people use the Bible.

The white horse pictures a true understanding of it from a desire to live according to its teachings, for the Lord will always enlighten us if we read the Word with this desire. So his rider had a bow to fight with and a crown to show that he was able to win in temptation. He went forth conquering and to conquer. The red horse pictures the false understanding of the Bible which people have who use it to excuse their own faults and to condemn other people. Such an understanding hurts rather than helps us. Black is the opposite of white; so the black horse pictures no real understanding of the Bible at all because of a lack of desire to study it seriously as a revelation from God. People of this kind often make a great fuss about little details in the letter of the Word, as the scribes and Pharisees did, but do not actually care much about truth and goodness. Read Matthew 23:23-24.

Finally at the opening of the fourth seal, a "pale" horse came out. This is a picture of those who have lost both the understanding of the truth and the desire to do right. You may remember in the parable of the Great Supper about the man who had married a wife and said that therefore he could not come. There is no hope of saving such people, because there is nothing in either their minds or their hearts to which the Lord can appeal to change them. So the rider on that horse was called Death, because when we turn altogether from the Lord, there is no life in our souls. And "Hell followed with him."

The opening of the fifth seal showed all those who could be saved, and the opening of the sixth showed those who could not. These last wanted only to be hidden from the Lord, as we try to hide when we are doing something which we know to be wrong.

Basic Correspondences

the white horse = a true understanding of the Word
the red horse = the understanding of the Word
when we do not wish to be good

    the black horse = an understanding of the Word
                            in which there is no truth
    the pale horse = understanding destroyed as to
                            both truth and good

Senior

There is so much in this lesson that all the teacher can do is to give its general meaning and discuss the quotation from the writings as a small example of the detailed interpretation. Try to impress the young people with the importance of cultivating a desire for all the spiritual truth we can get, and with the wealth which the Lord has put at our disposal.

The book of Revelation is the inspired record of a long vision given to the apostle John near the end of his life, when he was in exile on the island of Patmos off the coast of Asia Minor. It is the strictly prophetic part of the New Testament and treats of the spiritual states through which the Christian Church would pass, of its gradual decline, the final judgment upon it, and the establishment of a new and lasting Christian Church, which is pictured as the holy city, New Jerusalem, coming down from God out of heaven.

The book begins with John's vision of the Lord standing in the midst of seven lampstands and the messages which the Lord gave John for the seven churches in Asia Minor over which he was head. What we need especially to remember from chapters 2 and 3 for the purpose of our lesson for today is the fact that even as early as the time of the giving of this vision—somewhere around A.D. 90—the individual Christian groups were developing in different directions and were losing their first faith and zeal. Each of the seven churches had its good points and its faults; each of the seven messages of the Lord was couched in different terms; each church received a different warning, and each was promised a different reward for fidelity. People are different. They do not see things just alike. The Lord gives us the truth in His Word in such a way that we may choose to believe as much as we are willing to live by, and He holds us responsible for making the choice and for governing our lives accordingly. The choice is an all-important one, for it determines our life to eternity.

Chapter 4 gives us the vision of the great throne, which is the symbol of judgment, and chapter 5 gives the added picture of the book sealed with seven seals, which only the "Lion of the tribe of Juda," the lamb, the Lord Himself could open. In our study of that lesson we referred to Revelation 20:11-12, in which the judgment was accomplished by comparing the "books" which we write by our daily lives with the "book of life." The difference between a good and a bad life is just in whether we truly wish to be led by the Lord or to be led by our own desires and thoughts.

The opening of the seven seals pictures the opening of our understanding to see what the Word really teaches. The opening of each seal judges people who are in one or another attitude of mind toward the Word. The four horses are four different ways of regarding the Word.

The white horse pictures a true understanding of the Word which the Lord will always give us if our purpose in reading it is to find out what He really says and how He wants us to live, so that we can obey and serve Him. The rider on the white horse is able to conquer in temptation. Later in the book of Revelation (Revelation 19:11-13) the white horse appears again, and his rider is called the Word of God.

The red horse pictures an understanding of the Word with no desire to obey it. Without the desire to apply the truth to the discovery and correction of our own faults, we use our intelligence and the truth which the Lord gives us in the Word in such a way that they work harm to others and to ourselves, for truth used for selfish purposes becomes falsified and destroys us.

The black horse pictures the use of the Word by those who have no understanding of its real meaning nor any real interest in it. This rider had a pair of balances and was weighing everything and paying a very small price for everything he received. This is the attitude of mind of the scribes and Pharisees, elaborating on the letter of the law and ignoring its spirit.

The pale horse pictures those who have lost both their understanding of the truth of the Word and their desire to do right. Because they have left themselves no way of approach to the Lord, they are riding to spiritual death.

The opening of the fifth and sixth seals reveals the states in which the good and the evil find themselves in the judgment. The good are humble and long to draw closer to the Lord. The evil try to hide from the face of the Lord. We can sometimes tell whether or not we are doing right by our willingness or unwillingness to have our thoughts and intentions seen by others.

Every detail of this vision has, as always, its particular meaning, which we can further study at length in Swedenborg's works on the Apocalypse. The quotation given at the end of this lesson is merely an example of what is there for us.

Adult

The meaning of the four horsemen emerges so clearly in the light of correspondence that a consecutive study of the opening of the six seals seems indicated for this class rather than the usual topical discussion. If possible, the teacher should take time to read the whole chapter in *Apocalypse Revealed*, noting the cross-references in the Word, which are of particular interest.

The "four horsemen of the Apocalypse" have caught the imagination of the Christian world for centuries. They have always been recognized as symbols of a progressive judgment, and many attempts have been made to interpret them in terms of one or another world crisis.

But the fact is that their application is spiritual, not material, and that they have to do with the inner states of all of us who live in this age of the Second Coming. For the judgment which followed the opening of the seals is the final judgment made possible by the opening of the inner meaning of the Word.

In the *Apocalypse Revealed* Swedenborg gives us this very brief summary of the meaning of this part of our chapter: "The exploration of those upon whom the final judgment is about to come, is treated of; and what their understanding of the Word had been is discovered and hence what was the state of their life: that there were those who were in truths from good (verses 1-2); who were without good (verses 3-4); who were in contempt for the truth (verses 5-6); and who were altogether vastated as to good and truth (verses 7-8)."

The first type are those who will live in the heavens. They accept the truths of the Word and use them in combat against their evils. See Revelation 19:11-13.

The second type understand the truth but have no desire to live according to it.

The third type have no interest in or understanding of the truth, but wish to appear good and so, like the Pharisees, keep the letter of the law and argue about it.

The fourth type are wholly given over to self-love and the falsities which favor it.

All the last three types are destructive, and the forms of destruction are pictured in the powers given to the three riders.

In sharp contrast to them, the rider on the white horse had a bow in his hand, which is a symbol of doctrine. It is often called to our attention in the writings that the Word cannot be understood without doctrine. It is also stated that doctrine must be drawn from the letter of the Word and confirmed thereby. People have sometimes interpreted this to mean that we do not need the spiritual sense in order to understand the Word. But it is also pointed out in the writings that all the various Christian sects, like the Israelitish Church before them, have based their beliefs on the letter of the Word. So the question arises, "How are we to know what is the true doctrine?" The writings give us the basis of the answer in n. 91 of the *Doctrine of the Sacred Scripture*: "It has been shown above that the Word cannot be understood without doctrine, and that doctrine is like a lamp that enables genuine truths to be seen, the reason of which is that the Word has been written entirely by correspondences, and consequently many things in it are appearances of truth and not naked truths; and many things also have been written in adaptation to the apprehension of the natural and even of the sensuous man, yet so that the simple may understand it in that the appearances of truth in the Word, which are truths clothed, may be caught at as naked truths, and when they are confirmed they become falsities. But this is done by those who believe themselves wise above others, although they are not wise, for being wise consists in seeing whether a thing is true before it is confirmed, and not in confirming whatever one pleases. The last is done by those who excel in a genius for confirming and are in the conceit of self-intelligence, but the former is done by those who love truths and are affected by them because they are truths, and who make them uses of the life, for these persons are enlightened by the Lord, and see truths by the light of the truths; whereas the others are enlightened by themselves and see falsities by the light of the falsities."

We do not come at the truth without effort on our part. We must continually study the Word and the writings. But our study must be carried on with the mind humble and open to the Lord, and with the desire to learn the truth—even if it does not support our preconceived opinion—so that we may direct our lives by it. The rider on the white horse was given a crown, which is the symbol of victorious combat. The combat is against evil and falsity primarily in ourselves.

The rider on the red horse has no desire to see or to correct his own evils. His sword is truth falsified by being used for self-advantage. He uses this sword against others, and so destroys peace, and kills. Read Zechariah 1:8-15.

We know that darkness always pictures ignorance. The rider on the black horse had a pair of balances, which signify the "estimation of truth and good," and the value he placed on the wheat and barley was very small. The wheat and barley here represent exterior good and truth. He is not allowed to "hurt" the oil and wine because they represent interior good and truth which are hidden from him so that they will not be profaned. For an interesting and illuminating comparison read AC 7601 concerning the plague of hail in Egypt which destroyed the flax and barley but was not allowed to destroy the wheat and spelt (KJV: *rie*).

Finally compare the rider on the pale horse with the third excuse in the parable of the Great Supper (Luke 14): "I have married a wife, and therefore I cannot come."

In thinking of the correspondences involved in this story, it is also interesting to remember that the four creatures, or cherubim, are mentioned in order with the appearance of the horses, and that the creatures are described in order in chapter 5 as being like a lion, a calf, a man, and a flying eagle. The lion is the symbol of power, and the rider on the white horse went forth conquering and to conquer. The calf is the symbol of natural goodness, which the rider on the red horse is able to destroy. The man is the symbol of the intellectual, for which the rider on the black horse has no use. And the eagle is the symbol of spiritual knowledges which are killed out of the mind by the rider on the pale horse.

In the last part of our chapter the opening of the fifth and sixth seals reveals the effect of the opening of the Word upon the good and the evil gathered in the spiritual world during the centuries of the first Christian Church. Swedenborg tells us that the permanent Christian heavens could not be formed until the Second Coming of the Lord had taken place and that until that time all the good from the Christian world were kept, guarded by the Lord, in a part of the spiritual world called "the lower earth." These are the "souls under the altar" (verse 9). The evil who had called themselves Christians and expected to be saved were kept in "imaginary heavens." These were the heavens which "departed as a scroll when it is rolled together" at the opening of the sixth seal. The evil then saw themselves as they really were and sought a place to hide from the face of the Lord.

========

From the Writings of Swedenborg

Apocalypse Revealed, nn. 315-316: "*A measure of wheat for a penny, and three measures of barley for a penny*, signifies because the estimation of good and truth is so small as to be scarcely anything. These are signified because by 'a measure (*choenix*)' which was the measure and the quantity measured, is signified quality, as above (314); by 'wheat' and 'barley' is signified good and truth; and by a penny (*denarius*) which is a very small coin, that they are held in little or no estimation . . . *And hurt not the oil and the wine*, signifies that it is provided by the Lord that the holy goods and truths, which lie interiorly concealed in the Word, shall not be violated and profaned. 'Oil' signifies the good of love, and 'wine' truth from that good, therefore 'oil' signifies holy good, and 'wine' holy truth."

Suggested Questions on the Lesson

P. What is the name of the last book in the Bible? *Revelation*

P. To whom was this revelation given? *the apostle John*

J. Do you remember what was the first thing John saw? *the risen Lord*

J. For whom was he given messages? *seven churches*

J. What great symbol of judgment did he see? *throne*

J. Who were seated around the throne? *twenty-four elders*

P. Who sat upon the throne? *the Lord (the lamb)*

J. What other creatures appeared in the vision? *cherubim*

P. What was in the right hand of the one who sat on the throne? *a scroll or book*

P. What was this book? *the Word*

P. With how many seals was it sealed? *seven*

J. Who could open it? *the Lord (lion of Judah, lamb)*

P. What did John see when the first seal was opened? *white horse*

P. What did he see when each of the next three seals was opened? *red, black, pale horses*

J. Who were seen when the fifth seal was opened? *those slain for the Word*

J. What happened when the sixth seal was opened? *earthquake, etc.*

S. What in general is pictured by the four horses? *different ways of regarding the Word*

I. What does the opening of the seals mean? *opening of inner sense of Word to our understanding*

THE SEVENTH SEAL
Revelation 8; 9

This is a rather difficult lesson to teach, because the interest is almost entirely in the details of the correspondence. It is suggested that in each of the three younger classes the teacher, after taking up the review, read from the Word at least chapter 8 and let questions and comments help to determine the direction of the discussion for the rest of the period.

―――――

Doctrinal Points
Judgment is the laying bare of our real spiritual states when faced with the truth about ourselves.
It is always divine truth that judges us.
The Lord cannot forgive us unless we repent of our evils.

―――――

Notes for Parents
Our chapters for today contain visions of disaster, and again we must realize that it is spiritual and not physical disaster which is pictured. If we remember that the giving of the ten commandments from Mount Sinai was heralded by "thunders and lightnings, and a thick cloud upon the mount, and the voice of the trumpet exceeding loud; so that all the people that was in the camp trembled," we shall see that the sounding of the trumpets from heaven is a symbol of the proclamation of divine truth, and its effect shows us the spiritual devastation which is wrought in the souls of men by indifference to divine truth and denial of it.

In this world it is possible for us to put on the appearance of goodness when we are not good at heart. We all like to have others admire us and we like to think well of ourselves. But goodness which is put on for this reason has no real goodness within it. It is all on the outside and is left behind with the body when we pass into the other world. There we are seen as we really are, and if we

242

have not learned to be genuinely humble and loving and God-fearing, our inner states appear in all their ugliness. Our selfish ambitions, our pride, our resentment against those who do not favor us, our desire to be served by others, are pictured by the strange and terrible locusts of John's vision, and the false reasonings by which we have defended our selfishness are pictured by the destructive horses and their riders.

There is another very important lesson in our chapter. We like to imagine that we can put off serious thinking about spiritual things—that the Lord is so good and loving that He will in the end overlook all the evils we may have allowed to grow up within us, and will save us in spite of ourselves. But in this vision we are told plainly that in spite of the revelation of the ugly and destructive character of the things in their souls, the evil did not repent.

The Lord is indeed all-loving, but He is also all-wise. He created us in His own image and likeness, which means that He gave us the power to reason and the power to choose freely what we want to think and to be. He cannot take these powers from us without destroying our humanity. He cannot force us to love Him, because love must be freely given or it is not love. We know how this is from our experience with our children. We can make them behave, but we cannot make them like to behave. Our life in this world is our time of choice, the seed-time when we make ourselves what we want to be. The judgment in the other world is merely the harvest time, when we reap what we have sown.

———————

Primary

As we read this chapter to the little children, we need to keep in mind that the words are the Lord's and that the children are very close to Him as they listen. It is sometimes hard for us older people, whose minds are busy searching for the meaning of such a chapter as this, to realize that the children are not troubled about the meaning and are impressed and delighted by the words themselves, as they should be. Do not expect the children to remember the details from one reading, but after reading the chapter, take up the questions, having the children who are able to read find the answers.

We have been reading about some of the wonderful things which the apostle John saw in vision. The Lord was showing him a great moving picture acted out before his spiritual eyes. John did not understand what it all meant any more than you do, but he was told to write it down, and he obeyed.

Where was John when he was given the vision about which we read in the book of Revelation?

What book did he see?

With how many seals was it sealed?

Who opened the seals?

What did John see as the first four seals were opened?

The opening of the next two seals revealed the good and evil gathered to be judged.

Our lesson today is about the opening of the seventh seal.

What immediately followed?

What did the seven angels have?

What did the eighth angel have?

What happened when he filled it with fire and cast it into the earth?

What happened when the first angel sounded his trumpet?

What happened when the second angel sounded?

What happened when the third angel sounded?

What was the name of the star?

What happened when the fourth angel sounded?

What did the angel who flew through the midst of heaven say?

The sad things that happen in our chapter are pictures of things that happen in our minds and hearts when we are selfish and unwilling to learn and obey the Lord's truth.

Many years later, when the people of the Christian Church had gone through hard experiences and those who were good had learned that they needed more knowledge, which only the Lord could give them, the Lord showed to a man named Emanuel Swedenborg what John's vision meant, and commanded him to write it down. So now you will be able, as you grow older, to understand it.

Even now you can know that John's vision is a picture of the way in which the wonderful love and truth and power which the Lord is always offering us is received by different kinds of people. Good, unselfish people are made happy by it, but bad, selfish people hate it and are tormented by it.

Does this seem strange? When you are feeling naughty and trying to get your own way, how are you likely to behave when your mother tries to show you what is right?

In this world we can cover up our ugly feelings and thoughts, but in the other world they all come out and everyone sees them.

───────

Junior

The Junior notes suggest a line of thought in which this lesson can be meaningful for this age group. The thought of this meaning can be introduced in connection with the review and then developed after the striking pictures of the text have had their effect.

In our lesson today we have the beginning of the completion of John's vision with the opening of the seventh seal, which pictures the complete openings of the Word so that people can really be sure of what it teaches. Look up John 9:39-41. We all often do wrong things without realizing that they are wrong. Although such things may have very bad consequences, we feel that we shall be forgiven because we did not mean to do wrong. But when we know a thing is wrong and do it anyway, we do not want anyone to find it out because we know we are to blame. We like to think well of ourselves and to have other people admire us. When the real truth is known so that we cannot help seeing how selfish and foolish we have been, the pretty picture of ourselves which we have built up is destroyed. It is this kind of destruction which John was shown in his vision, and these two chapters will mean something to you if you will think that the things which are overthrown or burned up or drowned one after another as the trumpets sound are our ideas of our own goodness and wisdom.

We are told in chapter 7 that before the seventh seal was opened all the good people were marked or "sealed" by command of the Lord so that they would not be hurt by the things which were about to happen. Swedenborg tells us that the silence in heaven when the seventh seal was opened is an expression of the amazement of the angels when they saw how bad men of the church on earth really were.

How many angels did John see standing before God?
What were given to them?
What did still another angel have?
What happened when he cast his censer full of fire to the earth?
In our two chapters how many of the trumpets are sounded?

In the Word the sounding of a trumpet is always a symbol of the proclaiming of truth from the Lord. Look up Exodus 19:16 and read what happened just before the ten commandments were given from Mount Sinai. The blowing of the seven trumpets, like the opening of the seven seals, means the appearance of more and more of the truth. All these scenes are like a great moving picture which the Lord gives us to make us stop and think and not let our own hearts and minds get into such a state that we cannot bear to face the truth. Notice especially the last two verses in our lesson. Men and women can become so settled in selfish and evil ways that even disaster does not make them want to change themselves. Think how hard it sometimes is even now for you to acknowledge that you have been wrong and begin to behave differently. And the longer we go on closing our eyes to our own faults and just trying to have our own way the harder it is to change. But when you are young, good habits are just as easy to form as bad ones, and if we are wise, we can see that it is goodness and not selfishness which brings happiness to us as well as to others.

Intermediate

Much more can be done with this class on the general meaning of the two chapters, and the young people should be introduced to the thought that this is a picture not only of judgment on our individual lives but specifically of the Last Judgment, which took place at the time of the Second Coming. This is especially necessary as a preparation for the lessons that follow.

In the last lesson only the first six of the seven seals on the book of the Word were opened. Chapter 7, which we have not assigned, tells how the Lord, before allowing the seventh seal to be opened, had all the good souls sealed with His seal so that they could not be hurt by the things which were about to happen. There is a very plain and simple lesson for us in this. Other people cannot make us bad against our wills and we should never blame other people for our own weakness, because when we really want to do right, the Lord always makes it possible for us.

The opening of the seventh seal is the final revelation of the Lord's truth. You remember from our lessons on the Creation story that the six days represented the stages or preparation and development of the first church formed from the human race on earth, and the seventh day represented the completion of this development. The number seven signifies "all," and we think of it as a holy number because we connect it with the sabbath and because it is so often used of holy things in the Word. So here six seals are opened, and then there is a pause before the opening of the seventh. Then when the seventh seal is opened, two chapters are given to the story of the sounding of the first six of the seven trumpets, and then a new chapter and series of visions begins with the sounding of the seventh.

A trumpet in the Word represents "Divine truth manifested and revealed out of heaven." Look up Exodus 19:16, where the voice of a trumpet heralded the giving of the ten commandments from Sinai. When Joshua took Jericho, you remember, the people marched around the city, following the priests who bore the ark, once a day for six days and seven times on the seventh day, and then the priests blew their trumpets and the walls of the city fell. And perhaps you remember how in the story of Gideon (Judges 7:16-22) each of Gideon's men was given a trumpet and a lamp within a pitcher and when Gideon sounded his trumpet, all the others broke their pitchers so that their lights appeared suddenly, and blew their trumpets, and the enemy fell into confusion and was easily overcome.

In our lesson today, as each trumpet is sounded, destruction of one kind or another follows. We have seen that this vision given to John is a picture of the judgment which was to take place at the end of the first Christian Church. We have studied the successive churches on earth—the Most Ancient, the Ancient, and the Israel-itish—and have seen how each began with a new revelation of truth from the Lord, how this truth was received and used by the good and falsified and rejected by the evil, and how in each church the evil gradually increased until the Lord had to step in to save the remnant of good people and form them into a new church. The coming of the Lord into the world was the beginning of the first Christian Church, but the Lord Himself told the disciples (Matthew 24) that it would follow the same course as the others and that He would have to come again before the final Christian Church on earth could be established.

So the destructions which take place in our two chapters are a revelation of how falsities and evils gradually destroyed truth and goodness in the souls of most of the people in the first Christian Church. These people all thought that because they belonged to the church and professed to believe in the Lord, they would go to heaven. But you know that, although we can often hide our real feelings and thoughts while we live in this world, we have to leave all this "protective covering" behind us with our bodies when we die. The judgment is nothing more than the laying bare of our real spiritual states in the other world when we come face-to-face with the truth about ourselves.

We have not tried to take up the details of these chapters in a Sunday school lesson because there are too many of them. They are, however, all explained in Swedenborg's works *Apocalypse Revealed* and *Apocalypse Explained*, which you will want to study after you are grown up. You might notice now, however, that the first four destructions took place in the earth, the sea, the rivers and fountains, and finally the sun, moon, and stars, and you remember from other lessons that the earth pictures our life as to goodness, the sea the knowledges of truth gathered in the memory, the rivers and fountains truth as it comes to us from the Lord, and the sun, moon, and stars our love for the Lord, belief in Him, and knowledge about Him. In each case it is said that a third part was destroyed, and Swedenborg tells us that a third has the same meaning as the number three which refers to the three planes of the soul: will, thought, and act. So the sounding of these first four trumpets shows how the evil in the church destroyed in themselves all love, truth, and goodness.

In chapter 9, with the sounding of the fifth and sixth trumpets, the hells were opened to show the quality of those in them and the kinds of harm they do. Swedenborg tells us that those exposed by the fifth trumpet are those among the evil in the church who have considered themselves learned and wise and have desired to rule others, while those exposed by the sixth trumpet are those who did not pose as wise but who chose to believe that they could live as they pleased and nevertheless be saved in the end because they professed to believe in the Lord.

As we read chapters like this, we wonder how anyone could see such terrible destructions and still choose to reject the Lord's truth. But read the last two verses of our lesson. We should learn from this that while we may be kept by punishments from commiting outward evil deeds, our desire to commit them cannot be changed except by our own free choice. No one can be driven to love and serve the Lord or to love the neighbor.

Basic Correspondences

a trumpet = divine truth manifested
              and revealed out of heaven

Senior

This is a good lesson in which to arm the young people against the arguments of fundamentalists concerning the Second Coming and the Last Judgment. Our young people need such protection and we owe it to them. There are also in these chapters things which will help them to understand the chaotic conditions in the Christian world of today and to chart their course wisely and with charitable insight into the problems of young people in other churches.

We have seen that the four horses and their riders which appeared as the first four seals were opened picture different ways in which people look at the Word of the Lord. And the opening of the fifth and sixth seals revealed the general states of the good and of the evil with respect to their desire for divine truth.

There are many people in the Christian world who think that there is to be a judgment day on this earth, when the various prophecies in the Bible will be literally fulfilled, the dead will be raised, the evil cast into hell, and the good taken up to heaven. These people forget that some of these same prophecies were made in the Old Testament concerning the first advent and they were not literally fulfilled, although they believe the Lord came. The prophecies were all spiritually fulfilled, however, as all the prophecies in the New Testament will be.

The opening of the seventh seal marks the beginning of a long series of symbolic pictures of the judgment on the evil. There are two applications of these visions, one to the experience of the individual when he enters the other life, and the other to the general judgment on the first Christian Church which took place at the time of the Second Coming of the Lord in the middle of the eighteenth century. It is in this sense that it is called "the last judgment." We have seen in our lessons that at the end of each of the great dispensations—the Most Ancient, the Ancient, and the Israelitish Churches—there was a judgment, when the states of the people were revealed and the remnant of good people were separated from the rest, given a new revelation, and became the nucleus of a new church. In the twenty-fourth chapter of Matthew the Lord Himself tells His disciples the same thing will happen to the first Christian Church when He comes again "in the clouds of heaven with power and great glory." And this prophecy is directly connected with our lesson for today by verse 31 of that chapter: "And he shall send his angels with a great sound of a trumpet, and they shall gather together his elect from the four winds, from one end of heaven to the other."

Read here the first three verses of chapter 7 of Revelation. That chapter, which we have not included in our assignment, tells us that before the Lord permitted the seventh seal to be opened, He had all the good people sealed with His own seal so that the destruction which was to follow should not touch them.

From the book of Revelation we learn that judgment is no instantaneous process accomplished by a fiat of the Lord when one enters the spiritual world or at the end of a church on earth. We see this in the fact that there are many religions still in the world which are remnants of the Ancient Church, and the Jewish Church is still with us, and the first Christian Church is all around us. Only the Most Ancient Church has been completely removed from the earth. But in these churches which remain changes are going on, which we can see and understand in the light of our teachings. The Last Judgment took place in the spiritual world. Its effects on earth appear only gradually.

The same is true of our judgment as individuals. When we pass into the other world, our final choice has actually been made, but we are not immediately raised to heaven or cast into hell. If we have chosen to acknowledge and obey the Lord and to give up our own desires and thoughts whenever we found them to be contrary to the teaching of the Word of God, we shall find ourselves "sealed" with the divine seal, that is, protected against the assaults of evil spirits in the intermediate world, instructed, and led gently and happily toward the heavens. But if we have rejected the Lord's guidance and insisted on following our own way, the progressive destruction represented in our chapters will take place. Throughout the Word the sounding of a trumpet pictures the proclamation of divine truth, and it is in the light of divine truth that our evils appear and the falsities of the reasonings by which we have justified our selfishness are exposed. And we do not change from evil to good, as we learn from the last two verses of our lesson. We have to fit ourselves for the enjoyment of heavenly happiness. If the delights we crave are selfish, they can be found only in the hells.

The details of these visions are too many to be considered in a lesson, but they are all explained in the writings. An example follows the Adult notes.

Adult

The comparison of the gradual development of man into a church, as pictured in the Creation story, with the gradual judgment upon the man who has destroyed the church in himself is an interesting discussion topic. Another is Swedenborg's treatment of the Reformed Church, which we call Protestant. We all need to face this subject frankly, realizing that in talking about the first Christian Church we are speaking of it as an organization founded on certain doctrines and that we are not pronouncing judgment on any of its present members. We should hold the same thought in speaking of the Church of the New Jerusalem in the world. It is an organization founded on certain specific doctrines. If we profess to belong to it, we have the responsibility of studying and trying to live those doctrines. Our souls take their form from what we really believe, and it is this form which is revealed in the light of divine truth when we pass into the spiritual world.

We might begin our study of this lesson by noting some of the striking parallels it presents with other parts of the Word. We are familiar with the fact that the Bible begins and ends with accounts of the great river of water of life and the tree of life. We also realize that the great dragon of Revelation 12 is "that old serpent" which we first meet when he tempts Eve in the Garden of Eden. But we do not often carry our comparison further. Consider, then, the six days of creation, picturing the stages of the development of man into a true church, with the seventh day marking the completion of the process; then think of the opening of the six seals and the blowing of the six trumpets—with the seventh in each case set off by itself and signifying completeness—and realize that these mark the stages in the judgment upon those who reject the Lord and so refuse to be built into a church. Again, note that in the first chapter of the Bible we read that the sun, moon, and stars were created on the fourth day and that in our chapter on the judgment it was the sounding of the fourth trumpet which heralded the destruction of the sun, moon, and stars. Remember the "voice of the trumpet exceeding loud" which was heard from the mount just before the giving of the ten commandments from Sinai. Then there is the familiar story of the capture of Jericho, when the children of Israel marched around the city once each day for six days and seven times on the seventh day following the priests who bore the ark, and the walls fell when the priests sounded their trumpets. And there were seven priests—seven trumpets. In the story of Gideon, the Midianites were thrown into confusion by the sounding of the trumpets and the sudden flashing out of the lights as the pitchers which had hidden them were broken. And in the twenty-fourth chapter of Matthew—the so-called "little Apocalypse"—verse 31 tells us that at the Second Coming of the Lord—when He is to come "in the clouds of heaven with power and great glory"—"he shall send his angels with a great sound of a trumpet, and they shall gather together his elect from the four winds, from one end of heaven to the other." Compare this with Revelation 7:1-3. There are also many verses in the Prophets in which the sounding of a trumpet spells victory for the righteous and doom for the evil.

Even without a knowledge of correspondence it should be evident that these parallels are too many to be accidental, and that there is some meaning behind the letter, but in the light of the New Age we can see this meaning clearly. The sounding of a trumpet, we are told, represents "Divine truth manifested and revealed out of heaven" (AE 262). It is in the light of truth that evils and falsities are recognized in all their destructive and deadly character. We all tend to go along blithely believing what we want to believe, what is convenient for us to believe. This tendency in the Christian Church was evident as early as the time of the giving of the book of Revelation, as we learn from the Lord's messages to the seven churches in Asia Minor. The Second Coming took place—had to take place—when the perversion of the Lord's teachings had become so widespread and so entrenched that the simple good in the Christian Church could no longer find out the truth. The same situation existed, we remember, at the end of the Israelitish Church when the Lord made His first Advent. So while our chapters, like all the Word, have their application to the judgment on the life of every individual when he comes into the spiritual world, they refer specifically to what is called "the last judgment," the judgment which was executed in the spiritual world at the time of the Second

Coming upon all who had been gathered into that world from the
Christian Church since its beginning. We are told in the writings
that the permanent Christian heavens could not be formed until
the Word had been opened, and that the good who entered the
spiritual world from the first Christian Church were in the meantime kept in the part of the intermediate world which is called the
"lower earth," while the evil were gathered in "imaginary heavens."
The Last Judgment, made on the basis of the opened Word, was
executed upon these; the imaginary heavens were dispersed; the
evil, given to see their own actual states, found their places in the
hells; and the good were raised from the lower earth and formed
into permanent Christian heavens. The dispersion of the imaginary
heavens is what is pictured by Revelation 6:14. The condition of
the good and their protection by the Lord until the completion
of the judgment is described in Revelation 6:9-11 and 7:1-3.

A very brief statement of the general meaning of our two chapters for today is given at the beginning of these chapters in the
Apocalypse Revealed and is quoted here to help in our study of
these chapters:

On chapter 8: "The church of the Reformed is here treated of,
as to the quality of those therein who are in faith alone: the preparation of the spiritual heaven for communication with them (vers.
1-6). The exploration and minifestation of those therein, who are
in the interiors of that faith (ver. 7). Of those who are in its exteriors
(vers. 8, 9). What they are as to the understanding of the Word (vers.
10, 11). That they are in falsities and thence in evils (vers. 12, 13)."

On chapter 9: "Of the exploration and manifestation of the
states of life of those in the church of the Reformed, who are called
learned and wise from the confirmation of faith separated from
charity, and of justification and salvation by it alone (these are
treated of from verses 1-12).

"Of the exploration and manifestation of those therein, who are
not so learned and wise, and are in faith alone, and who live as
they please (from verses 13-19).

"Lastly, of those therein, who know nothing but that faith is the all by which man is saved, and not anything besides (verses 20, 21)."

From this we see that in this first part of John's vision the judgment is upon those who have confirmed themselves in the doctrine of "faith alone," the doctrine on which the Reformed, or Protestant, Church is founded. Some of the later visions deal with the Roman Catholic Church. We need to keep clearly in mind that Swedenborg is talking of the first Christian Church in its various divisions according to the doctrinal basis on which these divisions were made and developed. We sometimes choose to ignore such doctrinal foundations and to assume that "nobody believes those things anymore." But this is mere wishful thinking, growing, perhaps, out of our inclination to seem broad-minded and ecumenical. When people refuse to think about the teachings on which their church technically stands and continue to belong to it, believing anything they please, their allegiance is mere lip-service to a name and has no effect on their lives. There are plenty of people today who believe very firmly in the doctrine of faith alone although many of them do not live it. But any one of us may indeed be living in faith alone if we ride along on the assumption that we do not need to study the Lord's truth and live according to it—that the Lord is so kind that He will save us no matter what we think or do. We need to read our two chapters very thoughtfully in this light, for the destruction pictured in them is very real. It is the gradual destruction of all genuine goodness and truth in the soul of the person who chooses to lead himself instead of to be led by the Lord.

From the Writings of Swedenborg

Apocalypse Revealed, nn. 410-411: "*And the name of the star is called Wormwood; and the third part of the waters became wormwood*, signifies the infernal falsity from which their own intelligence is derived, and by which all the truths of the Word are falsified. By 'a star' is signified their own intelligence springing from pride from infernal love . . . By 'name' is signified its quality . . . ; by 'wormwood' is signified infernal falsity concerning which something will be said presently; by 'waters' are signified truths . . . , here the truths of the Word, because the subject relates to faith; by 'the third part' is signified all . . . A Christian man has spiritual life from no other source than from the truths of the Word, for in them there is life; but when the truths of the Word are falsified, and man understands and views them according to the falsities of his religion, then spiritual life with him is extinguished. The reason is, because the Word communicates with heaven; therefore when it is read by man, the truths therein ascend into heaven, and the falsities to which truths are adjoined or conjoined, tend towards hell, whence there is a rending asunder, whereby the life of the Word is extinguished. But this is the case only with those who confirm falsities by the Word, but not with those who do not confirm them. I have seen such rendings asunder, and have heard the noise like that of wood split by the fire on a hearth."

Suggested Questions on the Lesson

P. What was the book sealed with seven seals? *the Word*

J. Who opened it? *the Lord*

P. What did John see when the first seal was opened? *white horse*

P. What were the colors of the other three horses? *red, black, pale*

J. What was the rider on the pale horse called? *Death*

J. Who were seen when the fifth seal was opened? *the good under the altar*

J. Who were seen when the sixth seal was opened? *the evil*

J. What did these last people ask? *let the rocks hide us*

J. What happened immediately after the seventh seal was opened? *silence*

P. How many angels did John see standing before God? *seven*

P. What were given them? *trumpets*

P. What did an eighth angel have? *gold censer*

J. What did he first do with his censer? *put incense on it*

J. What did he then fill it with? *fire*

P. What happened when he cast it to the earth? *thunder, lightning, earthquake*

J. In the two chapters of our lesson how many trumpets were sounded? *six*

J. Can you tell some of the things that happened? *hail, fire, mountains into sea, star fell, third of sun darkened*

J. What was the name of the star that fell from heaven? *Wormwood*

J. What two names are given for the angel of the bottomless pit? *Abaddon, Apollyon (destroyer)*

P. Did the people to whom all these things happened repent? *no*

I. What do these two chapters treat of in their internal sense? *the gradual destruction of truth and goodness in first Christian era*

S. What is it which determines whether we go to heaven or to hell? *whether we follow or reject the Lord's guidance*

THE WOMAN AND THE DRAGON
Revelation 12

The powerful picture presented in this chapter contains very important lessons for our young people as well as for adults. To the younger children it may be given as one of the visions of John, the meaning of which they will study when they are older. They should be impressed with the details of the figure of the woman and of that of the dragon and led to look forward to the time when they can understand their meaning. The identity of the dragon with the serpent in the Garden of Eden should be stressed.

Doctrinal Points

The great red dragon of materialism is always present, testing our sincerity by trying to get us to ignore divine truth.

If we study our doctrines and remain true to them in our daily life, the dragon cannot harm us.

Even the New Church is not free from the temptation to live by the doctrine of "faith alone."

Notes for Parents

After the Last Supper the Lord charged His disciples to remain true to the teaching He had given them, as they went out to found the Christian Church. The apostles did remain true, but the churches they founded did not. We learn in Revelation 3 and 4 that even before the end of the first century A.D. both false teachings and evils of life had crept into the groups of Christians.

The visions recorded in the book of Revelation were given to the apostle John when he was a very old man. The whole book is a prophetic vision of what would happen in the first Christian Church—of how it would gradually become perverted, as all the churches before it had been, through the selfishness and worldliness of its members, and of how it would finally be judged and brought to its end and a new church raised up to take its place.

The vision which is the subject of our lesson for today tells of the beginning of this new church in heaven and the opposition it would meet on earth. In many places in the Scriptures the church is pictured as a woman—the bride, the Lamb's wife—whose husband is the Lord. So the woman in our chapter stands for the New Church. And all through the Scriptures love of self and especially love of the things of the world is pictured as a serpent, beginning with the story of the Garden of Eden, in which the serpent by his wily argument persuaded Eve to disobey the Lord. In our chapter we learn that the great red dragon is that same "old serpent, called the Devil, and Satan, which deceiveth the whole world."

The prophecy of this chapter was fulfilled some two hundred years ago, when the Lord in His Second Coming opened the seals of the Word and established the New Church on earth. If we think it strange that so few in the world realize this, we should remember that there are still millions who do not believe that the Lord made His First Coming nearly two thousand years ago. Knowledge of the Lord is never forced upon us. We have to open our minds to it by our own choice, and the old serpent, who over the ages has grown into the great red dragon, is always with us testing our sincerity by attempting with his subtle arguments to destroy the truth. But all those disciples of the Lord who try to "abide" in Him and keep His commandments are protected by the Lord and the angels and, like the woman, are given wings of spiritual understanding to lift them out of the dragon's reach.

―――――

Primary

Remind the children that the book of Revelation is the last book in the Bible and have them learn its name. Connect it with the Gospel of John. Then read the lesson as one of John's visions. If there is time, the teacher may also give the children further information about the dragon, based on verse 9, and tell them how much there is in this story for them to understand when they are older.

John was called "the beloved disciple" because he always seemed to be close to the Lord. John lived to be a very old man, at first in Jerusalem and later in Asia Minor, where he became head of the seven Christian churches which had been established there. When he was about ninety years old, the Roman rulers exiled him to the island of Patmos. There the Lord gave him a wonderful vision, which is recorded for us in the book of Revelation, the last book of the Bible.

First John saw the Lord—the same Jesus whom he had followed in the world—in a new and glorious form, and the Lord gave him messages for the seven churches in Asia Minor. Then he was taken up in the spirit into heaven and shown how the Lord and His angels control and put down evil when it threatens to become too strong for us to resist.

The visions John saw were like great moving pictures acted out in heaven to teach us about good and evil and to help us choose what is good and hate what is evil.

In our lesson for today what did John first see?
What was the woman standing on?
What was on her head?
What appeared to threaten her?
What can you tell about the dragon?
Where did the woman flee?
What happened to her child
Who fought against the dragon?
What were given to the woman to help her?
How did the dragon try to catch her?
How did the earth help her?

We are told that the great red dragon is the same old serpent which led Adam and Eve to disobey the Lord in the beginning of history. Whenever you are tempted to do wrong, you may know that this old serpent is whispering to you. Then just say, "Get thee behind me, Satan," and don't do the wrong thing. If you try hard to do this, the Lord and the angels will help you to do right.

Junior

This lesson may be used to.give the Juniors an idea of the fact that the Second Coming took place about two hundred years ago and was made known in this world by means of the writings of Emanuel Swedenborg. If you present the woman and the dragon as a picture of what is going on in the world now, you will help the children to be proud of their church and to feel a responsibility for resisting the dragon.

John is thought to have been the youngest of the twelve apostles and he outlived all the others. In his old age he was head of the seven Christian churches which had been established in Asia Minor, and during one of the persecutions of the Christians by the Romans he was exiled to the island of Patmos off the coast of Asia Minor. It was there that the Lord gave him the wonderful series of visions which are recorded in the last book of the Bible, the book of Revelation. This book is sometimes also called the *Apocalypse*, which is the Greek word for *revelation*.

We should read its first chapter regularly, for it tells of John's vision of the Lord and how the Lord commanded him to write down all that he was to see. The chapters which follow include the messages John was told to give to the seven churches in Asia Minor, the visions of the throne, the sealed book, and the four horsemen, and the opening of the seventh seal. Perhaps you remember that when the seventh seal was opened, seven angels appeared, each having a trumpet, and as each one sounded his trumpet, certain terrible destructions followed. The opening of the seals means the opening of the inner meaning of the Word and the sounding of each trumpet stands for the proclaiming of deeper truth as it was revealed, truth which showed up the evils which people were hiding in their hearts.

Our lesson for today is one of the visions which followed the opening of the last seal.

What did John see first?

What was under the woman's feet?

What was on her head?

What appeared next?

How many heads did the dragon have? How many horns?

What did his tail do?
What was the dragon waiting to do?
How was the woman's child saved?
Where did the woman go?
Who fought against the dragon?
What was the result?
What were given to the woman to help her?
How did the dragon try to destroy her?
How did the earth help her?

The book of Revelation is a prophecy of the history of the first
Christian Church and of how it would depart from the Lord, just
as former churches had done, until it had to be brought to an end
and a new church raised up on earth. In our lesson for today the
woman is a picture of the New Church which was to be established
by the Lord at His Second Coming, and the woman's child is the
pure truth of that church. You will study and understand this
better as you grow older. But you can understand now what the
dragon is. Read verse 9 and then go back to the beginning of the
Bible and read Genesis 3:1-5. You know what it is to be tempted.
There is something you want to do which you know is wrong.
Your conscience tells you it is wrong. But another little voice from
somewhere deep down inside you says: "Oh, that isn't really
wrong; everybody does it; your parents are just old-fashioned. Go
ahead and do it and see how much fun it will be." That little voice
is the voice of the old serpent of selfishness, and if we listen to
him and keep doing as he tells us, in time he grows into a great red
dragon which seems too powerful for us to fight.

You are fortunate to be brought up in this New Church which
John saw in vision and which began to be established on earth
about two hundred years ago, when the Lord made His Second
Coming. The truths which the Lord has revealed in His Word are
available to us now. But our selfishness—"that old serpent, called
the Devil, and Satan"—tries hard to destroy these truths as fast as
they enter our minds. The false arguments which rise in the mind
are the "flood" which pours out of the mouth of the dragon. "And
the earth opened her mouth, and swallowed up the flood which

the dragon cast out of his mouth." If we love the truths of our church and try hard to put them into practice in our lives, our minds will easily see how false the selfish reasonings are and will reject them.

––––––––

Intermediate

The book of Revelation has been called the "charter of the New Church." This lesson offers an opportunity to show our young people how this is true and to strengthen them for the opposition their beliefs will meet in the world, at the same time inspiring them by the picture of the origin of the New Church and the divine protection over it.

The book of Revelation is the record of a series of wonderful visions given by the Lord to the apostle John when, in his old age, he had been exiled by the Roman rulers to the island of Patmos, off the coast of Asia Minor. Throughout the history of the Christian Church people have felt the power of this vision. It is obvious from the letter (Revelation 1:19) that it has a very important meaning for the church and that it is a prophecy, and many have tried to puzzle out its meaning and to identify particular historical events—especially wars and conquests—with details of the prophecy. But only the opening of the internal sense of the Word by the Lord in His Second Coming has really enabled men to understand it.

The whole book is a prophecy of the history of the first Christian Church. This church was founded on the belief that Jesus Christ was the Messiah, the heavenly Father revealing Himself to men (Isaiah 9:6; John 4:25-26, 14:9). So the book of Revelation begins with a beautiful vision of the Lord. Then follow the messages which John is to give to the seven churches which had been established in Asia Minor, and these messages show that already—before A.D. 100—men were developing different ideas of the Lord and His teaching and were beginning to depart from true discipleship. Then John was taken up in the spirit into heaven and shown a great vision of the judgment which would be executed on the first Christian Church when these false ideas and evil practices had completely perverted it. In this vision the Word is shown first as a book sealed with seven seals and then, as the Lord opens one seal after another, deeper and deeper evils in men are revealed and judged. All these scenes are prophecies of the Last Judgment, to which many in some of the Christian churches around us are still looking forward, but which Swedenborg tells us took place in the year 1757.

Our lesson for today tells of the beginning of the New Church. Swedenborg tells us that on June 19, 1770, the twelve apostles who had been with the Lord in the world were sent out throughout the spiritual world to preach the doctrines revealed by the Lord in His Second Coming (TCR 791). By this the New Church was established first in the spiritual world, and this is why we call June 19 "New Church day." The New Church had to be established in the spiritual world before it could begin to descend to the earth.

The woman clothed with the sun portrays this New Church in the spiritual world and the moon under her feet symbolizes the faith of the New Church which would light the darkness of the minds of men on earth. The stars in her crown stand for all the beautiful truths which the New Church brings us. So, you see, near the end of the Word we come back to truth which the people of the Most Ancient Church had had by direct inspiration—the sun, moon, and stars which appeared on the fourth day of creation. The child which the woman was to bring forth represents the doctrine of the New Church.

Then appears the great red dragon. In verse 9 he is called "that old serpent, called the Devil, and Satan, which deceiveth the whole world." Again we go back to the beginning. Do you remember the argument of the serpent in the Garden of Eden (Genesis 3:1-5) which induced Adam and Eve to disobey the Lord and eat of the forbidden fruit and so lose their paradise? The serpent represented the love of the satisfactions to be obtained from this world and the love of reasoning from these material "appearances." He said to Eve in effect: "Don't believe what the Lord has told you; He is just trying to keep you from doing your own thinking." That was the beginning of all the falsity and evil in the world, and this old serpent grew with the growth of human selfishness, and his arguments gained in power as man's knowledge of the natural world grew, until we have the great red dragon with his seven heads and ten horns and seven crowns. Every time you try to present the doctrines of the New Church to those who do not really want them this great dragon rises up to fight you.

The dragon was cast out of heaven and the child was kept safe in heaven, and the woman was given wings—which picture spiritual understanding—to lift her up out of the dragon's reach, and the earth—the "good ground" of an honest and faithful heart—can dispose of the flood of falsity which pours out of the dragon's mouth. If you study your doctrines and remain true to them in your life, the dragon cannot hurt you, and your life will help to build the Lord's New Church on earth.

Basic Correspondences

the woman	=	the New Church
her child	=	its doctrine
the dragon	=	the love of the world
wings	=	spiritual understanding
a flood	=	false reasonings

Senior

The same suggestion applies to the Seniors which is made for the Intermediates. A few further points in the correspondence of the chapter are added in the Senior notes.

In the earlier chapters of Revelation the decline of the first Christian Church—by separating itself from the Lord, the true vine —is pictured, and this is followed by visions of a last judgment executed by the Lord's opening of the seals which had sealed the Word. John's vision was prophetic of what actually took place in the spiritual world at the time of the Second Coming of the Lord. Swedenborg tells us that the permanent Christian heavens could not be formed until the deeper truths of the Word were revealed and that all who in the world had professed to be Christians and so believed themselves to be "saved" were allowed to live in "imaginary heavens" until they should see their true states in the light of genuine truth. Then in the Last Judgment the good and the evil were separated, the evil found their way into the hells and the good were taken to their permanent homes in heaven. Swedenborg speaks of this Last Judgment as having taken place in 1757, and he also says that on June 19, 1770, the twelve apostles who had been with the Lord in the world were sent out through the spiritual world to proclaim the doctrines which established the New Church. Then the New Church could begin to appear on earth.

The woman clothed with the sun in our chapter for today is the symbol of the New Church. The sun corresponds to the glory of love to the Lord, in which the New Church appears in heaven. The moon under her feet pictures the intelligence and faith which would be in the people of the New Church on earth. The stars in her crown symbolize knowledges of divine good and truth possessed by this church. We know that often in the Word the church is called a bride and wife, her husband being the Lord.

The child which the woman brought forth stands for the doctrine of the New Church, and the great red dragon which threatened it symbolizes the resistance to the new doctrine from the worldly and selfish reasonings which had developed in the former church, on account of which it had come to its end. This is the same "old serpent" which was responsible for the origin of evil in the world (Genesis 3:1-5) and which caused the decline and fall of each succeeding church—the desire to be guided by self instead of by the Lord and to reason from natural instead of from spiritual considerations.

As New Churchmen you will meet this "dragon" again and again throughout your life in this world. He has grown with the growth of selfishness in man and has become more formidable with the increase of man's knowledge of the physical world and consequent pride in his own abilities. Swedenborg interprets the dragon as meaning specifically the doctrine of "faith alone" of the Reformed Church, which we call Protestant. The essence of this doctrine is that profession of belief in the Lord and reliance upon atonement for men's sins which His death on the cross accomplished will get a person into heaven regardless of what his life in the world has been. Although we know, of course, that many Protestants do not live according to this doctrine, it is still a part of their intellectual belief and serves as a refuge and excuse for those who care more for worldly than for spiritual values. It is also actually the basis of the idea we meet so often that the Lord is so loving and so all-powerful that He will certainly manage to get everyone into heaven someday. In fact we meet the dragon in many modern forms of thought. Since the time of Eden he has acquired seven heads and ten horns. The heads represent every variety of reasoning and the horns represent power. The crown on his heads are the statements from the Word which he twists to support his arguments.

But our chapter shows us plainly, too, how the Lord will help us if we really abide in Him. When the child was born, he was "caught up unto God, and to his throne." The doctrine of the New Church, being taught both in the letter and in the internal sense of the Word, is established in heaven. "Michael and his angels" fought against the dragon and cast him down to the earth. The quotation at the end of this lesson will tell you more of this. The angels are helping us when we resist the dragon. Then two wings of a great eagle were given to the woman and she was given a place in the wilderness where she would be nourished "for a time, and times, and half a time." The wings of an eagle represent the power and protection which come from intellectual sight and thought about spiritual things. The teachings of our church give us this higher understanding which lifts us above worldly things and enables us to see life in its true plan and proportions. And the nourishment of the woman for a time, and times, and half a time pictures the fact that the Lord is protecting and caring for His New Church on earth through its early stages when—so far as its members are concerned—it is small and weak and seems in danger of being destroyed. This is an encouraging thought for us all.

Finally, the earth opened her mouth and swallowed up the flood which the dragon cast out of his mouth to destroy the woman.

The flood, like the flood which destroyed the people of the Most Ancient Church, is the great body of falsity developed by selfishness and worldliness. The earth is another symbol of the church, but the church as it has been established in the life of every individual who accepts true doctrine and loves it. To such a person the falsity of the arguments of the dragon is immediately evident and the arguments are dissipated by the known truth in the mind.

Adult

The whole question of our attitude toward the ecumenical movement is involved in this lesson. We need to see the difference between cooperation with others on the natural level and trying to pattern our own church activities and attitudes on those prevailing in other churches whose fundamental concept of religion is quite different from ours.

Our lessons from the book of Revelation thus far have shown us the picture of the early states of the first Christian Church, the various ways in which its members began to depart from their first faith and life, and the prophetic vision of the condition of that church at the time when the opening of the seven seals would bring upon it the final judgment. We know from the writings that this judgment took place in the spiritual world in the year 1757. After this judgment the permanent Christian heavens were established, the good being brought into those heavens and the evil consigned to the hells. On June 19, 1770, the twelve apostles were sent forth throughout the spiritual world to proclaim the true Christian doctrine, and the New Church was begun in heaven, from which it was to descend to earth (TCR 791).

Our chapter for today is a prophetic vision of the preparation for this descent and of the opposition which would face the New Church on earth. Swedenborg's interpretation of these visions brings us face-to-face with the necessity for serious thought and important decisions concerning the nature and mission of our church, and its relation to other churches. The Rev. William Worcester's characterization of the book of Revelation as the "charter of the New Church" is not an idle epigram. Some time ago a Jewish rabbi who had been reading the writings of Swedenborg told a group of New Church ministers that when he first read what Swedenborg said about Jews, he threw the book aside, but later he took it up again and when he found that Swedenborg said even worse things about Protestants and Roman Catholics, he felt better about it. As New Churchmen we cannot ignore these statements of Swedenborg or doubt their validity.

The writings tell us that the woman clothed with the sun symbolizes "the Lord's New Church in the heavens, which is the New Heaven." She is clothed with the sun because "the church is in love to the Lord, for it acknowledges Him and does His commandments." The moon is seen under her feet "because the church on earth, which is not yet conjoined with the church in the heavens, is meant" and the moon signifies "intelligence in the natural man, and faith." Her crown of twelve stars signifies the New Church's "wisdom and intelligence from knowledges of Divine good and Divine truth from the Word." Throughout the Word a woman is often used as a symbol of the church—the bride and wife whose husband is the Lord. Read Isaiah 54:5, John 3:29, and Revelation 21:2, 9-10.

The child which the woman was to bear represents the doctrine of the New Church, and we should note that it was the child rather than the woman which the dragon really wanted to destroy. This is important for our later thought, for it means that the strength of the New Church will be in its doctrine. The child was saved by being caught up to God, and His throne. This, we are told, signifies that the doctrine is protected by the Lord and guarded by the angels of heaven.

Swedenborg identifies the great red dragon specifically as "those in the Church of the Reformed who make God three, and the Lord two, and separate charity from faith, and who make faith saving, but not charity together with it." The Church of the Reformed is the church afterward called Protestant. To make the Lord two is to "separate the Lord's Human from His Divine." Read here AR 537 ff. The dragon is red because red in this case signifies "falsity from the evils of lusts." His seven heads signify "insanity from the truths of the Word falsified and profaned." His ten horns signify "much power," and the seven crowns "all the truths of the Word falsified and profaned." We profane the Word when we quote it in support of arguments which permit or excuse selfishness and worldliness in us or in others. That the dragon's tail drew the third part of the stars of heaven, and cast them to the earth signifies "that by falsifications of the truths of the Word they have alienated all spiritual knowledges of good and truth from the church, and, by application to falsities, have entirely destroyed them."

AR 548 tells us that by Michael is not meant any archangel but the ministry in heaven performed by "those who confirm from the Word, that the Lord is the God of heaven and earth, and that God the Father and He are one, as the soul and body are one; also that men ought to live according to the commandments of the Decalogue, and that then men have charity and faith." Michael and his angels cast the dragon down out of heaven. So far as we are in truly heavenly states the falsities of the "faith alone" doctrine on which Protestantism was founded—the flood which pours out of the dragon's mouth—have no power over us, for the earth, which represents "the church as to doctrine," makes them "fall to nothing."

But the woman is still "in the wilderness." In AR 547 Swedenborg says: "It is of the Lord's Divine providence, that the church should at first be among a few, and that it should successively increase among many, because the falsities of the former church must first be removed; for before this, truths cannot be received, since truths which are received and implanted before falsities are removed, do not remain, and they are also dissipated by the dragonists."

This is where our lesson most closely touches our contemporary situation, and where honest thinking is most important. We are told sometimes that no Protestant Church any longer believes or preaches the doctrine of faith alone. This is simply not true. We know, of course, that there are many in Protestant churches who do not confirm this doctrine in their lives although they may still hold it intellectually and even rely upon it for comfort when they are thinking about their own evils and those of their friends and loved ones. But the whole "modern" attitude toward religion is an outgrowth of the faith alone doctrine: the idea that one church is as good as another, that we cannot really know anything about God or the life after death and so if there is a God and a life after death, that our eternal happiness will be taken care of; that it is God's responsibility, not ours, etc.

The fact that emphasis today is often placed on charity rather than on faith does not contradict this, for the "charity" meant is identified with what Swedenborg calls "benefactions," which may have no charity in them whatever, and "faith" is still identified with mere lip acknowledgment that Christ died to pay the penalty for our sins, which is essentially the doctrine of faith alone.

The New Church will grow on earth only as its members recognize and resist the temptation to identify charity with external works and the temptation to succumb to a weak acceptance of popular trends of thought. We face the dragon every day. Swedenborg tells us that good receives all its quality from truth and that truth cannot live with falsity.

From the Writings of Swedenborg

Apocalypse Revealed, n. 548: "By 'war' is signified spiritual war, which is of falsity against truth, and truth against falsity, for no other war can take place in heaven, where this is said to have existed . . . By 'Michael' is not meant any archangel; neither by 'Gabriel, and Raphael,' but ministries in heaven are meant; the ministry signified by 'Michael' is performed by those who confirm from the Word, that the Lord is the God of heaven and earth, and that God the Father and He are one, as the soul and body are one; also that men ought to live according to the commandments of the Decalogue, and that then men have charity and faith."

Suggested Questions on the Lesson

J. Who was John?   *the beloved apostle*

J. What island was he exiled to in his old age? *Patmos*

P. What did the Lord do for him there? *gave him visions*

J. What was the first vision given him? *the glorified Lord*

J. What does the whole book of Revelation prophesy? *the Second Coming*

J. How were the evils which grew up in the first Christian Church disclosed? *opening of seals*

P. In our chapter for today what does John first see? *woman clothed with the sun*

J. Can you describe this part of the vision? *moon under feet, crown of twelve stars . . .*

P. What next appeared to threaten the woman and her child? *dragon*

P. What can you tell about the dragon? *seven heads, ten horns, seven crowns*

P. How was the child saved? *caught up to heaven*

J. Who fought against the dragon? *Michael and his angels*

J. How was the woman saved? *eagle wings, fled to wilderness*

I. What do the woman and her child represent? *New Church and truth of that church*

S. What does the dragon represent? *doctrine of "faith alone"*

THE BEAST OVERCOME

Revelation 13; 19:11-21

This lesson should be tied in with chapter 12 to show how evil in the heart and falsity in the mind unite to oppose the development of the church in the individual and in the world. With the three younger classes the individual should be stressed rather than the world.

Doctrinal Points

Even today the "dragon" and his "beasts" try to persuade us that we can get to heaven no matter what kind of life we have lived. The Word has been opened to save us from such false reasoning. We are all invited to share in the "feast" the opened Word spreads out before us.

Notes for Parents

The vision of the two beasts which arose, one out of the sea and the other out of the earth, is a picture of the results in the hearts of men on earth when they listen to the false reasoning of the dragon. Deep down in our hearts we all know that we ought to acknowledge the Lord Jesus Christ as our God, study His Word, and obey His commandments. But our inherited selfishness is very strong, and we are prone to accept without careful examination any reasoning which favors the things we like to do. Some of these things, like the first beast, are obviously disagreeable. Ordinary intelligence prompts us to reject them. The beast received a deadly wound in one of his heads. But the wound was healed. We find some excuse which glosses over the seriousness of the offense. One very common excuse is: "Everybody does it."

Other bad tendencies of ours put on the appearance of goodness, as for instance when a man, moving into a town, looks around for the church whose congregation seems most likely to be useful to his business and becomes an active member of it. Or when we learn to quote Scripture so that we can condemn other people and impress them with our own goodness. This is like the second beast which had two horns like a lamb.

Only the Lord Himself, the rider on the white horse, could overcome the beasts. Only by honestly trying to find out what the Lord teaches in His Word and fighting such temptations under His leadership can we really recognize our secret selfishness and break down our false reasonings.

The Lord has opened heaven by showing us the inner meaning of His Word. This is the "feast" He offers us. We do not have to stumble along weakly through life, but can walk upright in the clear light of the Lord's truth. Like the woman in the last vision we can have wings which lift us up out of the fogs of human opinion into a higher and purer mental atmosphere.

Primary

The book of Revelation in its letter makes a deep impression on young children. If they can be led to associate these great pictures with their own little temptations, the Word is brought home to them with all its power to help. Children love to dramatize, and if we suggest how the dragon and the beast are at war with the Lord and the angels in each of us, their own imaginations will do the rest. We do not have to work out dramatizations for children. The adult imagination is likely to be a hindrance rather than a help to them.

In the vision of a woman clothed with the sun and of a great red dragon which threatened her, you remember that Michael and his angels fought against the dragon and cast him down out of heaven, and the woman and her child were saved.

The visions of John are pictures of things that go on in our hearts and minds. They are given in the Bible to help us see ourselves as the Lord and the angels see us.

The woman and her child we may think of as our good feelings and thoughts. The dragon—"that old serpent"—is a picture of the excuses we make in our thoughts for doing what we know is wrong.

Our lesson today shows us what goes on in our hearts.

What did John see rising up out of the sea?

How was this beast like the dragon?
What different animals seemed to be part of him?

That was a strange vision, wasn't it? The beast seemed to be made up of different kinds of animals, and the dragon was helping him. All the things John saw in his visions were pictures of things that go on in people's minds and hearts. The dragon was that same old serpent who has tempted people from the beginning of the world, and that whenever a little voice in your mind whispers to you to do something you know is wrong, you may know that it is the voice of the dragon.

But sometimes you do wrong without even stopping to think about it, don't you? Perhaps you get angry and strike somebody, or you snatch something which another child is playing with and enjoying. This is the work of the beast in your heart—the love of getting what you want no matter how much it hurts somebody else.

Perhaps you think you can't help doing these naughty things. But that isn't so. That is just the voice of the dragon helping the beast.

Who appeared out of heaven to oppose the beast?
What can you tell about this rider?
What three different names are given him?
Who were with him?
What happened to the beast?
In our hearts the beast is the love of getting the things we want regardless of other people's rights and happiness.

If you see how wrong these things are and try hard not to do them, the Lord will help you to overcome the beast, too, just as the rider on the white horse did in John's vision. The rider on the white horse is a picture of the Lord speaking to us in His Word, for the lesson tells us: "His name is called the Word of God."

Can you see why the rider on the white horse is called "the Word of God"?
Where do we find the Lord's help?

===

Junior

Try to lead the pupils to give examples of the beast and the dragon from some of their own daily temptations and experiences. You may be able to connect this chapter with problems involved in being a New Churchman by pointing out that the doctrines of the New Church show us the deeper evils in our hearts in addition to the evils of outward conduct, and so require more of us as well as offer us greater opportunities.

In our lesson from chapter 12, what did John first see?
What threatened the woman and her child?
How was the child saved?
Who fought against the dragon?
What was the dragon called?
How was the woman saved?
What happened to the flood the dragon cast out of his mouth?
What is the dragon in us?

The vision in our chapter for today follows immediately after the vision of the dragon and is tied in with it in several ways.

What did John see rising out of the sea?
How was the beast like the dragon?
What animals were part of him?
How did the dragon help him?
How was the second beast different from the first?
How were the followers of the beast marked?
What was the number of the beast?

In this chapter there are again many things which will have to wait for explanation until you are older, but you can understand now something of the difference between the dragon and the two beasts and their relation to each other. You may remember that the woman pictured the New Church, that her child was the true teaching of the church, and that the dragon was the selfish reasonings which would try to destroy the truth in our minds.

But there is something behind these reasonings—our selfish desires. These are the beasts. Notice that the first beast, though he has great power, is obviously ugly. In the Bible a leopard is always a picture of stealthy destructiveness and a bear of outward roughness. The first beast is our selfish desires which can easily be seen to be disagreeable. Each one of you knows what some of these are in yourself. The fact that this beast had one of his heads wounded to death means that we can't help admitting that these desires are wrong. But the second beast had two horns like a lamb, and a lamb is the picture of innocence. Some of our selfish desires can put on the appearance of being innocent and so defend themselves. This is why the Lord says to us: "Let him that hath understanding count the number of the beast." If we are really wise, we shall see through all the excuses we make for indulging our selfish desires, even when many of the people around us make these same excuses. We know how strong worldly reasoning is in the world today and how many people really believe that it is all right to think of yourself first. But we should know the beast's number.

Now let us think about how the beast was destroyed.

In chapter 19 what did John see when heaven was opened?
What was the rider first called?
What is the second name given him?
What is his third name?
Who is he?

John in the beginning of his Gospel tells us that Jesus Christ was "the Word made flesh." The Lord who speaks to us throughout the Word is the same Lord who created the world and all of us and who came into the world as Jesus Christ. He is the only one upon whom we can rely—He is "Faithful and True"—the only one who surely tells us the truth—"the Word of God"—and the only one whose power will always triumph in the end—"King of kings, and Lord of lords." We are all born selfish: the beast is in our hearts, and our minds are eager to accept the arguments of the dragon. But if we believe in the Lord, study His Word, and try to face the truth honestly and to correct our lives according to it, the Lord and the angels are fighting with us and will give us the victory without fail.

―――――

Intermediate

For this class the application of the lesson has been made in terms of the individual rather than of the church as a whole. The teacher may add the further application if he thinks the class is sufficiently mature to deal with it.

You remember that animals correspond to our affections. The two beasts in the vision in chapter 13 represent the kind of affections which develop in men on earth who listen to the dragon. When people stop looking to the Lord in His Word for the truth to guide their lives, ideas are developed which favor the selfish things they want to do, and these ideas in turn increase the evils in their hearts until everything in both their hearts and their minds becomes just the opposite of what it ought to be. For instance, it is natural for us, because of our inherited selfishness, to want things which other people have. As long as we remember the commandments "Thou shalt not steal" and "Thou shalt not covet" and think of them as the Lord's truth, and therefore binding upon us, we shall see our selfishness as wrong and fight it. But if someone tells us "We are born selfish, and cannot help it; so it can't be really wrong for us to try to get all we can for ourselves," and we let ourselves believe this, we shall become less and less honest and generous, and wealth and power will soon seem to us the only sensible things to work for. We know that many people, even church members, feel this way.

It was through this desire for selfish power that the first Christian Church declined, just as all those before it had declined. It did not "abide" in the Lord, but listened to the arguments of selfish men instead, although it still professed to worship the Lord and to call itself Christian. The great doctrine which was developed to excuse the indulgence of selfish desires is called the doctrine of "faith alone." This doctrine teaches that we cannot do anything to deserve heaven—we are all naturally sinners—but that Christ by His death on the cross paid the penalty for all man's sins and so appeased His angry Father; therefore all we really need to do is to acknowledge His sacrifice and by means of it claim the Lord's forgiveness, and if we do this, we shall get to heaven no matter what kind of life we have lived.

It is this doctrine which Swedenborg says the dragon represents, and the two beasts are the people who believe it and use it as an excuse for disobeying the commandments. He says the first beast pictures the laity and the second the clergy. You notice the second beast had "two horns like a lamb," which pictures the fact that they use quotations from the Word to make their doctrine seem true. There are plenty of passages in the Word which show that we cannot have goodness from ourselves, and if we use just this part of them, we can make them seem to teach what the dragon says. An example of this is found in Matthew 19:25-26. But if we read this carefully in connection with everything which is said in the same chapter, we find that we have something to do ourselves. We are saved not by merely saying we believe in the Lord, but by turning to Him for guidance and for help and strength to obey His commandments—help which He always stands ready to give us.

The description of the beast shows us what people are really like when they live according to the doctrine of faith alone. Read the interpretation of the three animals at the end of your notes. And the number six hundred and sixty-six—which is said to be "the number of the beast: for it is the number of a man"—shows us that if men look to themselves or to other men for their ideas of what they ought to feel and think and do, they will come into a state in which they will twist everything in the Word to support their selfish desires. People have often puzzled about this last verse of chapter 13, although we instinctively recognize that it must have a meaning, for it is natural for us to think of numbers in this way. When we believe we understand a person's motives and the way his mind works, we may say, "I've got his number, all right."

The other part of our lesson assignment—chapter 19—shows us what the Lord finally did to save men from this false reasoning which was growing stronger in the world and was making men beasts instead of men. We read: "I saw heaven opened." The Lord did open heaven, the heavenly or internal sense of the Word, and so came to men on earth for the second time as the Word to make clear to us what the Scriptures really are and teach. The white horse pictures the true understanding of the Scriptures, its rider—who was King of kings, and Lord of lords—is the Lord, and the "vesture dipped in blood" is the letter of the Word which had been so torn and misused. Verses 17 and 18 give us our invitation to share in the wonderful feast which this opening of the Scriptures spreads before us. If we accept this invitation, the beast can be cast out, and we shall see so plainly the falsity of all the interpretations of the Word which excuse selfish indulgence that we wonder how anyone could ever for a moment believe them.

Basic Correspondences

a leopard	=	love of falsifying truths of the Word
a bear	=	those who read the Word and do not understand it
a lion	=	(in a bad sense) evil in its power falsifying the Word
six hundred and sixty-six	=	every truth of the Word falsified

Senior

The teacher should keep in the pupils' minds the distinction between judging principles and judging individual people. The Seniors are already facing the temptation to "follow the crowd." This temptation takes many forms, often excusing weakness of will under the disguise of charity. Neither the individual nor the New Church is helped by ignoring the plain-speaking of the writings and assuming that "all this is changed since Swedenborg's day." The evidences of its continued presence are all about us. Our young people should be clear-sighted.

The vision described in chapter 12 represents the intellectual opposition which the New Church would find in the Christian world. The vision which follows it, which is the subject of our lesson for today, represents the deeper opposition which comes from selfishness in the heart when it is supported by the doctrine of faith alone of the former church. We might note here that this is the doctrine on the basis of which the "Reformed" or Protestant Church originally separated itself from the Roman Catholic Church. The Roman Catholic Church does not hold that doctrine, but separated from the Lord in another direction, by setting up the priesthood, and in particular the pope of Rome, as the spiritual authority on earth with power to save or to condemn men. This evil, together with its ultimate destruction, is pictured in the visions recorded in chapters 17 and 18 of Revelation.

Swedenborg interprets the two beasts of chapter 13 as the laity and the clergy of the Reformed Church, but we should note that he is not talking about all Protestant laymen and ministers, but about those who have "confirmed" in their lives the principal doctrine of Protestantism, which is "faith alone." To confirm a doctrine is to live according to it. No individual is either saved or condemned by membership in any particular church organization on earth. A person is saved by the development of love to the Lord and the neighbor in his heart and the carrying out of these two loves in his life. In every church organization there are people who are regenerating and people who are not. This is a matter of free choice. At the same time we should not fall into the popular fallacy that "one church is as good as another." If we are really trying to live as the Lord would have us live, we shall long for genuine truth to guide us, and the more genuine truth we can obtain the better and happier we shall be. Swedenborg tells us that the New Church is to be "the crown of all the churches." This is because it is founded on the acknowledgment of Jesus Christ as the only God of heaven and earth and on the genuine truths of the internal sense of the Word. We are New Churchmen only to the extent that we accept the Lord as our authority and try to study and live these truths.

Read carefully the quotation at the end of this lesson, which shows why the actual acceptance of the doctrine of faith alone makes a man a beast such as is pictured in our lesson. In the numbers which follow it Swedenborg tells us that a leopard "signifies the affection or lust of falsifying the truths of the Word," a bear signifies being "full of fallacies from the sense of the letter of the Word read but not understood," and a lion signifies "Divine truth in power . . . but here falsity in power appearing like truth by reasonings."

The deadly wound which one of the heads of the beast received relates to the obvious fact that charity and good works are so constantly commanded in the Scriptures, and the healing of this wound "signifies the healing of that head of the doctrine by this reasoning, that no one can do a good work of himself, and fulfil the law, and that there is on that account provided another means of salvation instead, which is faith in the justice and merit of Christ, who suffered for man, and thereby took away the condemnation of the law." That the second beast—who represents the clergy—had two horns like a lamb and spake like a dragon signifies "that they speak, teach, and write from the Word, as if it were from the Lord's Divine truth, and yet it is truth falsified."

From these quotations you can form a general idea of what the vision represents and of how much is involved in each detail of it. It would be impossible in one Sunday school session to go into all the details, but we should note verse 18. We may sometimes say, "I've got his number," when we think we have discovered a person's hidden motives and ways of thinking. If we are truly wise, we shall "count the number of the beast"; that is, we shall keep in mind the underlying falsity on which Protestantism was originally based and the lengths to which it still can lead the person who really accepts it. Of the number six hundred sixty-six Swedenborg says that it signifies that "all the truth of the Word is falsified by them."

We remember that Michael and his angels cast the dragon down out of heaven but that he still remained active on the earth. The two beasts were the result of the dragon's activity. In chapter 19 we find that, although heavenly societies of angels help, it is the Lord Himself who must overcome the beasts—Swedenborg identifies the "false prophet" with the second beast. The opening of heaven in verse 11 is the opening of the internal sense of the Word in the Second Coming, and all the details of the description of the rider on the white horse teach us about the Lord as He should appear to us in the Word. In opening the Word the Lord invites us to a feast. If we accept His invitation, He can give us power to recognize and overcome all the temptations presented to us in the modes of thought current in the world around us.

Adult

The quotation at the end of the lesson may offer additional material for discussion. The teacher should read all the notes from the Intermediate up in order to be able to answer questions on the correspondence of details of the vision, as some have not been repeated in the Adult notes. We need to define clearly the basis of our church and our own responsibility.

In the vision we considered from chapter 12, the principal action was on the plane of the heavens rather than of the earth. The vision of our lesson today shows the effect on earth of the dragon's presence and subtlety. The two beasts of chapter 13 picture those of the laity and those of the clergy in the Protestant Church who have confirmed in their lives the doctrine of faith alone. The first beast rises out of the sea and the second out of the earth because the laity are "in the externals of the doctrine of the church, and the clergy are in its internals." The various animals which form parts of the first beast are different manifestations of affections of falsity, the leopard "heresy destructive of the church," the bear "fallacies from the sense of the letter of the Word read but not understood," and the lion "falsity in its power appearing like truth by reasonings." The "two horns like a lamb" in the second beast signify that the clergy "speak, teach, and write from the Word, as if it were from the Lord's Divine truth, and yet it is truth falsified." It is the dragon which gives the first beast its power, and we read that the second beast speaks "as a dragon."

The interpretation of the deadly wound suffered by one of the seven heads of the dragon and its healing is particularly enlightening. In AR 576 and 577 we read: *"And I saw one of his heads as it were wounded unto death,* signifies that this point of doctrine, which is the head of the rest, that man is justified and saved by faith alone without the works of the law, does not agree with the Word, where works are so often commanded. . . . *And the stroke of his death was healed,* signifies the healing of that head of the doctrine by this reasoning, that no one can do a good work of himself, and fulfil the law, and that there is on that account provided another means of salvation instead, which is faith in the justice and merit of Christ, who suffered for man, and thereby took away the condemnation of the law."

The last verse of chapter 13 should be taken to heart by all of us. If we are New Churchmen we believe that the opening of the inner meaning of the Word was the Second Coming of the Lord, in which Swedenborg was merely an instrument, the true "servant of the Lord Jesus Christ." The interpretation of these visions in Revelation is not Swedenborg's therefore, but the Lord's. The conditions and states of thinking here atributed directly to he Reformed or Protestant Church are not merely conditions as Swedenborg perhaps saw them. They are conditions which the Lord saw and which are still evident today if we do not close our eyes to them. The same is true in regard to the interpretation of the visions recorded in chapters 17 and 18, in which the evils of the Roman Catholic Church are exposed and judged. If the New Church is to grow upon earth, its members must face facts, even when these facts are as unpleasant and threatening as the dragon and the beasts. Swedenborg says many times that falsities must be exposed and rejected before the truth will be generally accepted. Read AR 547.

If we are wise, we shall "count the number of the beast: for it is the number of a man; and his number is Six hundred threescore and six." This number, we are told, "signifies this quality, that all the truth of the Word is falsified by them." We meet this falsification of the Word in some of the works of modern scholarship, in theological magazines, in sermons, and in the arguments of fanatics. If we are wise, we shall recognize and face it, not try to close our eyes to its existence under the pretense of charity. We do neither the Lord nor the neighbor, nor yet the New Church, service by compromising with falsity.

The overcoming of the beasts is the work of the Lord in His Word. The opening of heaven (19:11) is the opening of the internal sense of the Word and the white horse is the interior understanding of it. The details of the description of the horse's rider are all familiar to us. His eyes as a flame of fire "signifies the Divine wisdom of the

Lord's Divine love." The diadems upon His head are "the Divine truths of the Word." The "name written" is the quality of the Word in its interiors, which only the Lord knows and is able to reveal. The garment dipped in blood is "Divine truth in its ultimate sense, or the Word in the letter, to which violence has been offered." The sharp sword going out of His mouth "signifies the dispersion of falsities, by doctrine from the Lord." The whole picture should impress upon us the fact that the New Church is founded on the truth that the Lord Jesus Christ is the only God of heaven and earth, that He conjoins Himself to man by means of the Word, and that the opening of the Word is His doing and necessary to the salvation of mankind. The church on earth has power only as it looks to the Lord in His Word for all its direction. The Lord has indeed spread a feast before us, food which our souls need if they are to have strength and wisdom to meet the demands of our age and to accomplish the work which the Lord has given us to do. Let us not be among those who "beg to be excused" from this feast.

From the Writings of Swedenborg

Apocalypse Revealed, n. 571: "*And upon his heads the name of blasphemy*, signifies the denial of the Lord's Divine Human and the doctrine of the church derived not from the Word, but from one's own intelligence. By 'seven heads' is signified insanity from mere falsities . . . and this insanity speaks blasphemy, when it denies the Lord's Divine in His Human; and also when it does not draw the doctrine of the church from the Word, but hatches it from its own intelligence. As to the first, that it is blasphemy to deny the Lord's Divine in His Human, the reason is that he who denies it is opposed to the faith received throughout the whole Christian world, namely from Athanasius, where it is expressly said, that in Jesus Christ, God and Man, that is, the Divine and the Human, are not two but one, and that they are one Person, united like soul and body . . . As to the second, that it is blasphemy not to draw the doctrine of the church from the Word, but to hatch it out of one's own intelligence, the reason is, because the church is from the Word, and its quality is according to the understanding of the Word . . . And the doctrine that faith alone, that is, faith without the works of the law, justifies and saves, is not from the

Word, but from a single expression of Paul falsely understood (Rom. 3:28...);
and every falsity of doctrine is derived from no other source than from one's
own intelligence. For what is more universally taught in the Word, than to
shun evil and do good? and what is more evident that that God and the neighbor ought to be loved? And who does not see, that no one can love the neighbor, unless he lives according to the works of the law, and he who does not
love his neighbor does not love God? for in the love of the neighbor the Lord
conjoins Himself with man, and man conjoins himself with the Lord, that is,
the Lord and man are together in that love."

Suggested Questions on the Lesson

P. In chapter 12, what did John first see? *woman clothed with sun*

P. What threatened the woman? *dragon*

J. What can you tell about the dragon? *seven heads, ten horns*

P. How was the woman's child saved? *caught up to God*

J. Where did the woman go? *wilderness*

P. Who fought with the dragon? *Michael*

P. Who won? *Michael*

J. How was the woman saved? *eagle wings*

P. In our lesson for today what first appears? *beast*

P. Can you describe the beast? *seven heads, ten horns, ten crowns*

J. What happened to one of his heads? *wounded*

P. What did the second beast look like? *two horns like a lamb*

J. What part does the dragon play in this vision? *gave power to the beasts*

J. What is the number of the beast? *six hundred sixty-six*

P. In the second part of our lesson, what appeared when heaven was opened?
   white horse

J. What can you tell about the horse's rider? *eyes like flame, many crowns,
   vesture dipped in blood*

J. What three things is he called? *Faithful and True, Word of God, King of
   kings*

P. Who followed him on white horses? *armies*

J. What invitation was given? *fowls to supper of great God*

J. What happened to the beast? *cast into lake of fire*

S. What do the two beasts picture? *(1) disagreeable selfish desires,
   (2) innocent-appearing selfish desires*

S. What does the number six hundred sixty-six mean? *every truth of
   the Word falsified*

I. What is meant by the opening of heaven? *revealing inner sense of
   the Word*

THE JUDGMENT AND THE HOLY CITY
Revelation 20:11-15; 21:1-7

In all classes mention should be made of why the Bible is called the Book of Life. It is easy to introduce this by reading the first verse of Genesis and then the first verse of Revelation 21, and finally verse 6. The teacher of each class—even the youngest—may well base his preparation of the lesson on a study of these three verses. All classes should learn that our church takes its name from Revelation 21:2.

─────

Doctrinal Points

We are all writing our own "book of life" daily by the moral and spiritual decisions we make.

This "book of character" will determine our eternal state, either in heaven or hell.

With the aid of the heavenly doctrines, the Word can be for each of us an inexhaustible source of truth about the way and purpose of life.

─────

Notes for Parents

There are two parts to the lesson for today, but they are very closely connected and both are very important. The picture of the judgment at the end of chapter 20 is a symbolic picture like all the parts of John's vision. When we die, we do not actually appear before a throne and have all the actions of our lives reviewed. But the judgment is nonetheless real. The books which are opened are the character we have formed by our inner choices here on earth— we are writing this book every day. Here we can often cover up our real feelings and thoughts, but in the other world they can be plainly seen, and if we have not learned to be unselfish and to love the Lord and the neighbor, we shall choose of our own free will to turn our backs on the happy, unselfish sphere of heaven and go

286

with others like ourselves. The lake of fire is also a symbol—it is the burning of selfish passions, which makes the sphere of hell.

Chapter 20 tells us of the new heaven which the Lord created from the good—those in whose hearts was found the unselfish love which is the very heart of the Word of God. The holy city descending from God out of heaven is a new church on earth founded on the basis of the opened Word. It is on this basis that our church was founded when the Word was opened two hundred years ago, and so the name *Church of the New Jerusalem* was given to it. In its teachings we find all the blessings described in our reading, because the Word becomes to us the "fountain of the water of life," an inexhaustible source of truth which enables us to understand the purpose of our life and to meet whatever hardships come to us as opportunities for spiritual development and progress.

Primary

The verses from each of the two chapters present a vivid picture which will appeal to the children. The emphasis should be on the books they are writing every day. The details of both parts of the vision should be impressed, and the reason why the creation of the new heaven immediately follows the judgment.

The apostle John had a wonderful vision of heaven. He saw the Lord—the same Lord Jesus whom he knew and loved—sitting on a throne with everyone bowing down before Him and singing praises to Him. And he saw in the Lord's right hand the book, which we know as the Word of God, sealed with seven seals. And he was promised that the Lord would open the Word. This vision of John's is described for us in the last book of the Bible, which is called the book of Revelation.

In the chapters which follow, the seals were opened one after another. As each one was opened, something new happened, each time more strange and terrible.
This is a picture of the judgment, in which deeper and deeper faults in our characters are searched out so that they may be destroyed.
At the beginning of our lesson for today, John again saw the great throne.

Whom did he see standing before God?

The books which were opened were the lives of the people which they had lived while they were on earth.

The other book, the book of life, was the Word.

The people were judged to see how well they had learned and obeyed the laws which the Word teaches.

You are writing the book of your life every day, because everything you think and feel and do becomes part of you, and someday—just as in John's vision—this book will be opened to see what you have written there and whether or not it agrees with the good and true things that are written in the Word of God. So you see that what you write in your book is very important.

It is very important for us to learn and do what the Lord wants us to do. This is what we come to Sunday school to learn.

In chapter 21 what does John see coming down from God out of heaven? Our church is named for this city.

It is a picture of heavenly character, and therefore of heaven itself.

How does the Lord assure us that we shall be happy there?

———————

Junior

A brief review including some account of the nature of chapters 6-19 so that the judgment may be seen as a deeper and deeper examination of our motives and thoughts will be of use. The importance of going to the Word for our principles and of making the choice of good day by day should be stressed.

What did John see in the right hand of Him who sat on the throne?

What is this book?

With how many seals was it sealed?

By whom is it said the book would be opened?

Why is the Lord called the Lion?

Why is He called the Lamb?

John saw the setting for a great prophecy of judgment. This is followed by the story of how the seals of the book were opened one after another. As each seal was opened, something strange happened, and more and more terrible things took place until with the opening of the seventh seal great wars and destructions began. This is a picture of what happens when we really begin to look deep into our hearts to see whether or not we love the Lord and the neighbor as the Word says we should.

Did you ever sit down and try to think just what made you do a particular thing? Let's take some good thing you did. Suppose you gave one of your friends something of yours which he liked. Offhand you would say you did it to make him happy. But were you really thinking of his happiness or of how he would thank you and admire you for your generosity and of how your mother would praise you when you told her about it? If such thoughts were in the back of your mind, there was really selfishness in your heart all the time.

We know that when we go into the other world, we shall no longer be able to hide our inmost thoughts and feelings. So now is the time for us to hunt out our selfishness and get rid of it. But this means a real struggle against temptation. It is this struggle which is pictured by the wars in the book of Revelation. Our natural selfishness is always trying to destroy the good in us and the Lord and the angels are fighting to destroy our selfishness.

In the first part of our lesson for today—the end of chapter 20—the final judgment is pictured, the time when we go into the spiritual world and see ourselves as we are, as just what we have made of ourselves in our life here.

What does John see again?
Who are standing before the throne?
How were the dead judged?
What happened to those who were not found "written in the book of life"?

It is not hard to understand that the book of life is the same book which has played so great a part in John's whole vision, the Word of God. And the other books are the books of our lives—our characters—which we have been forming day by day in this world. Those who are not found written in the book of life are those who have let themselves grow more and more selfish instead of trying to form their characters according to the teachings of the Word.

The "lake of fire" is a symbol picture like all the others. Are we happy when we are angry, or when we are hating someone, or when we are jealous, or when we are wanting something that belongs to someone else? These selfish loves are like fire burning inside us destroying all the happiness we might be having. The lake of fire is this burning of selfish desires which prevents the evil from ever being happy.

But those who have tried to learn and do the Lord's will and to overcome their selfishness have a very different future ahead of them. Chapters 21 and 22 tell about this future. We are studying today only the first few verses of chapter 21. The new heaven and new earth which John saw are an entirely new state of happiness in our hearts and minds and in our outward lives. Do you remember the first verse of the first chapter of the Bible? That tells us that the Lord made us with both a higher and a lower nature, and now we find that if we are good, in heaven we shall still have a higher and a lower nature, but both will be made new. Heaven is a place where everyone loves the Lord and the neighbor and no one is thinking of himself. So everyone is always happy inside and out.
What did John see coming down from God out of heaven?
What was the name of this city?

Our church takes this name because it stands for a new knowledge of what our lives ought to be, a knowledge which the Lord made available when He opened the Word and enabled Emanuel Swedenborg to write down for us truths which had been hidden within its letter. You have learned some of these deeper truths already, and you will learn more and more as you grow older. And if you continue to try to live according to all you learn, when you go into the other world you will be able to live in heaven, which is pictured by entering the holy city. Read the last verse of chapter 21 and also verse 14 of chapter 22.
In verse 6 what does the Lord call Himself?
What does He promise to give to him that is athirst?

Alpha and *omega* are the first and last letters of the Greek alphabet; so the Lord is saying that He is the beginning of everything and also the end or object toward which everything in creation looks. Do you remember the fourth blessing? If not, look up Matthew

5:6. Then look up John 4:13-14. The water of life is truth from the Lord. The Lord gives us this truth freely in His Word, and everyone who really thirsts for it will find all he needs there.

Read verse 7 and look up Matthew 25:34 and John 1:12 and 3:3. We know that we inherit many things from our parents and through them from our forefathers. Sometimes when you do something from this inheritance, you may hear someone say: "He's his father's own son." But the Lord is our heavenly Father. And the whole object of our life in this world is to overcome the many bad tendencies which we inherit from our earthly ancestors and to form our characters into the image and likeness of God; that is, to try to be as much like our heavenly Father as possible. This is to become *regenerate*, which means *reborn*, and so to become true sons of God.

Intermediate

The correspondence of the reading throughout will furnish plenty of material for the lesson. The Second Coming of the Lord should be identified with the opening of the seals, and the descent of the holy city with the beginning of the New Church.

The last book in the Bible, the book of Revelation, is, as we have seen, a prophecy of what would happen to the first Christian Church which the apostles founded. Evils and false ideas crept into it very soon. The greater part of the book is a symbol picture of the conflict that went on between good and evil and between truth and falsity, and the destruction which evil and falsity brought about in men's souls. A revelation means literally an unveiling. In this world we can to some extent veil or cover up the bad things that are in us by putting on a pleasant exterior. But when we come into the other world, our real character comes to view. And we make our character here. We cannot change it after we die.

In our lesson for today we are given a symbol picture of what finally happened in the other world when the Lord made His Second Coming two hundred years ago. All the people, good and bad, from the Christian Church had been living together in the other world much as they had lived in this world, waiting for the final judgment, which could not take place until the Lord had opened the Word. This is because it is the divine truth within the Word with which our characters have to be compared before good and evil can properly be separated. You can see how this is if you stop to think that a person can keep all the commandments in their literal meaning and yet not be a good person. For example, one may never actually kill anyone, but all the time one may want to murder but be held back only by fear of the law. The Lord, when He was in the world, showed men enough of this inner meaning of the commandments so that they could, if they wanted to, see and fight against their real evils. Read Matthew 5:21-22.

The character which we form for ourselves while we are in this world is the book which we take with us into the spiritual world. We are writing this book today and every day. If day by day we choose to try to do right—to learn and do what the Lord wants us to do—our book when it is opened in the other world will read like the book of life, the book which was in the hand of Him who sat on the throne in John's vision. This is what is meant by being found written in the book of life. In other places it is said that one's name is written in the book of life. In the Word a "name" means the *quality* of a person or thing. If, instead of this, we have chosen to go through life trying to get our own way, and merely putting on an orderly outward life because we could see that that would be more to our own advantage, then our names will not be found written in the book of life. The lake of fire into which the evil were cast in John's vision is a picture of hell, where people because they care only for themselves are constantly "burned up" with jealousy, covetousness, revenge, and hatred. Whenever you are tempted to say about something someone else has done, "That burns me up," stop and look into your heart and see if it is not really love of yourself and of having your own way that is the real fire you are feeling.

In chapter 21, the first heaven and the first earth refer to the state of life in which the Christians in the spiritual world were before the Second Coming and their final judgment. The new heaven and the new earth are the true Christian heaven which was formed of the good after the judgment; the heaven is their inner state and the earth their outer state.

Then we come to John's vision of the holy city, New Jerusalem, descending from God out of heaven. A city in the Word is the symbol of doctrine. Doctrine is another word for teaching, and a city pictures the system of teaching which one has accepted and in which he lives. The city of Jerusalem always pictures the church as to its doctrine. So the New Jerusalem is the church which has a new doctrine in which it lives. It is the New Church, and that is why the true name of the New Church is *the Church of the New Jerusalem*. Verses 3 and 4 of chapter 20 tell us the great blessings which the Lord can give to those who really choose to live in this new city of doctrine. We may know who God really is, our Lord Jesus Christ, and know that He is always present with us and caring for us. And, although we have the same problems and difficulties and disappointments and bereavements which others have, they will not make us doubtful or afraid or unhappy, because we shall understand them and why they are permitted to come to us. The Lord gives us the water of life freely, divine truth which leads to heaven. To be sons of God means to be regenerated or born again, by overcoming the selfish and evil tendencies which we inherit from our human ancestry and cultivating the unselfish love for the Lord and the neighbor which is our inheritance from our heavenly Father.

Basic Correspondences

name	=	quality
the "lake of fire"	=	the burning of self-love in the heart, which is hell
city	=	doctrine
Jerusalem	=	the church as to doctrine
fountain of the water of life	=	the Word

Senior

This lesson furnishes one of our best opportunities for discussing with young people the New Church, its basis and mission, and what our privilege and responsibilities as New Churchmen are.

The Bible begins with the words "In the beginning God created the heaven and the earth." And in our lesson for today we find that the first verse of the next to the last chapter in the Bible says, "And I saw a new heaven and a new earth: for the first heaven and the first earth were passed away." The Word in its letter is a tremendous drama treating of the life of man from his first creation through his spiritual decline until, with the coming of the Lord, his progress in self-destruction was checked and his course again turned toward heaven; and the book of Revelation in prophecy completes his course to the final separation of the good and the evil in the last judgment and the establishment of permanent Christian heavens through which divine truth can always flow to men on earth.

In the first few verses which we have for our lesson today the judgment takes place and in the rest of our lesson the new heaven and earth are established and from them a new church descends to the earth of this world. You perhaps remember from the account of creation that heaven and earth represent the internal and the external of man and that in the beginning they were both empty and dark, just as every person is born with both heavenly and earthly possibilities but with no knowledge or understanding. The new heavens and the new earth represent the fulfillment of the high possibilities of man both internal and external.

The simple picture of judgment is symbolic like all the rest of the book of Revelation. Swedenborg makes it clear that when we enter the spiritual world, we shall not find ourselves standing before a throne on which the Lord sits to judge us; neither will the Lord arbitrarily condemn us to hell or invite us into heaven. The throne, as we have already seen, is a symbol of judgment; the book of life is the Word; and the books that are opened are our inner characters, which we have been forming by our choices of good or evil day by day throughout our lives in this world. To have one's name written in the book of life is to find that one's inner character is in accordance with the teachings of the Word; that is, that one's ruling motives are love to the Lord and to the neighbor. This is the very sphere of heaven. If, when we enter the other world we are not in love to the Lord and the neighbor, we shall not choose to live in that sphere. Our judgment there is executed by our own free choice, as we gradually put off whatever disguises we may have been wearing to cover our real feelings and thoughts in this world, and show ourselves as we really are. The lake of fire mentioned in chapter 20:14-15 is indeed hell, but it is a symbolic picture of the company of all those who burn with hatred against everyone who does not serve them. The ruling love which makes hell is the love of self.

We know that the name of our church is *the Church of the New Jerusalem*, and that this name is taken from Revelation 21:2. A city always represents doctrine. Everyone lives in some city of doctrine, some system of thought and principle. The things he believes are the walls which limit his action and which shut out those he considers his enemies. If the things he believes are false, he is cut off from much that he might do and enjoy, and those who are shut out are those who would actually be his best friends. But if the things he believes are divine truth, he is prevented only from doing harmful things and he is protected from all his spiritual enemies. The city of Jerusalem throughout the Word is the symbol of the church as to doctrine, and the New Jerusalem is the church based on the new doctrine revealed to men by the Lord when He made His Second Coming in the opening of the Word. In *True Christian Religion*, n. 791, at the end of the chapter on the New Heaven and the New Church, Swedenborg says: "After this work was finished the Lord called together His twelve disciples who followed Him in the world; and the next day sent them all forth throughout the whole spiritual world to preach the Gospel that *the Lord God Jesus Christ* reigns . . . This took place on the nineteenth day of June, 1770." So we call June 19 "New Church Day."

What the Lord gave to men in His Second Coming is described in the remaining verses of our lesson. The opened Word helps us to see that the Lord Jesus Christ glorified is indeed the one God of heaven and earth, "the Alpha and Omega, the beginning and the end." It makes us realize that He is present with us and caring for us all the time. It removes all our doubts and fears and makes our griefs and disapointments easy to bear. The opened Word is to us "the fountain of the water of life" from which the Lord satisfies all our thirst for truth.

———

Adult

Here also the best discussion material is in the nature and mission of the New Church, although some of the younger and newer members may need to be given a clear understanding of how judgment takes place.

The middle chapters in the book of Revelation are a symbolic description of what happens in the church and in individual lives when the seals which have closed the inner meaning of the Word are opened one by one, bringing deeper and deeper truths to bear in the examination of the state of the church and of the individual heart. In this process the conflict between good and evil—between the forces of the Lord and the powers of the hells—increases, and the devastation becomes more and more extensive. If we are really examining ourselves in the light of the Word, we must go the whole way; we cannot take just the instruction we are willing to obey and ignore the rest.

The more one learns of the internal meaning of the Word, the more deeply it searches the mind and heart. It holds up high standards of spiritual thought and life, often diametrically opposed to common precept and practice. It never allows us to rest satisfied with ourselves, because when one temptation is overcome, a deeper one is always revealed to us. This is what is pictured by the fact that with the opening of each seal the devastation increased.

But the whole scene of conflict in the Apocalypse leads to final victory. Self-satisfaction is the badge of spiritual failure. Only those evils which we see and struggle against are overcome; the rest remain in us and limit our uses to eternity. We admire a person who wants to "die in harness." We cannot always succeed in this desire in our material occupations; physical age and weakness may prevent. But the soul does not grow old and weak with the body; it passes—if we are regenerating—"from strength to strength." We should wish to die in spiritual harness, to fight to the end against the evils and falsities within us, and against evil and falsity in the world. So long as the Lord permits us to remain in this world, we may be sure that there is still something for us to do in the way of spiritual progress, and we shall find the way to that something if we continue to read and study the opened Word, which will lead us daily to new conflicts, new victories, and fuller life.

But there can be no reservations, no halfhearted allegiance. The forces which oppose the work of the opened Word in the church and in us are pictured as the dragon—"that old serpent" who tempted Eve in the garden—and the beast, selfish and sensual desires in the heart and false ideas in the mind. These must be recognized and rejected little by little, day by day to the very end of life. The book of Revelation is given to show us these forces in their true aspect.

The last verses of the twentieth chapter sum up in brief and simple form the final judgment. Many people over the centuries have taken them literally, expecting to remain in their graves until some final day and then to be raised up and brought before a throne on which the Lord would be seated to judge them. And they have thought of the books as a record kept in heaven of all their acts, which would then be opened and read out. The writings give us a very different understanding of this scene. There is no need for anyone else to keep a record of our acts. We keep that record ourselves. For everything we do or think or feel affects us and goes into the formation of our character, and everything we choose freely, of good or evil, is written on our hearts. The character which we ourselves have formed by our free choices from day to day in this world is our "book" which will be opened when we pass into the spiritual world, not in any single judgment scene, but gradually, as we put off the external considerations which have restrained us in this world from giving full expression to what we really feel and think.

We shall judge ourselves by choosing in perfect freedom the kind of life which we have formed in our inner selves. Read Revelation 13:8, 3:4-5, and 2:17. We know that in the Word the name of anything always signifies its quality. Our names will be found written in the book of life if our inmost quality is found to be in accord with the divine truth of the Word. In that case our sphere will be the sphere of heaven where all live in love to the Lord and in mutual love for each other and no one wishes to exalt himself or to be served. If we are not so written in the book of life, if our final quality proves to be centered in self, our chosen sphere will be the sphere of hell, where all burn with the desire to exalt themselves and to be served by others. This is the "lake of fire."

We are all very familiar with chapters 21 and 22. The book of Revelation has well been called "the charter of the New Church." The formation of the new heaven and new earth and the descent of the holy city, New Jerusalem, are described as immediately following the opening of the books and the final judgment. The first verse of Genesis declares, "In the beginning God created the heaven and the earth." The ultimate result of this creation, desired and foreseen by the Lord from the beginning, is "a new heaven and a new earth." All the history of man as a race and as an individual lies between. In verse 6 of our chapter we read, "And he said unto me, It is done. I am Alpha and Omega, the beginning and the end." In TCR 791, at the end of the section on the New Heaven and the New Church, we read: "After this work was finished the Lord called together His twelve disciples who followed Him in the world; and the next day sent them all forth throughout the whole spiritual world to preach the Gospel that *the Lord God Jesus Christ* reigns, whose kingdom shall be for ages and ages, according to the prediction in Daniel (7:13, 14) and in the Apocalypse (9:15) . . . This took place on the nineteenth day of June,

1770." This is the only specific date so mentioned in the writings and we have every reason to observe June 19 as "New Church Day."

In AR 879 we read: "*And I John saw the holy city New Jerusalem coming down from God out of heaven*, signifies the New Church to be established by the Lord at the end of the former church, which will be consociated with the New Heaven in Divine truths as to doctrine and as to life." This should make us think very seriously about the basis of our New Church organization and its mission in the world. The new heaven is established in the spiritual world. It is the only Christian heaven there is and it is the eventual home of all the good—whatever their religion may have been in this world—but all the good people are not by virtue of their goodness members of the Lord's New Church on earth, because the New Church on earth must be "consociated with the New Heaven *in Divine truths* as to doctrine and as to life." Without good of life there is no church, but without true doctrine also there is no New Church.

The Lord said to His disciples (John 15:16): "Ye have not chosen me, but I have chosen you." He says the same to us in this new age. Is this an excuse for self-exaltation? Peter denied the Lord. Judas betrayed Him. Any one of us may and frequently does do the same. We deny and betray Him when we turn our backs on the truths which He has entrusted to us for the world's enlightenment— the Gospel He has given us to preach—and by all our failures to live these truths. "I have chosen you," He says, "and ordained you, that ye should go and bring forth fruit, and that your fruit should remain."

From the Writings of Swedenborg

Apocalypse Revealed, n. 876: "*And I saw a New Heaven and a New Earth*, signified that a New Heaven was formed from Christians by the Lord, which at this day is called the Christian heaven, where they are who had worshipped the Lord and had lived according to His Commandments in the Word, in whom therefore there is charity and faith: in which heaven also are all the infants of Christians. By 'a New Heaven and a New Earth,' is not meant the natural heaven visible to the eyes, nor the natural earth inhabited by men, but the spiritual heaven are meant, and the earth belonging to that heaven, where the angels are . . . It is called the Christian heaven, because it is distinct from the ancient heavens, which existed from the men of the church before the Lord's coming. These ancient heavens are above the Christian heaven; for the heavens are like expanses, one above another; it is the same with each particular heaven; for each heaven by itself is distinguished into three heavens, an inmost or third, a middle or second, and a lowest or first, and so it is with this New Heaven."

Apocalypse Revealed, n. 879: "*And I John saw the holy city New Jerusalem coming down from God out of heaven*, signifies the New Church to be established by the Lord at the end of the former church, which will be consociated with the New Heaven in Divine truths as to doctrine and as to life . . . it is said 'to come down from God out of heaven,' because it descends from the Lord through the New Christian heaven . . . for the church on earth is formed through heaven by the Lord, that they may act as one and be consociated."

Apocalypse Revealed, n. 881: "*Prepared as a Bride adorned for her Husband*, signifies that church conjoined with the Lord through the Word . . . By 'prepared' is signified clothed for her betrothal, and the church is no otherwise attired for her betrothal, and afterwards for conjunction or marriage, than by the Word; for this is the only means of conjunction or marriage, because the Word is from the Lord and concerning the Lord, and thus the Lord; for which reason it is also called 'a covenant,' and 'a covenant' signifies spiritual conjunction; the Word also was given for this end. That by 'Husband' is meant the Lord is plain from verses 9 and 10 of this chapter, where Jerusalem is called 'the Bride the Lamb's Wife.' "

───────────

Suggested Questions on the Lesson

P. What was the book which John saw in the right hand of the Lord? *the Word*

P. With how many seals was it sealed? *seven*

J. Who was to open the book? *the Lord*

J. In our lesson today who are standing before the throne? *the dead*

I. What are the "books" which are opened? *individual character*

I. How are the dead judged? *by the degree of love to the Lord and the neighbor*

J. What happened to those who were not found written in the book of life? *cast into lake of fire*

J. At the beginning of the next chapter, what does John see? *new heaven, new earth*

P. Where in the Bible did we first hear of the heaven and the earth? *Genesis 1*

P. What does John see coming down from God out of heaven? *holy city*

P. What is the name of the city? *New Jerusalem*

J. Why is this name so familiar to us? *name of our church*

J. What are some of the blessings people find in this city? *no tears, pain, death*

J. What does the Lord call Himself? *Alpha and omega*

J. What are *Alpha* and *omega*? *first and last letters of Greek alphabet*

J. What does the Lord promise? *water of life*

I. What kind of thirst is He speaking about? *for truth*

S. What is the "fountain of the water of life"? *divine truth in the Word*

S. What is meant by becoming a son of God? *developing in the image and likeness of God*

THE HOLY CITY
Revelation 21:9-27

In all classes above the Primary, a few minutes should be spent reviewing the Word as a whole. Some questions may also be asked, especially in the Junior class, but the review should be kept carefully within limits so that there will be time for the lesson proper, as it is very important for all the pupils to be impressed with the picture of the New Jerusalem as the culmination of the whole Bible story.

─────

Doctrinal Points

Our "holy city" is built of the heavenly principles we choose to rule our thoughts, feelings, and actions.

The New Jerusalem pictures the ideal of life toward which each of us should be striving every day.

─────

Notes for Parents

The Bible is one book, although it was written through many men over a period of more than fifteen hundred years. Its author is the Lord Himself and in it He tells us the story of His dealings with men from the time when He created them, showing us how in His love He followed them down as they departed from their first state of childlike trust and obedience, never leaving them without the knowledge they needed, and even—when they were about to destroy themselves—coming into the world Himself to fight their battles and show them the way to happiness.

We have seen that the final book of the Bible, given through the apostle John after the Lord's death and resurrection, is a prophecy, the revelation of what the further course of the world would be and also of what the result will inevitably be of the kind of life each of us chooses to live while we are in this world.

The greater part of the book of Revelation is concerned with the disastrous results of choosing to close our ears to the truth the Lord speaks to us in His Word. But the book does not end on this unhappy note. The last two chapters show us the wonderful happiness which is in store for all who will overcome selfishness and follow the Lord's guidance.

In our chapter for today the final state of the good is pictured in the beautiful vision of the "holy city, new Jerusalem, coming down from God out of heaven." We all know that we have an inner life as well as an outer life, that we may be very different in our secret thoughts and feelings from what we appear to other people to be. What we do not always realize is that our inner self is the really important one, not only because that is what will appear when we pass into the other world but also because it is the quality of our inner self which makes us happy or unhappy in this world. We all naturally like to blame our troubles on other people, but we know that people who have everything the world can give are often unhappy, and that many who have poverty and hardship to bear are nevertheless happy.

The "city" our souls live in is built of the principles which we have chosen to rule our thoughts and feelings. If we have chosen to learn and obey the Lord's truth, which He has given us in His Word, we live in the beautiful heavenly city described in our lesson. Its temple is the Lord and its light comes from Him, and every one of the truths of His Word is like a precious stone, beautiful with its own special brightness and color. The golden reed with which the city is measured is the Lord's own measuring stick of pure unselfish love, and our city is found to be "foursquare," sincere and just all through, rising toward the Lord higher and higher as our knowledge of Him and our love for serving Him—its breadth and length—increase. This is why the measure of the city is called "the measure of a man, that is, of the angel." It is a picture of the ideal life toward which each of us should be striving every day.

Let us keep this beautiful city always in mind. Its gates are open.

Primary

Little children love the very sound of this story as it is read to them from the Word, and it makes a much deeper impression than we realize. They should be taught to think of it as a picture of heaven and the heavenly life, and also to know and love the name of our church because it is named for this heavenly city. The children can also be given an idea of what the judgment really is. It is good to put in their minds the thought that the Lord always knows what they are feeling and thinking no matter how hard they try to cover it up, and that someday we shall have to appear openly as we really are. Read to them especially verses 16 and 17 and tell them that our ideal should be to "measure up" to the dimensions of this heavenly city.

You remember that the apostle John in his vision saw some very sad things, and that these were pictures of what happens in our hearts and minds when we do not want to learn from the Lord and to live as He wants us to live.

Most of the book of Revelation is a prophecy of the judgment.
Judgment is just the uncovering of what we are really like in our hearts.
This comes when we die because we leave behind us in this world everything we have "put on" for show.

But the Lord showed John also the beautiful things that happen to people who love to listen to His Word and to obey Him. Our story today is one of these beautiful pictures.

John finally saw the holy city, which is a picture of heavenly life.
How many gates did it have?
What were they made of?
What were written on the gates?
What were written on the twelve foundations?
What was the wall made of?
What were the city and its street made of?
What was the shape of the city?
What was the name of the city?
What is the name of our church?

Always remember that your church is named for the beautiful heavenly city. This is because it is in the church that we learn how to live heavenly lives like the angels in the beautiful city. See if you can remember the name, and try to be good. Then you may always live in the golden city.

Junior

Help the children to fix in their minds as many of the details of the vision as possible, with the understanding of what the city as a whole pictures, and tell them that every detail has a meaning which they will be able to learn in later years. The thought of what the "measure of a man" really is should be a helpful one to leave with them. If there is time, tie this in with the development of a man as pictured in the Creation story.

You remember that it was the opening of the seventh seal which began the different kinds of destruction, and that this was a picture of the fact that when we come face to face with the real truth, the bad things which we have allowed to work in our hearts and minds appear, together with the destruction they have caused. So when the seventh trumpet sounded, the very worst of people's selfish desires and thoughts appeared clearly and the evil were separated from the good and went away into hell, where selfishness reigns. Then the way was cleared for the good to see and enjoy the beautiful things prepared for them.

We finish our study of the Word with the beautiful vision of the descent of the "holy city, new Jerusalem," which is the ideal toward which all the Bible has been leading us. The people of Bible days, of course, thought of Jerusalem as the city which was their capital when they were a great nation, where the temple was built and all their worship centered. That earthly city with its temple was destroyed first by Nebuchadnezzar and again by the Romans in A.D. 70. But all through the centuries it has been clear to the Christian Church that in the Word Jerusalem is a symbol of something spiritual and eternal. Jerusalem means "place of peace," and we can think of it as the state of peace and happiness in which we can live if only we will learn the Lord's truth and try to live according to it. So it is a symbol of the church which is formed of those who love and serve the Lord both on earth and in heaven, and the New Jerusalem is a beautiful and fitting name for the church founded on the deeper truths which the Lord revealed when in His Second Coming He opened the Word. In John's vision it is because the seals were opened that everything could be put in order and the "holy city, new Jerusalem" could finally appear.

It is a beautiful vision and one which you will understand more and more as you grow older. But now you must try to get some of the details into your minds and have them to remember and think about.

Where was John taken to see the holy city?
How many gates did it have?
What were the gates made of?
What were written on them?
How many foundations did the wall have?
What were written on them?
What were the city and its street made of?
What were the foundations garnished with?
What was the temple in the city?
Where did its light come from?
Who may not enter it?
Who may enter it?

Now let us think a little about verses 16 and 17. What do we mean when we say that a person is "on the square" or a "square shooter"? We mean that he is sincere and just, always honest and fair to other people, a person whose word can be trusted. And we often speak of a person's "measuring up" to certain standards. So it is said of the holy city that its measure is the "measure of a man, that is, of the angel." A good man—who is an angel or messenger of the Lord—will be square, which means that he will try to learn what is right and will wish to live according to all the truth he learns. And he will also have another equal dimension: that is height, a reaching up toward the Lord for goodness and wisdom and strength of character. This is how a person comes to be "written in the Lamb's book of life" and to be one of the dwellers in the holy city, new Jerusalem.

═══════

Intermediate

Draw as much of the correspondence as possible from the knowledge of the young people themselves. It is an excellent lesson in which to spur them to an effort to work out the interpretation. Present the holy city as the ideal toward which each of them is working as a member of the New Church.

The opening of the seventh seal and the sounding of the first six trumpets exposed the true states of the souls of the people of the first Christian Church who had been gathered into the spiritual world from the time of the Lord's resurrection to the time of His Second Coming. These people had all believed themselves to be in heaven in the meantime because they had found themselves still alive and had been allowed to go on much as they had in the world. Swedenborg calls this state "imaginary heavens." The beginning of the breaking up of this state is described in verse 14 of chapter 6, where we read that after the sixth seal was opened, "the heaven departed as a scroll when it is rolled together."

With the sounding of the seventh trumpet the struggle began between the evil and the powers of heaven, in which the evil were finally brought into their true places in the hells. Then the good could be raised up out of the place where they had been kept in safety by the Lord, and they could be instructed in the deeper truths revealed by the Lord in His Second Coming and formed into the true Christian heaven, with which the new Christian Church to be formed on earth would be connected.

Our lesson today is about this new heaven and new church to which we may all hope to belong if we study the deeper truth revealed in the Word and try to live according to it. It is because the giving of this deeper understanding of truth is described in Revelation by the descent to earth of the holy city, new Jerusalem, that our church is named the "Church of the New Jerusalem" and is commonly called "The New Church."

The description of the holy city given in the verses assigned for our lesson today is a beautiful picture in the letter. It is still more beautiful when we understand the spiritual meaning of the details of the vision and think of them as qualities which are possessed by the New Church in heaven and by those who are true members of the New Church on earth. You already know enough correspondences to work out some of this meaning for yourselves. You know, for instance, that a city is the symbol of doctrine; so the

New Church has its form from truth. But the city was "pure gold, like unto clear glass," and you know that gold corresponds to love. So you can understand Swedenborg's own words about it: "By 'the city,' or Jerusalem, is meant the Lord's New Church as to everything of it interiorly regarded, or within the wall. By 'gold' is signified the good of love from the Lord . . . and 'like unto pure glass' signifies pellucid [transparent] from the Divine wisdom." The street of the city is also said to be "pure gold, as it were transparent glass." The street, where people walk, is the symbol of the way of life. If we truly belong to the New Church, we will walk in ways of loving service, directed by truth from the Lord.

The wall which bounds and protects the city is the letter of the Word. Its twelve gates are all the truths which introduce us to the understanding of what a good life is, and its twelve foundations are the great fundamental truths of Christianity. You have learned that the twelve tribes of Israel and the twelve apostles represent all goods and truths possible to us; so you can see why their names are written on the gates and foundations. The precious stones are the various truths of the Word as we come to see them one by one in all their clearness and beauty, as the Lord gives us light to appreciate them.

There were three gates on each side of the city, and it is said that they "shall not be shut at all by day." This is a picture of the fact that although every person in the world is different from every other, starting with a different endowment and a different environment, there is no one who does not have some knowledge of truth through which it is possible for him to find his way into the holy city, provided he is in the "daytime" state; that is, if he really wants truth from the Lord because he is eager to grow better all the time. If you think that in this case everyone will certainly find his way in eventually, read John 3:19 and then the last verse of our chapter. Everyone does not want to live in the light of the holy city, because it is the light that comes from the Lord only as we overcome selfishness and worship the Lord alone. This is what is meant by verses 22 and 23. We have already learned what it means to have the books of our lives compared with the book of life.

Another very important verse is verse 16. All through the Word length is used as a measure of love or goodness and breadth as a measure of the understanding of truth. Height represents "good and truth together in every degree," because it is by means of learning more and more truth and loving to do it that our souls reach up toward the Lord and that His spirit can come down to us. Now you can work out this verse for yourselves, and also see why the measure of the city is said to be "the measure of a man, that is, of the angel."

You may think of all the doctrine you have learned this year as part of the foundations and walls of the holy city. Those truths which you have understood clearly and welcomed into your thought and life are the bright precious stones, and if you keep on faithfully, the whole wall will someday appear to you to be made of "jasper," beautifully translucent.

Basic Correspondences

the city	=	doctrine
the street	=	the way of life
the wall	=	the sense of the letter of the Word
length	=	the measure of goodness
breadth	=	the measure of truth
height	=	good and truth together in every degree
the holy city, New Jerusalem	=	the New Church in heaven and on earth

Senior

Remind the Seniors of the fact that it is the ability to know and love the Lord which really distinguishes man from the animals, and tie this in with verses 16 and 17. Try to make the picture of the holy city an ideal which they may hold before them always as their ultimate goal, and stress the fact that without the truths given us by the Lord in His Second Coming, there can be no holy city in the individual or in the world.

Several chapters in the book of Revelation treat of the completion of the last judgment in the spiritual world, of the struggle of those in falsities and evils to maintain control, and of their defeat by the armies of the Lord and their final withdrawal to the hells whose delights they had chosen during their life on earth. So the spiritual world was reduced to order and the way opened for the descent of the holy city.

Swedenborg begins his interpretations of our chapter in the *Apocalypse Revealed* with this brief summary of its meaning: "In this chapter it treats of the state of heaven and the church after the Last Judgment; that after this, through the New Heaven, the New Church will exist on earth, which will worship the Lord alone (vers. 1-8). Its conjunction with the Lord (vers. 9, 10). The description of it as to intelligence from the Word (ver. 11); as to doctrine thence (vers. 12-21); and as to all its quality (vers. 22-26)." So the New Church is identified with the "holy city, new Jerusalem." We commonly speak of our church as the New Church, but we should always have in mind its full name and the source of that name. Never hesitate to use the full name when anyone asks you to what church you belong. If your hearer looks puzzled, say: "It is named for the holy city new Jerusalem, described in the twenty-first chapter of Revelation." This is often necessary because people today unfortunately do not know their Bibles as well as they should.

We can think of this holy city as the ideal according to which we, as New Churchmen, should be shaping our lives. In the first place it is pictured as a city, and we know that a city corresponds to doctrine. You do not belong to the New Church by merely in a vague way wanting to be good. Swedenborg tells us many times that good takes its quality from truth and that love has no power except through truth. So, although the city is pure gold—pure love—it is a city with foundations and walls and gates. And although it has twelve gates, three on each side, and so may be approached from various angles, and although its gates are always open, "There shall in no wise enter into it any thing that defileth, neither whatsoever worketh abomination, or maketh a lie: but they which are

written in the Lamb's book of life." We have seen that the judgment
on us as individuals is no more nor less than the comparison of the
books of our lives, which we have written by our daily choices in
this world, with the book of life, which is the Word of God.

The city is said to be of gold and its street of gold and the reed
with which the angel measured it was of gold. Love from the Lord
is the quality of the life of the New Church—the Lord alone is its
temple and its light—the paths in which the true New Churchman
walks are paths of loving service, and everything he thinks and
does must submit to the measuring stick of unselfish love.

But all the other details of the description have to do with truth.
The wall which defines the limits of the city and which also protects it is the sense of the letter of the Word, and it is said to be of
jasper, which is a translucent stone, because in the New Church
truth from the internal sense shines through the letter. The names
of the twelve tribes are written on the gates and those of the twelve
apostles on the foundations because the gates represent introductory knowledges and the twelve tribes all the truths and goods of
the church, while by the foundations are meant all things of Christian doctrine, and by the twelve apostles "all things of doctrine
from the Word concerning the Lord and concerning a life according to His commandments." The many and varied precious stones
which adorn the foundations are the particular truths of the letter
of the Word lighted up by the Lord from within as we come to see
and delight in them. Different truths in the Word have special
appeal for different people. We must always remember this when
we talk about the church to others, and be quick and sympathetic
in recognizing what each one needs most and so is looking for.
And the gates of the city were twelve pearls, "every several gate
was of one pearl." The pearl is "the acknowledgment and knowledge of the Lord." Read John 10:9 and then Matthew 13:45-46.
No one comes into the holy city except by the way of knowledge
and acknowledgment of the Lord. We cannot climb up some other
way, as the Lord tells us in John 10:1.

Of the city it is said that it is "foursquare" and that "the length and the breadth and the height of it are equal." This means that we must have as much truth as goodness and as much goodness as truth, and that both must be expressed in our lives from top to bottom—in will, thought, and act. We must not keep any part of our souls to ourselves, away from the direction and cleansing of the Lord's truth as it is given us through the Word. This is the "measure of a man, that is, of the angel." Angels and men alike must strive to live up to this heavenly ideal if they wish to dwell in the holy city, new Jerusalem.

Adult

Our lesson is more than a beautiful picture of an intangible heavenly vision. It is a searching and challenging statement of what we of the New Church may and should be and do. The teacher of the Adult class should be well versed in the details of the vision and their spiritual meaning and should make this lesson an especially thought-provoking and inspiring one. In preparation read, if possible, all of chapter 21 in the *Apocalypse Revealed*, but at least read the full five-page summary at the beginning of the chapter.

The Word in its letter begins with the account of the stages by which a truly human being is created, and it ends with a picture of the ideal form which it is possible for him to attain if he remains faithful to the Lord through all the temptations which are permitted to come to him. This form is pictured as the "holy city, new Jerusalem, coming down from God out of heaven, prepared as a bride adorned for her husband." It is a beautiful picture in the letter, one which children love to hear read for the very sound of the words, which set their imaginations to work and form a basis in their minds for the influx of the Lord's enlightening spirit. If with the years we have lost our love for this picture, there is something radically wrong in our souls, for the Lord says, "Except ye be converted, and become as little children, ye shall not enter the kingdom of heaven."

We in the New Church should love this picture above others, because under divine providence we have been brought in contact with the revelation of its meaning given to the world by the Lord

in His Second Coming. Our study now is centered on the details of
the description of the holy city. It is a description of our church as
it should be and of the soul of each individual one of us as it should
be. In his brief summary of the contents of chapter 21 in the
Apocalypse Revealed Swedenborg says: "In this chapter it treats
of the state of heaven and the church after the Last Judgment;
that after this, through the New Heaven, the New Church will
exist on the earth, which will worship the Lord alone (vers. 1-8).
Its conjunction with the Lord (vers. 9, 10). The description of it
as to intelligence from the Word (ver. 11); as to doctrine thence
(vers. 12-21); and as to all its quality (vers. 22-26)."

Our church organization was founded by a group of men and
women who had found in the doctrines revealed by the Lord in
His Second Coming the answers to their spiritual questions and the
true plan of heavenly living. They named their organization the
"Church of the New Jerusalem" because its purpose was to make
known these doctrines, which are the holy city, new Jerusalem.
Throughout the Word a city is the symbol of doctrine. "A city
that is set on a hill cannot be hid." The founders set their city on
a hill and the church grew. Today we ask ourselves why our organization is not growing and we run about studying the methods of
other churches and trying to copy them, soft-pedaling our doctrines for fear of seeming narrow and bigoted, trying to appear as
much like everyone else as possible. We say, "After all, our organization is not the New Church—the New Church is coming down
everywhere." If our organization is not the New Church, it has no
excuse for existence, and it is the New Church exactly to the
extent that we, its members, learn, live, and proclaim its doctrines.
If we try to dodge this necessity, we are like ostriches, hiding our
heads in the sand of current opinion. Because of our natural inheritance it is always easier to believe that if our intentions are
good, what we do will be right without any effort on our part to
study the truth which the Lord has given us. We really know better.
We see all about us the disastrous effects of misguided good intentions. But we persist in believing that our own are different.

True, the holy city in John's vision is made of gold and its street is of gold. The essential quality of the New Church in heaven and on earth is the good of love—but it is the good of love from the Lord, not natural goodness—and its ways are ways of loving service to the Lord and the neighbor and the city has a wall "great and high" and the wall—of jasper—is the symbol of truth from the sense of the letter of the Word "pellucid" [transparent], as Swedenborg says, from the understanding of the spiritual sense. The wall protects the city but it also imposes limits. We remember that the word *religion* means literally a "tying back." We cannot give free rein to our natural ideas and inclinations and dwell within the holy city.

True again, the city has twelve gates, three on each side, and they are always open. The gates represent introductory truths. People are different. Each one has a different inheritance, a different background, different problems. We need to remember this in all our missionary efforts. One may approach the city from any one of several directions and find a gate—a particular truth—which attracts him and affords access. But an angel or messenger of the Lord stands at each gate and a particular quality—expressed by the name of one of the twelve tribes—is written on the gate. The interest in the particular truth must be accompanied by a genuine recognition of the Lord and desire to be taught by Him. Though the gates of the city are always open, "there shall in no wise enter into it any thing that defileth, neither whatsoever worketh abomination, or maketh a lie: but they which are written in the Lamb's book of life." We have seen that judgment consists in the comparison of the books of our lives, as we have written them by our day-to-day choices in this world, with the book of life, which is the Word. And we cannot pattern our lives on the Word without studying what the Word teaches.

The foundations of the wall represent great basic truths, and because the new permanent heavens are Christian heavens, the names of the twelve apostles are written on the foundations. Of the jasper wall Swedenborg says, "that all the Divine truth in the sense of the letter of the Word, with the men of that church, is translucent from the Divine truth in the spiritual sense." Unless we are willing to make the effort to study the spiritual sense by means of the writings, our wall is not of jasper. And the same is true of the precious stones which garnish the wall, of which Swedenborg says that "all things of the doctrine of the New Jerusalem taken from the sense of the letter of the Word, with those who are in it, will appear in the light according to reception." Each of us knows certain particular verses from the Word which have been lighted up for us by our doctrines so that we really treasure them as precious stones. The more we study the Word in the light of the writings the more of these beautiful, varied precious stones we have.

The angel measured the city with a golden reed—the measuring stick of love from the Lord—and it was found to be foursquare: "The length and the breadth and the height of it are equal." In the Word length is the measure of love or goodness and breadth of truth, and height is the extent to which good and truth acting together govern all three planes of our lives from our outer conduct up through our thinking to our inmost will. The only way that the Lord's spirit can come down to us is as we form all the planes of our lives according to His Word.

This is the city which is "the measure of a man, that is, of the angel." We do not build the New Church. The Lord builds it in and through us as we deny *ourselves* and follow Him. The holy city, new Jerusalem, can descend to earth only as those who have been called to its service by the Lord are faithful and diligent stewards of the great riches entrusted to them. He says to each one of us, "Ye have not chosen me, but I have chosen you."

"Except the Lord build the house, they labor in vain that build it: except the Lord keep the city, the watchman waketh but in vain."

———

From the Writings of Swedenborg

Apocalypse Revealed, n. 914: "*And the foundations of the wall of the city were adorned with every precious stone*, signifies that all things of the doctrine of the New Jerusalem taken from the sense of the letter of the Word, with those who are therein, will appear in light according to reception. By 'the twelve foundations' are signified all things of doctrine (n. 902). By 'the wall' is signified the Word in the sense of the letter (n. 898). By 'the holy city Jerusalem' is signified the Lord's New Church (n. 879, 880). By 'precious stone' is signified the Word in the sense of the letter, pellucid [transparent] from its spiritual sense (n. 231, 540, 726, 911). And because this is according to reception, therefore it signifies that all things of doctrine from the Word with them, will appear in light according to reception . . . Interior thought is in the light of heaven, and is called perception, and exterior thought is in the light of the world; and the understanding of every man is such that it can be elevated even into the light of heaven, and also is elevated, if from any delight he wishes to see truth."

Suggested Questions on the Lesson

P. What is our lesson for today about? *the holy city*

J. Where did the city come from? *God, out of heaven*

P. What was its name? *New Jerusalem*

P. What was it made of? *gold*

P. How many gates did it have? *twelve*

J. What names were written on them? *tribes of Israel*

J. What was the wall of the city made of? *jasper*

P. How many foundations did it have? *twelve*

J. What were written on the foundations? *apostles*

J. What were they garnished with? *jewels*

P. What was the street of the city made of? *gold*

J. What is said about the temple in the city? *the Lord is the temple*

J. Where did its light come from? *the glory of God*

J. Who could not enter the city? *evil people*

J. Who could enter it? *those written in Lamb's book of life*

I. What does it mean to be written in the Lamb's book of life? *to have lived a good life*

P. What did the angel measure the city with? *gold rod or reed*

J. What were its proportions found to be? *"foursquare"*

J. Why was its measure called "the measure of a man, that is, of the angel"? *good person is "foursquare"*

J. Why should we in the New Church especially love this vision? *it pictures the ideal church*

I. What is pictured by the fact that the city and its street were of pure gold, like clear glass? *enables one to walk in loving ways, clearly understood*

S. What should we say when people ask to what church we belong? *Church of the New Jerusalem*

S. What should we say if they appear to be puzzled by the name? *see Revelation 21-22*

THE HOLY CITY
Revelation 21; 22

In this closing picture from John's vision the first thing to note in all classes is the fact that our church takes its name from the holy city coming down from God out of heaven. This should be an inspiration and a joy to all of us. After discussing the main features of the vision, the relation between the beginning of the Word and these closing chapters should be pointed out. It is very important that the pupils see the Word as one book, a complete picture of life and its development for good or evil as we choose to be led by the Lord or by self.

Doctrinal Points

The account of the holy city is a vision of the true form of life in which we may find lasting joy and peace.

Our "gate" into the city is through regular study of the Word and the writings, together with consistent efforts to apply the truths to life.

Notes for Parents

Many churches, taking statements in the Bible literally, think that there will someday be a great judgment at the end of the world. In the New Church we regard all the Word as a parable, though much of it is also history, and we believe that there have been several judgments, one on each of the various churches which have succeeded each other on earth, and also that each one of us is judged when at death he enters the spiritual world; that is, his inner life is revealed and he finds his place in heaven or in hell according to the character which he has formed in himself during his life in this world.

As verse 12 of chapter 20 tells us: "I saw the dead, small and great, stand before God; and the books were opened: and another book was opened, which is the book of life: and the dead were judged out of those things which were written in the books, according to their works." The books are the record of our lives which we write into our character day by day, and the book of life is the Word of God. A heavenly character is one patterned on the precepts of the Word.

John's vision in Revelation is a symbolic picture of this whole process of judgment, beginning with the vision of the Lord and the warnings and promises to the various kinds of people. After that, John saw a throne and the Lord sitting upon it with the book of life in His hand. The book was at first sealed with seven seals. This is a picture of the Word of God as we first read it, without understanding it. Then in the vision the Lord opens the seals one by one and as each is opened, strange and terrible things happen. The more deeply we see into the meaning of the Word the more we realize how many evils are in us, which we must fight and overcome with the Lord's help. But throughout the vision the good are also revealed and are protected by the Lord, just as He always seeks to preserve whatever good is found in us.

Finally in our chapters for today there comes the beautiful vision of the holy city New Jerusalem coming down from God out of heaven. It is a vision of the true form of life in which we may find joy and peace. We enter it by studying the Word of God and seeing and accepting its deeper truths and living according to them. The wall of the city is the literal sense of the Word, its foundations are the basic principles of a good life as laid down in the ten commandments. The precious stones are the varied and beautiful truths which appear to us as we study the Word, its gates of pearl the means of entrance through obedience to its teachings, its golden street the path of loving service in which we learn to walk.

The New Church is based on the revelation of the deeper meaning within the letter of the Word. So it takes as its name the "Church of the New Jerusalem." The way to the holy city has been revealed by the Lord. It is not always an easy way—it is not the way of worldliness and self-satisfaction—but if we choose to undertake it, the Lord and the angels are ever with us, enlightening, inspiring, and strengthening us. Verse 14 of chapter 22 tells us: Blessed are they that do his commandments, that they may have right to the tree of life, and may enter in through the gates into the city."

―――――――

Primary

Tell the children that John was given a vision of the beautiful city which is a picture of heaven, in which we shall all live someday if we are good. Then read from the Word as much of the actual description as possible. Be sure to include and comment upon 21:27 and 22:11, showing the children that it is the life they live here which determines whether or not they will enter the gates of the holy city of heaven. See how many of the details of the vision the children can remember afterward.

After John was given the messages to the seven churches, he was shown many wonderful and terrible things which teach us what happens in the other world to people who refuse to listen to what the Lord teaches us so lovingly and who insist on doing just as they please all their lives. And the vision shows us, too, how the Lord takes care of all who are good, and separates them from the evil.

After that John saw a vision of a sealed book which no one but the Lord could open.

As the seals of the book were opened one by one, a great judgment took place.

Finally what did John see coming down from God out of heaven?

How many gates and foundations did this city have?

What can you tell about them?

How was the city measured?

What shape was it?

What did John see flowing from the throne of God?

What grew on either side of the river?

Where have we heard of the river and the tree of life before?

Who cannot enter the city?

I wonder if you remember hearing about a river and about the tree of life in one of our lessons on the book of Genesis. They were in the Garden of Eden. Let us look back in our Bible and read about them. [Read Genesis 2:8-12.] When we are innocent little babies, before we have begun to do naughty things, it is like living in the Garden of Eden. But if we keep trying to stop being naughty and grow up to be strong, good men and women, when we die we shall live in heaven, and this is what the beautiful city of John's vision pictures.

———

Junior

After your review begin with the name of our church, and explain the general meaning of the holy city. Then take up such details as are mentioned in the Junior notes, having the class look up all the references to other parts of the Word. End with the lesson of 21:27 and 22:11.

With what vision does the book of Revelation open?

To whom was the revelation given?

Why did the seven churches in Asia need the messages that were given to John for them?

With what words do all the messages end?

The whole book of Revelation is really a picture of what happens in our lives as we begin to understand what the Lord says to us in His Word. Little by little we are led to see the wrong things that are in us, first in our conduct, then in our thoughts, and finally deeper and deeper down in our hearts. This is what is called the process of judgment. And if we acknowledge our faults as they are brought to light and try with the Lord's help to conquer them, we gradually become true children of God. This is what is called regeneration, which means rebirth. It is a long, slow process which goes on all our lives in this world. But if we are faithful, we come at last to the holy city toward which the Lord has all along been leading us.

So at the very end of the book—the end of the Bible itself—John is given a beautiful vision of this holy city, the New Jerusalem, coming down from God out of heaven. Our church is named for this city, because our church is founded on the opened Word. The description of the city in verses 11 to 27 of chapter 21 is very beautiful, and we like to read it over and over. See how many things you can remember about it. In each detail there is a wonderful meaning which you will learn gradually as you come to know more and more of correspondences.

Then in chapter 22 John is given a vision of what is within the city.

What does he see flowing from the throne of God?
What grows beside the river?
Where did we first read of this river and tree of life?

Read Genesis 2:8-17. And one of the Major Prophets also saw these things. Read Ezekiel 47:1-12.

Water is a picture of truth. The great river symbolizes the truth flowing from God to us in the Word. Everyone who really wants the truth can find it there. Read verse 17. Now read what the Lord said to the woman of Samaria in John 4:10-14. The tree of life which grows beside this river is a picture of the beautiful principle that everything we have comes to us from the Lord, and its fruit is genuine goodness. Read 22:14 to see how we may become truly good.

Now read 22:11. It teaches us that merely passing from this world into the spiritual world does not change anyone. A man who is evil here is just as evil when he wakes up in the world of spirits, and a man who is good here continues to be good there. After death no one can change his heart. We are put in this world just so that we can learn what is right and by choosing freely to do it make it our own forever.

There is one other point which we should notice especially. Read 22:8-9. Some churches teach that angels are a separate kind of creature, quite different from men and women. But here the angel tells John that he had himself been one of the prophets who had obeyed the teachings of the Word.

What does the word *angel* mean?

We are all angels when we are carrying the Lord's messages to others by our words or by our lives, and if we are the Lord's messengers in this way while we live here, we shall in time be beautiful angels in heaven. The holy city is a picture of the life that is built on obedience to the Lord's truth. Read 21:16-17. We know what we mean when we say that a person is a "square shooter." The good life is foursquare—equal in its understanding of what is right and in its performance of right—and it has another dimension also which is equal to the other two—its height. That means that it is a life that looks to the Lord as its source and director. That is why the measure of the city is said to be "the measure of a man, that is, of the angel."

Intermediate

Follow the same general outline as for the Juniors, but do more with the correspondence of the details. Stress the necessity of making our choice now and of looking to the Lord and the Word for our guidance all our lives.

Verse 2 of our first chapter for today is one which every New Churchman should memorize, because symbolically it gives us the reason for the name of our church. We have seen in the Old Testament and in the Gospels that Jerusalem stands for the church as to doctrine. The New Jerusalem is the New Church as to its doctrine, and every detail in the vision of the holy city refers to that doctrine and its glory and power. Life according to that doctrine makes the church also "the bride, the Lamb's wife."

The "great and high mountain" to which John was carried in spirit, we are told by Swedenborg, is the highest heaven. The "wall great and high" is the literal sense of the Word which contains and protects all truth. The twelve gates are all the knowledges of good and truth by which men are introduced into the church. The three gates on each side should not be thought of as three separate entrances, but rather as three gates one within another, representing the opening of all three planes to the Lord.* The foundations of the city are the things of doctrine in the literal sense of the Word, such as the ten commandments. The fact that "the length is as

---

*Although this is an appealing idea—with logic on its side—the editor is not aware of any direct statement to this effect in the writings. Cf., however, CL 11. One might also note that standard practice in Near Eastern cities—for defensive purposes—was to build walls with gates in depth. —Ed.

large as the breadth" means that in it good and truth are present in equal measure. The precious stones are all the beautiful truths of doctrine, which take different aspects to different minds. The gates all of one pearl picture the fact that all the knowledge about the Lord which we make our own by living it combines to bring us into the New Church. The street of gold is the path of loving service which enables us to see the beauty of truth. Verses 22 and 23 mean that all who are of the New Church in the heavens acknowledge gladly that they have no goodness or truth of their own but that all goodness and truth are of the Lord alone.

This same thought is carried out in the twenty-second chapter in the picture of the great river of water of life with the tree of life on either side. If we look to the Lord as the source of all wisdom and goodness, He enables us to do "good works," that is, acts which have genuine goodness in them, at every stage of our progress in knowledge of the truth. These are the twelve manner of fruits borne every month. The leaves of the tree, which are for the healing of the nations, are rational truths developed from the principle pictured by the tree of life. We can see that if the thoughts and acts of everyone in the world were constantly governed by obedience to the Lord, all the ills of the world would be speedily healed.

Notice that although the gates of the city are always open, nothing that "defileth" ever enters. This is because only those who really desire the truth for the sake of life ever approach the city. Many in this world learn the truth and talk about it, but if they do not want it to live by, it is only in their external memories, which are closed at death. Only what is lived out is written on the heart. This is what is meant by being written "in the Lamb's book of life." Read verse 12 of chapter 20. The other book which was opened is the Word, and men are judged according to the comparison between their lives and the Word. Each of us is writing his book of life day by day. Everything—every thought and feeling—which we choose to make our own becomes a part of our inner life, no matter how different we may seem on the outside, and when we leave this world, we leave the outside behind and appear as we really are inside. It is a fact that the Lord does not judge us at all: we judge ourselves. This is what the whole book of Revelation teaches us.

The warning in verses 18 and 19 of chapter 22 is a very serious one. As you grow older, you will find that people are constantly tempted to change the Word of God, to try to make it say what they think it ought to say instead of what it actually does say. This soon leads to the belief that the letter of the Word is not to be trusted, that it is the work of men and not of God. Then men begin to delve into the history of the Bible people instead of into the meaning of the Word itself. So they exalt the thoughts of men above the thoughts of God and cut themselves off from the light which the Word is given to bring to them. The fact that we do not always understand clearly what the Word is telling us does not mean that the Word is faulty—it means that we are ignorant and "slow of heart to believe all that the prophets have spoken," as the Lord said to the two disciples on the road to Emmaus (Luke 24:25). It is not an idle warning which is put in this prominent place at the very end of the Bible.

Basic Correspondences

the wall of the holy city	=	the literal sense of the Word
the twelve gates	=	all the introductory knowledges of good and truth
the foundations	=	the basic truths on which a heavenly character is built
precious stones	=	particular truths through which spiritual light shines
the holy city New Jerusalem	=	the true system of doctrine found in the opened Word
the street of gold	=	the path of loving service

Senior

Do more in this class with the outline of the Bible as a whole and the force of these concluding chapters as the culmination of the long spiritual history of mankind and of the individual life. What it means to be a New Churchman is a good general topic for discussion.

The Scriptures open with the Garden of Eden and close with the holy city. The Garden of Eden pictures not only the primitive state of the race man but the infant state of the individual. And the holy city pictures the ultimate goal of humanity and of each one of us. All the Scriptures in between the two describe the journey from what Swedenborg calls the "innocence of ignorance" to the "innocence of wisdom." The garden pictures the range of opportunities which the Lord sets before each of us; the city, our highest possible attainment.

In both the garden and the city we find the great river and the tree of life, but the tree of the knowledge of good and evil is not found in the holy city. We recall that the tree of life pictures the principle that all good and truth are the Lord's. This is the delight of the angels in heaven. The tree of knowledge of good and evil is the principle that man of himself is able to know truth and to do good. Those who have chosen this principle to rule their lives are forever outside of the holy city. The choice between these two principles is the fundamental choice which each of us must make while he lives in this world.

The fruit of the tree of life comes to us as nourishment for our souls in every possible state through which we must pass—the fruit yielded every month—and the leaves of the tree, which are for the healing of the nations, picture the thoughts and reasonings which spring from genuine acknowledgment of the Lord and desire to be led by Him alone. We can easily see that if all men were in this acknowledgment and desire, the nations would literally be healed. Injustice, strife, and oppression spring from the leaves of the other tree.

The beautiful picture of the holy city, with its twelve foundations, its walls great and high, its gold and precious stones, its gates of pearl which are never closed, its golden streets, and the Lord Himself its light is a picture of our inner lives in heaven if we are faithful in our effort to make the books of our lives read like the book of life (Revelation 20:21). We should also recognize that the life pictured by the holy city New Jerusalem is life according to the truths of the opened Word. It is the life of the New Church, the crown of all the churches. That is why our church was in its beginning named the "Church of the New Jerusalem." Each of us should be proud of this name and should try to live up to it, by studying the Word not only in its letter but in its spiritual sense and making the doctrines revealed for our church our own by learning and living them. This is the challenge which the name presents to us.

If we compare Genesis 2:16-17 with Revelation 22:11-12, we see that the law laid down at the beginning of our lives works out to its inevitable conclusion. The choice is ours. We make our lives good or evil, happy or miserable, by our own choice, and the choice made in this world cannot be reversed after death. The final judgment is merely the opening of our interiors to reveal what we have written there.

Adult

The identification of the holy city with the New Church and what this should mean to us is the especial lesson for the Adult class. We should recognize clearly that a city represents a system of doctrine and that, although we may not all enter the city by the same gate or be delighted with the same precious stone in its foundations, we do not enter it at all unless we see it as a city that is foursquare and compact together and wish to establish our lives within its walls.

Swedenborg tells us (AE 879) that "'a city' in the spiritual sense signifies doctrine." We have seen that our house is the house of our character. We build it within the city of certain doctrines or teachings through which we are associated with other men and women and can help them and be helped by them. Jerusalem is the city of the Lord's teachings, "the church as to doctrine." The temple was there, and there the worship of the Lord was carried on. We know that the actual city of Jerusalem was merely a representative and that when the inhabitants had perverted even the externals of their worship, Jerusalem and the temple were destroyed. So it has been with every church: when most of its adherents became selfish and worldly and no longer carried on their worship from a desire to serve the Lord and the neighbor, its city of doctrine was broken up and its people dispersed. Yet throughout the Word the Lord promises that in the fullness of time a church will be raised up which shall not perish, a system of truth will be revealed which shall not perish, a system of truth will be revealed which shall be adequate for all time. This is the stone which smote Nebuchadnezzar's image and then grew into a great mountain and filled the whole earth.

It is also pictured as the holy city New Jerusalem which John saw descending from God out of heaven "prepared as a bride adorned for her husband." Swedenborg (AE 881) beautifully explains this verse. He says that by Jerusalem is meant the church, and continues: "he [John] saw it first as a city, and afterwards as a Virgin Bride; as a city representatively, and as a Virgin Bride spiritually, thus in a twofold idea, one within or above the other; just as the angels do, who when they see or hear or read in the Word of a 'city,' in the idea of the lower thought perceive a city, but in the idea of higher thought perceive the church as to doctrine; and the latter, if they desire it and pray to the Lord, they see as a virgin in beauty and clothing according to the quality of the church. Thus also it has been granted me to see the church . . . The church is no otherwise attired for her betrothal, and afterwards for conjunction or marriage, than by the Word; for this is the only means of conjunction or marriage . . . From these things it may appear, that by 'Jerusalem prepared as a bride for her husband,' is signified that church conjoined with the Lord through the Word." The walls of the city, like the garments of the bride, picture the truths of the Word, which make of the holy Jerusalem "a city that is compact together" (Psalm 122:3). We build our house within the walls of the holy city New Jerusalem when we choose to allow the truths of the Word revealed for the New Age to define, circumscribe, and guard our thought and conduct.

This thought brings us to the consideration of the third of the fundamental doctrines of the New Church, the doctrine of life. Perhaps the most popular and most frequently quoted sentence ever written by Swedenborg is, "All religion is of the life, and the life of religion is to do good." (Life 1) This is a beautiful and true statement, but like all statements it can be falsified if it is taken out of the system of truth to which it belongs and used to support and defend ideas contrary to that system—like a single stone taken from the wall of Jerusalem and built into the wall of Babylon. This particular statement has been used sometimes to excuse lack of interest in "doctrine," and sometimes even to support the position that it is not necessary to go to church, to know about and worship the Lord, or even to keep the commandments, if only one is kind and charitable to his neighbors and active in so-called "good works." We need to know what Swedenborg means by "the life" and what by "to do good." "The life" is not outward conduct. Of the Pharisees the Lord said, "Ye are like unto whited sepulchres, which indeed appear beautiful outward, but are within full of dead men's bones." (Matthew 23:27) And at another time He said, "Except ye eat the flesh of the Son of man, and drink his blood, ye have no life in you." (John 6:53) "The life" is the inmost or heart of man. Religion must be primarily in the heart. And the Lord tells us what it is to do good in Micah 6:8: "He hath showed thee, O man, what is good: and what doth the Lord require of thee, but to do justly, and to love mercy, and to walk humbly with thy God?" "Good works" are not measured by the amount of money we give to charity or by our activity in social reforms, but by our personal righteousness, the justice, mercy, and humility before God which we show in every relation of life. "To do good" is to do not what I think is good or what my neighbors think is good but what the Lord says is good, and this involves a thorough and ever-growing knowledge of the Scriptures and their meaning, a constant effort to learn the Lord's will and do it and to avoid evils as sins against God. If a person's life lacks this inner quality of humility and obedience to the Lord, he cannot do good, whatever his outward acts may be. "If he does them from God they are good, if from self they are not good." (DL 9) And the only way to acquire this inner quality is to keep the commandments, to shun as sins against God the things which the Lord says we must not do. As long as we refuse to recognize our evils, as long as we excuse and defend them, we are not really looking to the Lord for guidance at all, and there is no life in anything we do.

The holy city New Jerusalem is the picture of a heavenly society, the New Church teaching lived. It exists in heaven, but also it is descending to earth to the extent that individual men and women learn and live these teachings. It is "foursquare," "the length, and the breadth, and the height of it are equal," and its measurements are those of a man, "that is of the angel." This is the full life with its three dimensions—love, wisdom, and act—perfectly equal: no good desire which is thwarted by ignorance, no knowledge of the truth which is not put into practice, no deeds which are not the expression of love and wisdom. All the good affections which men may have, represented by the twelve apostles and by the heads of the twelve tribes of Israel, are there as means of entrance and supports. The gates are not shut at all; all who wish may enter. And yet it is said, "And there shall in no wise enter into it any thing that defileth": those who do not wish to obey and serve the Lord see no beauty in the city and have no desire to enter it. For its beauties are all representative: the precious stones are beautiful truths seen in variety by different minds and translucent from the spiritual meaning. The golden streets are paths of loving service. The river of water of life is the truth proceeding from the Lord, the same living water which He promised to the woman of Samaria, and the fruits of the tree of life are all form of heavenly use. These things are beautiful only to those who love goodness for its own sake, thus who love the Lord, who is Good. The worship in the city is directed to the Lord alone, and all the light and glory of it are from Him. This is the picture of the crown and reward of a truly good life; and only a truly good life, lived according to the commandments in loving service of the Lord and the neighbor can see its beauty and glory.

We should all recognize in this last book of the Bible a stirring picture of the life of the true New Churchman, beginning with the beautiful vision of the Lord Jesus Christ reigning, and going on through the lifelong battle against the falsities and evils in oneself as they are gradually uncovered through deeper and deeper understanding of the Word, to the final victory of the established heavenly character with its enjoyments of the Lord's great gifts of love, truth, and heavenly usefulness. "Blessed are they that do his commandments, that they may have right to the tree of life, and may enter in through the gates into the city."

From the Writings of Swedenborg

Apocalypse Revealed, n. 897; *"Having the glory of God: and her light was like unto a stone most precious, as it were a jasper stone, shining like crystal,* signifies that in that church the Word will be understood, because translucent from its spiritual sense. . . . By these words is described the understanding of the Word with those who are in the doctrine of the New Jerusalem, and in a life according to it. With these the Word shines as it were when it is read: it shines from the Lord by means of the spiritual sense, because the Lord is the Word, and the spiritual sense is in the light of heaven which proceeds from the Lord as a sun."

Apocalypse Revealed, n. 935: "He who believes that a man does good that is acceptable to the Lord, which is called spiritual good, unless there are truths from the Word in him, is much deceived. Goods without truths are not goods, and truths without goods are not truths with man, although in themselves they may be truths: for good without truth is like the voluntary of man without the understanding, which voluntary is not human, but is like a beast's, or like that of a carved image which an artificer causes to operate. But the voluntary together with the intellectual becomes human according to the state of the understanding by which it exists. For the state of life of every man is such that his will cannot do anything except through the understanding, nor can the understanding think anything except from the will."

Suggested Questions on the Lesson

J. What did all the Lord's messages point out to the seven churches?
good and bad points, warning, promise
J. Why did the church of Laodicea receive the severest condemnation?
hardest problem to overcome
P. What has been named for this city (Revelation 21:2)? *our church*

P. How many gates did the city have? *twelve*

P. What did the angel measure it with? *gold reed*

J. What was its shape found to be? *foursquare*

P. What were seen in its foundations? *precious stones*

P. What were its gates made of? *pearl*

J. How was it lighted? *the Lord*

J. Who can enter it? *all who will to*

J. What was seen proceeding out of the throne of God? *river of water of life*

P. What grew beside the river? *tree of life*

P. Where have we heard about the river and the tree of life before? *Eden*

J. What did the angel tell John when John would have worshiped him?
worship God

J. How do we regularly use the last verse of the Bible? *benediction*

I. What does the holy city represent? *true system of doctrine found in opened Word*

S. What should the name of our church mean to us? *a challenge to live up to all it implies*

THE END OF JOHN'S VISION
Revelation 22:8-21

Certain great simple lessons are grouped together in the closing verses of the Bible and should be impressed upon all classes: (1) It is possible to all of us to become angels. (2) The Lord's truth is offered freely to all. (3) We must not from our own will and intelligence tamper with the Word as the Lord has given it. (4) To study the Word and obey its commandments is the way to heavenly happiness. (5) The choice is ours, but it must be made here and it is not changed after death. (6) Jesus Christ, risen and glorified, is the only God, the God who speaks to us in the Word, the alpha and omega, the beginning and the end, the first and the last.

Doctrinal Points

The Lord has opened the seals and revealed the inner meaning of His Word, for all who will to see.

The organized New Church is as necessary to the existence and growth of the inner church, as our bodies are necessary to the growth and regeneration of our souls.

Notes for Parents

In this closing chapter of the Bible is summed up all the teaching of the Word. We remember that the first verse in the Bible is: "In the beginning God created the heaven and the earth," and now the same God identifies Himself plainly as Jesus Christ and calls Himself "Alpha and Omega, the beginning and the end, the first and the last."

The heaven and the earth which He created in the beginning are not only the physical world but the heaven and earth in our souls, the heavenly and the earthly part of us. We all develop the earthly part in order to live in this world, but we are not always so careful to develop the heavenly part. And yet if we do not begin to develop

333

it here, we cannot begin after death, as the Lord plainly tells us in verse 11.

Near the beginning of the Bible we have the story of the Garden of Eden, watered by its great river and with the tree of life at its center. That is a picture of the beautiful state in which the people of the first church on earth lived, before they listened to the reasoning of the "serpent" (our sense appetites) and turned from the Lord to self. In the course of our lessons we have seen how far from the Lord they traveled and how the Lord in His mercy followed them down, teaching them and trying to save them from themselves, until finally He came into the world Himself, as the Word made flesh, to live out divine truth before men's eyes and so show them how to recognize and conquer their evils. His coming turned the tide.

Now in the closing chapters of the Bible we find the "river of water of life" and the tree of life again, this time in the holy city New Jerusalem, which was seen "coming down from God out of heaven, prepared as a bride adorned for her husband." This prophecy has been fulfilled. The Lord has now opened the seals and revealed the inner meaning of His Word. The holy city is the New Church which is developing as a result—the "woman clothed with the sun" of whom we have read. The Second Coming of the Lord which was promised in our chapter took place some two hundred years ago, and our church takes its name from this holy city New Jerusalem.

Let us not be of those who refuse to drink of this living water, or of those who try to add to or take away from the divine truth by their own selfish reasonings. Let us rather take or stand with those blessed who "do his commandments, that they may have right to the tree of life, and may enter in through the gates into the city."

Primary

The little children will be deeply affected by the beautiful picture of heavenly happiness and the possibility of becoming angels themselves. The lesson of the importance of their daily choices of right and wrong follows naturally. The teacher should have in mind the six points suggested at the beginning of the lesson.

The last vision that was given to John was of a beautiful city, which was called the holy city New Jerusalem, coming down from God out of heaven. You should always remember that our church is named for it: the Church of the New Jerusalem. This city is a picture of the heavenly life which the Lord gives us if we love and obey Him.

Our lesson today is from the very last chapter of the Bible. The chapter begins with a description of a river—"a pure river of water of life, clear as crystal"—on whose banks grew the tree of life, which bore twelve kinds of fruit. An angel had been showing John all these things, and now John tells us how his vision ended.

Do you remember another place in the Bible where we read about the river and the tree of life?

Do you remember how the Lord told the woman at Jacob's well that if she had asked Him, He would have given her living water?

"Living" water is pure truth from the Lord which comes to us in His Word.

What did we learn not long ago about bearing fruit?

Now read verse 14 and verse 17.

Does everyone enter the holy city?

The Lord invites us all, but some people refuse the invitation.

Can you think why?

What did John's angel guide say about himself?

The angel told John that he himself had been a man on earth; so we know that we may all become angels if we do right. We must learn the Lord's commandments and keep them so that we may "have right to the tree of life and enter in through the gates into the city." For although the gates of the city are always open, everyone does not enter.

You would think, wouldn't you, that everyone would want to live in that beautiful city, but you know some people really like to do wrong—sometimes we do ourselves—and that means that they like ugly and bad things better than beautiful and good ones. Which are you going to choose?

We can all be angels if we choose.

But we must learn the Lord's commandments and obey them.

Junior

With this class the lesson may be taken up a verse or two at a time. Impress upon them the comparisons between the beginning and the end of the Bible, calling attention to the fact that in the last verse God is specifically called "our Lord Jesus Christ."

Now we come to the end of John's vision, which is also the end of the Bible. We have studied chapter 21 and parts of chapter 22. If you do not remember them, you should read them over, for they tell of the beautiful vision of the holy city New Jerusalem—for which our church is named—coming down from God out of heaven, and of the "pure river of water of life, clear as crystal, proceeding out of the throne of God and of the Lamb," beside which grew the tree of life, "which bare twelve manner of fruits, and yielded her fruit every month." Perhaps you remember that the river and the tree of life were both in the Garden of Eden in the beginning of the Bible story. You want to put this away carefully in your memory, for it has a very deep meaning.

The holy city is a picture of the New Church as it is in heaven, the river is the truth which comes to us from the Lord, and the fruit of the tree of life is genuine goodness of all kinds. This city is descending to earth as fast as men and women on earth are willing to receive the truth and form their lives according to it; so it is symbolic of the true New Church on earth, to which we are all trying to belong.

An angel had been showing John all these things.

In verse 8 what did John do?

What did the angel tell him?

This is one of the verses in the Word which tells us plainly that the angels were once men and women on earth, so that we may know that we shall become angels if we live as we should. Notice that John was told not to seal this book as the books of the Word before had been sealed. This was a vision of the time when the Lord would open the Word so that anyone who really wanted the truth might understand it. And the next verse tells us that we are free to choose whether or not we will live the beautiful life the Lord wants us to live and be in heaven when we die. We must make our choice here in this world, for we do not change our essential character after death.

The Lord several times calls Himself the alpha and omega. These are the first and last letters of the Greek alphabet and, as we are told here, it means that He is "the beginning and the end, the first and the last." Do you remember the first four words of the first verse of the Bible? Now read the last two verses of the Bible. Jesus Christ is God, the first and the last.

Who have right to the tree of life?
Who may take the water of life?
In verses 18 and 19 what two things are we told not to do?

Do you remember how the Lord told the woman of Samaria at Jacob's well that if she had asked Him, He would have given her living water? In the Word, divine truth is offered freely to everyone and we are told plainly the conditions on which we may attain heavenly happiness. If we choose not to believe the Lord and not to learn His commandments and obey them, it is just because we do not want to. To add to the Word and to take away from it mean to think our own ideas are better than the Lord's as to what is right and wrong and what will bring us happiness. Whichever of these things we do, we shall suffer unhappy consequences, because the Lord is both all-loving and all-wise and His way is always best.

You have all learned the first verse of the Bible. You can easily learn the last verse because it is one you have heard so frequently in church. *Grace* means "acceptance," and so, as we begin with the acknowledgment that God created all things, we end with the prayer that what we make of the lives He has given us may in the end be found acceptable to Him. This is the real object of our whole life.

———————

Intermediate

The lesson should be used to re-emphasize our individual responsibility for our own spiritual progress and also for the development of the New Church in the world.

We complete our study of the Word with a lesson on part of the last two chapters of Revelation, John's vision of the holy city New Jerusalem, which he saw coming down from God out of heaven "prepared as a bride adorned for her husband." The holy city is the New Church in heaven, by means of which the New Church is being established on earth. You remember that the first verse of the Bible tells us that, "In the beginning God created the heaven and the earth," and that this really means the heaven and the earth in us, the heavenly and the earthly part of us. And in the Lord's Prayer we say, "Thy kingdom come, as in heaven so upon the earth." We have to have goodness and truth in our hearts and minds if we are to do genuine good on earth. The holy city, which is "the bride" of the Lord, and "the woman clothed with the sun," comes down from heaven to earth only as fast as individual men and women on earth learn the truths revealed by the Lord in the opened Word, live according to them, and come to love them.

This is our responsibility as New Churchmen. The New Church organization is necessary to the existence of the New Church in the world, as our bodies are necessary to our souls while we live here, but it is the true New Church only as it obeys the truth which comes down from God out of heaven.

Our lesson for today emphasizes this fact. In the beginning of chapter 22 we read of the "pure river of water of life" which John saw, on whose banks grew the tree of life—the same tree which in the beginning was in the center of the Garden of Eden. The tree of life is the Lord as to His divine love, and its fruits are genuine good works. The river is truth from the Lord coming to us in His Word— the same living water of which the Lord told the woman of Samaria at Jacob's well. Read verse 14 of our chapter. Unless we learn the Lord's commandments and do them, we are not really living in the holy city or doing genuine good here on earth, nor will we live in the holy city and eat the fruit of the tree of life after we die.

You notice that the angel who had been showing John the holy city and ts wonders was careful to prevent John from worshiping him, and told him that he was a mere man like John himself, who had kept the commandments of the Word. You will find that some churches teach that the angels are not men who have lived on the earth, but are a higher creation of the Lord's. This idea is apparently based on a single verse in the King James version of the Scripture, Psalm 8:5, which says of man: "Thou hast made him a little lower than the angels." We should know that this is a mistranslation, for the Hebrew word translated "angels" is *Elohim*, which means "God." We are all potential angels.

When we read in verse 10 that "the time is at hand" and in verse 12 "behold, I come quickly," we know that it is the Second Coming of the Lord that is meant. This is why John is told not to seal the book. For we know that in His Second Coming the Lord opened the Word and revealed its inner meaning. We wonder sometimes why our church is so small—why everyone does not see what wonderful things the Lord has revealed. The rest of our chapter shows us the reason.

Whenever we see a truth clearly and acknowledge that it is true, we become responsible for living according to that truth. Many people would rather remain blind to the truth for this reason. You remember what the Lord said to the Pharisees after He had opened the eyes of the man born blind. The Lord knew that the opening of His Word would not immediately change everyone. That is what verse 11 means. Each one of us has to choose for himself whether he prefers to be guided by the Lord or to follow his own will. The invitation which is given in verse 17 is addressed to everyone. The truths of the Word are available to all who want them. But in verses 18 and 19 we are warned that we must take them as the Lord has given them to us. The moment we begin to add ideas of our own or to reject some things the Lord says because we do not want to obey them, we are putting self before the Lord, and the Lord can no longer keep us safe and lead us to heaven. If we do not attain heaven, it is our doing, not the Lord's. The Lord once said to His disciples (John 12:47-48): "And if any man hear my words, and believe not, I judge him not: for I came not to judge the world, but to save the world. He that rejecteth me, and receiveth not my words, hath one that judgeth him: the word that I have spoken, the same shall judge him in the last day."

Basic Correspondences

tree of life	=	the Lord as to divine good
its fruits	=	genuine good works
the river	=	truth from the Word
angels	=	messengers of the Lord

Senior

The effort should be made in this lesson to impress upon the young people how this final chapter of the Bible brings out the three principal doctrines of the New Church: belief in Jesus Christ as the one God, belief in the inspiration of the Word, and belief in obedience to the commandments as essential to heavenly life.

We may think of the verses we have for today as the Lord's final charge to mankind. Although the Second Coming of the Lord did not take place until nearly seventeen hundred years after the time this book was written, it is foretold here, and the way in which the world would receive it is also foretold.

Our lesson contains statements which should encourage us as well as solemn warnings which we should heed. The Lord had said to His disciples: "Ye have not chosen me, but I have chosen you." Each one of us who has been brought up in the New Church or led into it has been chosen by the Lord. This does not mean that we are better than other people, but that the particular abilities with which we are endowed can be made useful to the Lord in the development of His New Church. Each of us has his own work to do for the church, and if we study its teachings and constantly look to the Lord in His Word for guidance, we shall be given wisdom and strength to carry out this work. It is perfectly possible for us to refuse to accept this responsibility. The choice is presented in verse 11 of our chapter. The Lord knew that many would not receive Him in His Second Coming. He does not force His truth upon those who do not want it and neither can we. Swedenborg tells us plainly that the New Church will grow slowly, that for a long time it will be with only a few.

This suggests one of the temptations to which New Churchmen are subject. We may become discouraged because our church is so small. And this discouragement brings with it another temptation, against which we are warned in verses 18 and 19. We are tempted to set up for ourselves objectives—such as large numbers, external activities, publicity, the praise of men—which have nothing to do with the spiritual church the Lord is trying to develop. This is a form of idol worship and may lead us to modify and interpret the teachings which the Lord has given us in the effort to make them more acceptable to our idols. When we do this, we are no longer New Churchmen at heart: we no longer worship the Lord Jesus Christ as our only God or look to His Word as divine truth or seek to obey His commandments. We worship self and the world instead.

In verse 13 the Lord says again, "I am Alpha and Omega, the beginning and the end, the first and the last." Our course takes us through the Word from beginning to end. In the beginning we have the ideal set before us: "In the beginning God created the heaven and the earth," the heavenly and the earthly natures in man, and developed them to the Garden of Eden state. A great river watered the Garden of Eden and the tree of life was at its center. But man chose to turn away from the Lord to self, departing further and further from the heavenly state, and the Lord's truth followed him down to lower and lower levels, until finally "the Word was made flesh, and dwelt among us" to turn back the tide of evil which threatened to destroy mankind. Then the slow, upward climb began and continued until in John's vision of the holy city New Jerusalem "coming down from God out of heaven" we again find the "pure river of water of life" and the tree of life.

In these last verses of Revelation we are left in no doubt as to who it is that we are to worship and obey. The angel guide whom John felt he should worship, told John at once that he was but another man, and in verse 16 we find that it is Jesus who sent the angel, and from there on the name of Jesus alone is used, so that at the end we have the response of all those who are of the church: "Even so, come, Lord Jesus" and the final benediction so familiar to us all: "The grace of our Lord Jesus Christ be with you all. Amen."

Adult

Several distinct discussion topics are outlined in the notes, any of which may be developed according to the interest of the class. The teaching of these last verses of the Bible is impressive and should be of deep concern to us all.

In the twenty-first chapter of Revelation we are told of the vision of the holy city New Jerusalem coming down from God out of heaven "prepared as a bride adorned for her husband." We have already had the New Church pictured as a "woman clothed with the sun." In AR 533 we read that by this woman the church is signified "because the church is called the Bride and Wife of the Lord" and further that she was seen clothed with the sun "because the church is in love to the Lord, for it acknowledges Him and does His commandments, and this is to love Him." But we are told many times in the writings that love gets all its "quality" from truth. So the final picture of the church is of a city, for a city signifies doctrine. And in the beginning of the twenty-second chapter John sees the "pure river of water of life, clear as crystal, proceeding out of the throne of God and of the Lamb." This river, like the river which watered the Garden of Eden, is divine truth from the Lord. On its banks grows the tree of life, the same tree which in the beginning was in the center of the Garden of Eden, "the Lord as to the Divine love," whose fruits are "the goods of love and charity," and whose leaves, which were "for the healing of the nations," are "rational truths therefrom, by which they who are in evils and thence in falsities are led to think soundly, and to live becomingly." (AR 926)

The final verses of chapter 22, which are the subject of our lesson for today, should be carefully studied and fixed in mind by all of us who profess to belong to the New Church, for they summarize the fundamental teachings of the Word, which are the basis on which the New Church rests, and also show us clearly certain important implications of these teachings which we are prone to forget.

First there is the incident of John's impulse to worship his angel guide and the angel's rejection of this worship. A similar incident is recorded in verse 10 of chapter 19. We know that we have angel associates from whom many of our thoughts come and we know that we can all help each other spiritually in many ways, but angels and men are all finite, and make mistakes, and each of us must himself study the Word constantly for his guidance in life.

In AC 5432 we read: "They who have arrived at maturity, and still more they who have arrived at old age, and have not viewed with their own eyes the truths of the church, which are called doctrinal things, and seen whether they are true, and then been willing to live according to them, retain them merely as they do all other memory knowledges; they are in their natural memory only, and thence on their lips; and when they utter them, they utter them not from their interior man or from the heart, but only from the exterior man and from the mouth. When a man is in this state he cannot possibly believe that the truths of the church are true, although it seems to him that he so believes. The reason why it seems to him that he believes them to be true, is that he relies on others, and has confirmed in himself the teachings of others. It is very easy to confirm things taken from others, *whether true or false;* for this needs nothing but ingenuity." For the New Churchman the sole authority is the Lord speaking in His Word.

This leads to another interesting and important lesson presented by our assignment. When one attends churches other than the New Church, one is struck by the frequent use of the Epistles sometimes rather than the Gospels, and when one examines the basic doctrines of these churches, one finds that they rest on the Epistles and on the decisions of men at the Council of Nicea in A.D. 325. The apostles and early leaders of the Christian Church had a feeling that the Lord was God, which came out occasionally in their writings, as in Paul's statement in Colossians 2:9 that "in him dwelleth all the fullness of the Godhead bodily." There are those in churches dating back to the first Christian Church today who have and occasionally express the same "feeling." But without the rational basis provided by the opening of the Word—the leaves of the tree of life—their minds remain clouded by natural concepts. Read the Epistles of John. John was the beloved disciple, apparently closest of all to the Lord. Yet from his own letters there is constant evidence that he habitually thought of God as other than Christ. In his Gospel—under inspiration—he recorded the words of the Lord to Philip: "He that hath seen me hath seen the Father," but when he wrote from himself, the thought of the Messiah as the Son of God—the mediator in the sense of a go-between—persisted. When one looks to the ideas of men—even of the apostles—for doctrine, one is not looking to the Lord. But in the book of Revelation under inspiration John recorded (21:5-6) that he that sat upon the throne said, "I am Alpha and Omega, the beginning and the end," and in our chapter these words are repeated by the same speaker who says, "I Jesus," and the response to the promise in verse 20 is: "Even so, come, Lord Jesus."

Another thing which is told us clearly in our chapter is that man has freedom to choose whether he will believe and follow the Lord or not, and that no presentation of the truth in this world or the next will reverse his choice. All do not enter the holy city, though its gates are open and its living water is offered to all.

Finally we have the solemn warning against adding to or taking from the book. This warning is spoken specifically to those who acknowledge the truth as coming from the Lord—those who profess to belong to the church—and it applies most of all to those who have accepted the Lord in His Second Coming. "Blessed are they who do His commandments." For those of the New Church "His commandments" include all that He has revealed of the way of life by the opening of the Word. Yet our selfishness and worldliness are constantly prompting us to misinterpret what we read in the Word and the writings so that it may teach what we want to believe. We are told that verse 18 signifies "that they who read and know the truths of doctrine of this book, now opened by the Lord, and yet acknowledge any other God than the Lord, and any other faith than in Him, by adding anything whereby they may destroy these two things, cannot do otherwise than perish from the falsities and evils, which are signified by the plagues described in this book." And essentially the same is said of those who "take away" from the words of the book. We should realize that worldly success and public approval may be "other gods" and must not be sought for ourselves or for our church organization at the cost of spiritual compromise and disobedience. When we begin to look to men instead of to the Lord for direction, we turn our steps away from the holy city. As the angel said to John: "See thou do it not . . . worship God."

––––––––

From the Writings of Swedenborg

Apocalypse Revealed, n. 954: "*I am the Root and Offspring of David, the bright and morning Star*, signifies that it is the Lord Himself who was born in the world, and was then the Light, and who will come with new light, which will arise before His New Church, which is the holy Jerusalem. 'I am the Root and Offspring of David,' signifies that He is the very Lord Himself who was born in the world, thus the Lord in His Divine Human; from this He is called 'the Root and Offspring of David,'and also the Branch of David' (Jer. 23:5, 33:15), also 'the Rod out of the stem of Jesse, and the Branch from his roots' (Isa. 11:1-2). 'The bright and morning Star,' signifies that then there was light, and that He will come with new light, which will arise before His New Church, which is the holy Jerusalem. He is called 'the bright Star' from the light with which He came into the world, wherefore He is likewise called 'Star,' and also 'Light,' 'a Star' (Num. 24:17), and 'Light' (John 1:4-12; 3:19, 21; 4:5; 12:35-36, 46; Matt. 4:16; Luke 2:30-32; Isa. 9:2; 49:6). And He is called 'the morning Star' from the light which will rise before the New Church, which is the New Jerusalem, from Him; for by 'star' is signified light from Him, which in its essence is wisdom and intelligence, and by 'morning' is signified His coming, and then the New Church."

––––––––

Suggested Questions on the Lesson

J. In our lesson today what did John think about the angel who showed him the vision? *that he should be worshiped*

P. What did the angel tell him? *worship God*

J. What do alpha and omega mean? *first, last*

P. Who have right to the tree of life and the right to enter the holy city? *those who obey*

P. Who is the Lord God? *Jesus Christ*

J. What invitation does He give us? *come unto me*

J. What does He warn us not to do? *add to or take away from words of book*

P. For what is our church named? *holy city*

I. Why is it so important for us to learn and do the Lord's will in this world? *because we make our eternal choice here*

S. What do (1) the river, and (2) the tree of life, represent? *(1) truth of Word, (2) divine love*

J. Why is the last verse of the Bible so familiar to us? *benediction*

APPENDIX I

SPECIAL "NEW CHURCH DAY" LESSONS

The five lessons that follow—never previously published—are intended for school or home use on the Sunday closest to June 19, New Church Day. The first four were written by the author of this set of lessons, the fifth (which is not complete) by the editor. This latter lesson is included because it bears the "stamp of approval" of Mrs. Dole. See below the photo-reprint of her note which was written on the original typescript.

This lesson was written by Rev. Wm. R. Woofenden in 1967.
O.K. of I pass away
Anita S Dole

NEW CHURCH DAY
Revelation 22:13-21

The emphasis in this lesson should be on the fact that the Second Coming of the Lord has been made and that this is His final revelation to mankind. The Lord has always given man sufficient knowledge of Himself and His will so that man has remained free to choose. Our opportunity is greater than ever, but the price of rejecting the Lord remains the same.

Doctrinal Points

The Second Coming of the Lord has been accomplished by opening the Scriptures. This revelation is to be the Lord's final great revelation to mankind.

Notes for Parents

We have read the description of the beautiful city for which our church is named, which the apostle John saw in vision descending from God out of heaven. It is not by chance that the Bible begins with the creation of the world and ends with the descent of the holy city: "In the beginning God created the heaven and the earth" and, as Jesus told John in the first verse of our lesson for today, "I am Alpha and Omega, the beginning and the end, the first and the last." Alpha and omega are the first and last letters of the Greek alphabet. The whole teaching of the Bible is summed up in this verse.

In the New Church the nineteenth of June is known as "New Church Day." This is because Swedenborg tells us in his last great work *True Christian Religion* (n. 791): "After this work was finished the Lord called together His twelve disciples who followed Him in the world; and the next day He sent them all forth throughout the whole spiritual world to preach the Gospel that *the Lord God Jesus Christ reigns*, whose kingdom shall be for ages and ages.

. . . This took place on the nineteenth day of June, 1770."

Almost everyone today speaks of our times as "this new age." But most of them are thinking in terms of cars, airplanes, medical and archeological research, space travel, and computers. Man has indeed learned more and more about the physical world in which he lives, but he did not and does not create that world; neither is he necessarily made happier by his new knowledge and use of it. In fact, every advance in physical knowledge creates new problems. Why?

The first verse of chapter 21 of Revelation tells us: "And I saw a new heaven and a new earth: for the first heaven and the first earth were passed away." This is indeed a new age, but it is the Lord and not man who has made it new. As we read through the Bible we find how man, created by the Lord in a first state of innocence and happiness—the Garden of Eden state—has again and again wrecked his world by choosing not to believe in and obey the Lord, preferring to direct his own life, choosing to put the tree of the knowledge of good and evil in the center of his garden in place of the tree of life planted there by the Lord.

The new knowledge of the inner meaning of the Word which the Lord has given to man in His Second Coming is to be His final revelation. The New Church will last for ages and ages because sufficient light has now been given to satisfy all who want to recognize the Lord and do His will no matter what arguments may be advanced by the "learned" men of the new age. We are still able to think rationally and choose the Lord's direction instead of our own. Each of us must study and think and choose for himself.

Primary

Speak of the Second Coming and of the new knowledge which has been given us, and the need of studying the Word more and more and choosing freely to try to behave as the Lord would have us behave. Review Revelation 1, emphasizing verse 11 as an introduction to today's lesson. The important lesson for this class is that the Second Coming has taken place, and how it took place.

What is the last book in the Bible?

Through whom was it written?

It was a vision of what would happen to the Christian Church founded by the apostles.

What person did John first see?

Do you remember what the Lord Jesus said first to him (Revelation 1:11)?

Today we are celebrating "New Church Day," which is the nineteenth of June. On that day, about two centuries ago, the Lord Jesus proclaimed that He was the sole ruler of the world, and that all who wished to recognize Him and live as He now clearly taught them might enter the beautiful city and live there forever.

This is a wonderful promise that has been given us. It seems as though we would all receive it with delight, doesn't it? But to receive it means much more than just saying, "Yes, I will." It means studying the Word of God day by day, learning more and more from it every day as we grow older. And it means saying "no" to ourselves very often when we want to have our own way, and learning to think of other people's convenience and happiness, and being pleasant and kind instead of cross and mean.

But if we do make this effort, we shall soon find that the harder we really try to be good the easier everything will get and the happier we shall be.

Now read the first verse of our lesson for today.

Alpha and omega are the first and last letters of the Greek alphabet.

So they stand for the beginning and the end of everything.

This means that we must all know that the Lord Jesus Christ is the one God, creator of the world and everything in it, and that the true object of our lives is to know and serve Him.

John was shown that, even though the Lord had taken on a human body in order to show men how to live, many would still choose not to believe Him.

So finally He had to make a Second Coming of a different kind, which would be His final revelation to man.

He would come again "in the clouds of heaven with power and great glory."

This means by opening the inner meaning of the Word so that the light of heaven could shine through.

This Second Coming actually took place about two hundred years ago.

It was first announced in heaven on June 19, 1770.

That is why we call the nineteenth of June "New Church Day."

We find the key to this inner meaning of the Word in the writings of Emanuel Swedenborg, whom the Lord chose as His publishing agent.

So we need to study the Word daily, and also to study the writings of Swedenborg, which enable us to understand it.

Then, if we live as the Lord teaches us to live, we shall be able to enter the gates of the beautiful city New Jerusalem and live there forever.

Notice the last verse of our lesson. It is often used in our church service as the minister's final blessing to the people. It is the most beautiful thing we can wish for anyone.

Junior

We have given the Juniors no questions to answer this time. The teacher may ask such questions as he thinks the class should be able to answer, before proceeding with the assignment for the day.

In one of our lessons from the book of Revelation we learned about the messages given to the apostle John for the seven Christian churches which had been established in Asia Minor by the time John was an old man. We saw that they were all different, just as each one of us is different, and we learned something of what those messages mean for us as individuals.

But these seven churches were real churches, the beginning of the first Christian Church on earth, and it was true that already they were showing bad as well as good qualities. So the whole of John's vision applies to the first Christian Church and its future as well as to our individual lives. The first Christian Church declined, just as all the earlier Churches had declined because many continued to put the tree of the knowledge of good and evil in the middle of their life instead of the tree of life, worshiping man instead of God. And John's vision showed that this would go on until men would think themselves so wise that the innocent good people who wanted to believe in God and serve Him could no longer answer their arguments. They needed more understanding of the Word, the "many things" which the Lord had told His disciples He still had to say to them (John 16:12). So the Lord had to make His promised Second Coming in order to save mankind.

The Second Coming actually took place about two hundred years ago, when the Lord opened the inner meaning of the Word through the agency of His dedicated servant Emanuel Swedenborg. This inner meaning was the light coming through the clouds. The beautiful vision of the holy city New Jerusalem descending from God out of heaven is the picture of the New Church on earth built in the lives of all who study the Word diligently in the light of this new knowledge and do their best to live as this new knowledge teaches them. The first essential of this new life is to recognize the Lord Jesus Christ as the one God of heaven and earth, the alpha and the omega.

Swedenborg tells us that on June 19, 1770, the twelve apostles were sent by the Lord throughout the spiritual world to "preach the Gospel that the Lord God Jesus Christ reigns." So we in the New Church celebrate June 19 as "New Church Day."

Intermediate

Stress the importance of our daily choices and the proof which history gives us the truth of verses 13 and 14 of our lesson for today. It is very necessary that children of this age be encouraged to think and act independently of what "everybody" thinks and does.

We are living in a new age. Our modern scientists often tell us this and young people are tempted to use it as an excuse for thinking that the ideas of right conduct which their parents and grandparents have are out of date. But the laws of God do not change. The commandments were known from the earliest times, and then thirty-five hundred years ago they were given from Mount Sinai in the ears of all the people by the voice of God and written on the tables of stone by the finger of God to prove that they are not man-made rules but the fundamental laws of God. And nearly two thousand years ago John was told in vision by the Lord Jesus Christ: "I am Alpha and Omega, the beginning and the end, the first and the last. Blessed are they that do his commandments, that they may have right to the tree of life, and may enter in through the gates into the city. This was said after the Lord had showed him the holy city descending to earth from heaven. John's final vision begins (Rev. 21:1): "And I saw a new heaven and a new earth: for the first heaven and the first earth were passed away." We are indeed living in a new age, but the laws of right feeling and thought and conduct are God's laws, the same for every age. Never forget this.

Day after day we are presented with choices to make. If we could not think and choose, we should be merely animals. Animals are governed by their instincts. They can never know the God who created them. Try to remember this, that whenever you choose to do as you please without thinking whether it is right or wrong, you are making an animal of yourself. Heavenly knowledge is eternal. It is much more important than earthly knowledge, which serves us only for a few short years. And each of us, by his choices day by day, is forming the character which will determine where he will live to eternity.

Swedenborg tells us that on June 19, 1770, the Lord sent the apostles throughout the spiritual world to proclaim that He alone reigned. The new earth and the new heaven are the new knowledge of heavenly and earthly life given us by the Lord in His Second Coming. This is why we call June 19th "New Church Day." May the new age mean for each of you a new heaven as well as a new earth.

Senior

Stress the difference between the New Church and all other churches and the reason why the Second Coming was made when and as it was.

We call the nineteenth day of June "New Church Day." What is the difference between the New Chuch and all the other churches in the world? We know that there are good people in all the churches, people who believe in God and are trying to live as they think God would have them live. This is true not only of the Christian churches but equally of Jews and Mohammedans and the people of what we call the pagan religions. Yet the different churches have always had different ideas of what a good life really was, different ideas of just who and what God is and of what His will is.

In preparing for your life in this world you do not say "I want to be a good and useful person" and then fumble along from day to day doing whatever happens to come your way, without study, thought, and practice in your chosen field. You study your own abilities and your own weaknesses and choose the best schooling for the work for which you think you are best fitted. But our life on this earth lasts only a few years. It is the spiritual world in which we shall all live to eternity. Does it make sense to imagine that we do not have to study and plan and practice for that life even more than for this?

Just as our homes and schools give us progressive instruction as we grow in age and ability to receive it, so the Lord from His first creation of man upon the earth has progressively provided all the instruction man was capable of receiving. The wise have recognized this instruction as coming from the all-wise God, have studied it, and have made use of it in their daily lives. The foolish have closed their eyes and ears and stumbled along on their own.

The Lord has now in His Second Coming given us the key to all the spiritual knowledge man can ever need. The New Church recognizes this and is founded on the belief that Jesus Christ glorified is the one God of heaven and earth and that His instruction can be found in His Word illumined by the new light from within it, now revealed to us. It is the revelation given two hundred years ago to meet the need of men of the new age when they were beginning to hunt for the reason back of everything and asking questions about the Word which they could not find answered in the literal sense. In the New Church we can find the answers to all of men's questions about the Lord, the purpose of our life here on earth, and the nature and reality of the spiritual world. It takes study and continued effort, as does anything that is worthwhile, but it makes us more and more useful to the Lord and to our fellow men and leads us into the holy city.

Adult

A brief verse-by-verse study of the lesson should be made in this class, after speaking of the reason for the name of this special day. Then ask for questions, and discuss whatever they bring out.

In our lessons from the book of Revelation, we have studied the nature and purpose of John's vision, the different types of reaction to the Lord and His Word which appear in the Lord's Church on earth and in each one of us individually, the nature of the final Church in heaven and on earth pictured as the holy city New Jerusalem, and what is required of each of us who wishes to live within that holy city.

In TCR 791 Swedenborg tells us the basis for celebrating "New Church Day." See the quotation below.

Our lesson for today, the last nine verses of the Word, gives us really a summary of the whole teaching of the Word and of our duty as members of the Lord's New Church. First (verse 13), we must recognize the Lord Jesus Christ as the one God of heaven and earth, our creator and our guide forever. Second (verse 14), if we wish to dwell in peace and happiness in the holy city both here and when we pass from this world, we must keep His commandments. Third (verse 15), we must be aware of the many temptations to evil which surround us in this world. Fourth (verse 16), the Lord has made available to us all the truth we need now and for all future time. Fifth (verse 17), the Lord offers us this truth freely to understand and to use from day to day. Sixth (verse 18), He tells us plainly that if we try to add our own ideas of what is true and right to what the Lord has said, we shall get into serious trouble. Seventh (verse 19), if we try to change and reject what the Lord says in order to make it suit our finite desires, we shall not be able to live in the holy city at all. Eighth (verse 20), we should accept gladly the fact that the Lord has made His Second and final Coming. And ninth (verse 21), we should all recognize our own weakness, and look to the Lord for forgiveness and love.

You will find very interesting statements in regard to the Second Coming in TCR 768-790, 846-847, and in AR 875.

From the Writings of Swedenborg

True Christian Religion, n. 791: "After this work was finished the Lord called together His twelve disciples who followed Him in the world; and the next day He sent them all forth throughout the whole spiritual world to preach the Gospel that *the Lord God Jesus Christ reigns*, whose kingdom shall be for ages and ages, according to the prediction in Daniel (7:13-14), and in the Apocalypse (11:15).

"Also that blessed are those that come to the marriage supper of the Lamb (Apoc. 19:9). This took place on the nineteenth day of June, 1770."

Suggested Questions on the Lesson

P. What special day do we celebrate today? *New Church Day*

S. Why do we call it that? *TCR 791*

P. What is the first thing the Lord says about Himself in our lesson for today? *I am alpha and omega*

P. What are alpha and omega? *first and last letters of Greek alphabet*

P. How do we know it is Jesus Christ who says this? *John recognized Him*

P. Where do we often hear the last verse of our lesson for today? *benediction in church*

J. Why did the Lord have to make a Second Coming? *men needed new insights into divine truth*

J. Why must the Lord always leave us free to choose whether or not we will do right? *love for the Lord and for what is good cannot be forced*

J. Why should we try to remember this even when we are children? *helps prepare us for heaven*

I. Why do men say that we are living in a new age? *great scientific advances*

I. What false conclusion do we sometimes draw from this? *Biblical laws "outdated"*

I. What laws will never change? *the Lord's laws*

S. What has the Lord done to meet our need in this new age? *opened inner sense of Word*

S. What obligation does this lay upon us? *regular study and continued effort to live up to the new truth*

NEW CHURCH DAY
Revelation 22:1-14

Start in all classes by asking the pupils if they know what we mean by New Church Day. If they do not know, remind those who should remember and tell those who have not been told before. In all classes, in addition to taking up the actual assignment, do as much as you can with the doctrinal basis on which the New Church is founded, and emphasize the feeling of gratitude and obligation to the Lord which we should have because He has given us this new knowledge.

———

Doctrinal Points
All in our church have an obligation to read and study the Word
daily in the light of the heavenly doctrines.

———

Notes for Parents
Swedenborg tells us that on the nineteenth day of June in the year 1770 the Lord sent His twelve apostles throughout the spiritual world to proclaim that "the Lord God Jesus Christ reigns," and that a new Church based on this fact was about to be established. This is why we think of the nineteenth of June as the birthday of the New Church and call it "New Church Day." For our New Church is based on the belief that the Lord Jesus Christ is the one only God of heaven and earth, not a mere man—even the best of men—who lived long ago, and not one of three persons in the Godhead, as most Christian churches teach. We believe that the Father, Son, and Holy Spirit of whom we read in the Bible are the three attributes of the one God, divine love, divine wisdom, and divine proceeding or activity, like will, thought, and activity in man. The Lord Himself said to Philip (John 14:9) when Philip asked Him to show them the Father: "Have I been so long time

with you, and yet hast thou not known me, Philip? he that hath seen me hath seen the Father."

Many people today still believe that those who die will lie in their graves until some future day when a last judgment will take place and they will be raised up, and then the good will be given new bodies and will go on living on a new earth which the Lord will form. In the New Church we know that when we die, we merely go to sleep in this world and wake up in the spiritual world, the real and much more beautiful world which is about us now, although we do not see it because our physical eyes focus our sight upon the material world. We also believe that the Last Judgment took place just before the New Church was begun in heaven, and that the Second Coming of the Lord took place then in the opening of the spiritual meaning of the Word, the "power and great glory" within the "cloud" of the literal sense, so that now, as we study the Word, we can learn more and more of its meaning to eternity, and if we sincerely try to live according to its teaching, we need have no fear, for we shall reach heaven and live there forever in peace and happiness.

If, as parents, we live in this belief, thinking and speaking as well as acting from it day by day, our children will grow up with an entirely different attitude toward life and toward the meaning and importance of their daily choices from that which they will encounter about them in the world, and will be greatly helped to recognize temptation and say "no" to it, and to develop into good men and women and eventually into angels.

Primary

This is a good lesson in which to tie the whole Bible together in the minds of the children as a continued story with a beginning and an end, and to show them what our life in this world is for and how important the way we behave from day to day is in determining whether or not we shall become angels. State the simple facts concerning the Second Coming and the New Church. Then go on to the lesson itself, and end with emphasis on verse 7 and its important meaning for our daily lives.

We of the New Church call the nineteenth of June "New Church Day." This is because it is the birthday of our Church, for we are told that on the nineteenth of June in the year 1770 the Lord sent His twelve apostles who had followed Him on earth throughout all the spiritual world to tell everyone that "the Lord God Jesus Christ reigns," and this is the teaching on which our Church is founded and the teaching which everyone in heaven knows and believes.

Our lesson for today is not a long one, but it is a very important one.

Do you remember the name of the first book in the Bible?

What does the word *Genesis* mean?

What is the last book in the Bible called?

What other word with the same meaning is sometimes used in speaking of it?

What do these words, *revelation* and *apocalypse*, mean?

When you were babies you did not understand the words you heard, did you?

Now, as you grow, you are able to understand more and more.

And you know that your understanding will grow steadily all your life.

Your parents can be wiser than you are, and your grandparents wiser than they.

And our growth in wisdom does not stop when we die.

Death is merely waking up in that beautiful world where we go on learning forever.

But you know also that you may choose to be foolish rather than wise.

When you disobey your parents, for example, you are choosing to be foolish.

To the end of our lives we have one Father whom we must obey. Who is He?

In what book does He teach us the way to wisdom?

At first we understand very little of the Bible.

Its meaning is like a cloud behind which we know the sun is shining.

Do you remember the lesson we had from the second chapter of Genesis, the very first book in the Bible? It was about the Garden of Eden where Adam and Eve lived. That garden had a beautiful river and it had a fruit tree growing in the middle of the garden which was called "the tree of life." Now here in the very last chapter of the last book of the Bible we find that that same river and tree are in heaven, the beautiful land where we shall all go to live forever when we leave this world if the books of our lives here are found to be written as they should be, according to the teachings of the Word of God.

Let us always be looking forward to that day, however long or short our lives here on earth may be. But let us not forget that we cannot ever reach that beautiful land unless from day to day we try faithfully to do what is right instead of just what we happen to want to do. We often think that having our own way will make us happy, but it won't: it will only get us into all kinds of trouble. The Bible word for "happy" is "blessed." And in the Bible the Lord has given us His Word so that we may know how we ought to live in order to be happy forever. As verse 7 of our lesson tells us: "Blessed is he that keepeth the sayings of the prophecy of this book."

The Lord has now, as He promised, come again to us "in the clouds of heaven with power and great glory."

This coming was announced to the angels on June 19, 1770.

So we call June nineteenth the "birthday of the New Church" or "New Church Day."

Junior

With this class emphasize the spiritual history of mankind as told in the Bible and the reason why the Lord had to give successive revelations to enable men better to know and understand Him. Tell them what a "dispensation" is and how John was called to be the prophet of the final dispensation described in Revelation by the descent of the New Jerusalem. Stress what verses 7 and 14 of our chapter should mean to each of us.

What is the first book in our Bible?

What is the last book?

By what other name is this last book called?

What does *apocalypse* mean?

What two things do we find in our reading for today which were found in the story of the Garden of Eden in the second chapter of Genesis?

This fact in itself shows us that the Word of God is one book, teaching us what the Lord intended for mankind from His first creation of them, what they chose to do with all the wonderful things He gave them, how from the beginning He supported the good and tried to teach the evil the folly of their ways, and how our life to eternity after we leave this world is going to depend on whether, while we are here, we choose to learn and obey the laws which He has given us for our happiness, or to turn our backs upon Him and do what we want to do from moment to moment, imagining that we are wise of ourselves.

Even as children growing up today you have an example of this. You know that when you decide to do something which your parents have forbidden, you either get into immediate trouble or are led into other wrongdoing such as lying or blaming others instead of yourself. What you have done does not make you happy. It was foolish, not wise. And if you do not face this obvious fact and correct your ways, you become worse and worse, more and more foolish, and get into more and more trouble.

Because of the increasing number of foolish people who imagined themselves wiser than the Lord, the world grew worse and worse and mankind more and more unhappy. The Lord did all He could, giving them new instruction from time to time, until finally He came and lived among them Himself to show to their physical sight the good way of life. The first Christian Church was founded on this example and turned the tide of evil in the world, but it was still not enough. Jesus knew that it would not be. He told His apostles (John 16:12): "I have yet many things to say unto you, but ye cannot bear them now." Men had still much to learn about the things of this world, and He knew that as science and philosophy developed, it would become harder and harder for those whom the world considered "learned" to believe many of the literal statements of the Word. So He promised to come again (Matthew 24:30) "in the clouds of heaven with power and great glory."

The church on earth is man's response to each new revelation from the Lord. As the first Christian Church was their response to His coming in person, the New Church is the response to His Second Coming. The prophecy of this coming was made through the apostle John in the book of Revelation. He did not come again in a physical body. That, as He had said on the cross (John 19:30), was "finished." The Lord does not have to do the same thing twice. His Second Coming was made for us by opening the clouds which are in our minds when we read the Word in its letter, and letting the power and great glory shine through as we begin to see the spiritual meaning which is within the letter.

John describes the New Church that would be formed on the basis of this new knowledge as the holy city New Jerusalem descending from God out of heaven. The new knowledge was given through the agency of a man specially prepared by the Lord to receive it, the famous scientist and philosopher Emanuel Swedenborg, who would be humble and faithful in writing and publishing it. As you grow older, you will read and study more and more of what Swedenborg tells us the Lord permitted him to see and hear, and to understand as he read the Word in this new light. And if you yourselves faithfully read and study the Word in this light and try to live as it teaches, you will not only realize more and more the blessings which the Lord has given you but you will become more and more true and useful members of the Lord's New Church, the Church of the New Jerusalem.

In the *True Christian Religion*, n. 791, Swedenborg tell us: "After this work was finished the Lord called together His twelve disciples who followed Him in the world; and the next day He sent them all forth throughout the whole spiritual world to preach the Gospel that the LORD GOD JESUS CHRIST reigns, whose kingdom shall be for ages and ages. . . . This took place on the nineteenth day of June, 1770." So we call June nineteenth "New Church Day," the birthday of the New Church.

Intermediate

Take up with this class the history of the Church among mankind from the beginning, and why each declined and a new one had to be instituted through a new revelation. Then take up the reasons for the breaking up of the first Christian Church as given in their notes, the importance of the new revelation, which we are told is to be the final one, and the duty of each of them to read and study the Word daily in its light throughout their lives, as well as to direct their thought and conduct according to its teachings. Illustrate from the chapter for today how much the new light enables us to find within the cloud of the letter.

In n. 791 of *The True Christian Religion*, one of Swedenborg's last writings, we read: "After this work was finished the Lord called together His twelve disciples who followed Him in the world; and the next day He sent them all forth throughout the whole spiritual world to preach the Gospel that the LORD GOD JESUS CHRIST reigns, whose kingdom shall be for ages and ages. . . . This took place on the nineteenth day of June, 1770." This is why we call June nineteenth "New Church Day," the birthday of the New Church, which we are told in TCR 788 "is to follow those that have existed since the beginning of the world, and that it is to endure for ages and ages."

You know that the first Christian Church, which started as a result of the travels of the apostles, has broken up into many sects, some of them having quite different beliefs even about who Jesus Christ really was. There are two reasons for this. One is that there are always people who choose to believe only what it is easy and convenient for them to believe. Such people simply refuse to believe many of the statements they find in the Bible. The second reason is that there are many who want to believe the Lord but have found puzzling statements and apparent contradictions in the literal story and, rather than give up all belief, have accepted explanations which do not agree and often do not even make sense. And as men have learned more and more about this natural world of ours, many have come to believe that it is the only world we can know anything about.

The book of Revelation was a prophecy of the state of the world as it would develop after the days of the apostles, and in its last chapters it gives the promise of a final judgment and the establishment of a New Church to which would be given an understanding of the real inner meaning of the Word of God which would explain both the past and the future history of mankind and enable us to worship and obey the Lord with understanding. We should be very thankful that we today live in this new age of the Church and have been shown these things by the Lord through the writings of His servant Emanuel Swedenborg.

For example, we can know that the river mentioned in the first verse of our chapter for today pictures truth from the Lord, the same river described in the story of the Garden of Eden in the second chapter of Genesis. All men have a "thirst" for knowledge of some sort, and for those who want knowledge of the Lord the Word has always provided this knowledge. The tree of life in our lesson is the same tree which in the beginning was in the midst of the Garden of Eden, the understanding that all good and truth are not our own but are given us day by day by the Lord. Men's first turning away from the Lord to self was pictured by their disobedience in eating of the fruit of the tree of knowledge of good and evil and so putting that tree in the center of their garden in place of the tree of life. We do this ourselves whenever we think we know better than the Lord what is good for us to think and do. Genuine goodness received from the Lord is the fruit of the tree of life, and the leaves of this tree are genuine truths from the Lord which alone can "heal the nations." We need very much to see and think of this in the present state of our world. Peace and happiness cannot come to any one of us or to the world in any other way than by obedience to the Lord. As verse 7 of our lesson tells us, "blessed is he that keepeth the sayings of the prophecy of this book."

Another thing which we should notice in our lesson is what the angel said when John fell at his feet to worship him. There is a verse in the Bible, Psalm 8:5, which in the King James and other translations says of man: "For thou hast made him a little lower than the angels." People assumed from this that angels were a higher form of creation than man. But this is not what the Word of God really says at this place. In the original Hebrew language, in which the Old Testament was dictated by the Lord, this verse says: "For thou hast made him a little lower than God"—angels are not even mentioned here. So we should note especially what the angel in our lesson told John. Angels are all men like ourselves, all originally born on our earth or some other earth in the physical universe, who are living in heaven because they chose to obey the Lord.

This is the world in which we make our choices, and we make them from day to day. So if we want to be happy and to become angels and live in heaven, in the holy city New Jerusalem, we need to learn and keep always in mind the last verse of our lesson for today: "Blessed are they that do his commandments, that they may have right to the tree of life, and may enter in through the gates into the city."

Senior

State briefly the facts concerning New Church Day and concerning the spiritual history of mankind as recorded in the Word and what the Second Coming of the Lord and the descent of the New Jerusalem man. Then try to be sure that the pupils know what the basic doctrines of the New Church are, encouraging questions and discussion.

The nineteenth of June is called "New Church Day," the birthday of the New Church.

All of you young people who read these notes, whether you were "born in the New Church" or not, have been providentially brought in contact with its teachings, for nothing ever happens which is not of the Lord's will or of His permission. This means that in each one of you the Lord sees the potential of understanding the teachings of the New Church and living according to them. This gives each one of you a serious responsibility of thought and conduct. Some people, even some members of the New Church, imagine that if we say that the church of which we are members is the one true Church, the final Church prophesied in Revelation, the New Jerusalem coming down from God out of heaven, we are setting ourselves up as better than other people. But if we do not so proclaim our Church and its teachings, what we are really doing is refusing the particular task to which the Lord in His wisdom has called us. We know that every individual is different from every other and that only the Lord knows each of us through and through.

It is only as we accept whatever of blessing and of trial is given us as a gift from the Lord and use it to the best of our ability in the service of the Lord for our own growth and for helping our neighbor that we can develop spiritually and eventually become angels. Notice how humbly John, even after all that the Lord had permitted him to see and hear in his vision, "fell down to worship at the feet of the angel." John did not set himself up. Yet John realized that it was his particular duty given him by the Lord to proclaim to the world what had been shown him by the Lord.

There are good people in every church and in every religion. We learn from the writings of Swedenborg* that every person who believes in a God and tries sincerely to live as he believes that God would have him live is a member of the "church universal" and will ultimately get to heaven, because, even if he has not in this world had an opportunity to learn the truth about God and the right way of life, he has desired it and will welcome it when he is told it in the other world; but those who in this world have persistently refused to learn or even try to learn because they preferred to think and do as they pleased will continue in the same desire when they reach the other world and so cannot be taught there. But the Lord has always provided that there be in this world a "church specific" which shall have access to all the genuine truth which the people of that age can understand. So there have been several "dispensations" of the Church in the course of history, all leading to this final one.

The opening of the inner meaning of the Word by the Lord in His Second Coming teaches us certain basic truths upon which no other church in the world is founded. The first and most important of these is that there is one God, the Lord and Savior Jesus Christ, and that the trinity called Father, Son, and Holy Spirit are not three separate persons but are in the Lord Jesus Christ—divine love, divine wisdom, and divine proceeding or activity—just as will, thought, and act are in each one of us. The second is that certain

---

*See, e.g., AC 6637, HH 328, 381, NJHD 244.

books of our Bible are the Word of God which, in their original languages, were verbally inspired by God in such a way that they express in earthly form—the forms in which God expressed Himself when He was creating the universe of nature—an internal meaning which we may study to eternity, always learning more about the Lord and what He would have us love and think and do. The third is that each of us is free to choose whether he will serve the Lord or himself, and that on our own free choice in this world will depend our state to eternity.

Adult

Be sure that all in this class know the facts concerning New Church Day and the Second Coming of the Lord. Then take up the correspondence of the Bible lesson, emphasizing verses 7 and 14 and their specific meaning for every member of the New Church.

As an adult each of us has his or her own life to live from day to day, his own background and abilities, his own tastes and temptations, his own education, his own daily work, his own friends, his own opportunities. Only the Lord knows just what each of us is and how far he is doing the best he can with his life. But wherever we go there are rules which we must observe if we wish to be accepted and liked, rules for the care and conduct of our homes, rules for our offices, jobs, schools, and laboratories, rules for our social activities, rules of the road. Rules are what make all our activities orderly and safe and enjoyable. Should we not expect to have rules for our inner spiritual life which will make our thinking and feeling as well as our actions orderly and safe and enjoyable?

The word "church" has several connotations: a building, a small group of people, a local organization, a national or world organization, religious thought in general, or a particular system of doctrine. But in every connotation the word "church" implies and assumes recognition of God, and churches differ primarily according to the concept of God to which they are dedicated, and this concept is a matter of doctrine, of specific belief. If we have no specific belief about God, about who and what He is and what belief in Him involves we are not really members of any church.

We know from the Word and from history in general as well as from the writings of Emanuel Swedenborg which, as members of the New Church, we professedly accept as authoritative, that every dispensation of the Lord's Church on earth has declined and come to its end because its own people refused to trust and obey the Lord as He had revealed Himself to them, and chose instead to worship "the gods of the nations round about."

Our New Church is still in its beginnings. It is small and not too widely known in the world. How sincere are we? Have we studied its teachings and accepted them freely and intelligently? Do they inspire us? Are we trying daily to live better lives by their help? When we come to church on Sunday, do we come willingly and eagerly to worship the Lord the Savior Jesus Christ as God, the one only God of heaven and earth? When we have a problem to solve, do we study it in the light of the teachings of the Lord in His Second Coming? Do we accept our difficulties and trials as opportunities to learn? Do we listen sympathetically to the troubles of our friends and neighbors and try to find and bring them thoughts from our doctrines which will really apply to their specific problems and help them? Do we refrain from criticizing and condemning others because they do not agree with us or do just as we do? It is the Lord who builds the Church, the church universal, which He sees as one man, and also the church specific, which He declares to be the "heart and lungs" of that man, a specific organ with a specific function. Our Church is the church specific for the new age. We help the Lord build it only as each of us tries continually and steadily to learn and live its teachings.

The New Jerusalem is the city of doctrine in which, as our chapter tells us is the "pure river of the water of life" and the tree of life whose leaves are "for the healing of the nations." "And there shall be no more curse: but the throne of God and of the Lamb shall be in it; and his servants shall serve him: And they shall see his face; and his name shall be in their foreheads." (Revelation 22:3-4)

From the Writings of Swedenborg

Apocalypse Revealed, n. 944: "Behold, I come quickly; happy is he that keepeth the prophecy of this book, signifies that the Lord will certainly come, and give eternal life to those who keep and do the truths or precepts of doctrine of this book now opened by the Lord."

Apocalypse Explained, n. 948[3]: "What the Divine Providence of the Lord was in revealing Divine truths can be seen from the successive establishment of churches. There have been several churches on our globe one after another. There was the Most Ancient, that was before the flood; there was the Ancient, that was after the flood; then the Hebrew; and then the Israelitish; after this the Christian; and now the New Church is beginning. Inmost Divine truths were revealed to those who were of the Most Ancient Church; more external Divine truths were revealed to those of the Ancient Church; and most external or ultimate Divine truths to the Hebrew Church, and afterwards to the Israelitish, with which church all Divine truth finally perished, for at last there was nothing in the Word that had not been adulterated. But after the end of the Israelitish Church interior Divine truths were revealed by the Lord for the Christian Church, and now still more interior truths for the church that is to come. These interior truths are such as are in the internal or spiritual sense of the Word. All this makes clear that there has been a progression of Divine truth from inmosts to ultimates, thus from wisdom to mere ignorance; and that now there is a progression of it from ultimates to interiors, thus from ignorance again to wisdom."

Suggested Questions on the Lesson

P. What special day are we celebrating? *New Church Day*

P. Why do we celebrate it? *[see TCR 791]*

J. What happened on the first New Church Day? *the Lord sent his apostles throughout heaven*

J. When was that? *June 19, 1770*

J. How did the Lord tell His disciples He would come again?
"in the clouds . . ."

J. What did this mean? *through the letter of the Word*

I. Why did the Lord have to make this Second Coming? *to reveal needed new truth*

J. Why did He not come again in a physical body? *not necessary*

P. From what book of the Bible is our lesson for today? *Revelation*

I. What is the book of Revelation? *closing prophecy of the Word*

P. To whom was this revelation given? *the apostle John*

P. At the beginning of our chapter what did John see? *river*

P. Where else have we heard of the river and the tree of life? *Genesis 1*

I. What does the river picture? *truth from the Lord*

I. What does the tree of life picture? *that all good and truth are from the Lord*

S. What did John teach us when he fell at the feet of the angel? *angels are men*

I. Why do some believe that the angels are a separate creation? *wrong translation of Psalm 8:5*

I. How may we know that they were all once men? *from what the angel told John*

I. Why did the first Christian Church break up into so many sects? *lacked truth*

S. What makes the Church on earth? *people loving and living divine truth*

S. What important instruction do we receive in our chapter for today? *the Lord has a use for us in His New Church*

S. What are the distinctive doctrines upon which the Church of the New Jerusalem is founded? *(1) Doctrine of the Lord, (2) Doctrine of the Word, (3) Doctrine of Freedom*

NEW CHURCH DAY
Revelation 21:1-12

This lesson is to be used only if you have Sunday school the third Sunday in June. Most of our Sunday schools close earlier. You will find the reason for this name for June nineteenth in the quotation at the end of the lesson. In all classes be sure the class knows the true name of our church and why it was given that name.

―――

Doctrinal Points
The whole world today needs the teachings of the New Church. It is part of our task as New Churchmen to help make the doctrines known.

―――

Notes for Parents
We have had lessons on the tabernacle, on the temple, and finally on the holy city, of which it is said (Revelation 21:22): "And I saw no temple therein: for the Lord God Almighty and the Lamb are the temple of it." When we are in our early adult years, we are like the Israelites "wandering in the wilderness," seeking our permanent spiritual home, led about from day to day by the pillar of cloud and fire, an acknowledgment of the Lord only vaguely understood. Our place of worship then is a movable tent, set up first in one place and then in another. If we faithfully follow the pillar until we reach a firm decision, our accepted belief, we build a more enduring place of worship, our temple in Jerusalem, our "possession of peace." Yet, as we progress in knowledge, we have more and more questions. We seek the answers in the Word of God, knowing they must be there, yet they elude us. Some become discouraged and give up the effort, turning to the worship of the earthly idols of the "nations round about." But some keep on seeking for true answers.

371

Such a one was Emanuel Swedenborg (1688-1772), a philosopher and scientist whom the Lord chose to be the instrument of His Second Coming. When the Lord came into the world the first time, taking on from the virgin Mary a body like ours, He came to show man the true way of life, and the first Christian Church was founded on this example. On the cross He said, "It is finished." He did not need to come in the flesh again. Yet He had told His disciples, "I have yet many things to say unto you, but ye cannot bear them now," and He had prophesied that He would come again "in the clouds of heaven with power and great glory." What was this Second Coming to be?

The "clouds of heaven" picture the letter of the Word. When our earthly sky is covered with clouds, we cannot see the sun but we know it is still there. Just as we are encouraged when the sun breaks through the clouds for a moment, so we are encouraged by those passages in the letter of the Word which give us a glimpse of its internal meaning as, for example, when the Lord Himself explains to His disciples the meaning of the parable of the sower (Matthew 13:1-9, Mark 4:14-20, Luke 8:4-15).

In the middle of the eighteenth century the Lord saw that mankind had reached a stage in their earthly learning when they not only could "bear" the "many things" He still had to say to them but needed them to keep from being carried away by worldly science and philosophy. So He opened Swedenborg's eyes to see the spiritual world in which all of us are inwardly living now and which we shall all see when we put aside our earthly bodies, and in which we shall go on living forever. And He instructed Swedenborg in the inner meaning of the Word so that he could write and publish the information for the use of all mankind. Swedenborg declared himself to be merely the "servant of the Lord Jesus Christ." His writings are the key which enables us to unlock the puzzling passages of the Word and see the sun shining through the clouds throughout.

We call June nineteenth "New Church Day" because Swedenborg tells us that on that day in the year 1770 the twelve apostles were sent throughout the spiritual world "to preach the Gospel that the Lord God Jesus Christ reigns, whose kingdom shall be for ages and ages." So the Lord Jesus Christ Himself is the temple in the holy city New Jerusalem, in which we may all live to eternity if we will.

Primary

Review what the pupils have learned about the holy city and speak of our church as a new church in which the Lord Jesus Christ alone is worshiped and love to the Lord as well as love to the neighbor are taught, and where we have given us by the Lord a wonderful new understanding of the Bible.

This Sunday we are celebrating "New Church Day." That is because on June nineteenth in the year 1770 the New Church began to come down from heaven to earth. Our chapter tells us about it. John saw it as a beautiful city called the New Jerusalem.

What can you tell about it?
Ask your teacher to read the first verse of our chapter for today.
This vision is a parable.
What is a parable?
The new heaven and the new earth mean a new understanding of the Lord and of what our life on earth is for.
This new understanding was given to the world two hundred years ago by the Lord by means of a man named Emanuel Swedenborg.
Swedenborg wrote and published it under the guidance of the Lord.
June 19, 1770, was the day on which the new understanding, the holy city, began to come down to earth.
Do you remember where Solomon's temple was set up?

Jerusalem means "place of peace." Do you know what peace is? It is being loving and happy, not quarreling or scolding, or trying to take things away from other people, not always trying to have our own way. When are you unhappy? Isn't it usually when you are naughty and have to be punished for doing something you have been told not to do? If we are sensible, we shall try harder and harder every day to do right instead of wrong, to try to make other people happy instead of always trying to have our own way. Then we shall have peace—we shall be living in the holy city.

What is the true name of our church?

This is because it is founded on the new understanding which is called the holy city New Jerusalem.

The new understanding is given through a new knowledge of the inner meaning of the Word of God.

We can study this all our lives with ever-increasing light.

This was the Second Coming of the Lord, prophesied in Mark 13:26.

The clouds of heaven mean the literal sense of the Word, and the power and great glory mean its internal sense.

Junior

Emphasize the reason for the Second Coming, the need of the modern world for the new knowledge given to this New Church, and the great responsibility resting on everyone exposed to this knowledge.

Who had a vision of the holy city?

What was the name of the holy city?

Earlier we have studied some of the details of John's vision of the holy city as they are given in the last part of chapter 21 in the book of Revelation. And we saw that this beautiful city is a picture of a heavenly state in which we may live if we study the truth which the Lord in His Second Coming has revealed to us in His Word in the light of its internal meaning, and try to live as He wants us to live. Today we are celebrating a special day, June nineteenth, which we call "New Church Day" because Swedenborg tells us that on that day in the year 1770 the establishment of the new Christian heaven was proclaimed in the spiritual world, from which the New Church on earth would descend. This is what the first verse of our chapter means.

You all go to school several days of each week. You all know that the things you have been learning in school this year could not have been taught you when you were babies, or even during your first years in school. And you all know that as you go further in school you will learn many more things, things which you would not be able to understand now. It is so with everyone and it was so with the human race. When they were first created, they were simple, innocent people, just as babies are now. The Lord gave them all the knowledge they needed. As the race grew older and people began to think for themselves, He gave them more instruction and of a more complex kind. And, just as it is with men today, those who chose to learn from Him and to do what He said was right became more and more wise, while those who just wanted to have their own way only made trouble for everybody and were unhappy themselves.

When the Lord was in the world He said to His disciples, "I have yet many things to say unto you, but ye cannot bear them now." Men learned more all the time about the physical world, however, and were finally becoming so proud of themselves and their learning that they would not even listen to the Lord, and the simple good people could not understand the Word well enough to meet their arguments. So finally the Lord came again, not in the flesh, but by showing us the inner meaning of the Word by means of the writings of His chosen servant Emanuel Swedenborg. You have all been blessed in being introduced to this knowledge in your early years. And the Lord has given each of you a great responsibility— to study the Bible in the light of this new understanding and to obey the Lord faithfully so that you may lead others to it and may yourselves dwell forever in the holy city.

Now let us reread our Bible lesson and think what it means in this new light. The holy city, as we have seen, is the New Church coming down from God to be established on earth. Those who truly belong to this Church will love the Lord as a true wife loves her husband (verse 2). The Lord is in this Church as its center (verse 2). We may now live happy, peaceful lives because we can understand how the Lord rules everything (verses 4-7). But if we know these things and do not try to obey the Lord, we shall live in hell instead of in heaven (verse 8). The wall of the city is the letter of the Word, especially that law which He has given to man from the beginning, the ten commandments, but now understood in new light and obeyed from love to the Lord (verses 9-12).

How many gates did the city have?
What were written on the gates?

Intermediate

These pupils are old enough to be given a clear statement of the origin and mission of the New Church and the need for it in the world of today. The teacher may be able to point out some of the temptations which they face, even at their age, in modern times. Stress the duty of each one of us to be faithful to the Lord and His commandments.

We have studied the general meaning of the holy city New Jerusalem, and the meaning of some of its details as described in the last part of our chapter.

Today let us think of the reason why this holy city, the New Church, had to come down from heaven just when it did, for we learn from Swedenborg that on June 19, 1770, the announcement was made in heaven which heralded the fulfillment of the prophecy given in the first verse of our chapter. So we call June nineteenth "New Church Day."

The letter of the Word has always puzzled people. Yet those who have read the Word for the purpose of learning about the Lord and living as He would have them live have always found shining through its clouds enough light to guide them, as well as the definite and unchanging laws of an orderly life, the ten commandments. This is because the earliest men were simple good people who knew they lived from the Lord and saw everything in nature as the expression of something in Him. With the good, those who chose freely to obey the Lord, this knowledge persisted almost until the time of Abraham, and formed the basis of the Ancient Word, from which the first eleven chapters of Genesis were drawn. But as men began to study and master the world of nature for themselves, they became proud of themselves, forgot about the Lord, and lost the knowledge of the true meaning of the Word. So they became less and less truly wise instead of more and more, until finally those who still wanted to obey the Lord could no longer be sure of the way, and the Lord had to come into the world Himself in a human body—which was called the "Son of God"—to show men the right way to live.

But He knew that even this would not be enough and He promised to come again in a different way, "in the clouds of heaven, with power and great glory." We know that everyone did not acknowledge Him in His First Coming. The proud and selfish who wanted to rule the world rejected and crucified Him. Even the first Christian Church, which had started among the good, soon began to break up into separate groups, each seeking to rule. And as men developed more and more worldly knowledge, through science and philosophy, the time finally came when again the good could not hold to their belief in the Word without more understanding. Then the Lord's Second Coming had to be made to give men once more the understanding of the inner meaning of His Word so that the good could not be deceived by those who called themselves wise because of their merely earthly knowledge.

This new understanding of the Word of God in the light of its inner meaning is the holy city New Jerusalem coming down to earth from God out of heaven, forming out of all good men and women a new heaven and a new earth. The mission of the Church called by this name is to help people to find and study and live according to this new light.

We see in our lesson for today that everyone will not accept the new light. There will still be those who are proud of themselves and do not want to be governed by the Lord, but for such people there is no place in heaven. Yet the gates of the holy city are forever open to all who sincerely want to live within its walls, within the boundaries of the teachings of the Lord in His Word, shining like jasper from the light within.

Senior

This is an excellent opportunity to warn our young people of the fallacy of assuming that our modern scientists and philosophers and psychologists are so learned that their pronouncements about the Bible and the spiritual world must be always accepted. Many young people are led astray by this idea.

In our study of the holy city we considered in some detail, as a description of the ideal of the Church to which we belong, the pattern of life given by the Lord Himself for this new age in which mankind is making such great strides in earthly science and philosophy. Why do we need this new ideal? It is because men, whenever they make new advances, are tempted to take credit to themselves, to forget that all their power to will, think, and do comes from the Lord and that, if they want to make good use of their achievements, they must look to Him for guidance and live according to His laws. As you go on through high school and college, you will find that there is so much to learn today about this natural world in which we live that you will often be tempted to forget how short our life here is in comparison with eternity, and how much more important is knowledge of the world in which our souls live. We indeed need knowledge of this world because our field of action for the time is here, and the Lord wants us to enjoy this world and to be useful in it. But we need to make sure that what we do from day to day here is not obscuring the higher plane of our minds which connects us with the Lord and with heaven.

So in the middle of our Bible reading for today, in verse 8, we find a condemnation of those who forget their duty to obey the laws of the Lord. Many people imagine that we can put off thinking about spiritual things until we have achieved what we want in this world, that the Bible is out of date, that it will be time enough to make up our minds about God when we die and find out if there is anything beyond this life. But this is not true. We are forming our eternal character from day to day. What we think and do today affects us and others tomorrow and forever. It is a serious thought, but ordinary common sense tells us it is true. The Lord leaves us free to make our own choices, because if He did not we should be mere animals acting on instinct. But from the very beginning of mankind upon the earth He has given them a progressive revelation of His existence and of His order, so that man would never need to choose blindly.

In our modern age we have more worldly knowledge to study and learn, but we also have more heavenly knowledge to balance and direct it. It will be our own fault if we make the wrong choice and take the road that leads to hell instead of entering one of the gates of the holy city and drinking freely of the "fountain of the water of life."

Adult

The need of the New Church teachings in our modern world and the responsibility of each member to study and live these teachings is the important lesson for the Adults. The teacher should ask for questions and answer them as clearly and fully as possible. The Church should be the center of life for all of us and the study of the Word our most important study.

John's vision of the holy city coming down from God out of heaven is the culmination of the Word of God. We have seen that the whole Word is the gradual revelation to mankind of the nature and will of God, as man developed from his first childlike state to his present state of expanding worldly knowledge. Just as a child cannot be taught everything at once, so man has developed from stage to stage and had to be instructed progressively until he reached his full adult capacity.

Man is different from the animals because he has rationality and freedom of choice. These qualities are what are meant by his being made in the image and likeness of God. The writings tell us that the one thing the Lord must preserve in man at all costs is his freedom of choice; the Lord could not have prevented the development of evils in the world without destroying man. Love which is not freely given is not love.

The final revelation needed by man was made when he reached his fullest mental development, about two hundred years ago. It was the Second Coming of the Lord—not an earthly reappearance, but a coming, as He Himself had prophesied, "in the clouds of heaven, with power and great glory." That is, a coming in the internal meaning shining through the clouds of the letter of the Word! Swedenborg tells us that this new understanding from the Word of the rule of the Lord Jesus Christ alone was proclaimed in the heavens on June 19, 1770. This is why we observe the nineteenth of June as "New Church Day."

We have only to read the philosophies of our day based on men's pride in their own scientific development, and to observe the progressive weakening of the doctrinal bases of Protestant sects and even of Roman Catholic claims to realize how essential the new revelation is to the preservation of knowledge and worship of the Lord in our new age. The mission of the New Church is a very important one and the responsibility of each one of its members is very great. Let us all make every effort to study and live the teachings of the holy city and to lead others to a knowledge of them wherever the Lord has seen fit to place us. The Church on earth is the bride, the lamb's wife. Let us all cleave to the Lord and serve Him first of all.

From the Writings of Swedenborg

True Christian Religion, n. 791: "After this work was finished the Lord called together His twelve disciples who followed Him in the world; and the next day He sent them all forth throughout the whole spiritual world to preach the Gospel that the LORD GOD JESUS CHRIST reigns, whose kingdom shall be for ages and ages, according to the prediction in Daniel (7:13-14), and in the Apocalypse (11:15). Also that blessed are those that come to the marriage supper of the Lamb (Apocalypse 19:9). This took place on the nineteenth day of June, 1770. This is what is meant by these words of the Lord: 'He shall send His angels and they shall gather together His elect, from one end of the heavens to the other.' (Matthew 24:31)."

Suggested Questions on the Lesson

P. What special day are we celebrating today? *New Church Day*

P. Why do we call June nineteenth "New Church Day"? *[see TCR 791]*

J. For what is our Church named? *the holy city New Jerusalem*

P. Who first saw the holy city coming down from God out of heaven? *the apostle John*

I. What does a city correspond to? *doctrine*

I. What do its walls correspond to? *letter of the Word*

P. What does the word *Jerusalem* mean? *place of peace*

J. Why did the world have to wait so long for the final revelation? *till men were ready*

I. Which is more important, knowledge of this world or knowledge of the Lord and His will? *knowledge of the Lord*

P. How did the Lord make His Second Coming? *by revealing inner sense of Word*

S. Why did the Lord have to give man freedom of choice? *love to Lord, neighbor must be freely chosen*

S. What does this teach us about His permission of evil? *necessary in order to preserve human freedom*

I. What is the great temptation we face in the world today? *pride of self-intelligence*

S. What is our duty as members of the New Church? *to help lead others to the Lord by means of the Word and the writings*

NEW CHURCH DAY
Revelation 22:1-14

"New Church Day" presents a good opportunity to emphasize man's fundamental need of recognition and worship of the Lord, constant study of the Word in the light of the writings, and the daily effort to live as the Lord teaches us to live instead of from our own selfish ideas of what is best. Try to keep this major objective in mind as you teach the various classes. None are too young to have it impressed upon them.

Doctrinal Points
Our first responsibility is to acknowledge the Lord and our complete dependence on Him.

The heavenly doctrines are the "key" to the eternal lessons for life to be found in the Word.

Notes for Parents
The New Church thinks of June nineteenth as a very special anniversary and calls it "New Church Day" because Swedenborg tells us that on that day in the year 1770 the proclamation was made throughout the heavens that "the Lord God Jesus Christ reigns, whose kingdom shall be for ages and ages." This meant that the time had arrived when the final revelation had been made by the Lord by His coming "in the clouds of heaven, with power and great glory," that is, by the opening of the inner meaning of the Word of God so that the light of a true understanding might break through the clouds of its literal sense.

In earlier lessons we have seen how the first Christian Church perverted the teachings on the basis of which it had been started by the apostles. We have also seen how each dispensation of the Church from the beginning of man has declined by similar perversion. Man must always be free to reject the Lord's teaching if he so chooses and to use his reason to support his own selfishness and pride, for without freedom and rationality he would not be man.

Many people today ask, "Why is it so important to acknowledge the Lord and the Word? Is not the really important thing to love others and do good works?" The answer is really very simple. If we do not acknowledge the Lord, we take credit to ourselves for any love of others we may feel, and if we do not study the Word of God to find out what the Lord teaches is good, our deeds are directed by our own ideas and there are as many different ideas of good as there are people. Left to ourselves we all make many mistakes even in trying to do good.

The Lord has now given mankind all the knowledge of Himself and His will that He needs to give. The New Church in the world is founded on the recognition of this gift. All of us who belong to the New Church have the obligation to study the Word of God in the light of its inner meaning, to examine ourselves in this light, and to seek to live from day to day as this light directs. If we do this, although as finite human beings we shall still have differences of opinion, we can discuss our differences in a loving spirit and work together as brothers and sisters, all looking to one all-wise Father for guidance. If we do this, we shall not only live to eternity in the beautiful city described in our lesson, but even in this world we shall be eating of the tree of life, drinking the living water, and walking the golden streets. Our life in this world is successful only if we view it constantly in its relation to eternal life. May we all make the wise choice.

"Blessed are they that do his commandments, that they may have right to the tree of life, and may enter in through the gates into the city."

Primary

This is the age when it is hardest for children to understand why they cannot always have what they want. The picture of the holy city may give them a new idea to help them begin self-control. Emphasize the effect of selfishness and disobedience both in this world and in the next.

Today we are celebrating a very special day for our Church, June nineteenth, which we call "New Church Day" because it was on that day in the year 1770 that it was announced to the angels that all was now in order for the establishment of the Lord's kingdom, which would last for ages and ages. This was what the apostle John prophesied in his vision of the beautiful city coming down from God out of heaven.

The picture John gives us of the holy city New Jerusalem is a beautiful picture, isn't it? We all think we would like to live there, don't we? And we all can live there if we try. Verse 14 of our chapter says: "Blessed are they that do His commandments, that they may have right to the tree of life, and may enter in through the gates into the city." You see, there is one requirement: we must "do his commandments." We do not get to the holy city all at once or without some effort. Isn't that true of most of the good things we have? We have to get up and dress ourselves in the morning before we can have our breakfast and go to school or out to play. We have to take care of our toys if we want new ones. We have to be kind and pleasant to other people if we want them to be kind and pleasant to us.

If we want to be able to enter the gates of the holy city, we have to do all these things, and as we grow older we shall find more and more to learn and do, and the longer we study the Bible the better we shall understand it. We shall love the Lord better the better we come to know Him. And we shall be more and more happy in doing His will the longer we practice it. The only thing that can hinder us and keep us out of the holy city is selfishness—always wanting our own way instead of the Lord's way.

This means that we ought to study the Bible all our lives.
When people will not study the Bible, it is because they do not really want to know about the Lord and what He wants us to do.
Why do you think anyone would feel this way?
Are you ever selfish?
Are selfish people happy together?
You can see then why selfish people will not be able to live in the holy city.
Can you repeat Revelation 22:14?

This tells us what we must all learn to do if we are to enter the holy city. Why not begin now?

―――――――

Junior

See how much the class remembers about the holy city and try to impress them with the importance of reading the Word and learning more and more of its internal meaning in order that they may live the true life of the holy city.

In verse 10 of our chapter for today the angel tells John that "the time is at hand" when his prophecy of the descent of the holy city would be fulfilled, and we have learned that this was to come about by the opening of the inner meaning of the Word so that everyone might see, if he would, that the Lord Jesus is the one God of heaven and earth. This would be the Second Coming of the Lord. And Swedenborg tells us that on June 19, 1770, the twelve disciples who had followed the Lord in the world were sent out to proclaim throughout the spiritual world that "the Lord God Jesus Christ reigns." This is why we call the nineteenth of June "New Church Day."

What is the full name of our Church?
From what does it take this name?
Do you remember any of the details of this city as John saw it in vision?
What did the wall represent?

In our worship services we say together what we call "the Faith of the New Church." Can you repeat it? This is a statement of the doctrine or teaching which the Lord has given us to be the wall of our holy city. We find all these teachings in the letter of the Word of God, but in order to understand them we need to see the light from within shining through. Read verse 18 of chapter 21. Jasper is a beautiful clear stone through which light can shine.

What man did the Lord choose to give us the information which will enable us to see this light?
Do we become New Churchmen by merely saying we believe these things?

The Lord gives us the answer to this question in verse 14 of our lesson for today. In order to live in the holy city both here on earth and forever in heaven we have to study the Word daily and, as we grow older, also study the writings of Swedenborg which enable us to see the light within, and we have to try day by day to live according to the teachings we find in this way. It may seem hard at first, but so does the acquisition and use of any knowledge. And the knowledge which we shall need forever is the most important knowledge of all.

―――――

Intermediate

With this class review the description of the holy city, stressing the correspondence of the river, the tree of life, the golden street, the gates, and finally the wall and the foundations, thus leading into the special lesson for today.

In our lesson on "The Woman and the Dragon" we learned why the nineteenth of June is called "New Church Day." This special lesson is written to help us keep that day in mind and realize more fully what it means to us.

Our lesson begins with the words, "And he showed me a pure river of water of life, clear as crystal, proceeding out of the throne of God and of the Lamb." This beautiful river is a picture of the pure truth as it comes to us from the Lord if we see and acknowledge that He is our king, the ruler of all the world. This new understanding of what the Lord says to us in His Word is the great gift which He has given to us in His Second Coming.

Throughout your study of the Bible in our Sunday School lessons you have been given glimpses of the light which makes the river clear as crystal, but you can see more and more of it only as you make it your own by continued study of the Word and of the writings of Swedenborg, the "servant of the Lord Jesus Christ," the man whom the Lord chose and prepared to be His agent in publishing the necessary knowledge so that all who sincerely wanted it could find it.

You are just beginning this study, as you are also just beginning the study of the material knowledges which will make you useful and successful in this world. You need both kinds of knowledge, but never forget that the knowledge of the Lord and His will is the knowledge which will determine your usefulness and success to eternity. The material world is all around us. It is easy to become absorbed in it and to close our eyes to the light that comes from the Lord. But that is really a very stupid thing to do, isn't it? For the spiritual world is all around us also. Our souls are living in it now. And true happiness for us in this world as well as to eternity can come only from receiving the Lord's truth in our minds and so living in obedience to Him that we may also receive His unselfish love in our hearts, which is to eat of the fruit of the tree of life.

Senior

Since for this class earlier lessons have brought out many of the points which are important for this special day, the teacher may give most of the lesson time to a review of these points, merely emphasizing the reason for the name given to this day.

We of the New Church call the nineteenth of June "New Church Day." You will find the reason for this in *True Christian Religion*, n. 791.

The first verse of the Bible reads: "In the beginning God created the heaven and the earth." And the first verse of John's final vision reads: "And I saw a new heaven and a new earth: for the first heaven and the first earth were passed away." Mankind in his beginning was like a newborn baby: he possessed a soul and a body but knew nothing of himself until he had been developed and instructed by the Lord. He was a man, however, not an animal. He was from his very beginning distinguished from the animals by the possession of two faculties, rationality and freedom of choice. The first chapter of Genesis teaches us how he was developed to full manhood and instructed directly by the Lord, and the second chapter describes the beautiful state in which he was able to live until he began to use his free choice to set himself up in place of the Lord.

Our lessons on the Bible have showed us how again and again the human race declined because of the many who chose to eat the fruit of the knowledge of good and evil—the exaltation of their own intelligence—instead of keeping the tree of life in the center of their garden. Each time a crisis was reached the many had to be destroyed or dispersed and a new beginning made with the remnant of faithful people by means of a new revelation of truth in a form suited to their state. When the Lord came into the world in a human body, mankind had reached its lowest state and the good could not have been preserved in any other way.

But you may remember that the Lord said to His disciples, "I have yet many things to say unto you, but ye cannot bear them now," and in another prophecy He promised that at a future time they would see Him coming "in the clouds of heaven with power and great glory." The Lord has now made this Second Coming by opening the inner meaning of the Word, so that anyone who will may now understand the many things He has to say to the men of this new age. It is His final revelation of Himself to man. How foolish we are if we in this age choose to be of those who imagine they know enough to live without God instead of learning of and living in the new heaven and the new earth!

Adult

The best lesson for the Adults is to help them to realize that the most important use they can serve—not only to their Church but to the world—is to study steadily and seriously the Word of God in the light of the internal meaning, to which the writings of Swedenborg are the key, and to try to live their daily lives in this light and be ready to help others from it as opportunity offers.

In our world today we face many frightening conditions: wars and rumors of wars, race hatreds, poverty and disease, lust for power, rebellious youth, drug addiction and insanity, business and political dishonesty, sex offenses and murder, decline of the churches. Many good people are staggered by these facts, completely discouraged, even sure the end of the world must be at hand. Many who believe in God fall into the temptation to blame Him, saying, "Why does God permit such things?" Others are drawn into so many kinds of external "good works" that they have no time to read and think, and fall into the habit of blaming everyone who does not do just the same things they do.

Yet the answer has been given us from the beginning: "And the Lord God took the man, and put him into the garden of Eden to dress it and to keep it. And the Lord God commanded the man, saying, Of every tree of the garden thou mayest freely eat: But of the tree of the knowledge of good and evil, thou shalt not eat of it: for in the day that thou eatest thereof thou shalt surely die." Man from his beginning was man, not an animal, because from his beginning he was given rationality and freedom of choice, the power to think above the level of this earth and so to recognize God, and freedom to choose on which level he would live.

If we study the history of mankind in the light of the Word of God, we can see that the decline of mankind from the first happy state to their present state has been the result of man's choice of self-intelligence and love of dominion in place of love to the Lord and the effort to learn of Him and do His will. Our reading for today repeats the fact of our freedom and points out the consequences of the selfish choice. But it also points out to us clearly that in this new age of ours the pure river of truth is still available to quench the thirst of all who really seek it, and the tree of life still grows in the holy city New Jerusalem, yielding fruit to satisfy the needs of every hungry person; and we are told plainly in the vision that "the leaves of the tree were for the healing of the nations."

The gates of the holy city are open. Let each of us honestly examine himself and face up to his own individual responsibility in the place where the Lord has seen fit to put him, remembering always the last verse of our lesson: "Blessed are they that do his commandments, that they may have right to the tree of life, and may enter in through the gates into the city."

―――――

From the Writings of Swedenborg

Apocalypse Revealed, n. 940: "*And there shall be no night there, and they have no need of a lamp and the light of the sun, for the Lord giveth them light*, signifies that there will not be any falsity of faith in the New Jerusalem, and that men there will not be in knowledges concerning God from natural light which is from their own intelligence, and from glory arising from pride, but will be in spiritual light from the Word from the Lord alone."

Suggested Questions on the Lesson

P. What special day do we celebrate today? *New Church Day*

J. Why is it so named? *[see TCR 791]*

I. Who tells us this? *Swedenborg*

S. Of whom was Swedenborg the agent? *the Lord in His Second Coming*

P. What did John see in the holy city? *river, tree of life*

J. Where did we first read of the tree of life? *Genesis 1*

I. What other tree was in the garden of Eden? *knowledge of good and evil*

J. What were men told about the two trees? *not to eat of latter*

P. What must we learn to do if we want to live in the holy city? *obey commandments*

P. Why must we study the Bible? *to learn how to live*

P. What is our other name for the Bible? *the Word*

I. What is the river of water of life? *pure truth coming from the Lord*

I. What is the only way to true happiness? *receiving the Lord's truth, living according to it*

S. What is our special duty as New Churchmen? *to learn and live the truths of the Word in the light of the heavenly doctrines*

NEW CHURCH DAY
Revelation 21:1-10
(True Christian Religion, nn. 791, 846-847)

This lesson is an additional special lesson to be used following the regular season, on June 19, or the nearest Sunday to that date. It is based on Swedenborg's statement in TCR 791 that "after this work [the book *True Christian Religion*] was completed, the Lord called together His twelve disciples who followed Him in the world; and the next day He sent them all forth throughout the whole spiritual world to preach the Gospel that the Lord God Jesus Christ reigns . . . This took place on the nineteenth of June, 1770 . . ."

Primary

Tell the children that when the Lord had finished revealing the teachings for a New Church, He sent His disciples all over heaven to tell this good news. Stress the term, "New Church Day." Look in some detail at the event described in TCR 791. Then follow the notes as a guide.

You know what fun it is to have something brand-new—a new dress or pair of shoes, or a new toy. It is even more fun when it is a surprise. You are delighted and jump for joy. Remember on your last birthday when you got some nice new things? You probably received something that you had never had before, something that was brand-new.

Have you ever wondered why you like new things? It is partly because you can always learn something from them. They may help you discover something that you didn't know anything about before. When you first learned how to ride a tricycle you discovered a new thing—it made it possible for you to go faster and more easily to more places. You learned to do something new.

This week is the birthday of something new in the world, something that the Lord has given to be enjoyed by everyone in the whole world. But not only enjoyed. It is intended to help us all learn things we never knew before and do good things that the Lord wants us to know how to do. What is this new thing? We call it the New Church. And June 19 is called New Church Day, for that was the day long ago when the Lord sent His disciples out to tell everyone in heaven the good news that the teachings of His New Church had been made known to men on earth.

When the Lord was on earth at the time of His first coming, He taught His disciples many new and wonderful things about Himself, and about the way people should live if they want to come at last into heaven and be happy forever. Before Jesus left His disciples, He told them to go and "make disciples of all nations, baptizing them in the name of the Father and of the Son and of the Holy Spirit, teaching them to observe all things that I have commanded you." (Matthew 28:19-20)

Those who believed these teachings and were baptized were called Christians, from the Lord's name Christ. They became like one large family, with the Lord as the Father, and so they were called the "church," meaning the Lord's family.

Many hundreds of years later, the Lord in his wisdom saw that the time had come to give to men a new understanding of His truth. Many of the teachings He had given before were being taught wrongly, and people did not know that what the church was teaching was often not what the Lord wanted at all.

For this reason the Lord made known to his children a new understanding of His teachings, which He called the doctrines of a New Church. When all of these teachings had been given, and written down in books, the Lord called together in the spiritual world all the disciples who had been with Him in the world and sent them out to tell everyone in heaven the good news that now men on earth knew that the Lord God Jesus Christ reigns.

Junior

Explain simply the spiritual meaning of Revelation 21:1-10 ("It treats of the state of heaven and the church after the Last Judgment . . . after [which] . . . the New Church will exist on earth [and] will worship the Lord.''–AR 875). Then connect this meaning with the event described in TCR 791.

Today we are celebrating the anniversary of something new in the world: something that the Lord has given for the benefit of all mankind. It was so important the Lord also told all the men and women and children in heaven about it.

What is this new thing that He gave us?
On what day did the Lord send out His disciples to tell everyone in heaven about this new thing?
What were they told to preach?

Our New Church teachings tell us that this was to fulfill a prophecy that was made in the Gospel. Look up Matthew 24:31 to see what that prophecy was.

Let us see if we can remember some of the new teachings which the Lord gave to the world to be used in His New Church:

1. He revealed that His Word has an inner spiritual meaning.

2. As we learn this spiritual meaning here in Sunday School and as we study at home, we find that the Bible really tells us all about heaven, all about the Lord, and all about the life that leads to heaven.

3. Although people had believed in a general way that there was a life after death, the Lord revealed through Swedenborg just what kind of life it would be. He described in full detail the way people live in heaven, and also in hell.

4. Another wonderful thing that the Lord revealed is that there is a new kind of love that is possible between a husband and wife if they truly love the Lord. He called this love conjugial love.

5. Many false ideas about what God wants of us were corrected. One very important doctrine the New Church teaches is that the Lord Jesus Christ alone is to be prayed to and worshiped, for there is no other God besides Him, and He alone has power to save us from our sins.

We celebrate New Church Day on or near June nineteenth, the anniversary of the day the Lord sent His disciples out to tell the good news.

Intermediate

Follow the same general outline as for the Juniors, but look in more detail at the summary of *news* given in TCR, nn. 846-847. If time permits, discuss part of chapter 14 of *True Christian Religion*, n. 768 et seq.

In Swedenborg's work, *True Christian Religion*, n. 791, which is at the end of the last regular chapter in the book, it says that when this last great summary work of the doctrines of the New Church had been completed, "the Lord called together His twelve disciples who followed Him in the world; and the next day He sent them all forth throughout the whole spiritual world to preach the Gospel that the LORD GOD JESUS CHRIST reigns, whose kingdom shall be for ages and ages, according to the prediction in Daniel 7:13-14 and Revelation 11:15. . . . This took place on the nineteenth of June, 1770."

Throughout the history of the organized New Church, this date has been celebrated as New Church Day. It is a day to remind ourselves of how much we have to be grateful for, in that the Lord has permitted us to know about the revelation He made as the basis of a New Church in the world.

In the supplement to *True Christian Religion*, nn. 846-847, Swedenborg records a remarkable conversation he had with some angels. It began when these angels asked him, "What is the news from the earth?" Here is an outline of his reply.

He said that the Lord had revealed many mysteries or secrets that had not been known before. Some of them are:

1. That in each and all things of the Word there is a spiritual sense corresponding to the natural sense; that by means of that sense the Word conjoins men of the Church with the Lord.

2. That the correspondences of which the spiritual sense consists have been disclosed.

3. That the Lord had made a new revelation about life after death.
    a. About the nature of heaven and hell.
    b. About the sun of the spiritual world.
    c. That there are three degrees of life, and consequently three heavens.

4. That many other things had been revealed: regarding the Last Judgment, the Lord as being the God of heaven and earth, God as being one in person and in essence in whom is a divine trinity, a New Church to be established by Him, the doctrines of that church, the holiness of the Sacred Scripture, that the Apocalypse (book of Revelation) had been unfolded, and many more things.

If you would like to learn how this revelation constitutes the Lord's Second Coming, read in *True Christian Religion*, nn. 768-790.

———

Senior

After discussing the significance of the event which led to naming June 19 as "New Church Day," and relating it to the first ten verses of Revelation 21, review briefly the new doctrines outlined in TCR, nn. 846-847. If any time remains, interesting details of the spiritual meaning of Revelation 21:1-10 will be found in AR 875, beginning at the subheading "THE CONTENTS OF EACH VERSE."

In Swedenborg's last great summary work, *True Christian Religion*, n. 791, which is the last paragraph at the end of the last regular chapter in the book, it says that when this work, this summary of the doctrines of the New Church, had been completed, "The Lord called together His twelve disciples who followed Him in the world; and the next day He sent them all forth throughout the whole spiritual world to preach the Gospel that the LORD GOD JESUS CHRIST reigns, whose kingdom shall be for ages and ages, according to the prediction in Daniel 7:13-14 and Revelation 11:15. . . . This took place on the nineteenth day of June, 1770."

This announcement heralded the descent of the Holy City from God out of heaven, described in Revelation 21:1-10. A summary of the spiritual meaning of these verses will be found in AR 875, beginning at the subheading "THE CONTENTS OF EACH VERSE."

Throughout the history of the organized New Church, June 19 has been celebrated as New Church Day. It is a day to remind ourselves of how much we have to be grateful for, in that the Lord has permitted us to know about the revelation He has made as the basis of a New Church in the world.

Following the last chapter, in a supplement to *True Christian Religion*, nn. 846-847, Swedenborg records a conversation he had with some angels, who had asked him, "What news from the earth?" Here is an outline of his reply.

He said that the Lord had revealed many mysteries or secrets of heaven that had not been known on earth before. Some of them are:

That in each and all things of the Word there is a spiritual sense corresponding to the natural sense; that by means of that sense the Word conjoins men of the Church with the Lord.

That the correspondences of which the spiritual sense consists have been disclosed.

That the Lord had made a new revelation about life after death: About the nature of heaven and hell; About the sun of the spiritual world; That there are three degrees of life and consequently three heavens.

That many other things had been revealed: regarding the Last Judgment, the Lord as being the God of heaven and earth, God as being one in person and in essence in whom is a divine trinity, a New Church to be established by Him, the doctrines of that church, the holiness of the Sacred Scripture, that the Apocalypse (book of Revelation) had been unfolded, and many more things.

If you would like to learn how this revelation constitutes the Lord's Second Coming, read in *True Christian Religion*, nn. 768-790.

Adult

Any or all of the above suggested materials can be the basis of stimulating discussion at the Adult level. After the reason for celebrating New Church Day is presented, the particular areas of interest expressed by the class can be a sufficient guide.

APPENDIX II

IN MEMORIAM

Mrs. Anita Sturges Dole
1889-1973

The author of these lesson notes was born on March 18, 1889 in Chicago, Illinois, to James Dwight and Anna Gertrude Cary Sturges. She received her education in the Chicago public schools, and received the A.B. degree from the University of Chicago in 1908, having been elected to Phi Beta Kappa the previous year on the basis of her academic achievement. As a child she attended an Episcopal Sunday school, and was confirmed in that faith in 1902. On completing her education, she was employed first as a cataloguer in the University of Chicago Library (1908-1910), and subsequently as secretary to Professor William I. Thomas (1910-1912), as a Research Assistant in the Chicago School of Civics and Philanthropy (1912-1914), and as Assistant Manager of a small publishing company (1914-1917).

During this period she studied voice and was in training under Herman De Vries of the Chicago Opera Company, considering a career in music, when in February of 1917 she was persuaded by her sister Alice to accept a teaching position at Urbana, a New Church high school and junior college in Ohio, to fill an unexpected vacancy. That summer, at the end of the term, she went with her sister to the New Church Assembly in Almont, Michigan. There she heard the Rev. Dr. Thomas King give a lecture in which he traced the correspondence of the ass in the Bible, illustrating its spiritual meaning with quotations throughout the Bible. She was fond of telling how, at the end of this talk, she was so convinced of the truth of the doctrine of the New Church concerning the Bible that she was ready to join the New Church. She was confirmed by Dr. King there at Almont, in August, 1917. That fall she made her decision to give up her promising career in music and devote herself to the teaching of the New Church doctrines, and to the work of the church. Her lovely soprano voice, though lost to the world at large, enriched the worship of her church to the end of her life.

She also loved to tell how, before she went to Almont, she had audited a course in philosophy being given at Urbana by its principal, Rev. Louis A. Dole, of how she had been most strongly attracted to him, and how Mr. Dole had apparently taken no notice of her at all. However, when she returned from Almont a confirmed and enthusiastic member of the New Church, Mr. Dole lost no time in becoming better acquainted with the new teacher on his staff. They were married on New Church Day—June 19, 1919.

In September of 1920 Mr. Dole accepted a call to serve the New Church society in Fryeburg, Maine, on a six-month trial basis; they stayed there for seventeen years. Almost immediately on taking up the Fryeburg pastorate, they discovered an interest among several Massachusetts New Church members who summered in Fryeburg, in establishing a summer assembly similar to that at Almont. It was through the on-the-scene efforts of the Doles, coupled with the fund-raising activities of the Massachusetts group, that the Fryeburg New Church Assembly became a reality in 1921, with Mr. Dole as its first president.

Time passed, and Mr. Dole was invested as General Pastor of the Maine Association of the New Church. In this capacity he became increasingly concerned at the decline of the Bath society where his father had once been minister, and where he himself had been confirmed. After several unsuccessful attempts to re-establish worship services in Bath by other means, he accepted a call to serve as its minister. The Doles moved to Bath in 1937.

In Bath, Mrs. Dole became active in the Parent-Teacher Association, serving several terms as president of her local chapter and as chairman of the Constitution and By-Laws Committee of the state organization; in the Girl Scout movement, serving as Commissioner for the Bath area for several years; in the Bath Council of Churches;

in the Maine Council of Churches, serving on its Constitution and By-Laws Committee; and in the Bath Council of Church Women, which she helped to found. During World War II she was Production Chairman of the Red Cross chapter in Bath, supervising the preparation of war relief materials sent overseas from the Bath area. Through these and other activities people of all faiths came to know and love her, and many found in her that rare combination of spiritual insight, practical advice, and personal interest which brought them again and again to her door. Many were still corresponding with her at the time of her passing on.

She was one of the most active members of the New Church, not only at the local level, but on the national scene. She served from time to time on the various committees of the General Convention and was elected to the Board of Managers of its theological school, from which she resigned when her son became a student there. She was active in the National Alliance of New Church Women, becoming one of its presidents and an ardent promoter of its Round Robin program—a system of circulating letters among particularly the isolated New Church women. She was for some years its Mother Robin.

She was best known, and will likely be longest remembered, for what she herself considered her life's work: the preparation of a comprehensive four-year course of Sunday school lesson notes based on the interpretation of the Bible in the light of the New Church teachings concerning its spiritual meaning. Although she did the research and writing for these lessons herself, she always sought her husband's opinion of her work, and would publish nothing which he had not read and approved. Working together, both in writing and in parish teaching, they passed on to their congregations and to their many church friends a rich heritage of Bible scholarship of a truly spiritual character, and they also achieved a degree of success rare in this century of widening generation gaps, in passing on to all three of their children not only their knowledge, but also their deep and lasting love for the Word of the Lord and for the church based on it.

In 1966, two years after the passing of her husband into the spiritual world, Mrs. Dole retired from parish work and went to live first with her son in Massachusetts and finally with her daughter in Edmonton. She never did retire from active service to the church, continuing to teach in the Sunday school and to participate in study programs, and carrying on a remarkably extensive and varied correspondence to the end.

In her old age she looked forward with increasing anticipation and some impatience to her passing into the spiritual world to join her beloved husband. This became her dearest wish, and it was granted by our Lord's divine mercy on April 7, 1973, shortly after her eighty-fourth birthday.

We rejoice today in her release from the increasing burdens of old age, and look forward to joining her when in due course we are called into that world where she has awakened and taken up her life's work in the health and vigor of her spirit.

She will always be held in loving memory by her three children, Rev. George F. Dole, Mrs. Louise Woofenden, and Mrs. Gertrude Tremblay; by her sons-in-law and daughter-in-law; by her thirteen grandchildren; and by her countless relatives and friends.

Edmonton, Alberta, April 13, 1973